# An Introduction to

## *Music*

## in Early Childhood Education

Join us on the web at

**EarlyChildEd.delmar.com**

# An Introduction to

# *Music*

# in Early Childhood Education

## Joanne Greata, Ed.D.

THOMSON

DELMAR LEARNING

Australia • Canada • Mexico • Singapore • Spain • United Kingdom • United States

**THOMSON**

**DELMAR LEARNING**

### An Introduction to Music in Early Childhood Education
Joanne Greata, Ed.D.

**Vice President, Career Education SBU:**
Dawn Gerrain

**Director of Editorial:**
Sherry Gomoll

**Senior Acquisitions Editor:**
Erin O'Connor

**Developmental Editor:**
Patricia Osborn

**Editorial Assistant:**
Stephanie Kelly

**Director of Production:**
Wendy A. Troeger

**Production Manager:**
J.P. Henkel

**Production Editor:**
Amber Leith

**Technology Project Manager:**
Sandy Charette

**Director of Marketing:**
Wendy E. Mapstone

**Channel Manager:**
Kristin McNary

**Marketing Coordinator:**
David White

**Composition:**
Pre-Press Company, Inc.

**Cover Design:**
Joseph Villanova

Library of Congress Cataloging-in-Publication Data

Greata, Joanne.
  An introduction to music in early childhood education / Joanne Greata.
      p. cm.
  Includes bibliographical references and index.
  ISBN-13: 978-0-7668-6303-3 (alk. paper)
  ISBN-10: 0-7668-6303-4 (alk. paper)
1. Music--Instruction and study--Juvenile. 2. Early childhood education. 3. Preschool music--Instruction and study. I. Title.
  MT1.G816 2006
  372.87'043--dc22

                                    2005027426

### NOTICE TO THE READER

# Brief Contents

# Table of Contents

**APPENDICES**

# Introduction

*An Introduction to Music in Early Childhood Education* is a tool for parents and teachers to musically nurture young children. Intended for early childhood education students, teachers, and parents, the book is written at an introductory level so readers do not have to know anything about music to be able to use the book. Material within the book is based on current research and developmentally appropriate practices, as well as the *National Standards for Arts Education.*

## Conceptual Approach

Thinking about writing a book and doing so are two different matters. My approach to the book has taken several turns as I contemplated the best way to present what I felt was important information. Studying the historical background of music's role in early childhood and understanding developmental theories are important steps to implementing appropriate music activities in early childhood classrooms. An equally important step is to acquire a basic knowledge in music.

Most adults have experienced a situation in which they feel uncertainty. Participating in a new game or attending a class before reading the assignment can cause apprehension and decrease the likelihood for participation. That same apprehension exists for early childhood educators when they are not prepared with a basic musical knowledge, and are expected to musically nurture young children.

To help alleviate that apprehension, I have formatted this book into nine chapters, each with two major parts: normal "textbook" information and a lab. Within the labs, the language is less formal, mirroring language I would use when speaking directly to students. Songs included in the text and appendixes feature autoharp or guitar chording, numbering to allow those who do not read music the ability to play the melody using numbers, and at least one verse of the song. Various cultures are represented in the songs.

Throughout the text, I use the phrase "music (or musical) nurturing." I have used the term for years, because it describes early childhood music education more accurately than to say we "teach" music. Early childhood educators are nurturers and facilitators of learning who create environments where learning can occur. Of course, they are a part of that environment and are actively engaged with the children. On the other hand, music teachers teach music. They teach musical notation and the techniques of singing or playing an instrument. They teach students how to combine the mental abilities of music, such as reading notes, with the physical abilities of music, such as finger or vocal placement, to end up with an emotional result, such as a performance. In early childhood, children are wrapped in music, calmed by it, played with to it and, yes, nurtured by it. Thus, I use the term music nurturing instead of music teaching.

## Organization

*An Introduction to Music in Early Childhood Education* is divided into sections that answer the questions Why, What, Who/How, and Where, and explore theoretical concepts, research, developmentally appropriate practices, and some activities. Within the sections, each chapter examines different aspects of early childhood music nurturing. Chapters 1 and 2 consider the "Why" of early childhood music education and include the thoughts of early childhood education pioneers on music as well as current supporting research. Chapter 3 is concerned with "What" types of activities can be used to musically nurture young children. Chapters 4 through 8 describe "How" to appropriately nurture those "Who" are involved in the process of early childhood music education: prenatal infants, infants and toddlers, preschool children, school-age children, and teachers and parents. Finally, Chapter 9 discusses "Where" musical nurturing occurs.

The lab in the second part of each chapter facilitates the student's exploration of music from the beginning of sound discovery to playing the autoharp. Students can use the labs to experience music for themselves and share the lab's activities with young children. While every lab ends with a section of music appreciation, individual lab topics include basic musical notation, musical terms, instruments of the orchestra, and making simple instruments. Chapters 1 through 5 take the student on a musical history journey that spans Western European music from the Middle Ages to the present. Chapters 6 through 9 address the music of Native Americans, the Middle East and Asia, Africa, and the Caribbean.

While some labs are directly tied to each chapter's main subject matter, all of the labs flow from one to the next, Chapter 1 through Chapter 9, building on the student's knowledge of music. Lab participation does not require musical talent or the ability to play an instrument, only an open mind and the ability to approach music in a playful and uninhibited manner.

The Appendices include a resource guide (see Appendix D), which lists books for children and the teacher's library, sources for obtaining instruments, suggested recordings, and special Web sites. Additionally, the Appendices include a glossary, child development charts (Appendix A), expanded information on prenatal music nurturing (Appendix B) and early childhood education theories (Appendix A), and songs (Appendix D), as well as instructions for the care and tuning of autoharps (Appendix C).

## Special Features

*An Introduction to Music in Early Childhood Education* includes several features to deepen the student's understanding of early childhood music nurturing:

- A Closer Look—found in boxes throughout the text and meant to provide in-depth information about an issue or topic introduced in the text
- Discovering Instruments—found within the labs and leads students to discover various rhythm and other orchestra instruments

- Including Children with Special Needs—gives suggestions for working with children who learn differently
- Key Terms—listed at the beginning of each chapter to denote new and important vocabulary
- Lab Activities—meant to allow students to experience music as they learn the technical aspects of the art; gives additional information for activities that are developmentally appropriate for infants, toddlers, preschool, or school-age children
- Making Musical Instruments—gives instructions on how teachers and children can make instruments from common materials
- Music of the World—presents musical customs of various world cultures
- Musical Elements—allows student to become familiar with musical elements and terms
- Musical History—takes students through the history of Western Europe from the Middle Ages to the present; additionally discusses the music of Native Americans, the Middle East and Asia, Africa, and the Caribbean
- References—listed at the end of each chapter to allow for further student exploration
- Snapshot of a Child—provides a snapshot of skills that typically developing children in the specific age group have developed
- Standards and Other Professional Guidance—presented to students as support for appropriate music activities for young children
- Suggested Activities—meant to give students further experience with the subject discussed in the first part of each chapter; each group ends with a journal reflection question that can be used for a personal writing assignment or classroom discussions
- Summary and Key Concepts—summarize the chapter and list key concepts after the first part of each chapter
- Try This One!—immediate and hands-on activities or music-related suggestions throughout the text that students can experience and share with young children

## Instructor's Manual

An Instructor's Manual to accompany *An Introduction to Music in Early Childhood Education* includes additional suggestions for instructional activities and resources as well as answers to questions posed at the end of chapters.

## Online Companion™

*An Introduction to Music in Early Childhood Education* features an Online Companion™ that provides additional instrumental resources and activities, including:

- Sample lesson plans to provide examples of developmentally appropriate music-nurturing activities in an early childhood classroom
- Suggested activities to build student knowledge and dispositions toward music
- Web sites for teachers and children to further expand their resources and learning

You can find the Online Companion™ at http://www.EarlyChildEd.delmar.com.

## About the Author

Joanne D. Greata received her EdD, specializing in early childhood curriculum and systems design, from Nova Southeastern University, an MA in Music from George Mason University, and a BS in Music Education from New York University. For years, her work has straddled the line between music education and early childhood education. In addition to over 20 years' experience in the early childhood classroom and 10 years as a director of early childhood programs, including programs accredited by the National Association for the Education of Young Children (NAEYC), she developed and taught a pre-piano course for preschool children and served as the music specialist for several child care centers. Joanne has taught music in the public schools, in private studios, in preschools, and at the college level. Her contributions to the early childhood field include serving as a validator and commissioner for the accreditation process for NAEYC, currently serving on the professional-development panel for NAEYC, serving The Council for Professional Development as an adviser and a representative, serving as the director of an early childhood education program at a community college, directing a statewide training project for TANF (Temporary Assistance for Needy Families) recipients wishing to work in early childhood education, presenting numerous workshops at local, state, and national conferences and, currently, teaching online courses for several community colleges and a university. Joanne brings the experiences and knowledge of a long and varied double career in music and early childhood education to this textbook.

Through her instruction and training with child care providers, Joanne came to realize that most providers were not prepared to nurture young children musically. Part of her doctoral work included a practicum that created musically nurturing environments for infants and toddlers by training caregivers. That experience provided more evidence that training in music was essential for early childhood educators, while supporting her belief that early childhood teachers would feel more confident about nurturing young children in music if they knew more about it. She came to realize the need for a book that not only discussed how to musically nurture young children, but also taught educators enough about music to help them feel empowered to do so.

## Acknowledgments

I want to thank Erin O'Connor for giving me the chance to realize my dream. I particularly want to thank Delmar's developmental editor, Patricia Osborn, for her guidance and support. Without her direction, I would still be floundering with Chapter 1. In addition, I wish to thank my dear friend, Beatrice Bright, an artist and author in her own right. Her support has been endless from the first time, many years ago, that I mentioned I wanted to write a book about music in early childhood.

## Reviewers

The editors at Thomson Delmar Learning and the author wish to thank the following reviewers for their time, effort, and thoughtful contributions, which helped to shape the final text:

Rhonda Clements, EdD
Hofstra University
Hempstead, NY

Jennifer Johnson, MEd
Vance-Granville Community College
Henderson, NC

Marilee Cosgrove, MA
ECLC School Readiness Program
Irvine, CA

Craig Lehman, MS
American River College
Sacramento, CA

Kathleen Cummings, MS
Suffolk County Community College
Riverhead, NY

Karen Roth, MA
National-Louis University
Evanston, IL

Berta Harris, MS
San Diego City College
San Diego, CA

Gilberto Soto, PhD
Texas A&M International University
Laredo, TX

Mary Henthorne, BS
Western Wisconsin Technical College
Lacrosse, WI

Becky Wyatt, MS
Murray State College
Tishomingo, OK

## Dedication

In memory of my parents, Amy and Howard Swick, who musically nurtured and supported me in musical endeavors throughout my life.

In honor of my loving and patient husband, Russell, who is truly the "Wind Beneath My Wings."

In tribute to Brian and Laura, Kevin, Sean and Dana, and Colin, my wonderful sons and daughters-in-law, who provided the inspiration to write this book and support during the long process. May you fully enjoy the melody, rhythm, and harmony of life and pass your love of music on to your children.

# Why?

Why is music a part of early childhood education? Why is music important to humanity? Why should music and other arts be recognized as fundamental academic subjects? Why is music considered good medicine? Why is music thought to be important for child cognitive development? Why is musical intelligence considered a separate intelligence? Why is it so important to begin musical nurturing at birth? Why, indeed! Section I examines these questions and more. This section contains two chapters.

Chapter 1, "Establishing Music in Early Childhood Education: A Historical Perspective," examines the philosophies and methods of several early childhood education pioneers. The chapter considers the importance of music to these pioneers as they shaped their curriculums. Was music used as a tool to further the educational process or was it considered an important part of the curriculum for its own sake? Additionally, the human development theories of prominent psychologists, educators, and theorists and the influence of these theories on early childhood music nurturing are examined.

Chapter 2, "Current Research Regarding Music and Music Nurturing," examines research and current thoughts regarding the musicality of man, the connections between music and the medical field, the connections between music and brain development, Gardner's theory of musical intelligence, and Gordon's music-learning theory. Newspapers and popular-magazine reports urge parents to take advantage of music education as a way to enhance their child's intelligence. What is the research behind these assumptions of intelligence building through music education? Are these assumptions correct? If so, when is the best time to involve young children with music?

The objective of Section I is to give those who work with young children an understanding of why music is an important element in early childhood education, not merely as an educational tool, but for its own sake. For years, early childhood education programs across the United States have recognized music as a valuable teaching tool. However, few who work with young children understand why young children should be nourished with music for its own sake. Adults who work with young children must change their thoughts about music's role in early childhood education. They must begin to value music for its own sake. Only then will they ensure that children under their care are musically nurtured and are given the personal resources necessary to engage in musical expression.

# Establishing Music in Early Childhood Education: A Historical Perspective

## Key Terms

| | | |
|---|---|---|
| accelerando | extrinsic rewards | Renaissance |
| advocate | formal operations | reversibility |
| anthroposophy | iconic | rhythm instruments |
| Baroque | improvisation | ritardando |
| Child Development Associate (CDA) credential | intrinsic rewards | scaffolding |
| | Middle Ages | sensorimotor stage |
| child study movement | monophonic | separation anxiety |
| classification | musical notation | seriation |
| concrete operations | object permanence | symbolic |
| conservation | polyphony | tempo |
| enactive | preoperational stage | zone of proximal development |
| eurythmy | recorder | |

Sarah and Marissa are good friends. They attended classes, received their **Child Development Associate (CDA) credential** at the same time, and are working in the same child care center as new classroom teachers. Together, they planned their lessons for the first month of school, which they are now sharing with their director, John (see Figure 1–1). Both of them know that they should include "a variety of music, art, literature, dance, role-playing, celebrations, and other creative activities from the children's culture" in their lesson plans (Council for Professional Recognition, 1996, p. 51). Sarah has planned to use music throughout her daily plans to help her teach the children. Marissa does not think that provides sufficient opportunities for children to "play with sound, rhythm, language, materials, space, and ideas in individual ways and to express their creative abilities" (Council for Professional Recognition, 1996, p. 50). John suggests that they examine what some of the early childhood pioneers had to say about music and how music should be used with young children. In addition, he suggests that they review child development theories that will help them select appropriate activities for the developmental ages and stages of the children in their classrooms.

***Figure* 1-1**  Sarah and Marissa discuss using music in the classroom with their director, John.

Why would examining the beliefs of early childhood pioneers regarding music in early childhood help Sarah and Marissa decide what to do in their classroom? Current thinking in any field of study is built on the foundation of historical viewpoints from the field's pioneers. Therefore, through reflection on historical viewpoints of early education pioneers, we arrive at a better understanding of where today's practices in early childhood originated. Not all of the historical persons mentioned in this chapter were educators. Some were practitioners who worked directly with children, while others were philosophers and theorists who suggested how other adults should work with children. However, all of them were **advocates** for young children and the education of young children by society.

## Historical Early Childhood Education Advocates and Pioneers

Throughout time, great thinkers contemplated the education of children. Beginning with Plato, Aristotle, and Socrates, society has received guidance regarding the upbringing and education of its future citizens. The following educational advocates and pioneers have influenced current early childhood

education. Additionally, and of specific interest for this textbook, they expressed opinions on the place of music in the education of children.

### Johann Amos Comenius (1592–1670)

Johann Amos Comenius was a Czech educator and bishop in the Moravian church. He believed that three reasons existed for educating children: "(1) faith and piety, (2) uprightness in respect to morals, and (3) knowledge of languages and arts" (Monroe, 1900, p. 111). His progressive educational philosophy included the belief that a child's education should start at birth. During the seventeenth century, formal schooling began at age six or seven and younger children received little education (Monroe, 1900). Comenius realized that if children were to be educated from birth, then the responsibility for this instruction must fall on the shoulders of their mothers (Monroe, 1900). However, he thought mothers were not prepared for this responsibility. To help them, Comenius wrote a guide for mothers called the *School of Infancy* that specifically outlined the training he felt mothers should begin as soon as their children were born (Monroe, 1900).

Some of the current early childhood principles of education that reflect the teachings of Comenius include:

- Early education is the foundation of future education.
- Learning begins at birth.
- Each child progresses through predictable stages, but at his own rate.
- Children learn through play.
- The child's physical development can affect his cognitive development.
- Children learn through hands-on, concrete manipulation of objects (Monroe, 1900).

The *School of Infancy* included music education to develop the child's musical sense. During the 1600s, only the nobility received an education in music, so this was a revolutionary move (Aries, 1962). Comenius believed that "music is instinctive and natural to the child" and that the child's first lessons in music were his vocalizations (Monroe, 1900, p. 119).

He called these vocalizations "complaints and wailings" (Monroe, 1900, p. 119). Comenius advised mothers to expose their infants to music so that "their ears and minds may be soothed" by the sounds (Monroe, 1900, p. 119). He also approved of the "banging and rattling noises" children make as "legitimate steps in the development of the child's musical sense" (Monroe, 1900, p. 119). He encouraged mothers to help their children develop a musical sense by allowing them to play drums, rattles, whistles, and horns and by making the children aware of rhythm and melody in music (Monroe, 1900). In addition, Comenius believed that music education assisted cognitive development (Monroe, 1900). Children can develop their language through the rhythms and melodies of nursery rhymes and songs. Comenius taught that although the children may not be able to understand the words, they will be attracted to the rhythm of the rhymes and songs (Monroe, 1900). Some principles of music education articulated by Comenius that are still used today include:

- Expose children to music, beginning at birth.
- Sing nursery rhymes and simple songs.
- Allow children to explore sounds.
- Allow children to explore instruments.

Although the care of young children was the responsibility of mothers in the seventeenth century, Comenius realized that some mothers were not able to care for their children. He recommended that children who must be cared for by others be entrusted only to those who made learning enjoyable. He felt that schools should not be "houses of torture"(Monroe, 1900, p. 112). Interestingly, he expressed this belief in terms of a musician who "does not dash his instrument against a wall, or give it blows and cuffs because he cannot draw music from it, but continues to apply his skill until he is able to extract a melody"(Monroe, 1900, p. 112). He encouraged teachers to use their skills to "bring the mind of the young child into harmony with his studies" (Monroe, 1900, p. 112).

As one of the first early childhood educational reformers, Comenius advocated the teaching of music for its own sake as well as for its use as a teaching tool. In addition, he used musical thoughts and musical terms to explain his ideas concerning good teaching practices.

## Jean Jacques Rousseau (1712–1778)

In 1762, Jean Jacques Rousseau, a French philosopher, wrote *Emile*, a literary work in which he presented his ideas regarding the education of an imaginary young boy, Emile. Some of his ideas for Emile's education that continue to be reflected in the early childhood field include:

- Children learn through concrete materials, not abstract thinking.
- Children learn through unstructured play.
- The environment should be appropriate for children.
- Children should spend a great deal of time in natural settings, outdoors.
- Learning begins at birth.
- Early education should be child-centered.
- Children think differently than adults.
- The curriculum should be appropriate for the level of the child's development. (Essa, 2003; Henniger, 2002; Rousseau, 1762/1928; Smith & Doyle, 1997).

Music education held an important place in Emile's education. Rousseau gave very specific instructions on how Emile should be taught. In reference to teaching him to sing, Rousseau (1762/1928) advised to "make his voice true, equal, flexible, and resonant, and his ear sensible to measure and harmony, and nothing more" (p. 137). Rousseau advised against requiring a child to use his voice beyond what he could naturally achieve. In other words, the music should be simple and within a range of notes that the child could sing without straining his voice. In addition, Rousseau instructed adults to avoid words when singing with children, because they might interfere with the enjoyment of the music. Concerning the use of words he said, "If he desired them, I should try to compose songs expressly for him, which should be adapted to a child's interest and should be as simple as his ideas" (p. 137). Rousseau wanted children to enjoy themselves through music and not worry about learning

**musical notation**. Rousseau asserted that Emile should not be taught to read until he was 12 years old (Closson, 1999). Concerning music, he expressed a similar desire that adults not teach young children to read music (Rousseau, 1762/1928). His assertion was that music is learned more accurately if learned first by ear, than by reading the music. Finally, Rousseau believed that to be good musicians, children should compose their own songs rather than just learn the songs of others. Rousseau advocated principles that current early childhood music education reflects and includes:

- Sing simple songs.
- Sing songs that reflect the child's interests.
- Sing songs without words.
- Have children compose their own songs (**improvisation**—to make up songs on the spot).
- Teach the child to listen to and reproduce music before teaching the child to read music (sound before symbol).
- Dance or move to music.

*Emile* was written during a time when singing secular songs was considered a crime and dancing was considered the "invention of the devil" (Rousseau, 1762/1928, p. 226). Work and prayer were considered the only proper activities for young girls. In a revolutionary move, Rousseau asserted that girls as well as boys should enjoy their youth and that they should also sing, dance, and play.

Rousseau was not an educator. However, his ideas did influence educational thinking, and current early childhood practices reflect his basic ideas. To Rousseau, music should be taught for its own sake. The inclusion of music in his educational plan for Emile was not a formal education in music, but a musical nurturing for the child's enjoyment. Eliminating structured, formal music lessons during the early years provides an appropriate foundation for young children's future music study.

## Johann Pestalozzi (1746–1827)

Johann Pestalozzi, a Swiss educator and "one of the greatest pioneers of modern education," was influenced by Rousseau's writings on education (Schwickerath, 1999). Pestalozzi became the first

person to be recognized as an early childhood educator. After opening a school at Yverdun, Switzerland, educators who were eager to learn from him flocked to the school. His educational plan for Switzerland was to make "moral men out of the children of his nation" (Walch, 1952, p. 139). He believed this could be accomplished by combining the philosophy of physical and intellectual development from the Greeks with the philosophy of Christian moral development (Walch, 1952). Early childhood education principles passed on by Pestalozzi to future generations of teachers include:

- Young children learn through sensory self-discovery and observation.
- Young children learn in a concrete manner by doing.
- Young children are individuals and they learn at their own rate and in their own manner.
- All children have the right to learn.
- Human relationships are important in the learning environment.
- Curriculum should be integrated (Barlow, 1977; Efland, 1983; Essa, 2003; Schwickerath, 1999; Walch, 1952).

Pestalozzi believed that mothers were important to the early education of their children. In his book, *How Gertrude Teaches Her Children,* he advised mothers about the education of their young children. Although he was not a musician, Pestalozzi believed that music was an essential element for his curriculum. He taught "that music should begin with lullabies the mother sings to the child in the cradle" (Walch, 1952, p. 138). Pestalozzi felt that music should be taught in a manner that enticed children to want to sing and left children with a love of music so that singing became "a natural and enjoyable activity" (Barlow, 1977, p. 60).

At Yverdun, music education was limited to singing. Through songs, children learned the fundamentals of music, including reading and composing music (Walch, 1952). In particular, Pestalozzi believed music was an aid to moral education (Walch, 1952). He believed that when schools or families used music to retain "the cheerful and chaste character," the existence of moral feelings and the ensuing happiness would "leave no doubt as to the intrinsic value of the art" (Walch, 1952, p. 138). Some of Pestalozzi's principles of early music education that are upheld in current music education include:

- Music education should begin at birth.
- Singing should be fun.
- Children should sing often.
- Children should learn to compose their own songs (improvisation).
- Teach the child to listen to and reproduce music before teaching the child to read music (sound before symbol).
- Begin with simple songs.
- All children should sing (Barlow, 1977; Efland, 1983; Walch, 1952).

To Pestalozzi music was important in the education of children from birth, for its own value as well as for helping to learn other subjects. Group singing of national songs and hymns was an important part of his school, and a former student reported that he enjoyed the singing in the halls as students went from class to class or on trips into the countryside (Barlow, 1977). Pestalozzi's principles continue to be used in the fields of early childhood and music.

## Friedrich Froebel (1782–1852)

Friedrich Froebel, a German educator, developed the first kindergarten in 1826. The German word *kindergarten* means children garden. Froebel's kindergarten curriculum was modeled on the trusting relationship a child has with his mother (Brosterman, 1997). Kindergarten teachers were to imitate loving mothers, the toys used in the classroom were called gifts, and the classrooms were like play gardens (Brosterman, 1997). In fact, gardens were an integral part of Froebel's original kindergartens (Brosterman, 1997). The early childhood education field continues to uphold many of Froebel's beliefs regarding how young children learn and how they should be taught. Some of those beliefs include:

- Children learn through play.
- Children learn through real experiences.
- Early learning sets a foundation for future learning.
- Children should have hands-on, concrete opportunities for learning.
- Children should draw their own conclusions, rather than be given an answer.
- Children should spend time with nature (Brosterman, 1997; Wiebé, 1923).

Upon visiting Pestalozzi at Yverdun, Froebel was influenced to make music and group singing a vital part of his kindergartens (Brosterman, 1977). Music and dance, particularly, were essential elements in Froebel's kindergarten games. Kindergarten games was the name of a group time during which the children sang and danced while they learned lessons about nature (plants growing, the sun rising, stars twinkling, etc.) or about occupations (shoemaker, farmer, baker, etc.) through dramatization (Wiebé, 1923).

Music was used as a transition aid as well as a teaching aid for these activities. The activities progressed in the following manner. The class would form a circle while singing about forming a circle. Another song might follow the first song and describe the circle with everyone standing "straight and strong" (Wiebé, 1923, p, 208). Finally, the children would play a singing and dancing game. For example, during one game, a child would stand in the center of the circle, while the other children sang a song about the child, asking about what he wanted to do. The child in the center would imitate an occupation or something in nature and then choose another child to take his place (Wiebé, 1923). The activity was then repeated. Currently, this type of activity is repeated in preschool classrooms every day.

After many years of teaching, Froebel became convinced of the importance of training very young children (Brosterman, 1997). He believed that by the time some children entered school at age seven, they were "too intellectually rigid to make good use of their subsequent lessons" (Brosterman, 1997, p. 33). In 1844, this belief led him to write his book *Mother-Play and Nursery Songs* (Brosterman, 1997), a guide for mothers to use with children as young as four months of age. The book featured 50 songs based on traditional German tunes with words added, a picture that illustrated a lesson, and a motto or instructions for the mother (Brosterman, 1997). These songs and games became the foundation for the songs we now sing in preschools and kindergartens, such as "Ring-Around-the-Rosies," "The Farmer in the Dell," and "If You're Happy" (Brosterman, 1997).

Froebel gave specific instructions on how to teach young children to sing. His instructions included:

- Sing softly.
- Sing to children, not with them—have children sing alone.
- Sing simple songs such as lullabies, often.
- Have children echo two or three notes sung by the teacher.
- Sing quickly and cheerfully—singing is fun.
- Have the children sit or stand straight while singing.
- Choose short songs with repetitions.
- Teachers should sing expressively and sing their words distinctly.
- Do not expect children to do too many things at once while singing (Wiebé, 1923).

Music played a fundamentally important part in Froebel's kindergartens. As stated earlier, music was used throughout the day as a teaching aid and as a transitional aid. Additionally, Froebel was concerned that children learn to sing well. Froebel's influence remains evident in many contemporary preschools and kindergartens.

## Maria Montessori (1870–1952)

Maria Montessori, the first woman doctor in Italy, was an advocate for young children (Driscoll & Nagel, 2002). Her work with young children and the schools that bear her name make her a well-known person in the early childhood education field. Originally, she worked with retarded or developmentally delayed children, believing that education rather than medicine could improve their development (Essa, 2003). She applied her techniques to working with these children, and they worked. In 1907, an opportunity to test her educational ideas on typically developing children presented itself. The city of Rome requested that she take charge of a day nursery in a poor tenement. She called the nursery "casa dei bambini" or children's house (Driscoll & Nagel, 2001). Throughout

the years, she shaped her educational principles and methods of working with young children. Current early childhood practices reflecting these principles and methods include:

- There are windows of opportunity for learning.
- The learning environment should be prepared to match the child's level of development (i.e., the furniture, materials, and equipment).
- Children learn through their senses.
- Children learn through hands-on experiences.
- Children learn differently than adults learn.
- Young children are capable of learning a great deal (Driscoll & Nagel, 2002; Essa, 2003; Faulmann, 1980; McDonald, 1983; Rubin, 1983).

When Dr. Montessori founded the Casa dei Bambini in Milan, Maria Maccheroni became the first director (Rubin, 1983). Maccheroni was a skilled and sensitive pianist, who worked closely with Dr. Montessori on the musical application of her philosophy (Faulmann, 1980). Together, they wrote 35 booklets on the subject of music education (Rubin, 1983). Some of these booklets were for the children's use and others were written as guides for the teachers. Unfortunately, many of these booklets are currently not available (Rubin, 1983). The work of Montessori and her friend, Maccheroni, was so entwined that when reading various writings, it is difficult to know who had the original thoughts that went into the philosophy (Rubin, 1983).

The Montessori music program consisted of listening, playing instruments, singing, and moving rhythmically to music (McDonald, 1983). The difference between the Montessori program and what was considered a normal general-music class was the individualization of the Montessori Method. Children did not have to join in and when they did, it was in a very individualized manner (McDonald, 1983). The individualization of music for and by the children explains why some people think that Montessori schools did not incorporate music, when, in fact, music was an important element in a child's education from Montessori's point of view (Faulmann, 1980). Although her individualized approach appears rigid in some aspects, her principles are recognized and accepted today (McDonald, 1983). Those principles of musical development include:

- Teach the child to listen to and reproduce music before teaching the child to read music (sound before symbol).
- Exploration is important—allow children to explore sounds through instruments and voices (hands-on exploration and learning).
- Allow children to experiment with orchestral instruments.
- Physical movement is important—teach children to move rhythmically.
- Teach children the difference between sound and noise (McDonald, 1983).

Although they lived at various times and places in history, these early childhood education pioneers and advocates agreed on various principles regarding both early education and early music education. Their points of agreement are illustrated in Tables 1–1 and 1–2.

## Discovering Instruments

### Recorders

A recorder is a simple instrument that is related to a flute (see Figure 1–2). It is played by blowing through a slit in one end and covering holes in the body of the instrument with the fingers. Recorders were widely used during the Middle Ages, Renaissance, and early Baroque eras. Recorders are made in various sizes including soprano, alto, tenor, and bass. Often, soprano recorders are used in late elementary school music classes to teach children how to read and play music. A revival of Renaissance and Baroque music throughout the world has led to the formation of many musical groups dedicated to playing recorders and early music (Dragon Early Music, 2004).

## Human Development Theorists and Their Influence on Early Childhood Music Nurturing

Now, let us briefly turn to the human development theorists who guide our thinking in early childhood

**Figure 1–2**  Soprano recorder

education. This portion of the chapter is not meant to substitute for an in-depth study of these theories. The theorists and their theories are introduced in this chapter and references are made to them throughout the text to illustrate how they guide our teaching methods when working with young children.

### Jean Piaget and Cognitive Developmental Theory

Jean Piaget (1896–1980) was a Swiss biologist and child psychologist. By studying his own children from birth, Piaget conceived a theory of how children develop cognitively. His theory of cognitive development was one of the first and most significant contributions to early childhood education and continues to be an influence on the field. Piaget believed that children's cognitive development occurs in four stages, sensorimotor, preoperational, concrete operations, and formal operations. Early childhood education is primarily concerned with the first two stages and part of the third. Each stage prepares the child for the subsequent developmental stage.

*Piaget's Stages of Cognitive Development*  The first stage is the sensorimotor stage, which begins at birth and continues through age two, approximately. During the sensorimotor stage, infants use their senses and motor skills to discover their world. They come into the

**Table 1-1**   Comparison of Beliefs in Early Childhood Education Advocated by Historical Advocates and Pioneers

| Beliefs in Early Childhood Education DSC | Johann Amos Comenius (1592–1670) | Jean Jacques Rousseau (1712–1778) | Johann Pestalozzi (1746–1827) | Friedrich Froebel (1782–1852) | Maria Montessori (1870–1952) |
|---|---|---|---|---|---|
| Learning begins at birth. | * | * | | | |
| Early education is the foundation for future learning. | * | | | * | |
| A child develops through predictable stages at his own rate. | * | | * | | |
| There are windows of opportunity for learning. | | | | | * |
| Physical development can affect cognitive development. | * | | | | |
| Children think and learn differently than adults. | | * | | | * |
| Children learn through unstructured play. | * | * | | * | |
| Children learn through real experiences. | | | | * | |
| Young children learn through their senses and observation. | | | * | | |
| Children should be allowed to draw their own conclusions. | | | | * | * |
| Early education should be child-centered. | | * | | | |
| Children learn through hands-on manipulation of concrete objects, not abstract thinking. | * | * | * | * | * |
| The environment should be prepared to match the child's developmental level. | | * | | | * |
| The curriculum should be appropriate for the child's level of development. | | * | | | |
| Young children are capable of learning a great deal. | | | | | * |
| All children have the right to learn. | | | * | | |
| Human relationships are important in education. | | | * | | |
| Curriculum should be integrated. | | | * | | |
| Children should spend a great deal of time in natural settings, outdoors. | | * | | * | |

**Table 1–2**  Comparison of Beliefs in Early Childhood Music Education Advocated by Historical Advocates and Pioneers

| Beliefs in Early Childhood Education | Johann Amos Comenius (1592–1670) | Jean Jacques Rousseau (1712–1778) | Johann Pestalozzi (1746–1827) | Friedrich Froebel (1782–1852) | Maria Montessori (1870–1952) |
|---|---|---|---|---|---|
| Music nurturing should begin at birth. | * | | * | | |
| Sing simple songs with young children, such as nursery rhymes and lullabies. | * | * | * | * | |
| Sing songs that reflect the child's interests. | | * | | | |
| Sing softly. | | | | * | |
| Sing songs without words. | | * | | | |
| Have children echo two or three notes sung by the teacher. | | | | * | |
| Sing often. | | | * | * | |
| Singing should be fun. | | | * | * | |
| Children should be encouraged to compose their own songs. | * | * | * | | |
| Teach children to listen to and reproduce music before teaching them to read music. | | * | * | | * |
| All children should sing. | | | * | | |
| Sing to children, not with them; have children sing alone. | | | | * | |
| Teachers should sing expressively and sing words distinctly. | | | | * | |
| Children should sit or stand straight while singing. | | | | * | |
| Allow children to explore sound through instruments and voices. | * | | | | * |
| Allow children to play instruments. | | | | | * |
| Do not expect children to do too many things while singing. | | | | * | |
| Dance and move to music. | | * | | | * |
| Teach children the difference between sound and noise. | | | | | * |

world with survival reflexes that are gradually replaced with intentional and complex movements. Over the first two years of life, infants begin to solve problems and realize they can have an effect on their environment. Around seven months of age, infants also develop **object permanence**, which allows them to understand that an object exists even when they cannot see it. This ability also leads to **separation anxiety** when the

## A Closer Look

### Waldorf Schools—Where Teaching Is an Art and the Arts Are Not Just Frills

Rudolf Steiner (1861–1925) was a philosopher, scientist, writer, educator, and Goethe scholar. He spent a great deal of his life striving to understand the spiritual world and was the founder of **anthroposophy**, "a philosophy with a spiritually-based world view" (Lenart, 2000, p. 1). "Anthroposophy holds that the human being is fundamentally a spiritual being and that all human beings deserve respect as the embodiment of their spiritual nature"(Mays & Nordwall, 2004, p. 1).

In 1919, when asked by the owner of the Waldorf-Astoria cigarette factory to open a school for the children of his employees, Steiner's philosophy of life and the spiritual world became the foundation upon which he built the curriculum for the school that became known as the Waldorf school. Worldwide, there are currently about 870 Waldorf schools. The schools include levels from preschool through high school.

#### Goals

The Waldorf schools' goals are "to produce individuals who are able, in and of themselves, to impart meaning to their lives" (Mays & Nordwall, 2004, p.4). The schools aim to educate the whole child with a broad curriculum that "balances academic subjects with artistic and practical activities" (Mays & Nordwall, 2004, p. 4).

#### Child Development Beliefs

Steiner believed that children go through three major developmental stages, each lasting seven years.

1. Birth–7 years old: the best way for children to learn at this stage is through physical activity and play.
2. 7–14: children learn through feeling and imagination. Children respond to the arts at this time.

3. 14 and up: This is the thinking stage when intellectual abilities are developed.

#### Distinguishing Features of the Waldorf Schools

- Academics are de-emphasized in the early school years. Pre-academic skills are developed in kindergarten, with minimal academics taught in first grade. Reading is not taught until second or third grade.
- Each grouping of children has the same teacher for grades 1–8.
- Art, music, gardening, and foreign languages are central activities in all grades. In the younger grades, all subjects are taught through the arts. Additionally, all children learn to play the **recorder** and to knit.
- There are no textbooks for the first five grades.
- Learning is noncompetitive with no grades given at the elementary level. Instead, teachers write summary evaluations on each child.
- Television and computers are discouraged for the young child.
- **Eurythmy** is a part of the curriculum in all Waldorf schools. Eurythmy is a dancelike bodily movement used to express music and speech with "specific movements corresponding to particular notes or sounds" (Mays & Nordwall, 2004, p. 4).

Waldorf schools have existed for 80 years, though not without controversy. The philosophical foundation of the school has led to misunderstandings. Although Steiner based his educational theories on his belief in anthroposophy, this philosophy is not taught in Waldorf schools. The schools are open to all children. For more information on these interesting schools, you can visit the sites listed in the Resource Guide in Appendix D.

Sources: Lenart, 2000; Mays & Nordwall, 2004.

---

infant realizes that mommy exists even when she leaves. Although the sensorimotor stage covers a short amount of time in the child's life, the rate at which a child grows and changes during the first two years of life caused Piaget to divide the sensorimotor stage into six substages. (See Appendix A for more details.)

The preoperational stage begins at approximately two years old and lasts until approximately seven years

old. It is a time of tremendous cognitive development. This stage witnesses the growth of the child's language and his problem-solving abilities. The child begins to classify his world for better understanding. **Classification** is the process of grouping people, animals, and things according to various attributes, such as shape, color, size, occupation, and use. Early in the preoperational stage, the child's limited sense of reality hinders his

---

## A Closer Look

### Child Study Movement

Around the end of the nineteenth century, there was an increasing demand for information about how children develop. Several societal factors contributed to this demand. To name a few, industrial advances required a better-educated workforce, society idealized motherhood as an important occupation, which caused mothers to seek information about their children, and their children's development, and recreational organizations developed after-school programs and public playgrounds.

In 1882, William Preyer wrote and published *Mind of the Child,* a book that described observations of his own son. As the

first of its kind, it was an immediate success and became the forerunner of many such books throughout the 1890s. About the same time, G. Stanley Hall, a founder of American psychology, began using questionnaires in his research on children. He believed that both teachers and parents would be more effective if they understood the child's level of development. Hall campaigned for the establishment of child study associations. He was convincing and, by 1911, the **child study movement** was an international movement with its own journal. Out of this movement sprang the theories on which the early childhood education field bases many of its beliefs (Wozniak, 1999).

---

perception of the world. In particular, he may not understand perceptions taken from any viewpoint other than his own. However, as he moves through the preoperational stage, he develops a more realistic view of the world and gradually begins to see things from another's point of view. (See Appendix A for more details.)

The **concrete operations** stage begins at approximately 7 years of age and lasts until approximately 11 years of age. During this stage, children continue to build on the concepts of classification and **seriation** that they began to explore and understand during the preoperational stage. Seriation is the process of arranging items in a series according to a particular attribute, such as height (from shortest to tallest or vice versa) or pitch (from highest to lowest). In addition, the skills of **conservation** and **reversibility** are achieved during this stage. Conservation is the understanding that an object's volume or quantity does not change regardless of whether its shape changes (a ball of clay has the same volume, even when it is flattened). Reversibility is the ability to think in reverse. By age 9, the child has left the realm of early childhood education and has entered late childhood. (See Appendix A for more details.)

The final stage of Piaget's cognitive development is the formal operations stage. This stage is well beyond the early childhood age range. During the formal operations stage, from approximately age 12 and

up, abstract thought is used to solve problems, wrestle with concepts, and develop ideas.

The ability to plan for and present developmentally appropriate activities to young children requires teachers to have a good understanding of child development. Studying Piaget's theory of cognitive development is just one step toward that understanding.

### Erik Erikson and Psychosocial Theory

Erik Erikson (1902–1994) was born in Germany and moved to Boston, Massachusetts, in 1933. As a follower of Sigmund Freud, Erikson is best known for his refinement and expansion of Freud's theory. His psychosocial theory was the first to include the entire age span of the human being and expanded Freud's theory from five to eight stages. The first four stages of Erikson's psychosocial theory embrace the early childhood years and extend from birth through age 11. (See Appendix A for more details.)

Erikson believed that each stage presents a task to the individual (Boeree, 1999). This task causes a conflict within the person or between the person and others, which must be resolved (Essa, 2003). The first four stages are described as conflicts between trust and mistrust, autonomy and shame, initiative and guilt, and industry and inferiority. To successfully complete each stage, a balance must be met between the opposing characteristics the person is confronting.

Understanding Erikson's psychosocial development theory is another step to understanding the complex subject of child development.

In early childhood music, it is important to have an understanding of Erikson's stages of psychosocial development theory so that teachers support each child's feeling of competence and success. When children have successful experiences with music, they will want to continue having similar experiences. Being able to help children build their trust, independence, initiative, and industry in music is an important step in helping children want to take music with them throughout life.

## Lev Vygotsky's Sociocultural Theory and Proximal Development Theory

Lev Vygotsky (1896–1934) was a Russian lawyer. He had no formal training in psychology but was fascinated by it, and his theory on how children solve problems has recently begun to influence early childhood education. During his short life, he wrote books and articles on psychology, but the Russian government rejected his ideas. After the Cold War ended, his students exposed his works to the world (Berk, 2001; Gallagher, 2004).

Vygotsky believed that culture plays a large part in a child's development. Among the various cultures, differences exist in children's thought and behavior. Vygotsky believed that children acquire their ways of thinking and behaving through their interactions with adults and older children. His theory looks at how culture, that is, values, beliefs, customs, and skills, is passed from generation to generation (Berk, 2001). Four basic principles of this theory include:

- Children construct their knowledge of the world.
- Development occurs within a social context.
- Learning can lead to development.
- Language is important for cognitive development (Gallagher, 2004).

An important concept in Vygotsky's theory is the **zone of proximal development**. Vygotsky believed that a child's learning takes place within this zone. The zone contains the child's potential accomplishments or those tasks the child has not yet mastered. The adult helps the child master a task by breaking it down into manageable units, giving verbal instructions, pointing out problems, and encouraging the child. The child interacts with the adult, picking up ideas for success, and begins to feel competent. Once the child begins to reveal his understanding, the adult lets the child assume more responsibility for completing the task (Berk, 2001). Vygotsky called the work of the adult to support children in their learning, **scaffolding.**

Vygotsky's theory has influenced the early childhood education field and, specifically, has generated additional research on the role of society in the development of children. In part, Vygotsky has influenced Russian education and the preschools of Reggio Emilia, Italy (Gallagher, 2004). In the United States and around the world, Vygotsky's theory is recognized and practiced. Music, as a part of each child's culture, supports the child's development. Therefore, it is important for each classroom's curriculum to reflect the culture of every child in the room through the music experienced by the children.

## Jerome Bruner and His Theory of Instruction

Jerome Bruner (1915–present), an American psychologist, has been a leader in educational reform for the United States and Britain since the early 1960s (Hollyman, 2000). As with Piaget and Vygotsky, Bruner's theory of how children learn is a constructivist theory, which means he believes that children construct their own knowledge. Bruner believed that learning is a process in which children are actively engaged. Children build new ideas and concepts using the knowledge they have acquired in the past and are currently acquiring (Kearsley, 2005).

Bruner believed that children use three different modes to obtain knowledge.

- **Enactive:** This refers to the manner in which children actively manipulate materials to discover their characteristics. Although this way of learning is used throughout a person's life, it is primarily used by children during the very early years.

- **Iconic:** This refers to the use of mental images such as pictures, diagrams, and models to learn, and is prevalent during the middle to late childhood years.
- **Symbolic:** This way of learning usually becomes prevalent during the adolescent years when abstract thinking is used to reason and solve problems (Hollyman, 2000).

According to Bruner, there are four major features of learning that should be addressed in a theory of instruction (Kearsley, 2005). These features include:

- A predisposition toward learning—in other words, children should be motivated to want to learn. Teachers must find a way to tempt a child's curiosity.
- A structuring of a body of knowledge so that the information is easily grasped—this relates back to the three modes of learning. It is up to the teacher to know the child and the best way in which to present information to the child, so he can grasp that information. In general, with very young children, the more concrete and active the learning, the better chance they have of learning.
- An effective sequencing of the material to be learned—in other words, lead a child through the content of material to be learned in a sequential manner that matches the child's mode of learning. Usually, this means to move from the concrete to the abstract.
- Establishment of a specific method of rewarding children—this means that children need feedback as they progress in the learning process. Teachers should give feedback in the form of praise (**extrinsic rewards**) as well as help children experience the reward of being able to solve a problem or understand a concept (**intrinsic rewards**).

As musical nurturers of young children, early childhood educators must learn to recognize the learning style and mode of learning for each child. They should motivate children to explore music and sounds in the world around them. Musical concepts must be presented in an effective manner and sequence so they can be grasped by every child. And finally, music nurturers must establish a way to provide children with feedback and encouragement while they guide them to a level of knowledge that allows the children to experience the intrinsic rewards of accomplishment.

## Summary

In answer to the question, why should music be a part of the early childhood curriculum, this chapter examined the work of early childhood pioneers and theorists. Early childhood education pioneers laid the foundations for the early childhood education movement, and kept music a vital part of that movement. Historically, music was used as an aid to develop character and to teach concepts. In addition, music was taught for its own sake. No matter how music was used, the reason behind its use was simply that the person who was writing about or implementing an early childhood educational theory believed that music was important. Near the end of the nineteenth century, the child study movement brought forth theories of child development that have guided the work of teachers with young children. This chapter explored the relationship of these theories to the use of music in the early childhood classroom.

Chapter 2 continues to explore why music is important in early childhood by discussing recent research in the music, early childhood, and related fields. Music Lab #1 begins your practical preparation to be a music nurturer of young children.

## Key Concepts

- An understanding of historical perspectives helps develop an understanding of current trends.
- Many of the practices in the early childhood field are not new ideas.
- Music has always been important to the field of early childhood education.
- An understanding of theories of child development helps teachers do their job.

## Suggested Activities

1. Choose an educational pioneer or theorist and further investigate his or her theories and ideas.
2. Visit several early childhood classrooms and identify the use of these early ideas.
3. Visit an after-school program. Is music used in the program? How?
4. Begin a journal for reflective thinking. Question 1: What do you think your strengths are as a musical nurturer for young children? What are your weaknesses? How do you plan to strengthen your weaknesses?

## Music Lab #1

Welcome to the music lab. I hope you left your inhibitions outside the door. That is a very important first step for each lab. If you approach each music lab as a child, uninhibited, you will begin to experience music in the same way that young children experience it, before they become self-conscious. This approach is a natural way to feel music and make it a part of your entire being.

Music Lab #1, as with all the labs in this textbook, will lead you to an understanding of music through simple music activities, many of which are appropriate for use with young children. Each lab ends with a musical journey of music appreciation. In this lab, the journey begins with Western European music of the Middle Ages and Renaissance and in subsequent labs continues through the twentieth century to the present. Additionally, the music of various other world cultures will be explored. This knowledge will help you select the music that you will use to nurture young children. It is my desire that your experiences in the music labs will help you feel competent and comfortable as you establish music in your classroom curriculum. Now, let's begin the activities for this lab.

### Activity #1: Listening to Sounds

Music is sound. Therefore, an exploration of sounds in the world is a good starting point for an introduction to music, both for you and for young children.

**For You**

1. Obtain recordings of sounds from nature such as rain, ocean waves, and animals, and man-made sounds such as household sounds and street sounds. These types of recordings are often found in the New Age music section. Choose recordings that are pure and do not incorporate music with the sounds, if possible. See the Resource Guide in Appendix D for suggested recordings.
2. Spend time listening to the sounds.
3. Think about what words you would use to describe the sounds to children. Are they loud, but musical, mysterious, noisy, tinkling, relaxing?
4. Use the relaxing sounds for relaxing before you go to bed.

**In the Preschool and in Out-of-School Programs**

1. In a quiet area, set up a tape recorder and headphones, so children can listen to sounds, both natural and man-made.
2. In a small group or at circle time, play various sounds for children and ask them to describe

Listening to sounds of nature can be soothing while children read books.

what they heard. Use descriptive words such as *loud, soft, high, low, long, mysterious,* or *noisy* with them.

3. At naptime, use nature sound recordings to help children relax.

## Try This One!

### Sound Detectives

Montessori taught children to listen through lessons in silence (McDonald, 1983). She asked children to sit in silence and she gradually introduced sounds into that silence (McDonald, 1983). In this same manner, Montessori also helped children distinguish between sound and noise. She felt this training would help them learn to prefer sounds over mere noise (McDonald, 1983).

This activity can be done with older preschool and school-age children. Prepare ahead of time by selecting a handbell for the exercise.

- Have the children sit in a circle.
- Tell them they are going to be sound detectives, but first they must close their eyes, be very quiet, and just listen.
- Allow them to listen in silence for about 15 seconds. (This can be a very long time for children

and may even have to be shortened the first few times you try this exercise.)

- Ask if they could hear anything while they were silent.
- Discuss the sounds they heard and the fact that they might not have heard these sounds if they had not been so silent.
- Tell them that they are to close their eyes once more and keep them closed while you make a sound for them. Tell them to just listen to the sound until it stops.
- Wait about five seconds and then ring the bell once. When the sound stops, wait a couple of seconds and have the children open their eyes and discuss what they heard.
- Repeat the exercise with the bell, again, to allow the children to hear what they have just discussed.

Many children are not used to sitting in silence, so the time you spend preparing them for the experience may vary from group to group. Plan the exercise at times when the routine usually calls for a quiet time and do not try to do it immediately following a loud and boisterous activity. Before naptime would be an ideal time to introduce the exercise. Repeat the exercise using various instruments such as a drum, tambourine, or triangle.

## Activity #2: Experiencing Rhythm Instruments

**Rhythm instruments** are found in most early childhood classrooms. Rhythm instruments can be divided into two categories, nonpitched and pitched. Many rhythm instruments come to us from other cultures and you will discover their origins along with the description of the instruments. In this lab, we examine nonpitched rhythm instruments only.

## Discovering Instruments

### Nonpitched Rhythm Instruments

- Maracas: Maracas originated in Latin America. They are dried gourds that still have their seeds inside. Play them by shaking like rattles. Often, maracas are made of plastic when purchased in early childhood rhythm kits.

- Rhythm sticks: These instruments have derived from primitive instruments made of sticks or animal bones. Their origin can be found in many cultures. Approximately 12 inches long, rhythm sticks come in two styles. Plain sticks are played by tapping against each other. Sticks with ridges can be rubbed against each other for a different sound. Rhythm sticks are usually found in basic early childhood rhythm kits.
- Woodblocks: These are blocks of wood that are partially hollowed out. A wooden mallet is used to strike them. When struck over the slot on the surface, the woodblock makes a very resonant "tick-tock" sound. The origin of woodblocks can be traced to many cultures. Not normally found in basic early childhood rhythm kits, woodblocks can be purchased separately.
- Tone blocks: These are similar to woodblocks, except that the surface has ridges. This instrument can be either struck or rubbed with a mallet. As with woodblocks, their origins can be traced to many cultures. Tone blocks are usually found in early childhood rhythm kits.
- Sand blocks: These are blocks of wood, covered with sandpaper. When they are rubbed together, they make a swishing sound. Sand blocks are excellent as one of the first rhythm instruments for young children. They are easy to hold and use.
- Claves: These are thick wooden sticks, approximately 1 inch in diameter and 6–8 inches long. They are made from hardwood, usually rosewood. Play claves by cupping one stick in the palm of your hand and striking it with the other stick. They make a bright clicking sound. These instruments are used extensively in Cuban music (Dolmetsch Online, n.d.). Not normally found in basic early childhood rhythm kits, claves can be purchased separately.
- Castanets: These are believed to have originated in the Orient (Iben, 1997). Instruments similar to castanets were played in ancient Egypt. They made their way to Spain from Africa during the Middle Ages where they became linked with Spanish dances. The dancers fasten the cord that

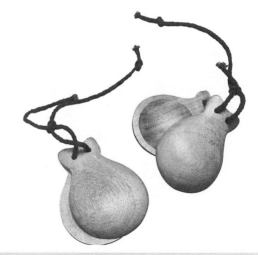

**Figure 1–3**   Castanets

holds the two halves together around the first finger and thumb. The castanets are struck together with the fingers. (See Figure 1–3.) In addition, castanets may be fastened to a handle. These are played by shaking or tapping in the palm of your hand. Castanets with handles may be found in early childhood rhythm kits.

Rhythm drums originate from nearly all primitive cultures. Usually they were made in a cylindrical shape and were covered with animal skin on one or both ends. Rhythm drums are played by striking with the hands or a mallet or stick. The following are common nonpitched drums.

- Hand drum: The hand drum comes in various diameter sizes, but the rim is usually less than 3 inches high. Hold the rim in one hand and strike the drumhead with the other hand or with a mallet. (See Figure 1–4.)
- Lollipop drum: This is similar to a hand drum, except it is on a stick and resembles a lollipop. It can also be played with the hand or a mallet.
- Tom-tom: This drum originated with Native Americans. The tom-tom comes in a variety of sizes and can sit on the floor or be held in a lap. The tom-tom can be played with the hand, a mallet, or sticks. The tom-tom is the drum most often found in early childhood rhythm kits.

**Figure 1–4**    Hand drum

**Figure 1–5**    Triangle

- Cymbals: These are metal disks with a handle in the center. Two can be played by striking or rubbing together. One can be played by striking with a mallet or wire brush. Cymbals are one of the oldest instruments and originated in Asia where they were used in religious rituals (Vienna Symphonic Library, 2002). They were brought to Europe during the Middle Ages (Vienna Symphonic Library, 2002). Cymbals are usually found in early childhood rhythm kits.
- Finger cymbals: These small cymbals are attached to the thumb and middle finger of one hand with elastic bands. They are played by striking them together. They can also be played by holding the elastic band of one cymbal and striking its rim with the other cymbal. This is the easiest manner for young children to play them. These instruments also originated in Asia, where they were usually used by female dancers who struck them together in a specific rhythm (Dolmetsch Online, 2002). Finger cymbals are not usually found in early childhood rhythm kits, although some kits have small cymbals mounted on a stick for shaking or hitting against the palm of the opposite hand.
- Triangle: This instrument gets its name from its shape (see Figure 1–5). It is a three-sided metal instrument with a string attached for holding it. Play the triangle by striking it with a metal or wooden stick. The origin of this instrument is not known. However, angels are depicted playing triangles in

paintings from the Middle Ages (*Explore Dictionary of Music*, 2005). This has led to the belief that it was used in religious ceremonies (*Explore Dictionary of Music*, 2005). Triangles are commonly found in basic early childhood rhythm kits.
- Tambourine: This instrument originated in the Mediterranean. There are two different types of tambourines. The first one is a wooden ring into which sets of metal disks are attached (see Figure 1–6). It is played by shaking or striking with the hand or against the leg. The second type has a drumhead that is similar to a hand drum as well as the inset metal disks. This instrument can be played in the same way as the headless tambourine and the drumhead can be struck with

**Figure 1–6**    Tambourine

the hand or a mallet. Often, tambourines found in early childhood rhythm kits are made of plastic.

Bells can be found in many sizes and shapes and are found in most cultures. Various materials including metal, wood, glass, and ceramic are used to make bells. The following are nonpitched bells.

- Jingle bells: These are small bells that are usually made from metal. They are played by shaking them. When attached to a band that can be fastened around the wrist or ankle, they may be called wrist bells. Many bells attached to a stick that can be shaken are usually called sleigh bells. Jingle bells are a common instrument in early childhood rhythm kits.
- Cowbells: This instrument gets its name from the tradition of placing the bells around the necks of cows to keep track of the herd (see Figure 1–7). When used as an instrument, it can be struck with a mallet or stick. A lower sound can be made by striking near the opening of the bell, while a higher sound can be made by striking near the top of the bell. Not normally found in basic early childhood rhythm kits, cowbells can be purchased separately.

**For You**

1. Obtain a set of rhythm instruments and experiment with them. What sounds can you make with

*Figure 1–7*  Cowbell

them? How would you describe the sounds to children?
2. How many different ways can you play the instrument?
3. Listen to compositions that incorporate rhythm instruments such as Steve Reich's *Music for Pieces of Wood,* a composition for five sets of claves, or the "Anvil Chorus" from *Il Trovatore* (Verdi), which highlights the tambourine and the triangle.

**In the Preschool and in Out-of-School Programs**

1. Place rhythm instruments on a low shelf for children to explore and play. This area should be away from quiet areas of the room. The variety of instruments available at any one time should depend on the age of the children. Several instruments of the same kind should be provided for young children who are just learning to share.
2. Allow children the freedom to explore the sounds they can make with the instruments. Do not expect them to participate in organized musical play until they have had a chance to explore the instruments.
3. Find an appropriate time to share recordings of music that highlights rhythm instruments with the children. See the Resource Guide (Appendix D) for other suggested recordings.

## Activity #3: Making Musical Instruments

The making of musical instruments by teachers and children is another element of the early childhood music program. One of the easiest instruments to make and one of the basic instruments for early childhood rhythm kits are sand blocks. Below are instructions to make sand blocks and an activity in which to engage children.

### Sand Blocks

**For You**
Collect the following materials:

- Stapler or tacks
- Two sanded blocks of pine for each set (Approximately: 4" × 3" × 1")
- Cabinet knobs or handles
- Sandpaper (medium or fine)

*Music of the World*

### Singing Bowls of Tibet

An unusual instrument comes from Tibet in the form of a bowl. Singing bowls have been used for centuries to help people relax and meditate. These brass bowls emit a calm tone when a stick is run around the outside of the bowl. See the Resource Guide in Appendix D for sources of singing bowls.

1. Obtain sets of two pine wood blocks that have been sanded.
2. Attach a cabinet knob or handle on the top of each block.
3. Cut the sandpaper to fit around the bottom of the block and up both sides.
4. Staple or tack the sandpaper on the block.

### In the Infant or Toddler Room

These instruments are not suitable for the infant and toddler rooms, except under meticulous teacher supervision. The teacher can play the instrument, or hold the infant's hands, while making the sound, but they should not be placed in a location for the children to use on their own. Toddlers enjoy making the swishing sound of the sand blocks, but at this age, they continue to place materials in their mouths. Not only is the sand not good for them to ingest, but these instruments cannot be sanitized.

### In the Preschool and in Out-of-School Programs

The children can make these instruments with some help from the teacher. The blocks of wood can be sanded as part of a woodworking project. If each child makes a set, he will have his own instrument for use during music time.

## Try This One!

### Playing Sand Blocks

Play the sand blocks by rubbing them together to make a swishing sound. Chant the following rhyme while playing the sand blocks.

**Choo Choo**

Choo, choo, choo, choo,
Goin' down the track.
Choo, choo, choo, choo,
Smokestack on your back.
Choo, choo, choo, choo,
Goin' down the track.
Choo, choo, choo, choo,
Clickety, clickety clack.

Variation:

1. Begin by chanting only the words, *choo, choo,* four or eight times. Swish the sand blocks on each word. Chant very slowly, as if the train is leaving the station, and then, gradually go faster and faster until you reach a medium speed to which you can say the rhyme.
2. Use the sand block as an accompaniment throughout the rhyme.
3. After finishing the rhyme, gradually slow down to a stop, saying *choo, choo,* another four or eight times, as if the train is pulling into a station and stopping.
4. Do not forget to blow your horn at the end— toot, toot!!

Be sure the children are very familiar with the rhyme before attempting this variation with them. What is being varied in this version is the **tempo**. Tempo refers to how fast or slow a piece of music should be sung or played. Tempo is discussed further in Chapter 3. In this exercise, the tempo was varied by starting at a slow speed and gradually getting faster at the beginning of the song to imitate the train leaving the station. This is called **accelerando**. At the end of the verse, the tempo is gradually slowed down to imitate the train coming into the station and stopping. This is called **ritardando.**

### Bowl Drums

**For You**

Collect the following materials.

- Various-size plastic or metal bowls or any other round container such as an oatmeal box, a Crisco can, or, for smaller drums, a snack tube.
- Pieces of plastic or fabric to fit over the opening of the bowl
- Large rubber bands or string
- Dowels—1 foot long and ¾-inch thick
- Cotton
- Fabric
- Rubber
- Small rubber bands or tape

1. Stretch a piece of plastic bag or fabric across the opening of the bowl and attach it around the body of your drum with a large rubber band or string.
2. Make mallets by wrapping various materials such as fabric, rubber, or cotton around dowels. Use tape or small rubber bands to hold it on the dowel.
3. Listen to the various sounds you can make with your drum.

**In the Infant or Toddler Room**

As with the sand blocks, these instruments are not suitable for infants and toddlers to use alone. The sticks are especially inappropriate in these rooms. You can make drums for the infants and toddlers to use under supervision, although they may not last very long. It is better to use sturdy drums that are made for infant and toddler use.

**In the Preschool and in Out-of-School Programs**

The children can make these instruments with some help from the teacher. Depending on the children in the group, you will have to decide whether to play the drums with hands or mallets. Either way, you should make mallets to demonstrate the various sounds made by the drums.

## Try This One!

### Dancing Drums

Depending on the age of the children, you can read or tell the story *Dancing Drum: A Cherokee Legend* by Terri Cohlene. Although the reading level is for 9- to 12-year-olds, this Native American legend can be told to younger children and the beautiful pictures shown. Have the children play either the drums they have made or they can use their laps as a drum (lapdrums) by slapping their thighs with their hands as you chant.

**Dancing Drums**

Dancing drum, dancing drum,
Play upon your dancing drum.
Dance, dance, dance,
Dance, dance, dance.
Fingers dance on dancing drum.

## Activity #4: Music Appreciation: Music of the Middle Ages and the Renaissance

Much of the music heard in concert halls around the world is influenced by traditional Western European music. As Western Europeans colonized various lands, they took their music with them. Folk music was handed down from generation to generation and some was mixed with the music of indigenous people living in these colonized lands. Additionally, the European method of writing down music (musical notation) allowed music composed in Europe to be played and enjoyed all over the world. On the other hand, music of many cultures is often an aural tradition and is not written down. Therefore, until recent history and the development of recording devices, it was difficult for music, other than traditional Western European–based music, to be experienced anywhere except in its own land.

Understanding the origins of music is merely another piece of basic knowledge that allows you to feel comfortable with music. Due to the influence of traditional Western European music, the history of this music will be examined in depth. However, we must keep in mind Vygotsky's theory of the importance of culture to a child's development and assure that the culture of every child in the classroom is reflected through the music experienced by the children. For that reason, several music labs will examine the music of other cultures in addition to Western European–based music.

**For You**

Each European historical era is reflected in the art of its time. In this lab, we begin with the history of the music of the Middle Ages (AD 450–1450) and the Renaissance (1450–1600). The sources for the music history presented in this activity are Gorman (1986), Kamien (2003), Sadie (1986), and Sherrane (2004).

## Musical History

Paintings on early man's cave walls, stories in the Bible, and Egyptian hieroglyphics all reflect music in the life of early man. With the exception of a few fragments, most early music did not survive. Other civilizations had music, some more complex than the music of Europe, but the Middle Ages are considered the historical beginning for music of the Western culture. Music of Western culture is based on traditions that came out of the social and religious developments of that time.

Sometime between AD 450 and 500, European civilization began to emerge from the Dark Ages into the Middle Ages. During the Dark Ages, Europe had been invaded by Huns, Visigoths, and Vandals, bringing about the fall of the Roman Empire. Gradually, as the Roman legions left and people were alone to defend themselves, a new system formed in medieval society called feudalism. Feudalism began in France, then spread to England and finally throughout Western Europe during the 11th century.

There were two types of feudalism, economic and political. Economic feudalism was an arrangement between the feudal lord and the people living on his land. The peasants pledged loyalty and service to the lord in exchange for the right to use the land and for protection from invaders. The feudal lord was the lawmaker, judge, and protector of his lands and the people on them. As feudalism grew, alliances formed and lesser lords came under the protection of stronger lords. Through struggles to obtain more land, hierarchies eventually formed with a king at the top. "Mini-kingdoms" were developed throughout Europe (Sherrane, 2004, p. 2). Political feudalism was the relationship between the king and the feudal lords or nobles under his protection. The Middle Ages were a time of cultural growth, when towns were built, churches, monasteries, and gothic cathedrals were erected, and universities were founded.

The Roman Empire left behind two legacies: the language of Latin and the Catholic religion. The church held absolute power during the Middle Ages and the kings were considered servants of God. The supremacy of the church gave it control of the arts and music in the Western world and, although secular music existed, the majority of music heard was sacred. Music was an important part of religious services and the church was the primary employer of musicians.

Early church music was in the form of chants or plainsong called Gregorian chants that evolved from Jewish and Byzantine religious chants. Gregorian chants were named after Pope Gregory I, who is credited with codifying the chants in the sixth century. These chants continue to be used in Western churches and are known for their spirituality. As the number of chants increased, it was necessary to write them down to ensure uniformity from one church to another. Monks were nearly the only ones who could read and write, therefore church music was the only music written down. The earliest examples of these chants are from about the ninth century. The musical style of the time was monophonic; in other words, there was just one melody usually sung without any instrumental accompaniment. Secular music was performed in the courts by French troubadours. This music was usually vocal music with instrumental accompaniment.

During the ninth century, composers began to experiment with music by writing for two or more melodies to be sung together. This practice is believed to have started earlier as improvisation, but it was never written down. (Remember, improvisation refers to the art of being able to make up music on the spot, as it is performed.) By the beginning of the Renaissance, a distinctly Western style of music known as polyphony, or many voices, had developed.

Now, two singers might sing two different tunes together, or an instrument might accompany a singer but play different notes than the singer sang.

Progressively, the Middle Ages blended into the Renaissance period (1450–1600). The word *renaissance* comes from the Old French word *renaistre* and means "to be born again" (Lexico Publishing Group, 2004). The Western world had climbed out of the Dark Ages, had gone through a thousand years of the Middle Ages, and was ready for rebirth. Discovery of ancient Roman and Greek writings inspired a renewed interest in learning. Science, education, and the arts flourished. A new invention called a printing press made information available to a larger public. The Renaissance was a period of creativity, exploration, adventure, and reformation. It was the time of Christopher Columbus, Vasco da Gama, Ferdinand Magellan, Leonardo da Vinci, Michelangelo, Martin Luther, Shakespeare, Palestrina, William Byrd, and Thomas Morley. The Catholic Church was losing its power in society. Musicians moved to the courts of the powerful kingdoms that had been established when medieval mini-kingdoms were consolidated during the eleventh century. During the Renaissance, instrumental music, specifically dance music, began to blossom. This music set the stage for the next period of musical history, the Baroque Era (1600–1750).

**For You**

1. Select at least one piece of recorded music from the Middle Ages or Renaissance. You will find suggestions in the Resource Guide in Appendix D.
2. As you listen to the music, reflect upon the history you have just read.
3. Do you think the music reflects the historical period in which it was written? Why?
4. Visit the Web sites listed in the Resource Guide (Appendix D) for the art of the Middle Ages and Renaissance. What characteristics do you think the art and music of these periods share?

**In the Preschool and in Out-of-School Programs**

1. Think of an appropriate time you can play the music to which you listened for the children you teach. Perhaps lunchtime or naptime would be appropriate times.
2. Read the book titled *A Medieval Feast* for the children while playing the music in the background. If you teach very young children, tell the story, rather than read it, and show the beautiful pictures that are in this book.

You have completed Music Lab #1. Occasionally, return to this lab and repeat the activities until you feel comfortable with them. During Music Lab #2, you will continue to explore sounds and rhythmic instruments.

## References

Aries, P. (1962). *Centuries of childhood: A social history of family life* (R. Baldick, Trans.). New York: Vintage Books. (Original work published 1960)

Barlow, T. A. (1977). *Pestalozzi and American education.* Boulder, CO: Este Es Press.

Berk, L. E. (2001). *Development through the lifespan.* Boston: Allyn & Bacon.

Boeree, C. G. (1997). *Erik Erikson.* Shippensburg University. Retrieved September 17, 2004, from http://www.shp.edu/%7Ecgboeree/erikson.html

Brosterman, N. (1997). *Inventing kindergarten.* New York: Abrams.

Closson, D. (1999). *A philosophy of education.* Probe Ministries. Retrieved September 16, 2004, from http://www.probe.org/docs/rousseau.html

Council for Professional Recognition. (1996). *The child development associate: Assessment system and competency standards: Preschool caregivers in center-based programs.* Washington, DC: Author.

Dolmetsch Online. (2002). Retrieved February 2, 2005, from http://www.dolmetsch.com/musictheorydefs.htm

Dragon Early Music. (2004). *The history of the recorder.* Retrieved January 31, 2005, from http://www.earlymusic.gil.com.au/history.htm

Driscoll, A., & Nagel, N. G. (2002). *Early childhood education: Birth–8.* Boston: Allyn & Bacon.

Efland, A. (1983). Art and music in the Pestalozzian tradition. *Journal of Research in Music Education, 31* (3), 165–178.

Essa, E. L. (2003). *Introduction to early childhood education* (Instructor's annotated 4th ed.). Clifton Park, NY: Thomson Delmar Learning.

*Explore dictionary of music.* (2005). Retrieved February 2, 2005, from http://www.explore-music.com/

Faulmann, J. (1980). Montessori and music in early childhood. *Music Educators Journal, 66*(9), 41–43.

Gallagher, C. (2004). *Lev Semyonovich Vygotsky. History of psychology archives.* Muskingham College. Retrieved September 18, 2004, from http://www.fates.cns.muskingham.edu/~psych/psycweb/history/vygotsky.htm

Gorman, B. (1986). *Medieval life: Squires, maidens and peasants.* Yale-New Haven Teachers Institute. Retrieved September 30, 2004, from http://www.yale.edu/ynhti/curriculum/units/1986/3/86.03.03.x.html

Henniger, M. L. (2002). *Teaching young children: An introduction* (2nd ed.). Upper Saddle River, NJ: Merrill Prentice-Hall.

Hollyman, D. (2000). *Jerome Bruner: A Web overview.* Retrieved January 31, 2005, from http://au.geocities.com/vanunoo/Humannature/bruner.html

Iben, H. (1997). *The guide to symphony orchestra instruments.* Retrieved September 15, 2004, from http://www.mathcs.duq.edu/~iben/auxil.htm

Kamien, R. (2003). *Music, an appreciation.* New York: McGraw-Hill.

Kearsley, G. (2005). *Constructivist theory.* Retrieved January 31, 2005, from http://tip.psychology.org/bruner.html

Lenart, C. M. (2000). *Waldorf schools: Educating the whole child.* Conscious Choice. Retrieved September 29, 2004, from http://www.consciouschoice.com/culture/waldorfschools1308.html

Lexico Publishing Group. (2004). *Dictionary.com.* Retrieved August 19, 2004, from http://dictionary.reference.com/

Mays, R., & Nordwall, S. (2004). *Waldorf answers on the philosophy and practice of Waldorf education.* Retrieved September 29, 2004, from http://www.waldorfanswers.com

McDonald, D. T. (1983). Montessori's music for young children. *Young Children, 39*(1), 58–63.

Monroe, W. S. (1900). *Comenius and the beginnings of educational reform.* New York: Scribner's.

Rousseau, J. J. (1928). *Rousseau on education* (R. L. Archer, Ed.). London: Edward Arnold. (Original work published 1762)

Rubin, J. S. (1983). Montessorian music method: Unpublished works. *Journal of Research in Music Education, 31*(3), 215–226.

Sadie, S. (1986). *Music guide, an introduction.* Englewood Cliffs, NJ: Prentice-Hall.

Schwickerath, R. (1999). *Pestalozzi and Pestalozzianism.* Catholic Encyclopedia. Retrieved September 16, 2004, from http://www.newadvent.org/cathen/11742b.htm

Sherrane, R. (2004). *Music history 102: A guide to Western composers and their music.* Internet Public Library. Retrieved September 16, 2004, from http://www.ipl.org/div/mushist/middle/index.htm

Smith, M. K., & Doyle, M. E. (1997). *Jean-Jacques Rousseau and informal education.* The Encyclopedia of Informal Education. Retrieved September 16, 2004, from http://www.infed.org/thinkers/et-rous.htm

Vienna Symphonic Library. (2002). *Instruments online.* Retrieved February 2, 2005, from http://www.vsl.co.at/english/pages/profile/news/product_news.htm

Walch, M. R. (1952). *Pestalozzi and the Pestalozzian theory of education.* (Doctoral dissertation, The Catholic University of America, 1952). Washington, DC: Catholic University of America Press.

Wiebé, E. (1923). *Golden Jubilee edition of the paradise of childhood: A practical guide to kindergarteners* (M. Bradley, Ed., including a "Life of Friedrich Froebel" by H. W. Blake). Springfield, MA: M. Bradley Co.

Wozniak, R. H. (1999). *Classics in psychology.* Thoemmes Continuum. Retrieved September 17, 2004, from http://www.thoemmes.com/psych/clap.htm

# Current Research Regarding Music and Music Nurturing

## Key Terms

absorption

acculturation

assimilation

audiate

aural perception

bell-shaped curve

biomusicology

diminishing intelligence

imitation

melody

Mozart effect

music aptitude

music-learning theory for
    newborn and young children

music therapy

musical intelligence

neurons

opera

oratorio

portfolios

preparatory audiation

purposeful response

random response

rhythm

rhythmic audiation skills

synaptic gap

theory of multiple intelligences

tonal audiation skills

windows of opportunity

S arah and Marissa found their research into the past interesting and it provided them with good reasons to integrate music throughout their curriculum. However, while doing their research, Sarah and Marissa began to notice references to current research on music and its relationship to early childhood. They decided to continue their search for answers by examining some of the current research in the fields of early childhood and music education for indications of why and how music should be used in the early childhood classroom.

Sarah and Marissa are correct to examine current research. In the past, educators used their instincts and personal experiences to form opinions concerning the role of music in early childhood programs. Beginning with the child study movement in the early 1900s, researchers have shed light on the developmental process of young children. Research on brain development, the influence of music on childhood development, the effect of music on health, and the development of **music aptitude** are just a few of the studies that have come to educators' attention as recently as the past 20–25 years. Current research continues to support the beliefs of many past educators as it solidifies the foundation of knowledge for future educational decisions. This chapter examines a wide range of research concerned with music. Through this research, we glimpse the importance of music to humanity in general and specifically the importance of music in early childhood. Subsequent chapters contain information regarding other age- or stage- specific research.

## Researching the Musicality of Man

Every known human culture incorporates music in one fashion or another. Why is music so much a part of our lives? Has music always been a part of the human experience? Researchers have studied these questions in an attempt to understand the musicality of man. Recently, the new field of **biomusicology** offered various explanations regarding man's musicality in the book *The Origins of Music* (Wallin, Merker, & Brown, 2001). Biomusicologists study why humans are musical and how music is used in the cultural and social rituals of various societies (Quinion, 2004). They also search for any evolutionary advantage for which music is responsible and research how the brain perceives music (Quinion, 2004). Most research in the field of music has been conducted by researchers with a musical background; however, biomusicologists are scientists researching music and its effect on humans.

*The Origins of Music* contains a series of articles written by scientists in fields such as biology, anthropology, neurology, psychology, musicology, and archaeology. In the book, interesting theories are posited and disputed regarding humans and music. For example, several articles theorized that humans are musical due to evolution. In other words, taking the Darwinian approach, musicality has to do with the "survival of the fittest." One theory suggested that early humans used music as a form of sexual selection (Merker, 2001). Merker studied male chimpanzees and discovered that they used sounds to attract females from neighboring groups into their group, thereby allowing for crossbreeding to strengthen their group. Another theory suggested that music evolved due to the interaction between mothers and their infants (Dissanayake, 2001). Some articles considered whether researchers seeking the origins of music could look to the origins of language for answers. They questioned whether music and language had a common origin, and discussed the regions of the brain that control music and language (Bickerton, 2001; Falk, 2001; Molino, 2001).

Research regarding why humans are musical is a new trend. However, as researchers continue to question what constitutes the humanity of humans and as they conduct studies to determine the origin of human traits, the future may bring more research on this interesting subject. Why should we care about the origins of music in humankind? Through an understanding of the origins of music, we begin to understand that music is an element of our humanity and, therefore, must be included in our lives from birth.

## Researching the Music and Medicine Link

Since the times of ancient Greece and Egypt, music and medicine have been linked (American Music Therapy Association [AMTA], 2004). References to the healing power of music are found in the writings of Plato and Aristotle (AMTA, 2004). During the Middle Ages and the Renaissance, physicians and musicians shared some of the same curriculum (Carpenter, 1958). Documents from that time indicate that lectures combined information about music and medicine and that before becoming a physician, a person had to study music (Pratt, 1991). The two areas of study moved apart over the years as each field became more specialized.

## The Beginning of Music Therapy in the United States

After World Wars I and II, hospitals sought music volunteers to entertain the convalescing war veterans (AMTA, 2004). When physical and emotional improvements became noticeable due to this musical entertainment, hospitals began to hire musicians to help other patients. Soon it was clear that these musicians needed prior training before working in a hospital (AMTA, 2004). In response to the need for training, colleges began to develop **music therapy** curricula. Michigan State University opened the first music therapy degree program in 1944 (AMTA, 2004), and over the past 60 years, music therapy has grown into a respected career field. Music therapists are allied health professionals who work in hospitals, both general and psychiatric, nursing homes, rehabilitation centers, mental health agencies, schools, and private practice (AMTA, 2004). Patients do not have to be ill to benefit from music therapy. It is also used to help children and adults find relief from stress (AMTA, 2004). Currently, there are more than 70 universities where candidates can earn a bachelor's or master's degree in music therapy. And in 1998, the AMTA was founded. In addition to supplying information to those interested in music therapy as a career, this organization encourages research that explores the benefits of music therapy.

## Other Biomedical Fields and Music

Various biomedical fields, such as psychology, neurology, psychiatry, and biology, have been involved in research that examines the effectiveness of music to promote good health. In fact, music has been defined as good medicine (Gideonse & Westley, 1998). In recent years, studies have found that playing music in the surgical waiting area relieved stress and anxiety in patients (Robb, Nichols, & Rutan, 1995; Winter, Paskin, & Baker, 1994). Some researchers asserted that participation in musical activities boosted the immune system (Bartlett, Kaufman, & Smeltekop, 1993; Kuhn, 2002). To demonstrate this finding, the amount of salivary immunoglobulin in the saliva of subjects before and after participation in musical activities, both passive and active, was compared. Other researchers look to music for help for Alzheimer's and Parkinson's disease patients, as well as for victims of stroke (Johnson, Cotman, Tasaki, & Shaw, 1998; Mazo & Parker, 2002).

Additional medical studies have sought ways to help children with disabilities through music. Researchers continue to seek help through music for autistic children, children with attention deficit hyperactivity disorder (ADHD), developmental disabilities, vision and hearing disabilities, and behavior problems. Research results point to the possibility that "music may very well be one of the most important influences of the mind/body relationship" (Pratt, 1991, p. 33).

***Performing Arts Medicine***    A relatively new field to link music and medicine is the field of performing arts medicine. Performing arts medicine is an occupational health care specialty for those working in the performing arts. The Performing Arts Medical Association (PAMA) was founded in 1989 to improve the health care of performing artists (PAMA, 2004). Their first meeting was so successful that it is now an annual event in Aspen, Colorado, called the Symposium on the Medical Problems of Musicians and Dancers (Jones et al., 2001). Each symposium disseminates research conducted regarding musical performance and related health problems. Topics discussed

## A *Closer Look*

### Music Therapy and Early Childhood

Recently, the AMTA began an online Early Childhood Newsletter, which features articles of interest to the early childhood community, including new research on the use of music therapy with young children. The newsletter can be accessed through the AMTA Web site at http://www.musictherapy.org.

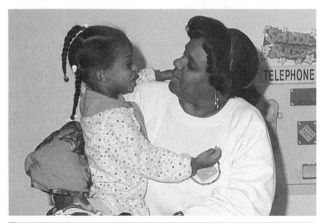

As allied health professionals, music therapists work in various settings, including schools.

address the problems of high demand and high stress on the performer's mind and body.

In the past, performance injuries were not publicly revealed and discussed. The ability to play an instrument well and make it seem effortless was an illusion to be guarded. Musicians are susceptible to injuries due to poor playing or practice habits, or overstressed body parts resulting from long hours of practice and playing. Numbness in fingers, cramped muscles, and sore throats are difficult for the nonmusician, but for the professional musician, these symptoms can affect her performance or worse, her career. The most famous case is that of Robert Schumann (1810–1856).

Today, music teachers are urged to be aware of their students' playing and practice habits as well as the postures they assume while playing (see Figure 2–1). Additionally, teachers are encouraged to work with physicians to solve performance problems that can strain and stress the body and mind (Jones et al., 2001). Musicians are advised to take care of their bodies as they do their expensive instruments, since their bodies are part of their instruments (Jones et al., 2001). Performers now seek the advice of medical specialists to help conquer performance-related aches and pains as well as performance anxiety. The objective for performing arts medicine is to prevent a problem from occurring, rather than trying to treat the problem after it has occurred.

## Research into Nonmusical Advantages of Music Education

In 1993, *Nature* published an experiment conducted by Rauscher, Shaw, and Ky that caught the attention of educators, parents, musicians, and scientists. The researchers experimented with college students and found that when the students listened to a Mozart sonata their spatial reasoning skills were temporarily raised. The term **Mozart effect** appeared in the press after this study, and refers to "the transformational powers of music in health, education, and well-being" (Campbell, 2004, p. 1).

Between 1993 and 1997, Rauscher, Shaw, and other researchers conducted further experiments into the effects of music on cognitive skills. Some of these experiments included preschool children. In 1997, *Neurological Research* published the results of a study in which preschool children who studied piano performed 34 percent better on spatial and temporal tasks than preschool children who spent the same amount of time using computers (Rauscher et al., 1997).

### A Closer Look

#### Robert Schumann (1810–1856)

While in his 20s Schumann noticed that the ring finger on his right hand was weaker than the rest of his fingers. He invented a gadget that he hoped would strengthen his finger. Not only did the gadget not work, but it also left his finger weakened and uncontrollable. With this permanent injury, his dream of becoming a virtuoso pianist was ended and he turned his musical energies to composing (Kamien, 2003; Sadie, 1986).

*Figure 2–1*   Music teachers must be aware of their students' practice habits, including posture.

The results of Rauscher and Shaw's original research in 1993 started a frenzy of activity aimed at making children smarter through listening to classical music. For example, Georgia and Tennessee legislators passed bills that gave a classical-music CD to each new mother as she left the hospital, and Florida legislators mandated that any child care center that received funding from the state had to play classical music. Mozart effect became a household term (Gladwell, 2000; Viadero, 1998).

Interest in the effects of music on brain development remains at a high level. The public continues to ask questions such as, If my child listens to Mozart, will she be more intelligent? or Can music increase the brain development of young children? Discussions on these subjects are found in popular magazines and on the Internet.

Rauscher and Shaw's research continues. And other researchers have attempted to duplicate the results of their original study, with mixed results. Some researchers have been successful in their efforts, while others have not produced the same positive results. Additionally, some researchers are conducting their own experiments. At this time, there is no agreement regarding how much effect or what effect music education can have on other areas of education (Weinberger, 1999). In fact, Dr. Rauscher was quoted as saying: "One of the things we have to be careful about is jumping to conclusions that we don't have data on at all. . . . I find that 'Mozart makes you smarter' thing is quite a bit of a leap." (Viadero, 1998, p. 4). However, she went on to say, "I think the evidence is solid enough to say, 'Let's improve and expand our music education programs for young children,'" (Viadero, 1998 p. 4).

The arts are often considered "frills" in the educational arena. Music suffers from this distinction along with art, drama, and dance. When funds are cut, frills are cut. For nearly a decade, funding for music education has been methodically cut in order to shift funding to traditional subjects such as reading, writing, math, and science. When studies show that music does enhance children's ability to learn, it is tempting for music educators to use this information to boost their programs. However, others warn that we should not lose sight of the fact that music should not be taught just for its ability to enhance other subjects—in other words, as a means to an end. Rather, it should be taught for its own worth (Weinberger, 1996). If we want to educate the whole child, the arts, including music, must be a part of her education (see Figure 2–2) (Fowler, 1990). Although there is evidence that music can affect cognitive development, music is worth teaching and learning for its own sake. If other benefits are realized from our musical experiences, that's wonderful.

## Howard Gardner and Music Intelligence

In 1983, Howard Gardner (1943–present), developmental psychologist and neuropsychologist at Harvard University, introduced his **theory of multiple intelligences** to the world. In his book *Frames of Mind*,

**Figure 2–2** To educate the whole child, the arts must be a part of her education.

he identified seven intelligences (linguistic, mathematical/logical, musical, spatial, bodily kinesthetic, interpersonal, and intrapersonal; see Table 2–1), adding that he felt there were more. He has since added an eighth intelligence—the naturalist—to his list. Gardner's theory sent ripples throughout the education community, changing the way teachers evaluate children's progress and plan for children's learning. In addition to the traditional practice of measuring a child's verbal and mathematical skills to determine her intelligence and achievement level, alternative assessment methods are now being used in various forms, such as **portfolios**. Gardner's theory forced educators to rethink the positive attributes of all students, not just those with good language and mathematical skills. The theory expanded the idea of intelligence to include the arts, and specifically included **musical intelligence**. This resulted in a renewed recognition that the arts are not just frills, but should be a part of each child's basic education (Fowler, 1990).

Gardner not only identified music intelligence as a separate intelligence among the original seven, but also stated that he believed it was the first intelligence to develop (1983). This intelligence may begin to develop as early as four or five months after conception. Caregivers of young children, parents, and early childhood teachers influence the development of children's independent intelligences both positively and negatively. It is the responsibility of these caregivers to ensure that each child is being fully nurtured from birth. In order to reach her fullest potential, all of a child's intelligences should be stimulated. A potential intelligence might not develop if it is not nurtured. In fact, if it is not nurtured, a potential intelligence might diminish (Gardner, 1983). This is called **diminishing intelligence**.

## Researching Brain Development

The first writing about the brain dates back to 4000 BC (Public Broadcasting Service [PBS], 2004). Humans have been fascinated with the brain for centuries, but the technology of the twentieth century allowed the research to blossom. Scientists have been able to watch the brain at work.

By the fourth week of gestation, the brain is busy making **neurons**, as many as 250,000 a minute (PBS, 2004). Neurons are brain cells. Eventually, the infant will have billions of neurons and trillions of connections among those neurons (PBS, 2004). Infants' brains are prewired to receive and process information from the world. Infants gather information from the world through their senses. Upon receiving stimulation through the senses, each neuron or brain cell passes the information on to nearby neurons. The cells do not touch while conveying these messages. There is a gap between the neurons called the **synaptic gap** (see Figure 2–3). Through electrical impulses or chemical reactions, the messages jump the synaptic gap from one cell to another. As the synapses are stimulated, networks are formed for future use (Baney, 2002). As the infant receives more stimulation, more neurons become a part of the network and the connections or pathways between brain cells become stronger. If the infant does not receive stimulation in a particular area of development, these pathways do not develop and the neurons begin to atrophy (Baney, 2002). In other words, the brain has a "use it or lose it" system. Some researchers believe that when children are not stimulated with music, the neurons that were originally designated for music

| Table 2-1   Gardner's Multiple Intelligences | |
| --- | --- |
| **Intelligence** | **Strengths** |
| Linguistic | • Quickly learns the words to fingerplays and songs<br>• Loves stories<br>• Sensitive to the meaning, order, and sound of words<br>• Enjoys talking |
| Mathematical/Logical | • Enjoys organizing<br>• Able to handle long chains of reasoning<br>• Recognizes patterns<br>• Quick to learn same and different<br>• Enjoys solving problems |
| Musical | • Drawn to sounds<br>• Enjoys music and musical activities<br>• Picks up melodies easily and remembers songs<br>• Can perceive pitch, tone, and rhythmic patterns<br>• Well-developed auditory sense and discrimination<br>• Ability to create and organize rhythmically |
| Spatial | • Ability to create complex mental images<br>• Can find their way mentally and physically around environment<br>• Ability to see the physical world accurately and translate it into new forms, such as art |
| Bodily Kinesthetic | • A fine-tuned ability to use the body and handle objects (fine and gross motor)<br>• Able to express emotions through bodily movement<br>• Expresses self with total physical response<br>• Have abilities in:<br>  • Physical movement and dance<br>  • Mime/creative drama |
| Interpersonal | • Respond to moods, temperaments, motivations, intentions, and facial and body cues of others<br>• Easily makes friends<br>• Recognizes and empathizes with other's feelings<br>• Cooperative<br>• Good communication and social skills |
| Intrapersonal | • Well-developed sense of self<br>• Talks about and understands emotions<br>• Self-reflective<br>• Excellent self-planners |
| Naturalist | • Enjoys being outdoors<br>• Is in tune with nature<br>• Sees patterns in the world<br>• Enjoys classifying plants and animals |

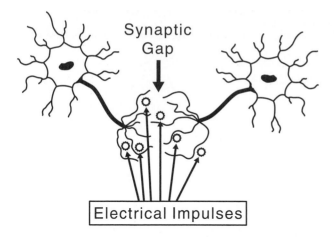

**Figure 2–3**  Messages jump the synaptic gap from one cell to another.

development begin to support other developmental areas such as language or vision (Gordon, 1995). Scientists are just beginning to understand how the brain develops (PBS, 2004). Some research includes the effects of music on brain development.

There are times during children's development when it is easier for them to learn particular skills. These developmental periods are called **windows of opportunity.** For example, around the age of two there is a window of opportunity for learning language. At this time, the language development portion of the brain is highly receptive. A two-year-old child learns language at an amazing rate and can learn several languages in what seems to be an effortless manner. However, once the window of opportunity has passed, learning a language is more difficult. Often, older students and adults struggle to learn a second language.

Questions have been asked and answers sought regarding music and windows of opportunity. Is there a window of opportunity, as with language, when musical skills are best learned? If there is a window of opportunity for developing musical intelligence and we assume that all humans are born with a biologic guarantee of musicianship, what is the overall effect on children who have a musically enriched environment versus children who have a musically deprived environment during the critical

early years? The next researcher looked for answers to these questions.

## Edwin Gordon and Music Aptitude

Edwin Gordon (1927–present), noted teacher, lecturer, author, and researcher in music education and the psychology of music research, supported the idea of diminishing intelligence. In other words, if a child is not stimulated in a particular area such as music, she will lose some of her natural potential in that area. Her music aptitude or musical potential will diminish.

Gordon developed a test to measure the music aptitude of children between the ages of five and nine. Music aptitude is a child's innate, but not necessarily inherited, musical ability (Gordon, 1999). Everyone is born with some music aptitude. According to Gordon (1990) this trait is normally distributed along the line of a **bell-shaped curve.** Some young children have more music aptitude than the majority of children the same age and some have less, but most children are born with an average amount of music aptitude. In other words, "just as there are no children without intelligence, so there are no children without music aptitude" (Gordon, 1990, p. 9).

The child's highest musical aptitude level is at the time of birth and begins to diminish immediately (Gordon, 1990). No matter how musically rich the environment, the child's music aptitude will never reach the birth level. However, the sooner a child receives music nurturing, the better the chance of her music aptitude approaching the birth level (Gordon, 1990).

Gordon's music aptitude test revealed that a child's music aptitude scores increased or decreased incrementally between ages five and nine, depending on whether the child received musical stimulation or not. In other words, the greatest increment of loss or gain in the level of music aptitude occurred between five and six years of age. Each successive year of age revealed less of a gain or loss until the age of nine. Gordon (1990) called the period between birth and nine years of age the developmental music aptitude period. During these years, the child's

## A Closer Look

### Bell-shaped Curves

The bell-shaped curve gets its name from its shape. The shape represents a theoretical distribution of natural occurrences such as the height or intelligence of a particular population (Lexico Publishing Group, 2004). For example, the average four-year-old boy's height is between 37 and 43 inches. The median height or the height in the middle of that range is 40 inches. That is the height at the top of the bell-shaped curve in Figure 2–4. Of course, some four-year-olds are shorter than 37 inches and some are taller than 43 inches. These children are at the ends of the bell-shaped curve. As with other natural occurrences, the musical aptitude of young children follows a bell-shaped curve (Gordon, 1990).

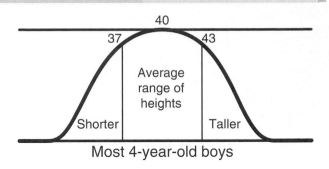

*Figure* 2–4    Bell-shaped representation of the heights of four-year-old boys.

---

music aptitude fluctuates and does not stabilize at a particular level.

At age nine, music aptitude scores stabilize and remain "the same through-out life" regardless of the amount of music stimulation a child receives (Gordon, 1990, p. 44). Remember, Gordon's early childhood music aptitude test only measured the aptitude of children five to nine years old. Gordon theorized that if the trend demonstrated between the ages of five and nine held true for the years from birth to five, then there could be a significant loss of music aptitude during the early childhood years before a child entered kindergarten and began to experience music education. The longer the lapse of time before a child is stimulated with music, the greater the loss of music aptitude might be. Gordon's aptitude test also indicated that once musical stimulation began in the primary grades, the gain of aptitude was less than if that stimulation had begun during the preschool years. Gordon believed a window of opportunity for developmental music aptitude exists and that it occurs between birth and age nine (Baney, 2002).

### Gordon's Music-Learning Theory for Newborn and Young Children

Research and observation led to the development of Gordon's **music learning theory for newborn and young children.**

"Music Learning Theory is an explanation of how we learn when we learn music" (Gordon Institute for Music Learning [GIML], 2003, p. 1). It is a guide to understanding the development of audiation.

Audiation is the cognitive process by which we hear and comprehend music in our heads, even when there is no music playing (Gordon, 1990). It is not the same as **aural perception.** Aural perception takes place when we hear music at the same time that the music is playing. "Audiation is the foundation of musicianship" (GIML, 2003, p. 4). Musicians must **audiate** all aspects of the music with which they are working. They audiate when they listen to music, read music, recall and write music they have heard previously, improvise music (make up the music on the spot during a performance), and compose music. As children develop their ability to audiate, they progress through a series of stages (GIML, 2003). The ability to audiate helps the child understand music, and being able to understand music is important to the child's ability to appreciate and perform it.

The music-learning theory specifically explains how children develop their **tonal and rhythmic audiation skills,** (GIML, 2003) (see Table 2–2). These skills allow us to hear a **melody** and the **rhythm** of a melody in our heads. During the early childhood years, most children are in the period of **"preparatory audiation"**

**Table 2–2    Gordon's Music-Learning Theory**

| | |
|---|---|
| **Acculturation** | Absorption |
| | Random response |
| | Purposeful response |
| **Imitation** | Shedding egocentricity |
| | Breaking the code |
| **Assimilation** | Introspection |
| | Coordination |

(Gordon, 1990, p. 25). Until they progress through this period of development, formal music training will be of little benefit to them (GIML, 2003).

There are three types of preparatory audiation: **acculturation, imitation,** and **assimilation** (see Tables 2–3, 2–4, and 2–5). Each type of preparatory audiation builds on the preceding type. In ideal situations, children progress sequentially through preparatory audiation from approximately birth to age six, at which time they enter school and participate in formal music classes. The musical age of a child is different from her chronological age. The type of preparatory audiation in which the child engages determines her musical age (Gordon, 1990).

**Acculturation**    Acculturation, the first type of preparatory audiation, has three stages: **absorption, random response,** and **purposeful response.** Acculturation is a readiness period. During this time, children learn primarily by listening to the music and sounds around them.

The stages progress as follows:

- Absorption, the first stage of acculturation, ideally lasts until approximately 18 months of age. In this stage, the child merely listens (Gordon, 1990).
- Random response, the second stage of acculturation, takes place between one and three years of age. During this stage, the child begins to participate in music in addition to being a listener (Gordon, 1990).
- Purposeful response, the third stage of acculturation, can take place anytime between 18 months and 3 years of age. During this stage, the child tries to match her movements and babble to the music in her environment (Gordon, 1990).

To support these important developmental stages, early childhood educators should

- play good music in a variety of styles for the children.
- encourage the child's babbling and movement to music.
- encourage children to create their own songs and chants.
- sing tonal and rhythmic patterns for the children as a way of encouraging them to try to sing them, but do not expect them to be able to imitate what is sung (Gordon, 1990).

**Imitation**    Imitation, the second type of preparatory audiation, has two stages: shedding egocentricity and breaking the code (Gordon, 1990). Ideally, the child should pass through the imitation type of preparatory

**Table 2–3    Stages of the Acculturation Type of Preparatory Audiation**

| Type: Acculturation, Birth to 2–4 | Stage | Characteristics | Musical Age |
|---|---|---|---|
| | 1. Absorption | Gathers musical sounds from environment | Birth to 18 months |
| | 2. Random response | Moves and babbles to musical sounds | 1 to 3 years old |
| | 3. Purposeful response | Tries to match movement and babble to musical sounds | 18 months to 3 years old |

**Table 2–4**   Stages of the Imitation Type of Preparatory Audiation

| Type: Imitation, Ages 2–4 to Ages 3–5 | Stage | Characteristics | Musical Age |
|---|---|---|---|
| | 1. Shedding egocentricity | Recognize that their movements and sounds do not match those of the people around them | Two to four years old |
| | 2. Breaking the code | Begin to imitate with precision the musical sounds in the environment through their singing and movement | Three to five years old |

audiation stages by five years of age (Gordon, 1990). The details of the stages are as follows:

- Shedding egocentricity, the fourth stage of acculturation and the second stage of imitation, should begin by three years of age. Some children may enter this stage of imitation as young as two years of age (Gordon, 1990). The child's level of music aptitude combined with the quality of music environment surrounding her will determine her ability to leave one preparatory audiation stage and enter another (Gordon, 1990). During the stage of shedding egocentricity, the child becomes aware of what she is singing or chanting, how she is moving, and how that differs from the way other children or adults are singing, chanting, or moving (Gordon, 1990). Some children may make the discovery quickly, in a matter of minutes, while others may take months (Gordon, 1990). Therefore, the amount of time a child spends in this stage can vary a great deal. The child must be able to gain this awareness in order to distinguish between accurate and inaccurate imitation (Gordon, 1990).
- Breaking the code, the fifth stage of acculturation, is the stage when children enter the musical world in which adults perform (Gordon, 1990). When a child enters the breaking the code stage, she learns to imitate tonal and rhythmic patterns (Gordon, 1990). Some children may move themselves from stage 4 to stage 5; others may need encouragement from an adult to move out of stage 4 (Gordon, 1990).

To support these important developmental stages, early childhood educators should

- sing simple tonal and rhythmic patterns.

**Table 2–5**   Stages of the Assimilation Type of Preparatory Audiation

| Type: Assimilation, Ages 3–5 to Ages 4–6 | Stage | Characteristics | Musical Age |
|---|---|---|---|
| | 1. Introspection | Recognize that their singing is not coordinated with movement and breathing | Three to five years old |
| | 2. Coordination | Coordinate their singing with their movement and breathing | Four to six years old |

- be observant and listen to the child as she tries to imitate the songs, chants, and moves the adult and other children make.
- be patient and allow children to make these discoveries at their own pace (Gordon, 1990).
- encourage children to move on to the next stage only when it is absolutely certain that they recognize that what they are singing, chanting, or how they are moving is different from others.

***Assimilation***    The third type of preparatory audiation, assimilation, contains two stages: introspection and coordination (Gordon, 1990). During assimilation, the child recognizes her lack of coordination between singing and chanting and body movement, including breathing, and begins to coordinate them (Gordon, 1990). Children can enter assimilation from three to six years of age. However, assuming an ideal situation where the child has an enriched music environment, this type of preparatory audiation should be passed through no later than the age of six (Gordon, 1990). The details of assimilation are as follows:

- Introspection is a stage when the child must discover whether she has coordinated her body movement with the rhythmic pattern that she is singing or chanting (Gordon, 1990). This discovery must be made by the child, alone, and is a prerequisite for success in the next stage. It cannot be taught to her. The child does not have to achieve coordination; she only needs to recognize that her movements are not coordinated with the rhythmic pattern she is performing. Once she is aware, she should be encouraged to enter the stage of coordination (Gordon, 1990).
- Coordination is the stage in which the child learns to coordinate her movements with the rhythmic pattern being chanted or sung (Gordon, 1990). Usually, before a child enters the stage of coordination, she is in kindergarten and, ideally, participating in formal music classes under the guidance of a trained early childhood music specialist. The music specialist

is able to evaluate each child's musical ability and give guidance as the child acquires new musical skills.

To support these important developmental stages, early childhood educators should

- sing simple tonal and rhythmic patterns.
- encourage children to move to the patterns.

Gordon's learning theory for music is an attempt to explain the music developmental process of a young child, beginning at birth. Understanding this process gives teachers and parents a perspective when selecting developmentally appropriate activities for young children. Parents and early childhood educators can and should be trained to nurture young children musically. Otherwise, thousands of young children will not receive this important nurturing.

## Summary

A great deal of research regarding the development of young children has emerged at the same time when, in the United States, 13 million children under the age of six spend each day with someone other than their parents (Children's Defense Fund, 2001). As more children enter child care settings at an increasing rate and at increasingly younger ages, this research shows that those who work with these children on a daily basis must be trained to work with them in an appropriate manner in all developmental domains, including music education. Research from the music education community confirms the importance of starting musical stimulation from birth. Music specialists must understand the unique qualities of early childhood in order to teach in the field and to guide early childhood educators regarding the musical nurturing of young children. Gordon's music-learning theory is a guide for musically nurturing young children and for developing their tonal and rhythmic audiation skills. When young children are musically nurtured, they can develop an understanding and appreciation for music that will add to their quality of life.

Research, which adheres to scientific principles, gives us a truer picture of the developing child. Until

## Standards and Other Professional Guidance

### K–12 National Standards and Pre-K Standards for Music Education

The Goals 2000: Educate America Act, the national education reform legislation, specifically recognizes the arts, music, visual arts, theater, and dance, for the first time as fundamental academic subjects. The act calls for the development of high standards for academic subjects. From June 1992 to June 1994, the Music Educators National Conference (MENC), on behalf of the Consortium of National Arts Education Associations, received federal funding from the U.S. Department of Education, the National Endowment for the Arts, and the National Endowment for the Humanities. The funding supported the establishment of voluntary national standards for arts education. The standards were to describe the knowledge, skills, and understanding students in grades K–12 should acquire in music, visual arts, theater, and dance (MENC, 1994). *The School Music Program: A New Vision* is the title for the K–12 National Standards and Pre–K Standards for music education. These standards also include information about what they mean to music educators. Throughout this text, the standards will be referenced as a guide to good teaching practices.

the child study movement began in the early 1900s and research followed, there was no proof that music was a necessary part of the early childhood curriculum. Past educators thought it was essential, but now research has established substantial proof of music's importance in the everyday lives of children.

## Key Concepts

- The child study movement initiated research into the development of children.
- Research indicates that music contributes more to our lives than aural pleasure.
- Music may enhance other developmental domains.
- Gardner identified music as an independent intelligence.
- Children should have musical experiences beginning at birth.
- The Goals 2000: Educate America Act recognizes the arts as fundamental academic subjects.

## Suggested Activities

1. Choose one of the studies mentioned above that interests you. Read more about the study and write a report about it.
2. Discuss Howard Gardner's multiple-intelligences theory with your class. What effect might his theory have on a classroom teacher's planning?
3. Search the Internet for new information on brain research. Report to your classmates and discuss the implications for teachers.
4. Journal reflection question 2: Has the information revealed by new research changed your outlook on the importance of music in our lives? How? Why?

## Music Lab #2

Music Lab #2 continues the exploration of sound and our journey into historical Western European music periods. During this lab, we will look at the Baroque period. As with the first lab, many of the activities presented in this lesson are appropriate for use with young children.

Remember: In the music lab, you should try to lose your inhibitions. You should try to approach the lab experiences in the same way children do, before they become self-conscious. In this way, you will begin to experience music in the same way that young children experience it.

## Activity #1: Explore Sounds

**For You**

Continue to use the activities from Lab #1 and explore sounds as much as possible. These labs are to help you gain experience with music, but you should also be exploring ways in which you can introduce children to sounds and music around them.

**In the Preschool and in Out-of-School Programs**

1. Think about how you can incorporate the sounds you are experiencing in your daily plans with the children. Brainstorm with your classmates about how you could use some of these sounds during
   a. naptime.
   b. transition time.
   c. circle time.
   d. lunch or snack time.
   e. outdoor time.
2. Can you use any of the sound effects to tell a story or enhance a nursery rhyme?

## Activity #2: Experiencing Found Sounds

For centuries, people have used whatever was available to them to make music. In the Caribbean, musical instruments are made from steel oil drums. Washboards are used in folk bands and by professional musicians as well. Other groups have used jugs as instruments. Cajun music uses spoons (gumbo spoons). Wooden spoons and metal measuring spoons on a string or chain also make good instruments, as many toddlers can tell you.

*Sound-maker Ideas*    Here are some ideas for making fun sounds:

- Washboards: small washboards are easier for young children to handle. Scrape them with a wooden spoon. (See Figure 2–5.)
- Various baby rattles: try to find rattles that make different sounds.
- Wooden spoons.
- Metal measuring spoons.
- Pots, pans, and lids.
- Jugs of various sizes: use these with older children.
- Kazoos.
- Slide whistles.

**For You**

1. Investigate various kinds of sound makers that are available in toy stores and in your own home.
2. Bring sound makers into your classroom to share with the children.

**In the Preschool and in Out-of-School Programs**

1. Bring the sound makers into the classroom and place on a shelf for the children to investigate.
2. Talk about the sounds they can make. Use descriptive words.

*Figure 2–5*  Washboard

**3.** Variation: have the children bring items from their homes that make sounds.

## Try This One!

### Crash! Bang! Boom!

1. Read the book *Crash, Bang, Boom*, by Peter Spier, to the children. This book is good for very young children through approximately age six. It talks about the sounds made by ordinary things and events in our lives.
2. When you finish the book, have the children go around the room and find items they can use to make sounds. They might find pot lids to crash together, or blocks to rub or smack together, or spoons to clack together.
3. Have them share the sounds they can make.
4. Play some marching music such as March of the Toys (Herbert), and have the children march about as they play their found sound instruments. See the Resource Guide (Appendix D) for other suggestions of marches.

### Activity #3: Experiencing More Rhythm Instruments

In Lab #1, we examined the rhythm instruments traditionally found in the early childhood classroom. In this lab, we will look at some of the less traditional and perhaps less well-known rhythm instruments.

## Discovering Instruments

### More Nonpitched Rhythm Instruments

- These rhythm drums are not usually found in the early childhood classroom:

  **a.** Bongo drums: Eastern Cuba, now known as Guantanamo, was the historical origin of bongo playing (Farley, 2001). The drum appeared around the late 1800s about the time slavery was abolished. Victor "Papo" Sterling, a bongocero (professional bongo player), believes the idea for the drum came from West Africa where a similar set of drums is used in religious ceremonies (RhythmWeb, 2001). Bongo drums are two drums, one large and one small, connected with a wooden piece and held between the legs to play. Play them with your fingertips, palms, and thumbs.

  **b.** Conga drum: Tumbadoras (conga drums) come from Cuba and Puerto Rico, but their roots are in the cylindrical drums of Africa (RhythmWeb, 2001). The idea probably arrived in the same way as the bongo drum, through the slave trade. This tall drum is shaped like a narrow barrel. It is played by striking the head in the middle and on the edge or by striking the wooden body of the drum. The drum is struck using the hand, fingertips, or sticks on the drumhead or on the side.

---

### *Music of the World*

**Tinga Layo**

This little song comes from the Dominican Republic. The rhythm is typical of music from the Caribbean. You will find the song in the Resource Guide in Appendix D.

1. Sing the song to the children.
2. Teach them the section "Tinga Layo" and ask them to sing it with you as you sing the song a second time.

3. The third time you sing the song add the second phrase for the children: Come, little donkey, come.
4. Depending on the age of the children, you may wait to teach more another day.
5. Select some rhythm instruments to play along with the song, such as a drum or guiro.

- Temple blocks: These instruments are originally from China, Japan, and Korea where they were used in religious ceremonies. Each block is hollow and shaped like a bulb with a large slit in it. The blocks vary in size, which changes the pitch of the block. They are mounted together on a stand, which is about waist high. The sound of the temple block is similar to but more hollow than the woodblock. Temple blocks are played by being struck with a mallet.
- Guiro: Another instrument with a Latin American origin, the guiro (pronounced: gwee-do) has a wooden ribbed body and is played by scraping it with a stick. In early childhood rhythm kits, the guiro may be made out of plastic. The washboard makes a similar sound when scraped.
- Nigerian Shekeré: This instrument is similar to the maracas. From Africa, this gourd has a covering of beads in netting (see Figure 2–6). The player moves the netting on the gourd with the hand to make a scrapping sound or it can be shaken.
- Cabasa: Originally from Brazil, cabasas were made from coconut shells or gourds with a lattice of seeds strung with wire. The original instruments were fragile and were eventually replaced with plastic for the shell, handle, and beads. The beads are strung with nylon. A piccolo cabasa is smaller and easier for children to play. Cabasas

are played by rubbing the palm of your hand across the beads, shaking them like maracas, or tapping them.
- Chilean rain sticks: Chilean Indians have used rain sticks for centuries in ceremonial rituals to bring rain to the desert. The sticks are made from cactus deadwood. Small pebbles are placed inside and when the stick is tilted from one side to the other, they trickle down through thorns on the inside. The sound is similar to falling rain. Rain sticks are now used as musical instruments.

**For You**

1. How many different sounds can you make with these instruments?
2. How would you describe the sounds?
3. How could you use these instruments in your classroom?

**In the Preschool and in Out-of-School Programs**

1. Gradually introduce these new rhythm instruments to the children and allow them to play and examine them.
2. Help the children describe the sounds they make.

## Activity #4: Making Musical Instruments

***Paper-Plate Tambourines***   This instrument is often made in early childhood classrooms. However, here are some different variations on the idea.

Collect the following materials.

- Paper, plastic, and styrofoam disposable plates
- Stapler or tape
- Cereal, dried beans, dried peas, oatmeal, pebbles, rice
- Hole punch
- Narrow ribbons of various colors

1. Face the tops of two plates together and staple or tape at least halfway around the rim. Use tape for the plastic plates or if you are using a fine-textured material inside the tambourine.
2. Place beans, rice, oatmeal, peas, cereal, or pebbles inside and finish stapling or taping the rest of the way around the rims.
3. Be sure the rim is sealed.

***Figure 2–6***   Shekeré

**4.** Punch holes around the rim and tie ribbons in the holes for a festive look.

**5.** The paper plates can be decorated, before or after constructing the instrument.

### For You

**1.** Collect various materials and make several tambourines.

**2.** Explore the different sounds that can be made with your tambourines. You will find that plastic disposable plates create a different sound from paper plates, even when filled with the same material.

### In the Preschool and in Out-of-School Programs

**1.** Depending on the age of the children, you can play the instruments you made for them, supervise their playing the instruments you made, or have the children make their own instruments and play them.

**2.** Discuss with the children what they put in their tambourine to make the sound.

**3.** Compare the various sounds that children can make on their tambourines.

*Rain Sticks*   Collect the following materials:
- Cardboard mailing tubes with end pieces—at least 2 inches in diameter (the longer the length, the longer the sound continues)
- Small pebbles, rice, unpopped popcorn, dried beans, dried peas, seeds
- Nails—1 $^3/_4$ inch long (If the tube diameter is wider, make the nails longer. However, make sure the nails are not too long, so they stay within the tube when hammered into it. A tube that is 22 inches long will require about 50 nails placed in a spiral. The nails should be placed about $^1/_2$ to $^3/_4$ inch apart.)
- Tempera paint
- White or simulated wood contact paper
- Colorful tape or glue

**1.** Tape or glue the end cap onto one side of the tube.

**2.** Hammer nails into the tube in a spiral pattern along the length of the tube. You may have to draw a line for children to follow with their nailing. The seam line is weak and should only be used as a guide. Do not nail into the seamline.

**3.** Select the material you would like to use from the list above.

**4.** Place approximately a half cup of the material inside your tube.

**5.** Place the second end cap on the tube and tilt it to hear the sound. Adjust the amount of the material inside until you are happy with the sound. Then place the end cap on the tube permanently by taping or gluing it. Cover the tube in contact paper and paint designs on your tube.

### For You

**1.** Collect the materials listed and make a rain stick.

**2.** Share the rain stick with children in your classroom.

### In the Preschool and in Out-of-School Programs

**1.** Play the rain stick for the children. Ask them what they think it sounds like. Tell them about the instrument and allow them to play it.

**2.** If the children are old enough to handle a hammer and nail, then they can make their own rain stick. This can be a woodworking project. It will probably require several days to complete.

**3.** Listen to the sounds made by various rain sticks. Are they all the same? Different? Discuss the sounds with the children.

**4.** Play the instrument and sing a song about rain, such as "Rain, rain, go away" or "It's raining, it's pouring."

## ▎ Try This One!

### Rain, Rain, Everywhere!

Using the rain sticks, orchestrate your own storm.

- Divide the children into three or four groups.
- Beginning with group 1, have them play their rain sticks.
- As group 1 continues to play, add all of the children, one group at a time, until they are all playing.
- Gradually, stop each group from playing until the storm is over.

Variations: Add cymbals for thunder. Sing rain songs during the "storm."

## Activity #5: Music Appreciation

**For You**

We continue on our musical journey into the Baroque Era. The sources for the music history presented in this activity are Kamien (2003), Lexico Publishing Group (2004), Sartorius (2004), Sherrane (2004), and Sony Music Entertainment (2001).

## Musical History

### Baroque Era (1600–1750)

The Baroque Era is divided into three phases: early (1600–1640), middle (1640–1680), and late (1680–1750). During the Middle Ages and the Renaissance, Rome was the musical center of Europe. This was primarily due to the influence of the Catholic Church. By the middle phase of the Baroque Era, the musical style of Italy had spread throughout Europe. Europe was strewn with many small kingdoms. Germany alone had 300 separately governed territories. The best jobs for musicians were in the courts, because music was the main form of entertainment. Nearly every court employed its own musicians and the number of musicians employed reflected the size and wealth of the kingdom. For example, the small court that Johann Sebastian Bach, the most famous family member of the Bach family, served in as music director had an orchestra of only 18 players. Larger courts might have 80 players, plus a company of **opera** singers. The music director was responsible for writing most of the music performed and new music was required for nearly every occasion. Therefore, the music director was a very important servant in the kingdom.

Many Baroque churches had an orchestra as well as a choir and the music was on a grand scale. There were few public concerts, so common people heard this grand music only in church. The church music director, like the court music director, also composed most of the music. In both the courts and the churches of the Baroque Era, the demand for new music was high. Often, music was composed for special occasions and was never heard again. Church musicians were not as well-off as court musicians were. They usually received an allotment of grain and firewood, which they supplemented with fees from weddings and funerals. Johann Bach once complained of suffering financially because there were not enough funerals. In addition to the courts and churches, large towns would often employ musicians for various occasions, such as graduations, visiting dignitaries, and processions.

Musical knowledge was handed from father to son during this time. Therefore, there were musical families, such as the Bach family, in which there were several generations of church and court musicians, teachers, and a few instrument makers. Training usually involved an apprenticeship to a well-known musician and often, young aspiring composers served as choirboys. The word *conservatory*, which is often linked to music, comes from the Italian word that means orphanage. It was the practice in Baroque Italy to attach music schools to orphanages, hire renowned composers as teachers, and train orphans and poor children as musicians.

Although there was a demand for good musicians, getting a job often involved more than talent. An applicant might be asked to contribute to the town's funds, or to marry the daughter of the retiring musician. Both Bach and Handel, two of the Baroque Era's most famous composers, are said to have turned down the same job, because it required marrying the organist's daughter.

During the Baroque Era, the violin came into prominence as the most important string instrument. Composers of the time began to write specifically for the violin, both as a solo instrument and in groupings with other instruments. The piano was not invented until approximately 1700 and it was not until after the Baroque Era ended that the piano developed enough to be a prominent instrument.

The leading composers and musicians of the time were Claudio Monteverdi (1567–1643), Henry Purcell (1659–1695), Elisabeth-Claude Jacquet de la Guerre (c.1666–1729), Antonio Vivaldi (1678–1741),

George Frideric Handel (1685–1759), and Johann Sebastian Bach (1685–1750). Of these composers, Handel and Bach stand out to the world. They were born within a month of each other in the late Baroque period. These two composers wrote much of the recognized music of the late Baroque Era.

***Birth of the Opera and the Oratorio***   Of the three Baroque periods, the early Baroque period was the most revolutionary. At that time, Rome was at the center of artistic development. Additionally, the seat of the Catholic Church was located in Rome. Music played an important part in the Catholic Church's attempt to invigorate itself during the Counter-Reformation, a time that followed the formation of many Protestant churches. Music also played an important part in the music of the new Protestant churches. Composers of the time believed that music could move people emotionally, and they selected passionate texts and wrote their music to express that passion. Melodies reflected the words being sung. For example, if the word being sung was *heaven*, the musical notes were high, and if the word was *hell*, the musical notes were low. Emphasis was placed on some words by using many notes on one syllable of a word. This style of ornamental singing also showed off the virtuosity of the singers.

Around 1575, a group of Italian composers, poets, and noblemen called Camerata wanted to develop a new vocal style based on ancient Greek tragedy. They created opera. Opera can be described simply as a story put to music. However, that statement is too simplified. Baroque operas were extravagant productions that required an orchestra, music director, costumes, scenery, lighting, and many singers. Several hundred people might be required to produce an opera. The storylines for Baroque operas were taken from Greek mythology and the ancient histories of Rome and Greece. These tales appealed to the aristocracy, because they identified with the characters. For that reason, and because the courts could afford the cost of these productions, early operas were seen only by those in the courts. Court operas were performed for special events, such as weddings and coronations. With the exception of Italy where the first public opera house was opened in Venice in 1637, opera was not available to the public in England and Europe until the early 1700s.

Handel studied and mastered the Italian operatic style. While Handel served as music director for Elector George Ludwig of Hanover, he visited London for the production of his opera *Rinaldo* (1710). He became famous throughout England and Queen Anne gave him an annual subsidy to remain in England; a political arrangement allowed him to remain there. When his employer, Elector George Ludwig of Hanover, became King George I of England in 1714 at Queen Anne's death, Handel's annual subsidy was doubled and he became the music teacher to the king's grandchildren.

Handel wrote 39 operas, but he turned to writing **oratorios** during Lent when operas were forbidden. Oratorios are similar to operas in that both are large musical productions, but an oratorio does not use scenery, acting, or costumes, requiring less money to produce. Additionally, oratorio storylines are usually biblical, making them acceptable during Lent. Handel's ability to write and produce oratorios was so successful that he never wrote another opera after 1741. His oratorio *Messiah* is probably the best known and loved of all oratorios.

**For You**

1. The Resource Guide in Appendix D lists several children's books about composers of the Baroque Era. Read at least one book.
2. Choose one composition listed on the resource page that the composer you read about wrote and listen to it.
3. Do you think the music you chose reflects the Baroque period? How?

**In the Preschool and in Out-of-School Programs**

1. Select an appropriate time to share the music you listened to with the children in your classroom.
2. After they have heard the music, you can tell the children about the composer by either reading the book or telling the story and showing the pictures.
3. Continue to play the music in your classroom, occasionally, so the children become familiar with it.

You have now completed Music Lab #2 and are ready to continue your pursuit of musical knowledge in Chapter 3. As with Music Lab #1, do not consider these activities as a single experience. Visit the lab and continue to explore the information. Listen to more music from the Baroque Era and play it for the children in your classroom. Music Lab #3 will begin our discussion of the musical elements rhythm, beat, and tempo.

# References

American Music Therapy Association. (1999). *A career in music therapy.* Retrieved October 1, 2004, from http://www.musictherapy.org/faqs.html

Baney, C. E. (2002). *Wired for sound: The essential connection between music and development.* Retrieved October 1, 2004, from http://www.gymboreeplayuk.com/wired.html

Bartlett, D., Kaufman, D., & Smeltekop, R. (1993). The effects of music listening and perceived sensory experiences on the immune system as measured by interleukin-1 and cortisol. *The Journal of Music Therapy, 30,* 194–209.

Bickerton, D. (2001). Can biomusicology learn from language evolution studies? In N. L. Wallin, B. Merker, & S. Brown (Eds.), *The origins of music* (pp. 153–164). Cambridge, MA: MIT Press.

Campbell, D. (2004). *The Mozart Effect Resource Center. Frequently asked questions.* Retrieved October 4, 2004, from http://www.mozarteffect.com

Carpenter, N. C. (1958). *Music in the Medieval and Renaissance universities.* Norman: University of Oklahoma Press.

Children's Defense Fund. (2001). *The state of America's children yearbook.* Washington, DC: Author.

Dissanayake, E. (2001). Antecedents of the temporal arts in early mother–infant interaction. In N. L. Wallin, B. Merker, & S. Brown (Eds.), *The origins of music* (pp. 389–410). Cambridge, MA: MIT Press.

Falk, D. (2001). Hominid brain evolution and the origins of music. In N. L. Wallin, B. Merker, & S. Brown (Eds.), *The origins of music* (pp. 197–216). Cambridge, MA: MIT Press.

Farley, B. (2001). *Bob's bongo basics.* Retrieved September 16, 2004, from http://www.bobfarley.com/bongo/history.html

Fowler, C. (1990, September). Recognizing the role of artistic intelligences. *Music Educators Journal, 77*(1), 24–27.

Gardner, H. (1983). *Frames of mind. The theory of multiple intelligences.* New York: Basic Books.

Gideonse, T., & Westley, M. (1998, September 21). Music is good medicine. *Newsweek, 132*(12), 103.

Gladwell, M. (2000). *Baby steps.* [Review of the book *The myth of the first three years*]. January 10, 2000. Retrieved October 12, 2004, from http://www.gladwell.com/2000/2000_01_10_a_baby.htm

Gordon, E. E. (1990). *A music learning theory for newborn and young children.* Chicago: G. I. A. Publications.

Gordon, E. E. (1995, Winter). The role of music aptitude in early childhood music. *Early Childhood Connections: Journal of Music- and Movement-Based Learning, 1*(2), 14–21.

Gordon, E. E. (1999, September). All about audiation and music aptitudes. *Music Educators Journal, 86*(2), 41–44.

Gordon Institute for Music Learning. (2003). *About music learning theory.* Retrieved September 19, 2004, from http://www.giml.org/frames.html

Johnson, J. K., Cotman, C. W., Tasaki, C. S., & Shaw, G. L. (1998). Enhancement of spatial-temporal reasoning after a Mozart listening condition in Alzheimer's disease: A case study. *Neurological Research, 20,* 666–672.

Jones, C. A., Norris, R., Palac, J., Sataloff, R. T., Sazer, V., Workman, D., & Brandfonbrener, A. (2001, October). Music and medicine: Preventing performance injuries. *Teaching Music, 9*(2), 22–30.

Kamien, R. (2003). *Music: An appreciation.* New York: McGraw-Hill.

Kuhn, D. (2002). The effects of active and passive participation in musical activity on the immune system as measured by salivary immunoglobulin A (SlgA). *Journal of Music Therapy, 39*(1), 30–39.

Lexico Publishing Group. (2004). *Dictionary.com.* Retrieved August 19, 2004, from http://dictionary.reference.com/

Mazo, E., & Parker, M. (2002). The medicine of music. *Health, 16*(5), 74–76.

Merker, B. (2001). Synchronous chorusing and human origins. In N. L. Wallin, B. Merker, & S. Brown (Eds.), *The origins of music* (pp. 315–328). Cambridge, MA: MIT Press.

Molino, J. (2001). Toward an evolutionary theory of music and language. In N. L. Wallin, B. Merker, & S. Brown (Eds.), *The origins of music* (pp. 153–164). Cambridge, MA: MIT Press.

Music Educators National Conference. (1994). *National standards for art education.* Reston, VA: Author. Retrieved September 24, 2004, from http://www.menc.org/publication/books/performance_standards/prek.html

Performing Arts Medical Association. (2004). *Performing Arts Medicine.* Retrieved October 1, 2004, from http://www.artsmed.org

Pratt, R. R. (1991, January). Music education and medicine. *Music Educators Journal, 77*(5), 31–36.

Public Broadcasting Service. (2004). *The secret life of the brain.* Retrieved October 18, 2004, from http://www.pbs.org/wnet/brain/index.html

Quinion, M. (2004). *World wide words.* Retrieved October 18, 2004, from http://www.worldwidewords.org/turnsofphrase/tp-bio1.htm

Rauscher, F. H., Shaw, G. L., & Ky, K. N. (1993). Music and spatial task performance. *Nature, 365,* 611.

Rauscher, F. H., Shaw, G. L., Levine, L. J., Wright, E. L., Dennis, W. R., & Newcomb, R. L. (1997). Music training causes long-term enhancement of preschool children's spatial-temporal reasoning. *Neurological Research,* 19, 2–8.

RhythmWeb. (2001). *History of the bongo drums.* Retrieved September 16, 2004, from http://www.rhythmweb.com/bongo/history.htm

Robb, S. L, Nichols, R. J., & Rutan, R. L. (1995). The effects of music assisted relaxation on preoperative anxiety. *Journal of Music Therapy 32,* 2–21.

Sadie, S. (1986). *Music guide, an introduction.* Englewood Cliffs, NJ: Prentice-Hall.

Sartorius, M. (2004). *Welcome to the wonderful world of Baroque music.* Retrieved September 16, 2004, from http://www.baroquemusic.org

Sherrane, R. (2004). *Music history 102: A guide to Western composers and their music.* Internet Public Library. Retrieved September 16, 2004, from http://www.ipl.org/div/mushist/middle/index.htm

Sony Music Entertainment. (2001). *Eras online.* Retrieved October 15, 2004, from http://www.essentialsofmusic.com/eras/baroque.html

Viadero, D. (1998, April 8). Music on the mind. *Education Week.* Retrieved October 2, 2004, from http://www.edweek.org/ew/articles/1998/04/08/30music.h17.html

Wallin, N. L., Merker, B., & Brown, S. (Eds.). (2001). *The origins of music.* Cambridge, MA: MIT Press.

Weinberger, N. M. (1999). Can music really improve the mind? The question of transfer effects. *MuSICA Research Notes, 6*(2), 5–7. Retrieved October 2, 2004, from http://www.musica.uci.edu/mrn/V6I2S99.html

Weinberger, N. M. (1996). Purists and Utilitians. *MuSICA Research Notes, 3*(2), 1–2. Retrieved October 2, 2004, from http://www.musica.uci.edu/mrn/V3I2F96.html#F96MoO

Winter, M. J., Paskin, S., & Baker, T. (1994). Music reduces stress and anxiety of patients in the surgical holding area. *Journal of Post Anesthesia Nursing, 9,* 340–343.

# What?

Early childhood teachers can exert a tremendous amount of influence on the development of the young children in their care. They have a responsibility to make it a positive influence so that each child will reach his fullest potential. Dedicated teachers accept this responsibility. In order to fulfill the responsibility, they must seek training on child development, curriculum planning, and ways to implement appropriate activities for children. Their training must be in all domains of early childhood development. When teachers have training in all developmental domains and understand how to apply that training in an appropriate manner to each individual child's developmental stage, there is a higher prospect that all children will reach their fullest potential.

Music is intertwined with all of the developmental domains, cognitive and language development, physical development, and social and emotional development. In addition to its impact on the child's total development, music is also important in our lives for its own sake. As discussed in Chapter 2, recent research demonstrates the importance of children receiving musical nurturing from birth.

With so many children under the age of six in child care on a daily basis and many more in out-of-school programs, the musical nurturing of these young children falls on the shoulders of those with whom they spend so much time. Training is required for teachers that addresses the best activities in which to engage young children. When teachers lack training, classroom music activities tend to occur in a haphazard and unplanned manner and at the impulse of the teacher (Greata, 1999). As a result, some children are nurtured and others receive little or no musical nurturing (Greata, 1999). When music activities are planned by teachers who lack music training, the activities tend to be limited in scope (i.e., singing a few songs or playing music in the background) and a majority of the music is limited in depth (i.e., the music sung or listened to is trivial) and not worthy of being considered an excellent musical experience (Greata, 1999). When teachers lack training, there are rarely planned objectives for the music activity or planned responses to the children's reactions (Greata, 1999). For example, the teacher may not have planned how to help a child who is having difficulty with the activity, or how to take a child who has mastered the activity to the next step in his development.

This section discusses the appropriate types of activities for musically nurturing young children. Many musical nurturing activities are not new to early childhood classrooms. What may be new is the purposeful planning of these activities and the understanding behind their selection that effective teachers must have. With this understanding and knowledge, each planned experience can be an excellent musical experience and each child can be musically nurtured in an appropriate manner.

# What Types of Activities Musically Nurture Young Children?

Last year, Isabelle earned her bilingual CDA certificate. This year, she continues her education as a candidate for an A.S. degree in early childhood education. The director of the child care center in which Isabelle works recognized her hard work and dedication to helping each child reach his full potential. This fall, she promoted Isabelle to the position of teacher in a classroom for three-year-olds. Although Isabelle has studied and read a little bit about music in the classroom, she has never taken a course about music in the early childhood classroom. She does know how important music is to each child's full development and wants to incorporate various types of music activities. What types of activities should Isabelle incorporate into her curriculum?

## Standards and Other Professional Guidance

### K–12 National Standards and Pre-K Standards for Music Education

The curriculum guidelines for the Prekindergarten Standards begin with a quote from the *MENC Position Statement on Early Childhood Education*: "A music curriculum for young children should include many opportunities to explore sound through singing, moving, listening, and playing instruments, as well as introductory experiences with verbalization and visualization of musical ideas. The music literature included in the curriculum should be of high quality and lasting value, including traditional children's songs, folk songs, classical music, and music from a variety of cultures, styles, and time periods." From *National Standards for Arts Education*. Copyright © 1994 by Music Educators National Conference (MENC). Used by permission. The complete National Arts Standards and additional materials relating to the Standards are available from MENC—The National Association for Music Education, 1806 Robert Fulton Drive, Reston, VA 20191.

The answer to Isabelle's question lies within this chapter. The chapter examines five different types of music activities for young children. These activities include sound exploration, singing with and to children, exploring rhythm, moving to music, and listening to music.

## Exploring Sounds

Sounds envelop us every day. Some sounds are more pleasant than other sounds, such as birds singing, trees rustling, and rain falling. Some sounds pollute the air, such as jackhammers, airplanes taking off or landing, and trucks backfiring. Some sounds warn us of danger, such as a fire alarm or the railroad-crossing bell. Other sounds help us get through the day, such as the alarm clock or the doorbell. When there is no sound, we may become uneasy, because being surrounded by sound is normal.

Music contributes to the sounds around us. It is "the art of arranging sounds" (Lexico Publishing Group, 2004). In music, sounds are arranged in an organized manner, thus setting music apart from other sounds. This organization uses musical elements combined in various ways to create each unique piece of music. Rhythm is an example of a musical element. Teachers of young children should become familiar with the elements used to create musical works of art. This familiarity will help them musically nurture young children. Do not worry! Be assured that learn-

ing about music is not as mysterious as it may seem. Throughout this text, and especially in the music labs at the end of each chapter, the musical elements are explored in an easy-to-understand manner.

Young children form a foundation for understanding the elements of music through sound exploration. They love creating their own sounds with whatever is available to them. They pound blocks together or on the floor, shake rattles, and "play" pots and pans with wooden spoons in the dramatic play area or on their own kitchen floor (see Figure 3–1). Through these activities, the young child begins to understand concepts such as loud and soft, high and low, and fast and slow.

*Figure 3–1*    Children love creating sounds with whatever is available to them.

Exploration is an important part of the young child's learning process. When first presented a new object, the young child spends time exploring the object to find out what the object can do (Mayesky, 1998). All five senses are employed. For example, when given a container with dry beans inside, a young toddler explores it by turning it over to look at it and feel it. He might smell it or put it in his mouth to taste it. Then, he might shake it or pound it on the floor. He explores all that the container can do and all that he can do with it. The teacher must recognize and support a child's exploration by giving the child appropriate materials to explore and sufficient time for his exploration. Teachers should model sound making with various materials and encourage the child to continue his exploration by commenting on the sounds that he makes. "The process of exploration and play is an essential part of an early childhood curriculum that promotes creativity" (Mayesky, 1998, p. 17). Children need the chance to explore objects before they can play or have other experiences with them. This includes the chance to explore sound in preparation for future musical experiences.

Play or experimentation is the next step in the learning process. Once the child knows what the object do, he can play or experiment further. For example, the container of beans can now be compared with others to determine which ones sound the same, or louder, or softer, or higher or lower in pitch. Pitch refers to the quality of a sound and the position of that sound in relationship to other sounds. In other words, is the pitch higher or lower or the same? Sound exploration is a simple starting point for nurturing children with music. However, often, it is not included in the daily curriculum plan. Yes, teachers must include sound exploration in their curriculum plans. From birth, exploring sounds should be a planned activity in the nurturing of children.

## Try This One!

### Shaking Tubes

You will need:

- Six small mailing tubes: 2 inches in diameter and 15 inches long

- Paper clips
- Buttons
- Marbles
- Toothpicks
- Coins
- Dried peas or beans
- Poster paper
- Electrical tape
- Colored markers

1. Fill the mailing tubes with the various items listed above. Tape the ends on the tube, so they do not come off when the tube is shaken.
2. Place the tubes on a table for the children to shake and hear.
3. Make a chart with the picture of each item on the chart, so the children can place each tube in the correct spot (ee Figure 3–2).
4. Make the activity self-correcting by placing a sticker on the tube that matches an answer code on the bottom of the chart. Tape a small piece of poster paper like a flap over the answers.
5. Keep track of the answers for each individual and make a chart to reflect the answers.

## Singing to and with Children

The second type of nurturing activity is singing to and with children. The most important sound to a young

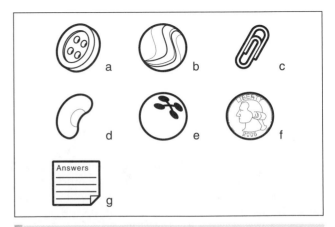

**Figure 3–2**  Sample Chart for Sound Game

child is his own voice. Infants spend long periods vocalizing, listening to the sounds they make, and imitating the sounds they hear. This is an important exercise for language development, as well as for musical nurturing. Singing to and with young children is not only a form of enjoyment, but is another form of sound exploration. As with language development, children need to hear sounds in order to reproduce them.

## Try This One!

### Books for Sound Making

Read any of the following books to the children in your classroom and make the sounds of the objects or animals in the stories. Obtain sound recordings and play for the children. See the Resource Guide in Appendix D for recording suggestions.

- *Gobble, Growl, Grunt* by Peter Spier (infant–preschool)
- *The Farmer in the Dell* by Ilse Plume (four- to eight-year-olds)
- *Moo, Baa, La La La!* by Sandra Boynton (infant–preschool)
- *Polar Bear, Polar Bear, What Do You Hear?* by Bill Martin Jr./Eric Carle (infant–preschool)
- *Tools* by Ann Morris (four- to eight-year-olds; this multicultural book shows the use of various tools around the world)
- *Cool Tools* (Spyglass Book) by Alison Auch (four- to eight-year-olds)
- *Noisy Workbench: My Electronic Sound and Lift-the-Flap Storybook* (Little Tikes) by Mary Anthony/Mike Giles (infant–preschool)

Imitation is one way in which teachers can explore the sound of the human voice with young children. As they play, children imitate the sound of a telephone, or a car, or an animal, or a monster. These are important exercises in the exploration of the human voice. The teacher can make the most of this childhood ritual by expanding the child's experience. The child can be encouraged to continue his exploration by simply commenting on the sound he makes. In addition, the child can be asked what sound he thinks a particular animal or a machine makes. The teacher should also demonstrate sounds for the children to imitate. Additionally, sound making can enhance storytelling. During story time, pause when appropriate to have children imitate the sounds of animals, machinery, or household appliances that appear in the story. This technique not only adds to the story, but also helps children discover their voices.

A second way that teachers can help children explore the sound of the human voice is through improvisation. Improvisation is the process of making up music on the spot. Teachers can sing about what the children are doing, seeing, feeling, or hearing and they can encourage children to make up songs as well. For example, the teacher can greet the children as they arrive or call the roll at circle time by singing the words to simple pitches instead of speaking to the children. (See Figure 3–3.) When the teacher continues this practice, the children will begin to answer by imitating the teacher's voice and improvising their own song. This technique is discussed further in Section 3.

In addition to enjoying their own voices, young children are comforted when their teacher sings to them. Children do not care about the quality of the teacher's voice. The important thing is that the teacher is singing to them (see Figure 3–4). Teachers

*Figure 3–3*   An example of a simple greeting sung by the teacher.

*Figure 3–4*    Children enjoy their teacher's singing.

should develop a repertoire of excellent children's songs. These songs should be memorized, so that teachers do not rely heavily on recordings. Knowing the song allows the teacher to sing it at anytime, with or without accompaniment, thus creating a spontaneous and enjoyable experience for the children. A basic song list for early childhood educators is in the Resource Guide located in Appendix D.

Singing with and to young children is an important part of a good music nurturing program. According to Zoltan Kodály (1882–1967), a prominent Hungarian musician and educator, the foundation of all musical training should be singing (Wicks, 2002). Singing should take place throughout the day. It can be a wonderful tool for teachers to use as they help children transition from one activity to another. A song can be a cue to move on to another activity and it facilitates the move by helping to remove stress. There does not have to be a specific time to sing a song such as at circle time and you do not have

to have a reason to sing a song other than the fact that you enjoy it. From birth, singing to and with children should become a planned element in the nurturing of children with music.

## Exploring Rhythm with Young Children

Rhythm permeates the earth and all living creatures. It is seen in the ebb and flow of the tides and in the changing seasons. Each individual has a unique rhythm and these unique personal rhythms are reflected in different personalities and temperaments. We feel the rhythm of our bodies throughout the day as we become hungry, tired, quiet, or energetic.

All forms of art have rhythm and each piece of art has a unique rhythm. If you were to compare a painting by Renoir with a painting by Picasso, you would find that they each have a unique rhythm. The architecture of the Greek Parthenon conveys a different rhythm than the architectural rhythm of a modern skyscraper. There is rhythm in the poetry, prose, and action of drama. Finally, we see and hear a variety of rhythms in dance and music.

What is rhythm? In this text, rhythm is examined as it relates to music. Sometimes, people refer to rhythm as the **beat**. Although rhythm and beat are related, they are not the same thing. Each piece of music has a beat and it has a rhythm as well. When you think of beat, think of your heart. Your heart has a beat. It is steady, unchanging, and keeps on going. Your heart might beat faster or slower depending on your activity level, but it remains steady and unchanging. You want your heart to behave that way. If the doctor tells you that your heart has "a rhythm," then you know it is doing something other than performing with a steady and unchanging beat. Maybe it is skipping beats, or maybe it is beating extra times. That gives your heart a rhythm.

So, what is rhythm? Rhythm is basic to music. When composers create their music, they use musical notation. These symbols and words communicate the music to the musician. Part of this notation tells performers to play or sing a sound longer or shorter than other sounds. This lengthening and shortening of musical sounds creates a rhythmic pattern or the rhythm of the music. Often, the rhythmic pattern repeats throughout a piece of music. Rhythm makes the music interesting and different from other music. Frequently, the rhythm is what first draws us to a piece of music. You hear a new song on the radio and the rhythm grabs you. Young children respond to music by "dancing" to the rhythm.

Rhythm can be explored with the youngest infant. In fact, because rhythm is also important to language development, exploring rhythm with infants, toddlers, and preschoolers serves a dual purpose. Chanting rhymes and poetry with young children helps them develop their language skills. Regardless of the child's background or ability, verbal experiences in rhythm, such as chanting rhymes and poetry, can be a positive language experience (Buchoff, 1994).

When it comes to musical development, experiences in rhythm are a must and being able to feel the musical beat is fundamental for later music education and enjoyment. Starting at birth and throughout the preschool years, children's brains are busy collecting and organizing information to use as they develop. If children are to have a sense of beat in music later in their studies, they must have experiences with rhythm and musical beats during this time (Feierabend, 1996). Rhymes, rhythmic chants, and fingerplays are the best ways to explore rhythm with very young children (Feierabend, 1996).

Rhythm is the basis of life. We feel it in our heartbeats and we see it in nature. Rhythm is also the basis of music. It is the life of the music. Without rhythm, a melody would be a long series of notes without meaning. When rhythm is added, the song comes to life. From birth, rhymes, rhythmic chants, and finger plays should become planned activities in the nurturing of children with music.

## Try This One!

### Trot, Trot to Boston Town!

Learn the following chant and use it when moving infants to or from the changing table, or as a transition for preschool children as they move from one activity to another.

#### Trot, Trot to Boston Town

Trot, trot to Boston Town
To buy a stick of candy.
One for you and one for me,
And one for Dilly Dandy.

When working with one child, substitute that child's name for "Dilly." The last line might then sound like this: "And one for Lisa Dandy" or "And one for Miguel Dandy."

## Moving to Music

Try to picture a young child who is awake, but not moving. This is difficult! At times, they seem to be in perpetual motion. Movement is important in the life of a child. Not only do they love to move, but also movement plays a crucial role in a child's development (Pica, 2000). It is easy to understand how movement enhances a child's physical development. As he moves, a young child practices the motor skills he will use throughout his life. What may be less obvious is that movement plays an important role in the cognitive, social, and emotional development of children as well (Pica, 2000).

## Try This One!

### Bubble Wrap Jumping

Combine sound exploration with movement by having the children jump on bubble wrap to hear the sound (see Figure 3–5). If you want to add music, make it soft enough for the bubble wrap to be heard.

Cognitive abilities develop as children move through their world, gathering information. As children move around the classroom or playground, they learn about the way their bodies work. They learn about balance as they walk on the balance beam, ride a seesaw, or stack blocks. They learn

**Figure 3–5**  Movement is important in the life of a child.

about cause and effect as they use their bodies to operate objects in their environment, such as riding a tricycle or turning the handle on a jack-in-the-box. As they climb the jungle gym, they learn about spatial concepts such as up and down, on top of and under, and high and low. The ability to move helps children make discoveries and enhances their cognitive development.

Movement brings children into contact with other children and adults and this helps their social development. As they participate in movement activities, children must learn to share space and materials. This includes learning to respect the space of other children and adults. Movement activities help develop cooperation. For example, it is important for children to cooperate when participating in games. One child can ruin a game for all of the children by not cooperating. Parachute play, for example, requires that all participants work together for a successful experience. Children learn to take turns on playground equipment and while playing games. As children move about their environment, they learn how to successfully participate in society.

A good sense of self is important for emotional development. First, children need to have a good **self-concept**. They need answers to the questions: Who am I and where do I belong in the world? Second, they need a good sense of **self-efficacy**. When a person has good self-efficacy, he has a "can do" attitude. Children need to feel that they have an effect on their environment and that they are not ineffective. Third, children need good **self-esteem**. They need to feel important and valued in the eyes of others. Movement enhances a child's sense of himself (Pica, 2000). As children develop better control of their movement and learn new movements, their self-esteem is enhanced (Pica, 2000). When they are successful in their movement attempts, their self-efficacy is strengthened. Teachers must plan movement activities that children can successfully accomplish. When teachers support children during movement activities, they begin to develop a good self-concept of who they are and what they can do.

## Try This One!

### The Rainbow Fish

1. Read the book *The Rainbow Fish* by Marcus Pfister to the children.
2. Ask the children to put their hands together and move their hands the way they think a fish moves.
3. Play about 15–30 seconds of "Aquarium" from Saint-Saëns's *Carnival of the Animals* for the children.
4. Ask them if they can move their hands like a fish to the music.
5. Replay the first 30 seconds.

6. Ask the children how they would move their whole body like a fish.
7. Replay the music and have the children move around the room to the music. How long you allow the music to play will depend on the age of the children and their involvement in the exercise. Be sure to listen to the music before playing it for the children.

---

Alone, these reasons are good enough for the inclusion of planned movement in an early childhood curriculum. When teachers set aside time for planned movement experiences in the classroom, children develop a larger repertoire of movement skills and improve the skills they already possess (Pica, 2000). For the purpose of music nurturing, another important reason to include movement in the early childhood classroom is its partnership with music. Music and movement go hand in hand. Once again, picture that young child and add music to your image. Maybe you thought of toddlers "dancing" to music or preschoolers moving while they sing or play a singing game or an infant being rocked to a lullaby. It is difficult to think about music without thinking about movement.

### Emile Jaques-Dalcroze and Eurhythmics

Emile Jaques-Dalcroze (1865–1950) was a Swiss musician and educator. He developed the "oldest of the modern music education methods" (Caldwell, 2002, p. 2). The method that he called *Rythmique* is known today as **Eurhythmics** (Caldwell, 2002). The philosophy behind this music education method can be traced to two other Swiss educators, Pestalozzi and Claparéde, who was Piaget's teacher (Caldwell, 2002). Dalcroze agreed with Montessori that it was important for children to learn basic skills and perceptions during the early years (McDonald & Simons, 1989). While serving as professor of harmony at the Geneva Conservatory, Dalcroze was disturbed by his students' lack of musicality and musical rhythm (Dalcroze Society of America, 2002). He believed that the best way to teach these basics was through kinesthesia (Caldwell, 2002), which means to sense through movement or the muscles. "To put it succinctly, in order to

perform any music well we need to first train the instrument that performs it: the body" (Caldwell, 2002, p. 5). From birth, moving to music should become a planned element in the nurturing of children with music.

## Listening to Music

Music is an art of sound. If children are to become attentive music listeners, then teachers must help children learn to listen to music, perceptively. "**Perceptive listening** is the essence of musical intelligence" (McDonald & Simons, 1989, p. 43). When a piece of music is played, a perceptive listener not only hears the music, but listens with an understanding of the music. He is able to hear, appreciate, and understand the elements of the music. Additionally, the perceptive listener understands how the elements combine to make the music unique.

A newborn arrives ready to listen, even though his listening ability is not fully developed. Researchers have noted that children as young as two months stop their activity and give fixed attention to musical sounds produced with the human voice or an instrument (McDonald & Simons, 1989). Learning a language can be compared to learning about music. An infant listens for a long time before being able to speak words. It is the same with music. Children need to hear music for a long time before being able to reproduce it in a musical manner (Feierabend, 1997).

Every day most of us are exposed to sound pollution, especially in urban areas. The sounds of traffic, construction, road repair, and machinery assail us. Often, we are surrounded with "audible wallpaper" in stores and elevators to the point that we are not even aware of it (Baney, 2002, p. 4). When we are in an environment in which we are bombarded with sound, we learn to shut it out (Baney, 2002). To be perceptive listeners, children must develop "**attentive listening**" (Baney, 2002, p. 3). Attentive listening is the same as focused listening or, in other words, paying attention to the music being played. Teachers should give children an opportunity to develop this important skill. Not only is attentive listening a vital skill in musical nurturing, but also "in every part of life and learning" (Baney, 2002, p. 3). If we want children to learn to listen attentively, it is important that we do not turn off their listening abilities with "audible wallpaper" (Baney, 2002). Merely playing a radio or tape recorder in the background all day does not fulfill the objective of exposing children to music. Occasionally, teachers must provide a time for focused, attentive listening to music. From birth, focused listening to music should become a planned element in the nurturing of children with music.

## Try This One!

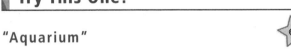

### "Aquarium"

Play "Aquarium" from Saint-Saëns's *Carnival of the Animals* for the children when they are put down for naptime and during other times such as lunchtime. If the children have heard the music prior to moving to it, there is a greater chance that it will hold their interest for a longer period of time.

## Summary

There are five types of activities for musically nurturing children, sound exploration, singing to and with children, exploring rhythm, moving to music, and listening to music. Often, these activities are used in an early childhood classroom without careful planning on the part of the teacher. Musically nurturing young children should not be done in a haphazard manner. Teachers must recognize the importance of these activities in the development of children's musical intelligence and carefully plan for their use. Section 3 (Who? and How?) of this text examines activities that are developmentally appropriate for children in various ages and stages of development.

## Key Concepts

- There are five appropriate types of musical activities for use in early childhood classrooms: exploring sound, singing to and with children, exploring rhythm, moving to music, and listening to music.
- Musical nurturing activities should be included in curriculum plans.
- Through sound exploration children form a foundation to understanding musical concepts such as high and low, loud and soft, fast and slow.
- Singing to and with children not only helps them learn to use their singing voice, but is another form of sound exploration.
- Rhythm is basic to music and all art. Exploring rhythm with young children is an important activity to help children feel the rhythm and beat of music.
- Moving to music helps children develop musicality and rhythmic feeling.
- Listening to music helps children learn to be perceptive listeners.

## Suggested Activities

1. Visit an early childhood classroom. Observe the musical activities that take place in the classroom. Are the activities planned? If not, how does the teacher engage the children in these musical activities? Does the teacher offer a variety of activities to the children? Are all of the children involved in music activities during the day? Do you see or hear children engaging in music on their own?
2. Discuss with your classmates the various ways in which you can involve children with music.
3. Choose one type of activity such as sound exploration, rhythmic exploration, singing, or listening and/or moving to music and decide how you would implement that type of activity in your classroom. For example, would you use it during circle time, transition time, or naptime?
4. Journal reflection question 3: Is there any music activity in which you are more comfortable or uncomfortable? What do you need to do to feel more comfortable?

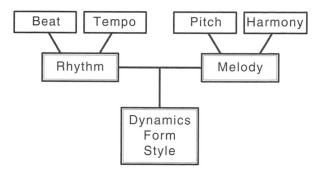

**Figure 3–6**  Diagram of the relationship of musical elements to each other.

## Music Lab #3

Welcome to Music Lab #3! With this lab, we begin to explore the basic music elements, rhythm, beat, and tempo. These elements are used in activities for you and for young children. Additionally, our music history journey continues into the Western European Classical period.

## Basic Musical Elements

When we dissect a song, we find certain elements that make up that song. Two elements that create a song's uniqueness are the rhythm and melody. Both rhythm and melody have other musical elements closely related to them. Beat and tempo are related to rhythm, while pitch and **harmony** are related to melody. Both rhythm and melody are related to **dynamics**, **form**, and **style**. Figure 3–6 illustrates the relationships of these musical elements.

This lab addresses rhythm and its related elements, beat and tempo. Earlier in this chapter, rhythm and beat were introduced, explaining the difference between them. Tempo refers to how fast or how slow a piece of music is played. Tempo affects how fast or slow the beat is. In subsequent chapters, the elements of melody, pitch, harmony, dynamics, form, and style, among others, will be explained. Following are several activities that will help you and children learn to feel the beat, rhythm, and tempo of music. All songs and rhymes referred to are in the Resource Guide in Appendix D.

## Musical Elements

### Rhythm

Rhythm refers to the pattern created when long and short sounds are combined, such as when we chant words in a rhyme or play pitches in a piece of music. For example, clap the words of "Mary Had a Little Lamb" while you sing the song in your head. This is the rhythm of the song. Rhythm combines with melody to make each song unique.

### Beat

Beat refers to the steady pulse of the music. It is like a heartbeat. It might become faster or slower, but it remains unchanging in reference to the space of time between each beat. Grouping beats differently, such as four in a group or three in a group, and accenting the first beat of a group can change the music. For example, begin to clap a steady beat. Now, group the beats into groups of four by counting, **1**, 2, 3, 4 - **1**, 2, 3, 4, etc. For added effect, say the number one louder than the rest of the beats. This is the grouping of beats for a march. Try marching to your beat. Next, group the beats into groups of three by counting, **1**, 2, 3 - **1**, 2, 3, etc., and again, say the number one louder than the rest of the beats. This is the grouping of beats for a waltz. Can you waltz to your beat?

## Tempo

Tempo refers to how fast or slow a piece of music should be sung or played. *Tempo* is the Italian word for "time." Traditionally, musical terms are written in Italian, although in recent years, the trend has been to break away from that tradition. Many words are used to tell musicians how fast or slow to play a piece of music. For example, largo (lar-go) means to make the beat very slow, as if a king or queen or even a bride were entering. Moderato (mo-der-a-to) means make the beat the same as a medium walking pace, as you might want for a march. Presto (pres-to) means make the beat very fast as if there were a hive of bees buzzing around.

## Activity #1: Clapping the Beat

### For You

1. Clap your hands in a steady, unchanging manner. You are clapping a beat.
2. Keep clapping that steady, unchanging beat, and sing, "Mary Had a Little Lamb."

As you sang and clapped, did you notice that sometimes you clapped on each word you sang? Did you also notice that sometimes there were extra notes between your claps and sometimes you clapped while you held a long note? You were clapping the beat or pulse of the song.

1. Do this activity again and listen carefully for those extra notes in between your claps and for the long notes that you sing while you continue to clap.
2. Next, begin to clap a beat and then chant the nursery rhyme "Hot Cross Buns" to your beat.
3. What did you notice this time?

### In the Preschool Program

1. Begin clapping a steady beat. The children will follow.
2. Begin to sing a song and the children will join in. Young children can and should be engaged in this activity on a daily basis. For young children, the experience should be fun and without much discussion. By leading the children in this type of activity, the teacher is helping them begin to feel the beat in music. The teacher should tell the children they are clapping the beat.

### In the Out-of-School Program

This activity is a good activity to use to gather children together. However, songs chosen for early elementary children should be appropriate for their age. Songs such as "Kookaburra," "Looby Loo," and "Clap, Clap, Clap Your Hands" are good songs for this age. Jump rope rhymes make good rhythmic rhymes for older children. You will find these songs and some chants as well as suggested reference books in the Resource Guide in Appendix D.

## Activity #2: Walking the Beat

In this chapter, you were introduced to Emile Jaques-Dalcroze. Dalcroze taught the importance of feeling the musical beat with our bodies, because our bodies are a part of our musical instruments.

### For You

1. This activity requires room to move about the room. Play a walking beat on a drum or other instrument such as a wood block or rhythm sticks, while you walk in a large circle, stepping on each beat. As you walk, sing, "Mary Had a Little Lamb." As with Activity #1, notice that as you walk, you sing some of the notes in between your steps and other notes you hold while you continue to step.
2. Sing "Twinkle, Twinkle, Little Star" and then chant "Hot Cross Buns" as you continue to step to the beat. Although the activity is nearly the same as Activity #1, in this activity, you are using more of your body to respond to the music.
3. Try to clap and walk the beat at the same time as you sing and chant. Use other songs and chants

you know as a part of the activity. What was different or what was the same with each song and chant?

**In the Preschool and in Out-of-School Programs**
It is more difficult for young children to walk to the beat than to clap it. That does not mean that you should not try this activity with them.

1. Begin by playing the beat on a drum or other rhythm instrument.
2. Once the children are all walking to the drum-beat, you can begin to sing or chant a song. The children may not be able to sing and walk at the same time. The purpose of this activity is to allow young children to experience the beat of a song. Discussion is not necessary. Again, use the word *beat* to tell the children that they are walking the beat of the song or chant.

## Activity #3: Playing the Beat on Rhythm Instruments

**For You**

1. Choose a rhythm instrument.
2. Establish a steady, unchanging beat, as you did when you were clapping or walking.
3. Sing several nursery rhymes or songs or chant various nursery rhymes while you play the beat.
4. Use your ears to listen for those extra little notes in between the beats and for the long notes that you sing while the beat continues in a steady manner.

Children must have a chance to explore rhythm instruments at great length before teachers try to do an organized instrument activity. Otherwise, they cannot resist exploring the instrument instead of doing what you would like them to be doing.

**In the Preschool and in Out-of-School Programs**

1. Allow the children to first play the beat using their "lap drums." Have the children sit with their legs crossed. They can then slap their laps for a drum.
2. After they have had sufficient experience with rhythm instruments, you can have them play the beat on instruments.

In Activities #1, #2, and #3, you have experienced clapping, walking, and playing the beat of songs. Just as it is important for our hearts to beat in a steady and unchanging pulse, it is important for music to have a steady, unchanging beat or pulse. The tempo may change from one song to the next. For one song, the beat may be slower than another song and some songs have similar tempos. Can you think of a song that has a slow beat? Maybe it is a lullaby, such as "All the Pretty Little Horses." Can you think of a song with a fast beat? Maybe it is a fast dance, such as "Clap, Clap, Clap Your Hands." Additionally, the tempo may change within the same song. For example, the song might begin slowly and get faster.

## Activity #4: Clapping, Walking, and Playing the Rhythm of Songs

During Activities #1, #2, and #3, you noticed extra notes that you sang and did not clap, walk, or play. In addition, there were long notes that you sang, while you continued to clap, walk, or play. What you were hearing was the rhythm of the song.

**For You**

1. Try this experiment: Begin to clap a beat. Now try to sing "Twinkle, Twinkle, Little Star" by singing only on the clapped beat. Repeat the experiment, but this time, sing "Mary Had a Little Lamb." How boring songs would be if we only sang on the beat! Rhythm is a combination of musical notes, some long sounding and others short sounding, that form a pattern. Rhythm makes each song unique. Rhythm gives life to music. Activity #4 helps you experience the rhythm of the music.
2. Use the same songs and chants that you used in Activities #1, #2, and #3. This time, clap, walk, or play an instrument when you sing or say the words. Now you are clapping, walking, or playing all of the notes you are singing, such as those little notes in between the beats. Additionally, you hold the long notes, even when you are not clapping. You sense how long you should hold the note, because you feel the beat. Try this activity with

several songs and chants. You are experiencing the rhythm of the song.

### In the Preschool and in Out-of-School Programs

1. Have the children do the same activity. Be sure to tell them they are clapping, walking, or playing the rhythm.
2. Begin by only clapping the rhythm. Depending on the age of the children, this may be difficult for them at first. Ask them to have their hands clap the words. Again, as with the earlier activities, this should be a fun activity. Do not insist that the children do it perfectly. Many will not be able to do it at first. Exposing the children to the concept is the most important point. With practice, they will be able to do it. The idea of clapping the rhythm should be established without a lot of discussion.
3. When the children are accomplished at this, you can play a game by changing from clapping the beat to clapping the rhythm to various songs. Tell the children that you are going to clap the rhythm or beat while they sing a song. Ask the children to guess whether you are clapping the rhythm or the beat. This can be done only after many weeks of experience and most likely with older children.

## Activity #5: Clapping Names

As with songs, names also have their own rhythm.

### For You

1. Spend time clapping the names of your classmates.
2. Notice the different rhythms for the various names.
3. Notice the names that have the same rhythm.
4. Try guessing a name someone else claps.

A child's name is very important to him. Clapping the names of children is one way in which you can introduce them to rhythm.

### In the Infant and Toddler Rooms

1. Bounce a baby or toddler on your knee to the rhythm of the names of various children in the room.

2. You can also tap their backs or hold their hands and clap their hands to the rhythm of various names.

### In the Preschool and in Out-of-School Programs

1. Clap the names of various children when you gather them in a group.
2. Have the children clap the name back to you while they say the name.
3. Have individual children clap their name for the rest of the class to clap back to them. Make this a game for them. Some names have the same rhythm as others. Children will begin to notice this as they gain sufficient experience.
4. When the children have had a great deal of experience, clap names for them and have them guess whose name you are clapping.
5. With older children, clap songs for them to guess.

## ▌ Try This One!

### Roll Call Clap

During roll call, clap the rhythm to the following chant and have the children clap back to you.

| Teacher: | Who is John? Who is John? |
| Child: | I am John! I am John! |
| Teacher: | Who is Melissa? Who is Melissa? |
| Child: | I am Melissa! I am Melissa! |

## ▌ Try This One!

### Variations on "Ah, vous dirais-je Maman"

Play Mozart's *Variations on "Ah, vous dirais-je Maman"* for the children and see if they can guess the name of the song. The tune is the same as "Twinkle, Twinkle Little Star." Mozart did not write the tune. It is an old French country tune. In fact, Haydn used the tune in the second movement of his *Surprise Symphony*. A **theme and variations** is a musical form in which the melody is stated as the theme of the piece and then

## Making Musical Instruments

### Sound Cans

Collect the following materials:

- At least six 6-oz. orange juice cans with tops
- Colorful tape
- Contact paper
- Rice, beans, cotton balls, bells, rocks, sand, or any other materials that make sounds

1. Thoroughly wash and dry the cans and lids.
2. Place a different material in each can. Very little of any material is needed to make a sound. Experiment to make sure the sounds vary. Cotton balls alone are soundless, but you can feel them moving inside. Placing cotton inside the can with another material changes the sound. Experiment with different materials to obtain a variety of sounds.
3. Tightly tape the lid on the can.
4. Cover the can with contact paper.

#### For You

1. Make several sets of sound cans to share with the children in your classroom.
2. Make two identical sets of cans. Place matching colored dots on the bottoms of identical cans.

#### In the Infant or Toddler Rooms

Children will enjoy exploring the sounds they can make by shaking or pounding these cans. This should be a teacher-directed activity in case the child becomes curious and tries to get to the material inside. Talk to them about the sound they are making. Is it low or soft? Is it high or low?

#### In the Preschool and in Out-of-School Programs

1. Children who are old enough should be included in the process of making sound cans. Depending on the ease of obtaining sufficient materials (in particular 6-oz. cans with lids), each child can make his own sound can collection.
2. After the children have had a chance to explore the various sounds of single cans, give them identical cans to match sound sets. The activity is self-correcting, if the matching cans have the same colored dot on the bottom.
3. Initially, introduce the children to a limited number of sound sets. I suggest that you start with six cans or three sets for young preschool children to match. Additionally, make the three sets very different from each other, so the children can easily distinguish them from each other.
4. As they gain more experience with sound matching, children can match larger numbers of can sets and sounds that are closer to each other without becoming frustrated.

### Egg Shakers

In addition to the sound cans, make music shakers out of plastic eggs filled with the items listed for the sound cans. Be sure you tape the egg halves together very well. The plastic eggs are a good size for little hands and make excellent rhythm shakers. In addition, they are small enough for easy storage. Each child can also make his own egg shakers to use during music time.

---

the composer writes several (in this case 12) variations of the theme. This is an excellent piece for you to experience the theme and variations form. The familiarity of the tune makes it easier to hear how Mozart varied it.

## Music Appreciation: The Classical Period (1750–1827)

#### For You

Our journey through musical history continues, as we move into the Western European Classical period.

The sources for the music history presented in this activity are Kamien (2003), Kendall (1985), Sadie (1986), and Sony Music Entertainment (2001).

The age of discovery during the Baroque Era led to a period of enlightenment in the Classical Era. The industrial revolution made goods available to a larger mass of people and the middle class was on the rise. The individual was recognized as capable and able to make decisions about his future, including political decisions. Rousseau, Voltaire, and Jefferson expressed these ideals in their writings. It was from this thinking that the American and French revolutions began. The ability to pursue happiness was

## Music of the World

**Mein Hut (My Hat)**

This song is fun to sing and not difficult for the children to learn the words, because they just keep switching around.

Here is the pronunciation of the German words.

Mein (mine)
hut (hoot)
es (ess)

hat (hot)
drei (dry)
ecke (eka)
und (oont)
war (var— are with a v in front of it)
nicht (neekt)
meine (myna)

For an art activity, you can make three-corner hats in the art corner.

Voice

| 5 | 6 | 5 | 4 | 3 | 4 | 2 | 2 | 3 | 4 | 5 | 6 | 5 | 3 |
Mein Hut es hat drei Ec - ke.    Drei Ec - ke hat mein Hut. -
My hat, it has three cor-ners.    Three cor - ners has my hat.

| 3 | 5 | 8 | 5 | 4 | 3 | 4 | 2 | 2 | 3 | 4 | 5 | 6 | 5 | 1 |
Und hat es nicht drei Ec - ke,    es war nicht mei - ne Hut.
And had it not three cor-ners,    it would not be my hat.

Song "Mein Hut es hat drei Ecke"

available to more people as the general wealth rose and music was considered a luxury many wished to pursue. Composers began to write more for the common people and less for the courts and churches. The music they wrote was simple and balanced in form and reflected society's interest in the natural. Three composers stand out during this period of Western music—Haydn, Mozart, and Beethoven.

Franz Joseph Haydn (1732–1809) was born in Austria. By the age of 29, he was invited to serve as composer for the Esterházys, the most powerful and wealthiest of Hungarian nobles. In this position, Haydn was a servant. However, for musicians of the time, this was a sought-after position because it provided a steady income and an outlet for their music. A normal week for Haydn consisted of two concerts, two opera performances, and daily chamber music, most of which he wrote.

Haydn is affectionately known as "Papa Haydn." This is due to the influence he had on the development of the symphony and string quartet. Haydn is famous for his use of humor in his symphonies. One story is told that when he heard a group of young children playing bird whistles, drums, and rattles in the town market, he went back to the palace and composed his *Toy Symphony*. Along with the string instruments of the orchestra, Haydn used bird whistles, rattles, a ratchet, a toy drum, a toy trumpet, a triangle, small cymbals, a cuckoo horn, and a harpsichord as his instruments. His *Farewell Symphony* and *Surprise Symphony* have similar stories attached to them.

As the middle class grew, had more leisure time, and wanted to enjoy some of the pleasures available only to the aristocracy, such as music, concerts and operas began to be presented to the public. With this change, musicians no longer had to work for a patron in order to make a living. In addition, their music was heard by a greater number of people.

Wolfgang Amadeus Mozart (1756–1791) was born at this time in Salzburg, Austria, where his father was a court musician and composer. Surrounded by music, his natural musical aptitude was stimulated. By four, he played music he heard his sister play on the harpsichord. When he was five, Wolfgang composed his first two pieces of music, minuets. He could play both the harpsichord and violin by age six and he read music perfectly at first sight. Wolfgang's father, Leopold, took his talented son and daughter on a tour of Europe to show them off to the courts. Mozart was busy composing and taking lessons as they traveled to play for the aristocracy. The two children played for Louis XV in France, George III in London, and Empress Maria Theresa in Vienna. By the time he was 8, he had written a symphony and by age 11, an oratorio. The family visited Italy several times and here Wolfgang studied the latest operatic style. He mastered the form so well that he wrote his first opera at age 12 and began writing operas for production in Milan, Italy.

Unfortunately, Wolfgang was not as successful as an adult as he was as a child prodigy. His life of travel left him dependent on his father for decision making and feeling just above the level of servanthood. When his efforts to find employment elsewhere failed, at age 25, Mozart left for Vienna to become a freelance composer. At first, he was very successful. His opera, *The Marriage of Figaro,* was a huge success. Mozart wrote to his father that everyone was talking about *Figaro*. However, the fickle aristocracy of Vienna turned against him when they heard his opera, *Don Giovanni*. Mozart was commissioned to write the opera by an opera company in Prague. It was a huge success in Prague, but in Vienna, it was too dark and dissonant for the aristocracy. He began to lose students and the aristocracy refused to attend his concerts.

Ironically, success returned in his final year of life. He received two commissions for compositions that year. The first was for his comic opera, *The Magic Flute*, which was another triumph. The second was an anonymous request for a requiem. A requiem is a mass for the dead. Through his illness, Mozart came to believe that the requiem was for him and worked feverishly to finish it before he died. He died before his 36th birthday, without finishing the requiem. It was later finished by his student.

Although Mozart died at a young age, he was a copious composer and left the world vast numbers of compositions. He composed every type of music over his brief lifetime, but opera was his passion. The three most famous of his operas are *The Marriage of Figaro, Don Giovanni,* and *The Magic Flute.* Worldwide, audiences continue to be enthralled with them.

Music historians disagree as to when the Classical Era ended. Some believe it ended with Beethoven's death in 1827, while others believe it ended in 1820 and that Beethoven actually led the way into the Romantic period.

Although the printing press had been invented in 1450, many court and church composers continued to hand-write their music because they were composing so quickly for immediate events. Sometimes there was only one copy of the music. Stories are told of music being handed to court musicians with the ink still wet. However, during the late Classical Era, musicians began to work independently and not under the patronage of a court. Performers were compensated for concerts and composers were compensated by submitting their work to music publishers. By the end of the Classical Era, most of the instruments we know today had been invented and the piano was in the process of being perfected. Beethoven took advantage of all of these changes. He was one of the first composers to submit his work to music publishers. Letters to his publishers regarding the publishing and his payment for his compositions continue to be studied by music researchers. His piano compositions demonstrate the growth of the piano during his lifetime.

Ludwig Van Beethoven (1770–1827), an undisputed musical genius, was born into a family of musicians in Bonn, Germany. Beethoven's father hoped to use Beethoven's talent to bring income to the family in the same manner that Mozart's father had used his children's talents. However, a European tour did not materialize. By the time he was 11 years old, Beethoven was assistant to the court organist in Bonn. In this way, he helped support his family. Beethoven was already composing musical works and had several works published by the time he was 14.

At the age of 17, he moved to Vienna to study with Mozart, but had barely arrived when his father sent for him to return to Bonn because his mother was dying. In 1789, after his mother's death, Beethoven took charge of the family—his father and two brothers. He returned to the court in Bonn and played the viola for the chapel and theater orchestras. When Haydn's journey back to Vienna from London brought him through Bonn, in 1792, Beethoven was sent to Vienna to study with him. Although Beethoven did not study long with Haydn, he would have hot chocolate with him on Friday afternoons. Vienna was to be Beethoven's home for the rest of his life.

Beethoven earned his living giving lessons and concerts. He was very popular as a performer and publishing houses eagerly bought his compositions. At age 29, he discovered he was going deaf. This increasing disability caused fits of depression throughout his remaining years. His deafness did not bother him as a composer, because he could hear the music in his head. In fact, he composed his music as he sat at his desk, instead of at the piano. However, it gradually affected his ability to perform and conduct his music, although he continued to conduct long after he could do it effectively. Socially, he was devastated. In letters, he expressed his despair.

Beethoven's depression and personal difficulties caused irregularity in his writing. He would go for a period without any composition and then a sudden burst would appear. In a burst of creation after 1818, he composed some of his greatest works. During this time, he composed his late piano sonatas and string quartets, and the *Missa solemnis*. In particular, the composition of his Ninth Symphony with its *Ode to Joy* stands out as a great accomplishment. Not only was Beethoven the first composer to include voices on equal par to the orchestra in a symphony, but he composed it while totally deaf.

The power of Beethoven's music demands that it be heard. Within the range of his compositions, Classical music reached the height of its development. Within that same range of compositions, Beethoven in his deafness lifted music beyond the compositional practices of the time and moved it into the Romantic period where his music influenced future composers.

## For You

1. The Resource Guide in Appendix D lists several children's books about Haydn, Mozart, and Beethoven. Read at least one book.
2. Choose one composition listed in the Resource Guide (Appendix D) by the composer of the book you read and listen to it.
3. Do you think the music you chose reflects the Classical period? How?

## In All Early Childhood Classrooms

1. Select an appropriate time to share the music you listened to with the children in your classroom.
2. After they have heard the music, you can tell the children about the composer by either reading the book or telling the story and showing the pictures.
3. Continue to play the music in your classroom occasionally, so the children become familiar with it.

You have completed Music Lab #3. You now understand the music elements of rhythm, beat, and tempo and are ready to move on to Lab #4 and the music elements of melody, pitch, and harmony. Occasionally, return to Lab #3 to practice the activities.

# References

Baney, C. E. (2002). *Wired for sound: The essential connection between music and development.* Retrieved April 4, 2004, from http://www.gymboreeplayuk. com/wired.html

Buchoff, R. (1994). Joyful voices: Facilitating language growth through the rhythmic response to chants. *Young Children, 49*(4), 26–30.

Caldwell, J. T. (2002, July). *A brief introduction to Dalcroze eurhythmics.* Retrieved April 4, 2004, from http://www.jtimothycaldwell.net/resources/ pedagogy/makingsense.htm

Dalcroze Society of America. (2002, July). *A short biography of Emile Jaques-Dalcroze.* Retrieved April 4, 2004, from http://www.msu.edu/user/ thomasna/dalbiog1.html

Feierabend, J. M. (1996). Music and movement for infants and toddlers: Naturally wonder-full. *Early Childhood Connections: Journal of Music and Movement-Based Learning, 2*(4), 19–26.

Feierabend, J. M. (1997). Developing musical literacy: An aural approach for an aural art. *Early Childhood Connections: Journal of Music- and Movement-Based Learning,* Retrieved April 4, 2004, from http://www.giamusic.com/music_education/ feierabend/articles/aural.html

Greata, J. D. (1999). *Creating musically nurturing environments in infant and toddler childcare setting by providing training to caregivers.* Unpublished doctoral practicum report, Nova Southeastern University, Florida.

Kamien, R. (2003). *Music: An appreciation* (8th ed.). New York: McGraw-Hill.

Kendall, C. W. (1985). *More stories of composers for young musicians.* Edwardsville, IL: Toadwood.

Lexico Publishing Group. (2004). *Dictionary.com.* Retrieved August 19, 2004, from http:// dictionary.reference.com/

Mayesky, M. (1998). *Creative activities for young children.* Clifton Park, NY: Thomson Delmar Learning.

McDonald, D. T., & Simons, G. (1989). *Musical growth and development: Birth through six.* New York: Schirmer Books.

Music Educators National Conference (MENC). (2004). *The school music program: A new vision.* Retrieved September 3, 2004, from http:// www.menc.org/publication/books/prek12st.html

Pica, R. (2000). *Experiences in movement with music, activities, and theory.* Clifton Park, NY: Thomson Delmar Learning.

Sadie, S. (1986). *Music guide, an introduction.* Englewood Cliffs, NJ: Prentice-Hall.

Sony Music Entertainment. (2001). *Eras online: Baroque 1600–1750.* Retrieved September 2, 2004, from http://www.essentialsofmusic.com/ eras/baroque.html

Wicks, D. (2002, August). *What is Kodály teaching?* Retrieved April 4, 2004, from http://www. kodaly.org.au/Teaching/description.htm

# Who? and How?

Section 3 of this textbook examines the "Who" and "How" of early childhood music. The "How" will be addressed in each chapter of this section, as it relates to the age of the children being presented. Developmentally appropriate activities will be discussed to help teachers learn to musically nurture the children in their care. The developmental traits of various ages and stages of child development, including children with special needs, will be presented. This is not meant to substitute for an in-depth study of child development, but merely to give a perspective of the developing child in light of early music education.

Of course, "who" in an early childhood education book normally would include children from birth through the primary grades and, of course, they are included in this book. In general, early childhood educators do not encounter infants in child care centers until they are at least six weeks old. However, community-based home visitor programs work with pregnant and new mothers and, in 1995, Early Head Start was established to work with pregnant women and infants. In 2004, the federal Early Head Start Program provided services for pregnant women and 62,000 infants up to three years of age (Administration for Children and Families, 2005). As the number of pregnant mothers in these programs increases, the need for more early childhood educators to be knowledgeable in all areas of fetal development increases. To help more early childhood educators understand prenatal music nurturing, I chose to address prenatal music in this textbook as well as the normal early childhood age range.

Beyond the children, the adults who care for them, teachers and parents, will be considered. Chapter 8 looks at this important group. Partnerships between parents and teachers significantly improve children's chances for success. These partnerships are particularly important during the early childhood years, when children are building their sense of self and need to feel secure in the knowledge that all the adults in their lives care about them. For an early childhood music program to be successful, parents must be involved and educated as well as the teachers. This chapter will look at the roles of parents and teachers as facilitators, evaluators, and students of early childhood music.

The following six chapters examine the musical potentials of each group involved in early childhood music. Activities and resources that are specific to each group are discussed and explored. Music labs at the end of each chapter help the student continue to grow in his or her musical ability, so that musically nurturing young children will be an enjoyable and rewarding experience.

# 4 Musically Nurturing Infants (Birth–18 Months of Age)

## Key Terms

| | | |
|---|---|---|
| absorbent mind | nationalism | taikyo |
| études | pitch pipe | verismo |
| frequency | sound wave | vibration |

In the infant room, Luis is rocking three-month-old Angela while he feeds her. Luis sings a Spanish lullaby as he rocks and gently pats the baby. Angela stops sucking, stares at Luis, listening; she smiles and then continues her sleepy contented sucking. In the same room, Joan is standing at the changing table with Hassan (see Figure 4–1). Hassan is six months old. He is protesting against his wet diaper. Joan sings a simple tune to him— "Hassan, Hassan, Why are you fussing?" Hassan stops and looks at her. As she works, she imitates the sounds that Hassan makes and when she finishes changing his diaper, she washes his hands and then claps them together saying, "Shoe a little horse, shoe a little mare, but let a little colt go bare, bare, bare!" Hassan smiles at Joan.

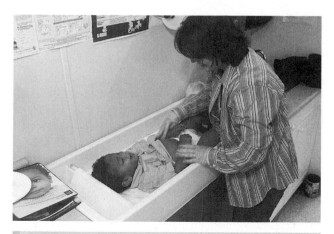

**Figure 4–1**   Infant teachers musically nurture children during normal routines.

Before the 1980s, most children remained at home with their mothers until they were at least two years old. Today, more than 6 million infants and toddlers, beginning as young as six weeks, are cared for by someone other than their parents for up to 40 hours a week or more (Children's Defense Fund, 2004). During the late 1980s and into the 1990s, more mothers with increasingly younger children entered the workforce. To answer the growing demand, more child care centers began offering infant care. Concurrently, new information on brain development was available to the public. Research projects revealed the first three years of life as a crucial period for establishing foundations in all domains of child development.

Additionally, technology made it possible to enter the world of the prenatal child. New information about this special time replaced some of the mystery concerning the prenatal period. For example, parents can obtain the first picture of their child and might know its gender before it is born. Developmental problems are detected and can be corrected with surgery performed in the uterus. This new information does not take away the wonder and awe of the prenatal period, but knowing the answers to certain questions can relieve the anxiety of expectant parents. As technological advances allow, more information is sought by researchers who study how the unborn child develops and how that development can be stimulated before birth. One field that has exhibited a great deal of interest in the unborn child is the field of music.

## Research and Prenatal Music

Reportedly, Kodály once said that music training for a young child should begin nine months before the birth of that young child's mother (Meier, 2003; Zemke, 2001). Whether this is a true story or not, Kodály believed that training in music should begin as early as possible (Choksy, 1981). In *Frames of Mind*, Gardner (1983) not only identified music as one of the original seven independent intelligences, but he also theorized that music was the first intelligence to develop. Could this development begin before birth? Some contemporary music educators point to the beliefs of Kodály and Gardner and believe that music nurturing should occur before birth (Meier, 2003). Although prenatal music nurturing may seem extreme or even ridiculous, recent research tends to support it.

The world of the prenatal infant is important to the medical and educational fields. Through research in the fields of music therapy, general music, and early childhood education, the medical and educational fields enjoy a clearer picture of fetal development in all domains. Researchers have studied the possibility of enhancing infants' cognitive development and emotional development before birth and the effects that music nurturing may have on that development (Sallenbach, 1998; Whitwell, 2003). For example, some studies indicate that language development begins before birth and that singing to the unborn child contributes to her future language ability (Whitwell, 2003).

Other researchers have investigated prenatal music nurturing as a means to facilitate bonding between the unborn child and her parents (Whitwell, 2003). Prenatal bonding between a mother and her unborn child is not a new idea. Many ancient cultures established traditions that incorporated music as a means for a mother to bond with her unborn child (Whitwell, 2003). The ability of a mother and her child to form a good attachment is important to the child's total development and many believe this

## Music of the World

### Ancient to Modern Prenatal Bonding Traditions

For thousands of years, Eastern cultures have recognized the effect of music on human beings. Additionally, they recognized the connection between the well-being of the expectant mother and the well-being of her unborn baby (Whitwell, 2001).

Confucius believed that the human character was shaped in the womb (Logan, 2003). Through Confucian influence, 2,000 years ago the Chinese established tranquility clinics for expectant mothers (Logan, 2003). Pregnant women were separated from their husbands and taken to rural centers where they were encouraged to seek peace and serenity (Whitwell, 2001). Expectant mothers received instructions regarding a healthy diet, cleanliness, and stress reduction (Logan, 2003). These sessions were accompanied by calming music played on stringed instruments and woodwinds (Logan, 2003). The women walked by the banks of rivers, meditated, and listened to poetry and songs (Whitwell, 2001).

Sometime around 1000 AD, the Chinese practice of tranquility clinics found its way to Japan (Logan, 2003). Expectant mothers were counseled to avoid disharmony. This ancient technique of prenatal stimulation called **taikyo** continues to be recognized and used in Japan (Logan, 1990). It is believed that the feelings and thoughts of the parents as well as other family members can influence the fetus (Whitwell, 2001).

In India, ancient Hindu scriptures refer to prenatal education (Indian Gyan.com, 2000). According to Hindu teaching, in the same manner that the expectant mother's food affects her unborn child, her thoughts affect his mental development (Indian Gyan.com, 2000). Expectant mothers are advised to refrain from anything that will affect the forming child negatively (Indian Gyan.com). In the past, Hindu mothers were trained by special teachers in this philosophy as well as how to transfer their positive thoughts to their fetuses (Whitwell, 2001). These techniques were taught in "Thought Rooms" (Whitwell, 2001).

Ancient traditions of nurturing the unborn child for months preceding birth continue to be used throughout New Guinea, Madagascar, Africa, Polynesia, and Asia (Logan, 2003). In recent decades, Western cultures have begun to adopt many of these techniques (Logan, 2003). Frederick Leboyer (2002), author of *Birth Without Violence*, encourages expectant mothers to transform pregnancy and childbirth into a spiritual experience through Indian chanting. Overtone singing, used for thousands of years by Tibetan monks and Mongolian shamans during their spiritual ceremonies, is also encouraged for its soothing ethereal sound (de Gast, 2004). Today, as in ancient times, expectant parents can find many prenatal music programs available across the United States to help them attain intrauterine stimulation of their infant.

---

bonding should begin as soon as the mother knows she is pregnant.

Of specific interest to the music educators, researchers have learned that hearing is the first sense to develop and that the fetus can hear by the fourth or fifth month of gestation (Tomatis, 1991). Additionally, fetuses as young as 16 weeks respond to music (Chamberlain, 1994; Hepper, 1991; Sallenbach, 1998; Shetler, 1989). Responses have been observed as changes in heart rates or changes of movement from, for example, tranquil to excited or vice versa (Verny & Kelly, 1981).

### Parents and Prenatal Music

Through periodicals and the Internet, prenatal research findings have reached the public. Parents are especially interested when they hear of studies that indicate ways in which to make their children smarter. For example, in one study, children who received prenatal music stimulation were followed through their fifth birthday. At five years of age, these children showed a significantly better vocabulary and higher-ranking IQ than the control group that did not receive the prenatal stimulation (Manrique, 1995). Parents want to do the best for their unborn children and the Internet brings an endless number of resources to expectant parents. Information concerning prenatal music, music-enhanced birth preparation, and prenatal music classes is available. Usually, there is a monetary charge for participation in these classes, but expectant parents do not have to join a prenatal music class or spend any money in order to musically stimulate their babies. More information on this subject can be found in Appendix B along with several Web sites to visit.

## Standards and Other Professional Guidance

### Pre-K Music Education Standards

The National Music Education Pre-K Standards are intended for age four. However, guidelines are given for infant and toddler music experiences. These guidelines include:

1. "Singing and chanting to them, using songs and rhymes representing a variety of meters and tonalities.
2. Imitating the sounds infants make.
3. Exposing them to a wide variety of vocal, body, instrumental, and environmental sounds.
4. Providing exposure to selected live and recorded music.
5. Rocking, patting, touching, and moving with the children to the beat, rhythm patterns, and melodic direction of the music they hear.
6. Providing safe toys that make musical sounds the children can control.
7. Talking about music and its relationship to expression and feeling."

From *National Standards for Arts Education.* Copyright © 1994 by Music Educators National Conference (MENC). Used by permission. The complete National Arts Standards and additional materials relating to the Standards are available from MENC—The National Association for Music Education, 1806 Robert Fulton Drive, Reston, VA 20191.

## Try This One!

Ask a pregnant mother who is at least six months along in her pregnancy if she would be willing to stand near a tape or CD player while you play some music. Tell her what you are going to play and that you want to know the reaction of her baby. Turn the volume loud enough to be clearly heard. First, play rousing rock music. Play the music for at least a couple of minutes to see if the baby reacts. Second, play a soothing song, such as a lullaby, for several minutes and see if the baby reacts to that.

## Exploring Sounds with Infants

When a child takes her first breath, she begins the most important period of her intellectual development in which she will build the foundation for all learning to follow. Piaget defined this period as the sensorimotor period. It ranges from approximately birth through two years of age. During this time, the child is trying to understand her world. She does this through her senses and physical manipulation of objects with which she comes into contact. She will taste, bang, smell, touch, and observe everything she contacts in her world. The more exposure a child has to stimulating experiences, the stronger the networks become in her brain and the more information she has to draw upon in the future.

From birth, the child is in a period of absorption (Gordon, 1990). Montessori called this characteristic of the young child an "**absorbent mind**" (Essa, 2003, p. 117). Commonly, we say that children's minds are like sponges. They soak up everything around them. This is how the young child learns. For example, a child learns to think in her native language through an informal process that begins at birth or possibly before. This informal process includes all of the speech that surrounds the child, as well as books, poetry, and nursery rhymes that are read or recited to her. The brain is stimulated in this rich environment and forms a network of neurological cells that allows the child to process language information. Language is only one type of the many sounds the child absorbs from her environment. When she absorbs musical sounds, her musical intelligence is engaged. In this way, her brain builds the neural network necessary for her to think musically (Feierabend, 1995).

## Snapshot of a Child

### Birth to 18 Months Old

*Birth Through Four Months Old*  The young infant comes into the world prepared to survive. Nature provides her with reflexive movements that protect her and help nurture her. These reflexes include, among many others, a sucking reflex that helps the young child eat and a blinking reflex that remains with the child the rest of her life. The infant responds to sound by becoming quiet or moving her entire body, kicking her legs, and moving her arms. She is interested in the human voice and can recognize her own mother's voice within the first month. During these first four months of her life, the infant will progress physically by first lifting her head, then rolling over from stomach to back and then back to stomach. Eventually, she is able to lift her head and shoulders while on her stomach. Most infants can hold their heads steady when held in a sitting position by the age of four months. The infant progresses from clenching her fists most of the time, to being able to hold and shake a rattle, to reaching out for objects she sees. This is a time of enormous change.

*Five Through Eight Months Old*  At this age, the infant is becoming more mobile. During these four months, the infant goes from sitting briefly while supported to being able to sit and pull herself up to a standing position. She delights in games such as peek-a-boo and is becoming a social being. She smiles at people and recognizes familiar people. During this time, the infant begins babbling to entertain herself and she imitates the sounds she hears, including other voices. By the end of this period of growth, the infant will combine syllables and consonants to make sounds such as bababa, mamama, and dadada. She also begins to explore the sounds she can make with objects in her environment. Intentionally, she will make sounds with objects such as pots and pans and their lids. At this time, the infant begins participating in her musical world.

*9 Through 12 Months Old*  Physically, within this time frame, most infants can sit alone, crawl, pull up on furniture, and cruise holding on to furniture. Some may walk holding onto an adult's hand and others may begin to take steps alone. Now, the infant will make motions with her arms and hands such as waving bye. Her babbling continues as she talks to herself and others. Words begin to emerge from her babble and she babbles as if she is speaking in sentences. The infant's babble sounds like singing. Now, she can make sounds that imitate animals and she enjoys reading books and singing songs that repeat this skill. The cruiser enjoys manipulating objects, including musical objects. At this age, the infant begins to demonstrate her musical self.

*13 Through 18 Months Old*  As the infant proceeds through these six months, she turns into a young toddler. Gradually, the infant gains her ability to walk steadily, walk up and down stairs, and walk backward. She is beginning to perform self-help chores such as trying to dress and feed herself. At this age, the infant is interested in her body and can point to parts of her body when asked. She can understand many words and enjoys pointing to familiar objects. The walker's vocabulary is growing and she babbles long sentences sprinkled with familiar words. The infant is still in the sensorimotor period and continues to absorb the information about her world through her senses and her movement about in her world. The material in this snapshot is from Berk, 2001.

---

Infants come into the world ready to learn about sound. According to Andress (1980),

Children learn about sound in four steps:

1. They become aware that sounds exist.

2. They learn that there are differences among sounds.

3. They discover that they can make sounds like those they hear.

4. They realize that sounds can be organized to communicate ideas and feelings. (p. 87)

Infants are aware of the sounds around them and if they are presented with the right opportunities, they will learn the differences among sounds. For example, a young infant is intrigued by the sound of a rattle.

What would happen if an infant were given rattles that had different sounds? Perhaps a better question would be: how often do teachers listen to the sounds of the rattles they give infants, notice whether one rattle is different from another rattle, and then purposely vary the rattles they give to infants? This is the sort of thinking that teachers must use if they want to facilitate infants' exploration of sound.

Young infants prefer soft sounds to raucous ones. Booties with bells attached, soft-sounding rattles with various sounds, music boxes, musical crib mobiles, and soft-textured balls with bells inside are just a few of the musical toys that appeal to young infants (see Figure 4–2). Placing a soft-sounding wind chime near the baby gives her another sound experience. As the infant matures, she can be held up to the chimes and allowed to touch them and make them chime.

## ▌Try This One!

### Sound Exploration Activities for Infants

*Birth to Four Months Old*    Shake a rattle in different directions about 6–12 inches from the baby's face. The baby will learn to follow the sound. Shake the rattle at different tempos (fast and slow) and different dynamics (loud and soft).

*Four to Eight Months Old*    Place an instrument such as two or three resonator bells or a tambourine on the floor. Play the instrument with a thick stick. Do not use a normal mallet, because it could be dangerous for a child this age. Offer the stick to the child and ask her to play. Assist her as she tries to make a sound by striking the instrument. You may have to demonstrate again. Then hand the stick back to the child and ask her to play.

*8 to 12 Months Old*    Select one of the following sets of two resonator bells; C and G, or F and C, or G and D. Sit on the floor with the bells in front of you. With a mallet, play the two bells, demonstrating the high and low sounds. Play the high bell twice and sing "high sound," then play the low sound twice and sing "low sound." Allow the child to try to play the bells. When the child makes a sound on the bells, label whether she is playing a high sound or a low sound.

*12 to 18 Months Old*    Place various rhythm instruments, such as a tambourine, jingle bells, hand bells, and triangles, on the floor for a small group of children to explore. Comment on the sounds that they are able to make.

## Including Children with Special Needs

### Children with Hearing Loss

Infants and toddlers with hearing loss benefit from the vibrations of instruments. Resonator bells are particularly good to use with these children. After striking the bell, hold it close to the child's ear so she can feel the vibrations.

Once the baby can sit by herself, she can be a more efficient sound-making participant. For generations, mothers have entertained their infants with materials from the kitchen, such as sets of measuring spoons on a ring, wooden spoons, pots and pans, and lids. At this stage, infants begin to play with musical toys and

**Figure 4–2**    Young infants should be given soft toys with bells and other sounds inside.

enjoy a jack-in-the-box played by an adult. Children are delighted by many musical toys and music boxes and want to hear them, repeatedly. This is such an important time for infant sound gathering that teachers must supply a variety of safe, appropriate, sound-making toys and materials for infants to experience (see Figure 4–3). Additionally, it is important to capitalize on the child's interest in music during the first year of life, because once the child is 18 months old, she is compelled by her new ability to verbalize her language and may begin to lose interest in music (Gordon, 1990).

## Singing with Infants

After birth, one of the first sounds a child hears is that of the human voice. During the first month of life, the infant distinguishes the human voice from other environmental sounds and orients toward the human voice. Infants can differentiate their mothers' voices from other voices within the first month of life (Scott-Kassner, 1993). In fact, in the video, *The First Years Last Forever*, Dr. T. Berry Braselton, a well-known pediatrician and author, demonstrated that immediately following birth an infant would turn her head

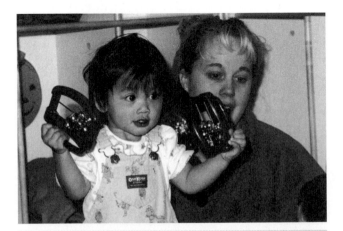

*Figure 4–3*  Teachers must supply a variety of safe, appropriatae, sound-making toys and materials for infants to experience.

toward the sound of her parents' voices (New Screen Concepts, 1997).

By the sixth month of life, the child's interest in the sounds around her is so intense that she wants to participate. Ostwald (1973) designated this time as a period of vocal contagion. During this time, the child also learns to listen while others talk. As she babbles, the child's voice converges with another person's voice and she stops her vocalization and listens (Ostwald, 1973). From this point on, the infant begins to engage in conversations with the adults in her life. These conversations are a give-and-take of cooing sounds by both participants (Zimmerman, 1984). Listen to adults as they coo and talk with an infant. Male or female, their voices take on a higher pitch and a melodic sound. Infants are attracted to this type of talk—motherese—and respond by cooing back. Motherese is similar to a song with its rising and falling pitches and rhythmic patterns. Some music educators believe that these cooing conversations are an infant's first music lessons (Zimmerman, 1984).

As the infant coos and makes sounds, she attracts the attention of family members and teachers. Her vocalizations not only stimulate her brain, but imitate sounds in her world. When people in her environment respond by imitating her sounds, they are validating the infant's importance, which in turn encourages her to continue her vocalizations and to listen and imitate the sounds made back to her. This is an important first step in the child's development of her singing voice.

During these early years, children begin to develop their singing ability. Somewhere between birth and six months of life, infants begin to imitate the sounds they hear (Fenson & Ramsay, 1981). As young as three months of age, infants can match tones sung or played for them (Scott-Kassner, 1993). In one study, after only three sessions of having a pitch sung to them or played on a **pitch pipe**, infants were able to imitate the pitch (Kessen, Levine, & Wendrich, 1979). Infants who are five months of age are capable of hearing and differentiating between simple melodic contours and rhythmic patterns (Chang & Trehub, 1977). During months 7 through 12, the infant's ability to repeat her own vocalizations and to mimic others increases (Ostwald, 1973). They not

## A Closer Look

A pitch pipe is a round disc, about 2¹/₂ inches in diameter and about ¹/₄ – ¹/₂ inch thick. Around the edge of the pipe, there are holes with letters written above them. The letters stand for notes. When you blow into a hole, the pipe plays that note.

only mimic pitch, but they also mimic rhythms and accents (Ostwald, 1973).

When the newborn enters the world, she may already recognize her mother's as well as her father's voice, if her father actively communicated with her before birth. The child has listened to the rhythm and melody of her parents' voices for at least six months. They have soothed her in the womb and now they welcome her into her new world. The bonding that began in the womb continues to develop into a trusting relationship, as mother and father care for their infant and meet her basic needs.

Studies have shown that when sung to, infants maintain a more intense level of interest than when they are spoken to (Trehub, 1999). Singing to infants helps build the necessary secure and trusting relationships between infants and their caregivers, whether the caregivers are parents, grandparents, or teachers. The power of singing probably comes from its relationship with motherese. Upset infants are soothed with singing. In fact, very young infants are comforted by simply crooning two notes (see Figure 4–4) (Honig, 2001).

When an infant enters a child care situation, the teacher can help the child feel more secure and comfortable by asking her parents if they sing or play a particular song to her. By learning and singing the same song, teachers can make the day more pleasant for the

**Figure 4–5**  Teachers can use familiar songs to comfort distressed infants.

infant and may help reduce separation anxiety in older infants (over six months of age) (see Figure 4–5).

Hush          now,          Ba  –   –   – by. –   –   –

**Figure 4–4**  Very young infants are comforted by simply crooning two notes.

## A Closer Look

### Lullabies

Lullabies are recognizable around the world, because their qualities are universal (Glausiusz, 2001). They help relax and soothe babies and facilitate getting them to go to sleep more easily. Any gentle song or piece of music, whether it is called a lullaby or not, can calm a child and encourage her to sleep (Honig, 2001). A mother's lullaby lowers the stress hormones in her infant (Glausiusz, 2001). They also soothe the singer, after a long day of work. Lullabies are simple, repetitive, slow, and have a steady beat.

Lullabies often sound melancholy. These lullabies are written in a minor key and this makes them sound melancholy. Most children's songs are written in a major key and that makes them sound happy. However, the quality of lullabies seems to bond the listener with the singer. In addition to the sad quality of sound, the words of some lullabies sound violent. For example, reflect upon the final line of *Rock-a-Bye Baby*, "Down will come baby, cradle and all" or the final line of the Mexican lullaby, "Senora Santa Ana," "Here comes an old man to take you away." The foreboding words are possibly a "blessing in the form of a curse" that are meant to keep the unthinkable from happening (Warner, 1998, p. 94).

Interestingly, recent research indicated that few mothers and fathers in the United States sang lullabies to their infants (Trehub, Unyk, Kamenetsky, Hill, Trainor, Henderson, & Saraza, 1997). Many parents never even sang the traditional lullabies to their infants, such as "Rock-a-Bye Baby." On the other hand, cultures in other countries chose lullabies as the foremost song to sing to infants, even when they were not trying to put the infants to sleep (Trehub & Trainor, 1998; Trehub, Unyk, & Trainor, 1993).

Regardless of their melancholy sound, or perhaps because of it, lullabies soothe children, and help them go to sleep, even those who fight against sleep. On a historical note, a child who did not respond to a lullaby by cuddling was called "a lullaby cheat," in the seventeenth century (Warner, 1998).

---

If the song is not familiar to the teacher, she can ask the mother to record her favorite song. This situation may occur if the song is from a culture that is different from the teacher's. Not only can the teacher learn a new song, but also she can play the recording for the mother's infant to soothe her. The other children will also benefit from this recording. If the infant's parents do not sing to her, the teacher can educate the parents about the importance of this activity and teach them songs that they can sing to their children. This can also be done with recordings. A lullaby is a form of song often linked with infants. Lullabies are gentle songs that are sung to encourage a child to sleep. Many lullabies are folk songs that have emerged in their present form after being passed down over many years from generation to generation.

In addition to using songs to calm an upset infant, teachers should sing or chant during routine

---

## Music of the World

Every culture has a way to quiet a baby. Here are some interesting books that feature lullabies of various cultures.

- Delacre, L. (2004). *Arrorro Mi Nino: Latino lullabies and gentle games.* New York: Lee & Low
- Feierabend, J. M. (2000). *The book of lullabies.* Chicago, IL: Independent Publishers Group
- Ho, M., & Meade, H. (2000). *Hush!: A Thai lullaby.* New York: Orchard Books
- Jaramillo, N. P. (1994). *Grandmother's nursery rhymes/Las nanas de abuelita: Lullabies, tongue twisters, and riddles from South America/Canciones de cuna, trabalenguas y adivinanzas de Suramerica.* New York: Henry Holt and Company.
- Jordon, S. (2001). *Lullabies around the world: Multicultural songs and activities.* Niagara Falls, New York: Sara Jordan Publishing
- McGill, A. (2000). *In the hollow of your hand: Slave lullabies.* Boston: Houghton Mifflin

activities such as diapering, feeding, or when transitioning from one activity to another (Honig, 2001). Between 20 and 35 percent of a child's day can be spent transitioning from one activity or routine to another. Due to the custodial nature of their care, infants are usually on the higher end of that range. Transitions consume a lot of time that could be used to musically nurture young children. Songs can be made up that match the activity (Honig, 2001). This takes a little practice, but infants are a forgiving audience. If teachers are not sure how to make up songs, they can start by using the tones of what has been called the 'universal child's song.' This melody is frequently heard as a taunt on playgrounds and is usually sung to words such as "nanny, boo-boo" or "see if you can catch me."

## Try This One!

### Improvising with Familiar Tunes

Using the tune to a familiar song such as "Here We Go 'Round the Mulberry Bush" or "Mary Had a Little Lamb," add words to sing about what you are doing with the child. Figures 4–6 and 4–7 are two examples.

Although recorded songs can be used in the infant room, an infant tends to be more involved in the music if the teacher holds her while singing (Boyd, 1989). For infants, music nurturing needs to be delivered in an interactive rather than passive form. Teachers should sing as much as possible to infants. However, if the teacher wants an infant to concentrate on the melody and rhythm of the song, it is best to use nonsense syllables such as "loo" or "la, la." This practice is recommended by both early childhood and early childhood music education experts, because infants can concentrate on only one attribute at a time and the words get in the way of the music (Ball, 1995; Honig, 2001).

## Listening and Moving to Music with Infants

For young children, listening and moving to music often go hand in hand. Due to the overlap between these two types of activities, they will be discussed together in regard to infants. Infants respond to music with movement at a very young age with their whole bodies (Pica, 2000). As we learned earlier, this is the sensorimotor period of cognitive development. Children in this period learn through their senses and through movement.

During the infant and toddler years, a child develops her listening vocabulary (Gordon, 1999). What is a listening vocabulary? It is all of the music she can absorb before she begins to participate in music. The most important time for the music-listening vocabulary to develop is before the age of 18 months (Gordon, 1999). However, many children enter school

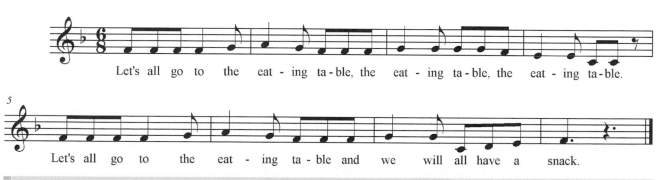

*Figure* 4–6    Song sung to the tune of "Here We Go 'Round the Mulberry Bush."

**Figure 4–7** Song sung to the tune of "Mary Had a Little Lamb."

without a music-listening vocabulary. As a result, there has been a decline over the past two decades of kindergarten children who are able to sing (Levinowitz, 1998). To build listening vocabularies, teachers must expose children to a rich variety of music. Often children will arrive in the child care center without a listening vocabulary. By the time a child is three, it is almost too late for some children to acquire a music-listening vocabulary (Gordon, 1990). Therefore, engaging infants in listening to music is very important.

## Try This One!

### Moving and Listening Activities for Infants

***Birth to Four Months Old***    When you place the infant on the floor to play or in the crib to sleep, place a tape or CD player nearby to play soothing music for the infant. Try "Sea Gulls" and "Tickly Toddle" by Hap Palmer, or "Brahms' Lullaby," or Mendelssohn's "Nocturne" from *A Midsummer Night's Dream.*

***Four to Eight Months Old***    Bounce the infant on your knee as you say the following:

> Ride a cock horse to Banbury Cross,
> To see a fine lady upon a white horse;
> Rings on her fingers and bells on her toes,
> She shall have music wherever she goes.

***8 to 12 Months Old***    Play "Papageno's Song" from Mozart's opera *The Magic Flute* for the children. Hold younger infants' arms and flap them to the music. Older infants will imitate your movement of flapping your arms. Others may want to dance to the music.

***12 to 18 Months Old***    As the infant is able to move about by herself, you can play singing games with her such as "Ring Around the Rosies" or "I Wiggle My Fingers." You can find the song "I Wiggle My Fingers" in the Resource Guide in Appendix D.

Moving to recorded music is an important way to learn to listen to music. However, music for listening and moving should be selected very carefully. Teachers are responsible for stimulating infants with music and must ensure that the sounds and music presented are of the highest quality. When selecting music for the listening and moving experiences of young children keep these things in mind.

- Typical recordings of children's songs are not appropriate for facilitating the development of listening vocabularies (Gordon, 1999). Instrumental music is the best for developing listening vocabularies.
- Musical excerpts should be very short in length for listening and movement activities (Cave, 1998). The attention span of young children is limited and they enjoy repetition. Therefore, teachers should select musical pieces that can be played or sung repeatedly in a short amount of time. It is better to repeat a short listening activity many times

than to lose the children's interest in the middle of a long excerpt. A good rule of thumb is to play musical pieces that are no longer than three minutes.

- Children should experience a wide variety of excellent recorded music. The music should not only vary by style (baroque, classical, country and western, rock, etc.), but also by dynamics (loud or soft), tempo (fast or slow), tonality (major—happy sounding, or minor—sad or lonely sounding), harmonies (the tones of the music fit comfortably together or they are dissonant), and meters (e.g., waltz, march, or swing).

Dalcroze believed that children developed their love and appreciation of music through rhythmic movement (Caldwell, 2002). He felt that the experience of movement to music should begin in the first year. Except for moving their arms and legs, young infants cannot move themselves. Therefore, teachers must facilitate the movement of young infants to songs, rhythmic chants, and recorded music. Teachers should gently move the infants' arms and legs to music. Rocking, bouncing, swaying, and dancing to music with infants are all appropriate activities. These activities create a "hearing-feeling connection" (Weikart, 1995, p. 7). This connection helps the child develop a steady beat later in her music education (Weikart, 1995).

Newborns require more support of their heads than older infants require. While sitting on the floor, the adult can place the newborn on her outstretched legs. The adult's knees can be gently lifted on the beat while she recites a rhyme or sings a song. Eye contact is maintained by having the infant face the adult. Move the baby's arms and legs up and down, gently, or wiggle her toes or fingers to the music of a song or recording (Honig, 2001).

Older infants who can hold their heads up should be placed on the adult's knee and gently bounced to the beat of a rhyme or song (Feierabend, 1996; Fox, 1989). As they grow and gain more control of their arms, legs, and heads, their responses to music become more purposeful.

When clapping songs or rhymes such as "Pat-a-Cake" with infants younger than six months, it makes no difference whether you hold their hands or not (Feierabend, 1996). After six months of age, rather than holding their hands and clapping for them, it is better to begin eliciting movement from the child (Feierabend, 1996). The teacher should place the child's hands in front, palms down, and clap up onto the child's palms (Feierabend, 1996). The child will soon engage in the movement by clapping down onto the adult's palm. Once the child is engaged in movement, the adult should set the tempo of the rhyme or song to match the movement of the child (Feierabend, 1996).

Whenever possible, songs and rhythmic patterns should be vocally performed by the teacher (Bolton, 1996). Infants attend to music better when there is interaction with the teacher, while they sing, chant, or move to music. Remember, infants cannot attend to or focus on more than one attribute at a time. Therefore, when focused listening is desired, the teacher must facilitate the infant's success at focusing. To do this, the teacher should sing songs and chants without words by using a neutral syllable such as "la" to sing the song or by humming the song. Of course, infants listen when songs are sung and music is played that contain words, but focused listening is facilitated when the words are not there. When music with words is played for infants, "the child cannot directly focus on either the music or the words" (Gordon, 1990, p. 41).

Dancing with an infant not only creates a wonderful bonding experience, but also is an appropriate musical activity. Hold the infant on your shoulder and gently tap the beat on her back as you move or dance about the room (Feierabend, 1996). A similar activity requires the adult to draw circles on the infant's tummy (Honig, 2001). Gently sway or rock infants while cuddling and singing a lullaby. Listening and moving to music with infants is an important part of the infant music-nurturing program.

## Summary

As early as four months after gestation, the prenatal infant can hear and respond to sounds. Parents, both mothers and fathers, can begin bonding with their infant before birth through songs and chants. When infants are musically stimulated during their prenatal

Dancing or rocking an infant creates a wonderful bonding experience.

period, they continue the process of bonding with their parents after birth by recognizing the songs and chants they heard before birth.

As with other domains of development, these first months of life are important to building the foundation of the child's musical development. During this time, she becomes aware of the sounds in her environment, begins to imitate those sounds, begins to develop her singing voice, starts to respond to music with movement, and begins to develop her listening vocabulary. With the help of the adults in her life, the infant moves from an absorber of music to a participant in the music of her environment.

## Key Concepts

- Research has shown that the fetus can hear by the fourth or fifth month of gestation.
- Expectant parents should sing, move, and listen to music with their unborn baby.

- Mothers and fathers should dance with their unborn baby.
- Babies show a preference for music they heard in the womb, so choose the music carefully.
- Fathers as well as mothers should sing to their unborn babies.
- Infants should be stimulated with a variety of good music.
- Music can be a natural part of the daily routine.
- Music helps transition children from one routine to another.
- Infants need the time and materials to explore sounds.
- Singing, chanting, moving, and listening to music are all important activities in the infant room.

## Suggested Activities

1. Review some of the materials that are available for prenatal music nurturing. If possible, visit a prenatal music class. Interview the expectant parents about whether they use music to stimulate their unborn baby. Report your experiences to the class.
2. Read about various prenatal music programs and write a report about them.
3. Observe an infant child care room. Note the various ways in which music is used in the room.
4. Visit an infant store to observe what sound toys are available for infants.
5. Research some of the books listed in the Resource Guide in Appendix D. Find a suitable book to share with infants and prepare an activity that incorporates the book.
6. Journal reflective question 4: If prenatal music stimulation does enhance a child's cognitive development, should this type of program be made available to all pregnant women?

## Music Lab #4

Welcome to Music Lab #4! This lab discusses the musical elements melody and pitch. The lab activities will incorporate these elements, as well as rhythm,

beat, and tempo. You will explore pitched rhythm instruments, make your own instrument, and continue to explore musical history as you enter the Western European Romantic Era.

## Musical Elements: Melody and Pitch

In Lab #3, you discovered that rhythm and melody contribute to a song's uniqueness. You explored rhythm and beat in the lab's activities. In this lab, you will explore melody and pitch, which are closely related.

## Musical Elements

Pitch refers to the relationship between sounds in regard to their highness or lowness of sound. Now we have to get a little scientific. We are surrounded by air. When an object is moved back and forth, this is called **vibration**. The vibration of the object causes the air around it to move and this starts a wave, which we call a **sound wave**. A sound wave is the wave of movement that is caused by a vibrating object. Sound waves can occur in other mediums, such as water, but for our purposes, we will only consider sound waves as they pass through air. The object that causes this disturbance in the air could be the movement of our vocal chords as we speak or sing. We exhale as we speak or sing; the air rushes over our vocal chords, which are vibrating, and they begin a sound wave. A vibrating string and sound board, such as on a guitar or violin, can cause the air around it to vibrate, causing a sound wave. The pitch of the resulting sound is dependent on how fast the object (in this case, a string) is vibrating and on the size of the object that is vibrating. On a stringed instrument, such as a guitar or violin, the thinnest string will vibrate faster than the thicker strings. Therefore, the thinner the string is, the higher the pitch its sound will be. If you look inside a piano, you will find that the strings for the higher sounds are not only thinner, but they are shorter. By shortening the thinner strings, the pitch becomes even higher.

Melody refers to what we normally call the tune of a song. Melody consists of pitches that follow one

## A Closer Look

### Understanding Frequency and Sound Waves

Our ears are designed to be detectors of sound. There are also man-made detectors that can measure the pressure produced by sound waves, so we can actually see what the sound looks like. Figures 4–8 and 4–9 are examples of a pressure–time plot that a monitoring detector might show. Notice that on Figure 4–8 the monitor has measured more waves than Figure 4–9, in the same amount of time. The sound measured by Figure 4–8 has a higher **frequency** than the sound measured by Figure 4–9. Each wave is a vibration; the

object that causes the sound in Figure 4–8 is vibrating faster than the object was vibrating when it made the sound in Figure 4–9. This causes a higher frequency of sound waves. Frequency is measured in units called Hertz and 1 Hertz equals one vibration per second. Therefore, if a sound is measured at 50 Hertz, the object that caused the sound is vibrating 50 times per second. Pitch is the relationship between sounds—the higher the pitch, the more vibrations or the higher the Hertz, and the lower the pitch, the lower the vibrations or the lower the Hertz. (Henderson, 2004; Kurtus, 2002).

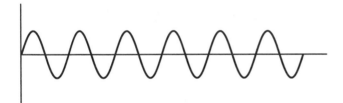

*Figure* 4–8    High-Frequency Sound Wave

after the other. Sometimes a pitch is higher than the one before it and sometimes it is lower. This movement of pitches up and down gives a shape to the melody. When we combine the pitches of the melody with a rhythmic pattern, it becomes a unique tune.

## Activity #1: Exploring Pitched Rhythm Instruments

In the previous labs, we have explored nonpitched rhythm instruments. The description, "nonpitched," does not mean that the instrument has no pitch, but instead that the instrument's pitch cannot be changed or tuned to match other instruments. Sometimes these instruments are referred to as untuned instruments and pitched rhythm instruments are referred to as tuned instruments. For example, one triangle will always have the same pitch. However, two triangles may have different pitches from each other. The pitch of the two triangles cannot be controlled. You can control the pitch of the sounds you make on pitched rhythm instruments.

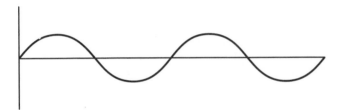

*Figure* 4–9    Low-Frequency Sound Wave

## Discovering Instruments

### Pitched Rhythm Instruments

- Xylophones (see Figure 4–10): Historically, this instrument was first used in southeast Africa in the fourteenth century and was first seen in Europe about 1500. Performers used the instrument in various forms throughout Europe and it was first used in an orchestra in 1874. The name comes from the Greek words *xylon*, which means wood, and *phone*, which means sound. All xylophones are constructed in the same basic manner. Wooden or metal bars of varying lengths are mounted on a platform usually made of wood. They are played by striking with a mallet. Xylophones can be found in varying sizes from an 8-bar child's xylophone to an orchestral xylophone with 49 bars that begin with the pitch middle C.
- Metallophones: A metallophone consists of metal bars that have been tuned and placed over a resonator box. The metallophone has been used for hundreds of years to make music. Balinese and Javanese musicians use several different types of metallophones in their ensembles. The glockenspiel is a type of metallophone,

*Figure* 4–10    Xylophone

although usually the word *metallophone* refers to an instrument that has a single row of tuned metal bars.

- Glockenspiels: The name of this instrument is German and literally means "play of bells." However, in Germany the word *glockenspiel* refers to a Carillon. The Carillon is a musical instrument made up of 23 bells. This instrument has a keyboard to play the bells. For the purpose of this textbook, glockenspiel refers to an instrument that is also called the orchestra bells, or a lyra when played in a marching band. The glockenspiel is similar in looks to the xylophone, yet it is smaller. The pitches of the glockenspiel are also higher than that of a xylophone. The glockenspiel is played by striking it with mallets. It makes a pure, bell-like sound.
- Resonator bells or tone bars: These are bars of varying lengths made from bell steel or aluminum alloy. The length of the bar affects the pitch of the tone. Each bar is accurately pitched. The bar is fastened to a box chamber, usually made of high-impact plastic. This box chamber is the resonator that enhances the sound of the bell when it is struck. Normally, the bells are sold in sets of 20 to 30 bells. Each bell is a different pitch. The set includes notes found just below the center of the piano keyboard (G below middle C) or from middle C on the piano keyboard and up 20 or 25 keys (both black and white keys). The bell set can be played by one person, or several children can each play a single bell. The bells are played by striking with a mallet.
- Hand Bells (see Figure 4–11): These bells come in a variety of sizes and have a handle attached for holding them. Each bell has a different pitch. The larger the bell, the lower its pitch is. Hand bells are usually played by a group of musicians who hold a bell in each hand or set the bells on a table in front of them and pick up different bells to play them. Hand bells come in sets of 6 to 60 bells. These bells are often used in church services. However, hand bells are available for use by young children and are usually made of plastic.

**Figure 4–11**   Hand Bell

### For You

1. Experiment with the various pitched instruments.
2. Ask yourself questions about your experience:
   a. What sounds can you make with them?
   b. How would you describe the sounds to children?
   c. How many different ways can you play the instrument?
3. Examine the instruments. For example, what makes the pitch on one bell higher than the pitch on another bell?
4. Strike a resonator bell and then a triangle or hand bell at the same time. Which sound lasts longer? How would you describe the bell's sound as it continues? Does it get louder, softer, stay the same?

### In the Preschool and in Out-of-School Programs

1. Allow the children to freely explore and experiment with the instruments by locating them in an accessible place.
2. Ask questions as they become involved in exploration. Which makes the highest sound, lowest sound, softest sound, loudest sound?
3. Encourage the children to improvise on the instruments.

## Activity #2: Experiencing Vibration: Connecting Music with Science

This activity helps you connect music with science as you explore the vibration of various instruments.

**For You**

1. Strike a bell and then gently touch it. Can you feel the vibration?
2. When the vibration stops, such as when you touch the bell and press on it, the sound stops. The vibration of the instrument creates a sound wave. When the instrument no longer vibrates, there is no sound.
3. Try this experiment with a variety of instruments such as triangles, cymbals, or xylophones.

**In the Preschool and in Out-of-School Programs**

Go through the same activity with the children. There are other connections between music and science, but this one is easily understood by young children and is a good way to introduce children to the concept of vibration.

## Try This One!

## Milk Carton Guitars

Collect the following:

- Half-gallon cardboard milk carton
- Two $\frac{1}{4}$-inch pieces of dowel that are 6 inches long (two pencils also work). They have to be able to lie across the width of the carton.
- Two or more rubber bands of different thicknesses.

1. Begin with two rubber bands, one thick and one thin.
2. Place them around the length of the milk carton. Separate them from each other by a couple of inches.
3. Lay the carton on its back.
4. Slip a wooden dowel under the rubber bands. Place one dowel at the top of the carton and one dowel at the bottom of the carton. You do this so the rubber bands are lifted off the carton and they can vibrate freely.

5. The dowels should be straight so that the space between the dowels is the same for both rubber bands.
6. Pluck the rubber bands in the middle, one at a time. Can you see the rubber bands vibrate? What do you hear? Is there a difference in the sound between the rubber bands? What is it?
7. Notice that the rubber bands only vibrate between the two dowels.
8. Move the dowels closer together so the vibrating portion of the rubber bands is shorter. What do you hear now? Why do you think that is?
9. Add more rubber bands of various thicknesses and listen to the differences of the sounds.

You have demonstrated two things with this exercise.

1. The thicker rubber band sounds lower than the thin rubber band.
2. When the vibrating rubber band is shorter, it sounds higher than when the same rubber band is longer.

## Activity #3: Using Instruments Throughout the Day

You can use instruments as tools in your classroom throughout the day. For example: Use a signal of three notes on the tone bars near the end of free-play time to signal the children that they will need to clean up their materials and toys in a short time. This is more pleasant than yelling, "Five more minutes." A different signal using bells, rhythm sticks, or triangle might alert the children to clean up for lunch. By using two distinct signals, the children learn to listen for different sounds. In addition to using sound signals throughout the day, instruments can be used to enhance stories or rhymes.

**For You**

1. Brainstorm alone or with your classmates to select books or nursery rhymes that might lend themselves to the use of instruments for enhancement.
2. Examine the various books and nursery rhymes you thought of in your brainstorming session and discover how you can use any rhythm instruments to enhance the story or rhyme.

**In the Preschool and in Out-of-School Programs**

1. Read the book or rhyme you chose to the children and use instruments to enhance the story.
2. Leave the book with the instruments in the music center for the children to read and use the instruments themselves.
3. A recording of the story helps younger children with this exercise.

## Try This One!

### Tick, Tock, Tick, Tock!

Read *The Completed Hickory Dickory Dock* by Jim Aylesworth to the children in your class. Use a resonator bell to chime the hour as the story goes around the clock. Older children can play rhythm sticks, tone blocks, or wood blocks to represent a ticking clock when the rhyme is read. Children in the out-of-school program who enjoy performing can develop this book into a performance for the younger children.

See the Resource Guide in Appendix D for other books to use with instrument enhancement.

## Try This One!

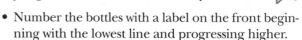

### Playing the Bottle Glockenspiel

- Number the bottles with a label on the front beginning with the lowest line and progressing higher.
- Play the bottles with a mallet to make sure they are "tuned."

---

## Making Musical Instruments

### Bottle Glockenspiels

Collect the following materials:

- Eight identical glass bottles at least 8 inches tall (e.g., glass soda bottles)
- A funnel
- Water
- A small wooden mallet
- Ruler
- Permanent-ink marker

1. Measure from the bottom on each bottle and mark with a line.
   a. Bottle 1: $\frac{3}{4}$ inch
   b. Bottle 2: $1\frac{1}{2}$ inches
   c. Bottle 3: $2\frac{1}{4}$ inches
   d. Bottle 4: 3 inches
   e. Bottle 5: $3\frac{3}{4}$ inches
   f. Bottle 6: $4\frac{1}{2}$ inches
   g. Bottle 7: $5\frac{1}{4}$ inches
   h. Bottle 8: 6 inches
2. Using the funnel, fill each bottle to the line you have drawn. When the bottles are placed in a row with the lines on the bottles sequentially going up, they will form a musical scale.

3. Now you are ready to play your bottle glockenspiel.
   a. Use the wooden mallet first to gently strike each bottle.
   b. Try blowing across the lip of each bottle. This is how sounds are made with jugs.

#### For the Preschool Program

1. Have the children help you make a bottle glockenspiel.
2. Mark the glass bottles ahead of time with the permanent-ink marker.
3. Have the children pour the water.
4. If they pour past the line, let them hear what sound the bottle makes before pouring out the extra water.
5. Since the bottles are made of glass, a teacher should always supervise this activity with young children.

#### For the Out-of-School Program

1. This is a good activity for older children and can be tied into a science project.
2. As a listening exercise, place the bottles out of order and have children place them in order according to sound. You will have to cover the lines, but you can place a circular label with a number on the bottom of the bottle for a self-correcting exercise.

- You should be able to sing a scale, as in the song "Do, Re, Mi" (Do, a deer, a female deer. Re (ray), a drop of golden sun.)
- To tune the bottles just add or remove a little water. Sometimes the water is a little over or under the lines that you drew.
- Using the numbers in Table 4.1, play the tune on your glockenspiel.
- Write the numbers on a large chart for the children to play the song.
- Use the same chart for children to play the songs on the xylophone, the resonator bells, or the hand bells.

## Activity #4: Music Appreciation

With this lab, we leave behind the Classical Era and move into the Romantic Era of Western European music history. The sources for the history presented in this activity are Kamien (2003), Sadie (1986), and Sherrane (2004).

## Musical History

### Romantic Era (1820–1900)

The early 1820s brought about the cultural movement of romanticism. This movement stressed emotion, imagination, and individualism. The Western world had undergone social changes, due to the American and French revolutions. The middle class was growing and monarchs were afraid of losing their kingdoms. The Romantic Movement occurred at the same time as the Industrial Revolution, which brought about an interest in the plight of the working class and the poor. Artists of all venues reflected the reality of life in their works. Additionally, nature

became an important subject in art as an escape from reality. Poetry, painting, and music all reflected nature. Most artists, including musicians, viewed themselves as being romantic and strove to express their personal feelings in their works.

Additionally, Napoleon's invasion of Europe inspired patriotism, which brought about a nationalism movement. This movement revived national languages, cultures, and histories. Interest in the arts of peasants became widespread. Composers found inspiration in folk tales and wove folk songs into their compositions. Compositions were no longer merely named by number, such as Symphony No. 1. Instead, names such as *Finlandia* and *The Moldau* appeared as compositional titles. Countries where the music of France, Germany, and Italy had been dominant experienced the greatest transformation as their composers began to explore the cultural heritage of their own countries.

With Beethoven as their inspiration, composers of the Romantic Era proclaimed to be free artists and they strove to compose music for posterity, unlike those before them who composed for specific functions. In actuality, they were free artists, because the aristocracy could no longer afford to maintain their private opera houses, orchestras, and composers. Most of the composers of the Romantic Era came from the rising middle class, for whom they wrote, and had to earn a living by selling their compositions, performing, teaching, conducting, and writing critiques of musical performances for publications.

The growth of the middle class saw, among other things, the development of subscription concerts and a piano in nearly every middle-class home. This growing interest in music brought about the development of music conservatories in the United States and Europe. During the Romantic Era, more instruments were added to the orchestra and there was a growth

| Table 4–1    "Mary Had a Little Lamb" by Numbers | | | | | | | |
|---|---|---|---|---|---|---|---|
| **Mary Had a Little Lamb** | | | | | | | |
| 3, 2, 1, 2 | 3, 3, 3 | 2, 2, 2 | 3, 5, 5 | 3, 2, 1, 2 | 3, 3, 3, 3 | 2, 2, 3, 2 | 1 |

in orchestral works, which included symphonies, ballets, and concertos.

The many composers from this era make it impossible in this limited space either to introduce all of them or to do justice to the ones that are introduced. My purpose is to give you a humanistic view of some of the better-known composers of the era in the hope that you will be inspired to seek out more information on your own. You will find a list of suggested books in the Resource Guide in Appendix D for that purpose.

Franz Schubert (1797–1828) was born in Vienna, where he taught at his father's school to earn a living until age 21, at which time he immersed himself in his music. Schubert was a composer and not a conductor or a virtuoso. His musical income came from the sale of his compositions. His love of poetry led him to compose songs. In fact, he is the first master of the art song. At the age of 19, while still teaching school, his musical productivity peaked and he composed 179 works. These works included two symphonies, an opera, and a mass. Some of his songs brought him recognition during his lifetime, but his true genius was not recognized until after his early death at age 31.

Robert Schumann (1810–1856) was born in Zwickau, Germany. He gave up the study of law to become a piano virtuoso. As we read in Chapter 2, his dream of becoming a concert pianist did not materialize due to an injury to the fourth finger of his right hand. He fell in love with Clara Wieck, the 17-year-old daughter of his piano teacher. She was a talented pianist in her own right. Her father was against their marriage and they had to go to court to get permission to marry. Schumann's early works were only works for the piano, but in 1840, during his first year of marriage, he was inspired to write 150 songs. Clara introduced Robert's works to the public in her solo concerts. Robert's mental and physical health was not good. After trying to drown himself, he was committed to an asylum in 1854 and died two years later at the age of 46.

Frédéric Chopin (1810–1849) was born in Warsaw, Poland, to a Polish mother and a French father. He attended the Warsaw Conservatory and moved to Paris at 21 years of age. Here he became friends with many of the leading French writers and painters of the time. He taught piano to the children of aristocrats and performed at intimate gatherings in their salons. Chopin was the only great composer to compose exclusively for the piano. Chopin had poor health and died of tuberculosis at the age of 39.

Born in Hungary, Franz Liszt (1811–1886) was a piano virtuoso of outstanding ability and considered the greatest pianist of his time. Chopin is said to have wished he could play his own piano **études** the way Liszt could play them. Much of the music Liszt wrote during his early years was to show off his virtuosic abilities. At age 36, he left the concert stage behind to become the court conductor at Weimar. It was his intention to compose and to be recognized as a serious composer. Liszt gave free lessons to talented youth, wrote books on the music of Chopin, and critiqued music for publications.

Felix Mendelssohn (1809–1847) was born in Hamburg, Germany, into a wealthy Jewish family, where he and his sister Fanny were raised Protestant in an effort to avoid persecution. His musical talents were recognized early, since he was a gifted pianist by age 9 and by 13 had written incredibly fine symphonies, concertos, sonatas, and vocal pieces. At age 20, he conducted Bach's *St. Mathew's Passion*. This was the first time the work had been performed since Bach's death; it was not only an historical event, but also rekindled an interest in Bach's compositions and earned Felix international acclaim. He was 26 when he became conductor of the Leipzig Gewandhaus Orchestra and 33 when he founded the Leipzig conservatory. Hard work and travel brought on a stroke and he died at age 38.

Peter Ilyich Tchaikovsky (1840–1890) is the most famous Russian composer. At age 30, he composed *Romeo and Juliet*, his first great piece for the orchestra. Beginning in 1877 and for 14 years afterward, he received an annual annuity from a wealthy benefactor whom he never met. This annuity allowed him to leave his teaching position at the Moscow conservatory, devote himself to composition, and travel through Europe, conducting his own works.

Johannes Brahms's (1833–1897) father was a struggling musician and the family lived in the slums of Hamburg, Germany. By age 13, Brahms was studying music and composition by day and earning money for those studies at night by playing in the bars and brothels. During his first concert tour at age 20, he met Robert and Clara Schumann and began a lifelong friendship. When Robert Schumann was committed to an asylum, Johannes moved into the Schumann home to help care for their seven children when Clara was on tour. Not only was he famous for his own compositions, such as "Brahms' Lullaby," but he also conducted a Viennese music society where he reintroduced the works of Bach, Handel, and Mozart to the public.

Born in Paris, Camille Saint-Saens (1835–1921) was not one of the greatest composers of the Romantic Era, but one conductor called him the best second-rate conductor in history. During his lifetime, Saint-Saens was a respected and influential musician of France. He spent his life teaching, performing, and writing. Ironically, one of his most popular pieces, *The Carnival of Animals*, was written for a group of friends and was never intended for publishing. This piece is often played for young children.

Giuseppe Verdi (1813–1901) and Giacomo Puccini (1858–1924) were two leading opera composers of the Romantic Era. Both came from poor families. A wealthy patron took Verdi in and supported him while he studied and paid for his studies in Milan. Verdi later married the patron's daughter. Puccini was born into a long line of composers and church organists. He struggled with poverty while studying in Milan, but his first successful opera, which appeared shortly after his graduation, brought him commissions and an annual salary from Italy's leading music publisher. Both composers wrote popular Italian operas, but Verdi is considered the most popular of all Italian opera composers. His works, such as *Aida, Il trovatore, La traviata*, and *Un ballo in maschera*, dominated the Italian opera scene throughout the nineteenth century and many are standard repertoire for opera companies today. Puccini's works, such as *Madame Butterfly* and *La Boheme*, largely fall into a category called **verismo**, which means "realistic" opera. The characters are everyday people who live, love, and suffer. Puccini became wealthy and world famous during his own time, due to the popularity of his operas.

**For You**

1. From the list of children's biographies written about composers of this period, choose a book to read.
2. Listen to at least one composition by that composer.
3. Do you think the music you chose reflects the Romantic Era? How?

**In the Preschool and in Out-of-School Programs**

1. Read the book you have chosen to the children, or tell the story and show the pictures, depending on the appropriateness of the book to the age level of the children.
2. Select an appropriate time to share this composer's music with the children. You can play the composer's music while you tell them about the composer and his music.

## References

Administration for Children and Families. (2005). *Head Start Program Fact Sheet*. Head Start Bureau. Retrieved July 16, 2005, from http://www. acf.hhs.gov/programs/hsb/research/ 2005.htm.

Andress, B. (1980). *Music experiences in early childhood*. Fort Worth, TX: Holt, Rinehart & Winston.

Ball, W. (1995). Nurturing musical aptitude in children. *Dimensions, 23*(4), 19–24.

Bolton, B. M. (1996). Was that a musical response? Eliciting and evaluating musical behaviors in very young children. *Early Childhood Connections: Journal of Music- and Movement-Based Learning*.

Boyd, A. E. (1989). *Music in early childhood*. (Report No. PS-018264). East Lansing, MI: National Center for Research on Teacher Learning. (ERIC Document Reproduction Service No. ED 310 863)

Caldwell, J. T. (2002, July). *A brief introduction to Dalcroze eurhythmics*. Retrieved October 21, 2004, from http://www.jtimothycaldwell.net/ resources/pedagogy/makingsense.htm

Cave, C. (1998). Early language development: Music and movement make a difference. *Early Childhood*

*Connections: Journal of Music- and Movement-Based Learning, 4*(3), 24–29.

Chamberlain, D. B. (1994). The sentient prenate: What every parent should know. *Pre- and Perinatal Psychology Journal, 9*(1), 9–31.

Chang, H., & Trehub, S. E. (1977). Auditory processing of relational information by young infants. *Journal of Experimental Child Psychology, 24,* 324–333.

Children's Defense Fund. (2004). *Child care basics.* Retrieved September 11, 2004, from http://www. childrensdefense.org/earlychildhood/childcare/basics.asp

Choksy, L. (1981). *The Kodály context.* Englewood Cliffs, NJ: Prentice-Hall.

de Gast, I. (2004). *Mother and baby sound connection.* Retrieved October 11, 2004, from http://www. ilkadegast.com/HTML/motherandbaby.html

Essa, E. L. (2003). *Introduction to early childhood education.* Clifton Park, NY: Thomson Delmar Learning.

Feierabend, J. M. (1995). Music and intelligence in the early years. *Early Childhood Connections: Journal of Music- and Movement-Based Learning, 1*(2), Retrieved September 11, 2004, from http://www. giamusic.com/music_education/feierabend/articles/intelligence.html

Feierabend, J. M. (1996). Music and movement for infants and toddlers: Naturally wonder-full. *Early Childhood Connections: Journal of Music- and Movement-Based Learning, 2*(4), 19–26.

Fenson, L., & Ramsay, D. S. (1981). Effects of modeling action sequences on the play of twelve-, fifteen-, and nineteen-month-old children. *Child Development, 52*(3), 1028–1036.

Fox, D. B. (1989). MusicTIME and music times two: The Eastman infant-toddler music programs. In B. Andress (Ed.), *Prekindergarten music education.* (pp. 13–24). Reston, VA: Music Educators National Conference.

Gardner, H. (1983). *Frames of mind. The theory of multiple intelligences.* New York: Basic Books.

Glausiusz, J. (2001, August). The genetic mystery of music: Does a mother's lullaby give an infant a better chance for survival? *Discover Magazine, 22*(8).

Retrieved October 11, 2004, from http://www. spiritsound.com/mystery.html

Gordon, E. E. (1990). *A music learning theory for newborn and young children.* Chicago: G. I. A. Publications.

Gordon, E. E. (1999). All about audiation and music aptitudes. *Music Educators Journal, 86*(2), 41–44.

Henderson, T. (2004). *Lesson 2: Sound properties and their perception: Pitch and frequency.* Retrieved October 11, 2004, from http://www. glenbrook.k12.il.us/gbssci/phys/Class/sound/u1l2a.html

Hepper, P. G. (1991). An examination of fetal learning before and after birth. *The Irish Journal of Psychology, 12*(2), 95–107.

Honig, A. S. (2001). Building relationships through music. *Scholastic Early Childhood Today, 15*(4), 24–25.

Indian Gyan.com. (2000). *Harmony of body and mind.* Retrieved October 11, 2004, from http://www. indiangyan.com/books/yogabooks/yoga_preg/harmony_body_mind.shtml

Kamien, R. (2003). *Music, an appreciation.* New York: McGraw-Hill.

Kessen, W., Levine, J., & Wendrich, K. A. (1979). The imitation of pitch in infants. *Infant Behavior and Development, 2,* 93–99.

Kurtus, R. (2002). *General wave motion. School for champions.* Retrieved October 11, 2004, from http://www.school-for-champions.com/science/waves.htm

Leboyer, F. (2002). *Birth without violence.* Rochester, VT: Healing Art Press.

Levinowitz, L. M. (1998). The importance of music in early childhood. *General Music Today, 12*(1), 4–7. Retrieved September 11, 2004, from http://www. westsidemusictogether.com/importance.html

Logan, B. (1990). *The science of BabyPlus.* Retrieved October 11, 2004, from http://www.babyplus.com/science/infant2.html

Logan, B. (2003). *Learning before birth: Every child deserves giftedness.* Retrieved September 11, 2004, from http://www.brentlogan.net/

Manrique, B. (1995). *Prenatal and postnatal stimulation research.* Make Way for Baby! Retrieved October 11, 2004, from http://makewayforbaby. com/research.htm

Meier, J. (2003). *Prenatal music classes?* Retrieved October 11, 2004, from http://www.firstbabymall.com/expecting/pregnancy/prenatalmusic.htm

Music Educators National Conference. (1994). *National standards for art education.* Reston, VA: Author. Retrieved September 24, 2004, from http://www.menc.org/publication/books/performance_standards/prek.html

New Screen Concepts (Producer) in association with The Reiner Foundation. (1997). *The first years last forever* [Film]. (Available from Parents Action for Children, formerly the I Am Your Child Foundation, at http:// www.parentsactionstore.org)

Ostwald, P. F. (1973). Musical behavior in early childhood. *Developmental Medicine and Child Neurology, 15*(1), 357–375.

Pica, R. (2000). *Experiences in movement: With music, activities, and theory* (2nd ed.) Clifton Park, NY. Thomson Delmar Learning.

Sadie, S. (1986). *Music guide, an introduction.* Englewood Cliffs, NJ: Prentice-Hall.

Sallenbach, W. B. (1998). Claira: A case study in prenatal learning. *Journal of Pre- and Perinatal Psychology and Health, 12*(3–4), 175–196.

Scott-Kassner, C. (1993). Musical characteristics. In M. Palmer & W. L. Sims (Eds.), *Music in prekindergarten: Planning and teaching* (pp. 7–13). Reston, VA: Music Educators National Conference.

Sherrane, R. (2004). *Music history 102: A guide to Western composers and their music.* Internet Public Library. Retrieved September 16, 2004, from http://www.ipl.org/div/mushist/middle/index.htm

Shetler, D. J. (1989). The inquiry into prenatal musical experience: A report of the Eastman Project 1980–1987. *Pre- and Perinatal Psychology Journal, 3*(3), 171–189.

Tomatis, A. A. (1991). *The conscious ear.* New York: Station Hill Press.

Trehub, S. E., Unyk, A. M., & Trainor, L. J. (1993). Maternal singing in cross-cultural perspective. *Infant Behavior and Development, 16*, 285–295.

Trehub, S.E., Unyk, A. M., Kamenetsky, S. B., Hill, D. S., Trainor, L. J., Henderson, J. L., & Saraza, M. (1997). Mothers' and fathers' singing to infants. *Developmental Psychology, 33* 500–507.

Trehub, S. E., & Trainor, L. J. (1998). Singing to infants: Lullabies and playsongs. *Advances in Infancy Research, 12,* 43–77.

Trehub, S. E. (1999). Singing as a parenting tool. *Early Childhood Connections. Journal of Music- and Movement-Based Learning, 5*(2), 8–13.

Verny, T., & Kelly, J. (1981). *The secret life of the unborn child.* New York: Summit Books.

Warner, M. (1998). "Hush-a-Bye Baby": Death and violence in the lullaby. *Raritan, 18,*(1), 93–114.

Weikart, P. S. (1995). Purposeful movement: Have we overlooked the base? *Early Childhood Connections: Journal of Music- and Movement-Based Learning, 1*(4), 6–15.

Whitwell, G. E. (2001). *Prelude.* Center for Prenatal and Perinatal Music. Retrieved October 11, 2004, from http://www.prenatalmusic.com/prelude.htm

Whitwell, G. E. (2003). *The importance of prenatal sound and music.* Life Before Birth. Retrieved October 11, 2004, from http://www.birthpsychology.com/lifebefore/soundindex.html

Zemke, L. (2001). *Lovenotes: Music for the unborn child.* Retrieved October 11, 2004, from http://healthythoughts.com/ht19/lovenotes.htm

Zimmerman, M. P. (1984, June 28–30). *State of the art in early childhood music and research.* (Report No. PS014616). Paper presented at the Music in Early Childhood Conference, Prov., UT. (ERIC Document Reproduction Service No. ED 250068)

# Musically Nurturing Toddlers (19 Months–36 Months of Age)

## Key Terms

| | | |
|---|---|---|
| eighth note | middle C | quarter note |
| forte | musical alphabet | staff |
| half note | musical comedy | whole note |
| jazz | piano | |

In the toddler room, 11-month-old Jessica is standing, holding onto a chair and "dancing" to the recording her teacher, Miguel, is playing. Sixteen-month-old Carlos runs over to join Miguel. He points at the recorder. "Do you like the music?" Miguel asks, "Can you dance?" Carlos begins to bounce to the music, stops and runs to a shelf containing musical instruments, picks up a drum and begins to pound on it.

Fourteen-month-old Jelani arrives with his mother. He recently began coming to the child care center and hangs back behind his mother. Hana welcomes Jelani. He knows her and peeks out from behind his mother. "Jelani, come with me and we'll show Mommy how the Lady rides." Jelani gives his hand to Hana and toddles with her over to a chair where she sits. She places Jelani on her knees and bounces him, saying:

> This is the way the Lady rides
> Trot, trot, trot, trot
> This is the way the Gentleman rides
> A-gallop, a-gallop, a-gallop, a-gallop.
> This is the way the Farmer rides
> Hobble-dee-gee, hobble-dee-gee.

Jelani laughs. Mommy says good-bye and Hana begins to bounce Jelani again.

Toddler teachers musically nurture children during normal routines.

These toddler teachers are nurturing the children in their care with music throughout the day. In addition, they are using music to transition from one routine to another and in the process are helping the children adjust to changes.

The toddler months begin during the sensorimotor period when children learn through their senses and physical manipulation of objects and continue into the preoperational period in which the child uses symbols such as language to express his world. He begins to classify his world for better understanding and to make recall easier.

## Snapshot of a Child

### 19- to 36-Month-Olds

*19- to 24-month-Olds*    Physically, the child is still not proportioned as an adult. His head remains the largest part of his body and throws off his balance at times. The young toddler can use a spoon, can move quickly in a toddler run, can throw a ball underhand, and continues to develop self-help skills, such as undressing. Near the end of this period, he will begin to dress himself. As the child moves through the next six months, he will begin to walk upstairs and some children will walk downstairs. The child will learn to kick a ball forward and some will learn to throw a ball overhand. In the block corner, the child will develop the ability to build a tower of four blocks.

Cognitively, a child this age is adding words to his vocabulary at a rate of 10 words per day. By the end of this period of development, most toddlers can follow two-step directions, name familiar objects in a book, name at least six body parts on a doll, speak in

## Standards and Other Professional Guidance

### Pre-K Music Education Standards

The National Music Education Pre-K Standards intend that by age four, children have been prepared to learn music at the kindergarten level, when they enter school. Guidelines for musical experiences for two-, three-, and four-year-olds are articulated:

Two-, three-, and four-year-old children need an environment that includes a variety of sound sources, selected recorded music, and opportunities for free improvised singing and the building of a repertoire of songs. An exploratory approach, using a wide variety of appropriate materials, provides a rich base from which conceptual understanding can evolve in later

years. A variety of individual musical experiences is important for children at this age, with little emphasis on activities that require children to perform together as a unit. As a result of their experiences with music, four-year-olds should initiate both independent and collaborative play with musical materials, and they should demonstrate curiosity about music.

From *National Standards for Arts Education*. Copyright © 1994 by Music Educators National Conference (MENC). Used by permission. The complete National Arts Standards and additional materials relating to the Standards are available from MENC—The National Association for Music Education, 1806 Robert Fulton Drive, Reston, VA 20191.

three- or four- word sentences, understand opposites, and complete simple puzzles. During this time, many children will begin to classify objects.

Socially and emotionally, at this age the child likes to imitate others. The dramatic play area becomes more interesting to him as he tries on the roles of the adults in his life. He also enjoys being a helper around the home or classroom. Many children will begin to take a greater interest in other children.

**25- to 30-month-Olds**   Physically, this age child is beginning to lose his "baby fat" and starting to look like an older child. His head is becoming more in proportion with his body. His self-help skills are improving and many children begin to dress themselves. With help, this child can brush his teeth and wash and dry his hands. By the end of this period, he can jump off the ground and many children this age can balance on one foot. Fine motor skills have advanced enough for the child to draw a straight line and make a vertical line.

Cognitively, this age child continues to work on classification skills. His vocabulary continues to grow and many children speak clearly all the time by the end of this period. Additionally, he is learning his colors and many can name at least one color.

Socially, the child's interest is growing and many children will name one friend by the end of this time.

**30- to 36-month-Olds**   Physically, the toddler is changing into a small child. By the end of this period, his proportions are closer to adult proportions. This allows him better balance and coordination. There remains a wide range of abilities in this age group, but many children can throw a ball overhand, balance on each foot for three seconds, wiggle their thumbs, and complete their potty training. If the clothes are easy to handle, many children can dress themselves. In the block corner, some children can build towers of eight blocks. A very few children may be able to hop and draw a circle.

Cognitively at this age, most children can name at least one color, describe how two objects are used, use four to five words in a sentence, and name two actions such as running or jumping. Some children will

begin to uses prepositions such as *on, in,* and *over.* Many of the children this age can follow a two- or three-part command.

Socially and emotionally, the children are changing as well. Some children can express a wide range of emotions by this time. Many children will name a friend by name. By the end of the period, children in this age group separate from their parents somewhat easily. The end of this period ends the toddler stage and the child moves into the preschool years. The material presented in this snapshot is from Berk, 2001.

# Sound Centers

Every early childhood classroom, including toddler rooms, should have a "sound corner" to satisfy the natural curiosity of children. Although materials that make sounds can be incorporated in many areas of the classroom, a specific area should be set aside for the exploration of sound. This area should be placed away from quiet activity areas, because the children will definitely make loud sounds as they explore. In the toddler room, little cubbyholes can be used for a toddler to sit alone and absorb himself in the sounds he can make. These little areas naturally attract toddlers, because they enjoy sitting in small places and playing. Make sure that the walls are low enough to allow the teacher to observe the child using the center. Observation is important, first, for safety and, second, for gathering information on the child's development.

## Toddler Sound Exploration

Many of the materials used by infants will continue to attract the attention of toddlers. For instance, a set of wind chimes placed on the playground in a quiet area gives the children a serene area outdoors. On the playground, the chimes can be louder than the ones selected for young infants. Toddlers also enjoy music boxes and some of the musical toys that infants enjoyed. However, toddlers are more independent in their hands-on exploration process. At this age, children begin to operate music boxes, jack-in-the-boxes, and other musical toys on their own (Figure 5–1). Not all materials in the sound center need to be purchased. Teacher-made sound toys can be introduced to toddlers. These toys are easy to make and very inexpensive. The possibilities of sound materials are limited only by the caregiver's imagination.

Toddlers usually engage in parallel play. This means that they will sit beside or near another child and play with a duplicate or similar toy, without interacting with the other child. The two children may imitate each other's play, but they play by themselves. Sharing is not in the toddler's job description. No matter how much we want them to learn to share, we cannot expect it. Therefore, teachers must make sure they provide an adequate supply of child manipulated musical toys. It is a good idea to have two of each kind of soundmaker out on the shelves at any one time. Rotating the various toys keeps a sense of newness.

**Figure 5–1**   Toddlers enjoy musical toys.

## Try This One!

### Playing Sound Cans

Place several sound cans in the music area for the toddlers to explore. By the age of two, children are beginning to classify. As toddlers become aware of the differences in sounds, teachers should name those differences for the children. Using words such as *loud* and *soft* or *fast* and *slow* not only helps children classify the sounds they make or hear, but these descriptive words are added to their vocabulary. For example, "Wow! You made a loud sound! Can you make a soft sound?" By using inflection in your voice and by asking the question in a softer tone, you illustrate the concept of loud and soft with your voice.

Demonstrate to the children different techniques for making sounds with the cans such as shaking, tapping, and banging. Label the sounds with words such as *clanking*, *tinkling*, *swishing*, and *thumping*.

Select a particular sound to accompany a chant or poem. For example, the sound of sand or rice swishing in a can could represent rain for either of the poems "It's Raining" or "Rain, Rain Go Away." Say the poem for the children and use the sound can to accompany you. Next, allow one of the children to play the sound can for you while you say the poem.

Sounds of nature can be very soothing. In fact, various manufacturers have developed sound machines to help people relax and sleep. Recordings have been made of rainstorms, brooks bubbling, and ocean waves rolling onto the beach. Perhaps you experienced some of these sounds in Music Labs #1 and 2. Playing nature sound recordings at nap time will help relax the children. Do not allow the recordings to merely play in the background. Comment on what the child might hear. For example, if birds are singing after a storm, point that out. You might simply ask, "Do you hear the birds?"

The child's job during these early years is to absorb as much as he can from his world. To build a good musical network, he must absorb as much musical sound as possible, including the music of his culture. Even when he does not seem to be paying attention, the child is aware of most of the sounds in his

## Making Musical Instruments

### Sound Toys for Toddlers

Before creating any sound toy, be sure the material is durable and safe. A variety of found materials can be used to create sound toys. Here are just a few.

- Plastic bottles in several sizes
- Pint-size milk or cream cartons
- Oatmeal boxes
- Potato chip tubes
- Toothbrush holders
- Plastic eggs
- Film canisters
- Frozen-juice cans
- Ice-cream containers

The list could go on and on. The list of what you can put in the containers is also endless, depending on the sounds you want to make. For young children, I have used colorful cereal in a small water bottle to make a soft sound. Eventually the cereal must be replaced, because it begins to crumble after a lot of shaking. Besides the normal beans, rice, and seeds, here are a few materials that are not used often.

- Corks
- Nails or screws
- Buttons
- Various cereals
- Bells in various sizes
- Paper clips
- Colored beads
- Coins
- Small marshmallows
- Cotton
- Nuts in the shell

Making sure that the children cannot get to the materials is of utmost importance. When possible, hot-glue the lid on the container and use colored tape over the lid. For those containers you cannot see into, such as frozen-juice cans, cover them with contact paper. I use white contact paper and then place a picture on the outside to suggest the sound. For example, a picture of a horse might tell me that when the can is shaken it could sound like a horse galloping. Depending on how many and how large they are, corks do fine for that sound.

Once you have made your sound toys, they are not just for the children. You should think of ways you can use the sound canisters to enhance your storytelling.

environment (Gordon, 1990). The teacher's job is to provide a rich and varied musical environment that allows time for him to absorb the sounds of his world.

## Singing with Toddlers

By the time children are 19 months of age, they are responding to music more actively. From this point forward, children are in the process of learning to engage in music through singing and moving to music (Levinowitz, 1998). Research studies concerned with the complex development of the singing voice have shown that singing is a learned skill that starts during early childhood (Levinowitz, 1998). More than half of the kindergarten children in a recent study were found lacking in the ability to sing (Levinowitz, 1998). These results suggest that many children are not being musically nurtured. In particular, no one is singing to

them. Just as children must be talked to from birth if they are going to learn to speak, they must be sung to if they are going to learn to sing. Children who have been in a singing environment will begin to develop their own singing skills.

If the environment is musically rich, somewhere between the ages of 18 months and 3 years, children try to imitate the songs and chants they have heard. At 19 months of age, young toddlers are capable of matching fragments of melodies (Scott-Kassner, 1993). Listening continues to be the toddler's primary mode of learning, but he is beginning his transformation from being merely a listener to a participant in music (Gordon, 1990). Whether the child is normally developing or not, these responses are dependent on the musicality of the child's environment. To help toddlers develop their singing voices, adults should sing "to them, with them, and for them" as much as possible (McDonald, 1989, p. 89).

## Including Children with Special Needs

### Children with Learning Disabilities

Children with learning disabilities may not progress at the rate described here. They will progress, but at their own rate. When the teacher sings to them, they are provided with enjoyable stimulation. Whether they respond or not at this young age, they benefit from this interaction. "The issue of environment stimulation is urgently important" when addressing the needs of children with cognitive disabilities (Bowe, 2000, p. 363). Singing to young children with learning disabilities helps stimulate their brains. Often, as with typically developing children, these children can learn skills and concepts more easily through music than through other teaching methods.

The techniques and song selections vary according to what is developmentally appropriate for various ages and stages. However, a variety of songs should be sung to children of all ages and these songs should incorporate a variety of keys and styles (Cave, 1998; Feierabend, 1996). Additionally, children need to hear songs that are beyond their singing ability (Cave, 1998). All of these practices will help children establish a good musical foundation and help children's brains form an extensive neural music network that will prepare them for future musical experiences.

## Try This One!

### Making Sounds to Accompany a Book?

Encourage toddlers to participate in the reading process by making sounds to accompany a book you are reading. This is one way to help them discover their voices. Many books are suitable for this activity. Choose a book, read it to the children, and have them make sounds where appropriate. When working with young children, you will have to demonstrate the first few times through the story. Here are some story suggestions.

*Fiddle-I-Fee* by Melissa Sweet
*Old MacDonald Had a Farm* – three different books by Pam Adams, Frances Cony, and Carol Jones
*Moo, Moo, Brown Cow* by Jakki Wood
*Polar Bear, Polar Bear, What Do You Hear?* by Bill Martin Jr.

### Music Babble

After listening to his language from birth, the child begins to babble in the sounds of that language. He is rewarded by the attention and responsive sounds of the adults around him. This encourages him to continue his babbling. The music development process also includes a music babble period. This is an important activity, because the child expands his ability to audiate, or in other words, to hear and understand music in his head, as he produces music babble.

Often, children's music babble has nothing to do with the music they have heard. At this stage, they are moving and music babbling to their own sounds (Gordon, 1990). With encouragement from the adults around him, words begin to emerge from the child's language babble and he moves through the language babble period. Similarly, when he receives encouragement and support for his music babble, fragments of songs begin to emerge from the music babble and the young child moves through the music babble period. Teachers can encourage music babble in the same way they encourage language babble, by responding to it, by imitating the sounds the child is making, and by applauding his attempts at music. This attention validates what the child is doing. By paying attention, the teacher is showing her approval and telling the child that he is doing something important.

Unfortunately, unlike the child's language babble, music babble often is not recognized by parents and teachers. As a result, many children do not experience the same level of encouragement and guidance for their music babble as they do for their language babble. Additionally, many children are not sung to, nor do they experience music in their environment at the same consistent level that they experience language. Therefore, these children are unable to move easily through the music babble stage (Gordon, 1990).

## A *Closer Look*

### Criteria for Quality Song Selection

In the same manner that caring adults select high-quality food to nurture children's physical development and select high-quality books to nurture children's reading development, they must also select high-quality songs to nurture children's musical development. Excellent songs for young children meet several criteria Feierabend (1996):

- The text relates to the child's make-believe world and is still fun to sing after many repetitions. The story is about an adventure or animals talking such as "The Bear Went Over the Mountain."

- The words and the melody fit together in such a way that they imitate spoken inflections. For example, if a person were to speak the words, using dramatic inflections, this would be mirrored in the rise and fall of the melody.

- The rhythm in the song is similar to the rhythm of the words when spoken.

---

Songs that have been handed down generation after generation meet the criteria of quality songs. Because they are the best songs for young children, these songs have stood the test of time and become favorites. Songs composed to help teach a concept are fine, but often they are not the best songs to help children learn to sing (Feierabend, 1996). Even when the song meets all these criteria, it is not enough. Adults must use expression when singing to children. This is the only way children will learn to sing with expression (Feierabend, 1996).

Repetition is very important to toddlers. This characteristic is seen in the young child's desire to read a favorite story repeatedly or to endlessly repeat the same song. Since they are in the process of developing their language skills, toddlers will pick up snatches of songs, especially the repetitive sections. Songs such as "The Farmer in the Dell" are ideal songs for toddlers. Because they are short songs, "Rain, Rain Go Away" and others like it are favorites for toddlers. Songs that name the parts of the body, such as "Head, Shoulders, Knees and Toes," are good to sing with toddlers as well as infants. Most toddlers can name six body parts (National Association for the Education of Young Children [NAEYC], 1997). This is a time when children are forming their self-concepts. Songs about themselves hold the interest of toddlers. Changing the name used in a song to a child's name is fun for them. For example, sing "Johnny Works with One Hammer" by changing the name to Bobby or Miguel, and create a playful time

for the children. Songs that incorporate movement, such as "London Bridge Is Falling Down" and "Ring Around the Rosies," help young children feel the rhythm, beat, flow, and phrasing of music (Heyge & Sellick, 1998).

You do not need a reason to sing a song other than the fact that you enjoy it and the children enjoy it. When selecting songs to teach children, teachers should choose songs that children may have a chance to sing at home with mom, dad, or other family members or friends. The most beneficial songs for helping children learn to use their singing voices are generally short, simple, narrow in pitch range, repetitive, and sung in the range of the young child's voice. Simple songs such as folk songs and nursery rhymes are the best songs to sing with young children (Aronoff, 1969; Feierabend, 1996).

The toddler teacher's song repertoire does not have to be extremely large. However, it must be of a quality and variety that is worth repeating endlessly. As when singing to infants, teachers should improvise songs with toddlers that describe what they are doing. This can be done in a singsong manner. For example, toddlers are experimenting with their independence and may not always be cooperative. By cheerfully singing what you want them to do, they may respond to you in a more positive manner during routines and transitions (Honig, 2001). Children do not care about the quality of their teacher's voice. They simply enjoy an adult singing to them.

## Music of the World

### A Lullaby from Dominica

Dominica is an island 29 miles long and 16 miles wide at its widest point. The island is part of the Windward Islands in the Caribbean. Politically, it is tied to France and those ties are reflected in its culture. While traveling, a young woman sang a Creole lullaby for me. Now you can sing it (see Figure 5–2). It was explained to me that the Majoo mentioned in the song is a playful spirit.

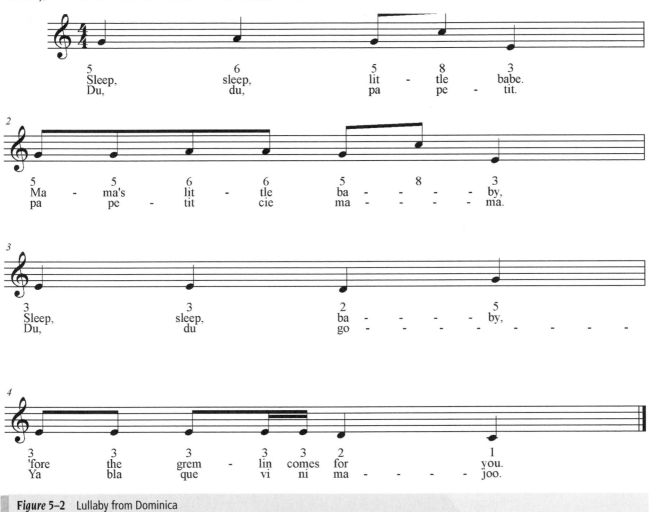

**Figure 5-2**  Lullaby from Dominica

## Rhymes, Rhythmic Chants, and Finger Plays

Chanting is included in this section because chants have similar characteristics to songs. Both rhythmic chants and songs have beats, unique rhythms, and melodies. Rhymes and finger plays differ from songs in that they do not possess a predetermined melody, as a song does, but the language is melodic and comes alive for the children when presented by an enthusiastic teacher.

Past generations used rhythmic chants as the fundamental means of playing with infants and toddlers. When performed well they exhibit a steady beat and provide a good rhythmic experience. The rhymes and songs that were once passed from generation to generation were, and still are, the perfect musical stimulation for young children (Feierabend, 1996). Unfortunately, they are no longer being passed on to the future generations (Feierabend, 1996). What was once a natural occurrence, to sing and play with a baby using rhymes and songs, has nearly become obsolete. Part of the reason for this trend is the redefining of the family into a smaller family unit. There are fewer adults to do chores, leaving little time to play with the baby. In addition, family units have been geographically dispersed, taking young families away from grandparents and other extended family members. When extended family members lived close to each other, younger adults learned by observing grand- and great-grandparents interact with the younger members of the family.

## Try This One!

### Chants and Finger Plays for Toddlers

Toddlers are interested in themselves and in their bodies. Any finger plays, songs, and chants that acknowledge this interest are winners in the toddler room. Perform the following rhyme with the children. Be sure to practice by yourself first.

**It's Me!**

I have ten little fingers (Wiggle fingers.)
And ten little toes. (Wiggle toes.)
Two little eyes (Point to eyes.)
And one little nose. (Point to nose.)
Two little ears (Pull on ears.)
And one little chin (Point to chin.)
One little mouth (Point to mouth.)
Don't put your fingers in! (Put hands behind back.)

Songs such as "I Wiggle My Fingers" complement this rhyme. You can also sing the song "Put Your Finger in the Air," but change the words to put your finger on your nose, or eyes, or knees, and so on. Additionally, the books *From Head to Toe* by Eric Carle and *Hand, Hand, Fingers, Thumb* by Al Perkins can be used with this rhyme.

---

John Feierabend, a national leader in early childhood music education, spent years interviewing senior citizens throughout the United States. He asked them about the songs and rhymes they used when playing with a baby (Feierabend, 1996). He found that people over the age of 80 had the largest repertoire of songs and rhymes to use with a young child. The younger the person, the smaller the repertoire they had. Those who were younger than 40 years old had little or no repertoire. "Those songs and rhymes that demonstrated community affection and endorsement—and were orally transmitted from one generation to the next—are being replaced by commercially imposed 'ear candy,' literature that provides a temporary rush but lacks long-term nutritional value" (Feierabend, 1996, p. 20).

The same rhythmic chants used with infants can be used with toddlers and preschool-age children. Each teacher should develop her own repertoire of rhythmic chants and rhymes and practice performing them for children (see Resource Guide in Appendix D).

## Listening and Moving to Music with Toddlers

Listening and moving to music go hand in hand for toddlers as they did for infants. Toddlers are in constant motion. Working with them can be like trying to herd cats. However, toddlers still love to crawl into a lap and be rocked or bounced on a knee. In the toddler years, these activities continue to be good bonding activities. Advantage should be taken of these special times, because toddlers grow up very quickly!

During the toddler stage, children are developing their fundamental movements. They are exploring what their bodies can do. They not only learn to walk, but also bend, stretch, sway, stamp, clap, shake, and wiggle parts of their bodies. These body movements can be explored to music. By incorporating these movements into songs and to recorded music, teachers give children a movement repertoire.

Toddlers also need models and ideas for movement. Teachers can model movements by moving for children to songs, chants, and recorded music. The movements the teachers use should be developmentally appropriate and match the abilities of the children. For teachers of toddlers that means to keep movements simple. Although toddlers may try to imitate the teacher's movements, their movements should not be expected to be precise. They are learning to move and the focus must be on the process of moving to music rather than the product. Movement can occur in many forms.

- It may involve the movement of fingers or toes to a finger play or rhythmic chant.
- It may involve the movement of arms and legs, or the entire body, while a song is sung or a recorded piece of music is played.
- It may involve structured movement to a song or instrumental piece of music. By structured movement, I mean movement that has been decided on before the music is played. Usually, the teacher makes this decision and makes an announcement such as "let's all march to this song."
- It may involve creative movement to a piece of music, sung or recorded. By creative movement, I mean that the children are told to move the way the music makes them feel.

## Including Children with Special Needs

### Moving Toddlers with Physical Disabilities

Toddlers with physical disabilities cannot participate in all of the movement activities. Teachers should adapt their activities so that every child can participate in all activities. However, if the child is small enough, the teacher can carry him while moving to music (Bailey, Cryer, Harms, Osborne, & Kniest, 1996). When the child is too large to be carried

around the room, the teacher should sit with the child on her lap and swing or rock to the music. This adaptation will allow the child to feel the beat of the music through movement.

Some motions that can be used with music include swinging arms, bending knees, shaking hands, slapping legs, tapping toes, tapping heads, bending from the waist, and clapping hands. Numerous songs, such as "If You're Happy and You Know It" or "Make a Pretty Motion," ask children to shake, stamp, clap, or swing parts of their body. When conducting bouncing activities with toddlers, it is best if their feet can touch the floor so that they can initiate the beat (Feierabend, 1996). The adult can do this by crossing one knee over the other and having the toddler ride on the adult's foot. When they become too large to carry, teachers can still hold their hands and dance with them.

## Try This One!

### Moving to Songs

Make up words to the tunes of familiar songs such as "Row, Row, Row Your Boat," "Hot Cross Buns," and "Rain, Rain Go Away" for moving with toddlers. Here are some examples.

1. To the tune of "Hot Cross Buns":

   Stomp your feet! Stomp your feet!
   Stomp, stomp, stomp, stomp.
   Stomp, stomp, stomp, stomp.
   Stomp your feet!

   Continue with other verses: Clap your hands; wiggle your fingers; slap your knees; nod your head.

2. To the tune of "Row, Row, Row Your Boat":

   Swing, swing, swing your arms,
   Swing them all around.
   Swing them right and swing them left.
   Swing them round and round.

   Continue with other verses: Shake your leg; wiggle your fingers; turn your body; shrug your shoulders.

**3.** To the tune of "Rain, Rain Go Away":

Jump, jump, jump up high.
Jump until you reach the sky.
Run, run, run away.
Run until the end of day.

Young toddlers respond to music by "dancing" when they hear music (see Figure 5–3). This is a natural response for toddlers. Children also make movements as they babble music to themselves (Gordon, 1990). Chanting rhymes and finger plays that incorporate movement are enjoyed by toddlers. In fact, many of the listening and moving activities that were begun with infants can and should continue with toddlers (Feierabend, 1996). The difference is that while infants were passive in their participation, toddlers participate more actively in the music activities.

When they can toddle around, children can participate in simple circle games. Games such as "Ring Around the Rosies" (Figure 5–4) and "Here We Go 'Round the Mulberry Bush" are excellent beginning songs to involve children in movement to music. Kodály advocated using singing games, circles and dances, rhymes and nursery rhymes, and folk songs for movement. He believed that the best way for children to learn to identify the beat of the music was through self-produced music (Choksy, 1981). He felt that the child's body responded better to music that the child sang than to music from an external source. The slower the music the more difficult it is for children to feel the beat. When working with children who are just beginning to learn to move to music, play selections that are moderate to fast in tempo.

## ▌ Try This One!

### Moving to Chants

Toddlers are experimenting with their bodies and finding out what they can do with them. This jump rope chant is a good one to use with toddlers. You can introduce it to the children by using a teddy bear to do the movements. Then, tell the children they are all teddy bears. Stand and lead the children through the chant. Be sure to practice so you can say the chant rhythmically.

Teddy bear, teddy bear, (Clap on the first syllable of Teddy.)
Turn around. (Turn around.)
Teddy bear, teddy bear, (Clap on the first syllable of Teddy.)
Touch the ground. (Touch ground.)
Teddy bear, teddy bear, (Clap on the first syllable of Teddy.)
Turn out the light. (Pretend to turn off the light.)
Teddy bear, teddy bear, (Clap on the first syllable of Teddy.)
Say good night! (Say good night and wave.)

Around 18–24 months of age, the toddler begins to use his imagination. With this ability, they can pretend to move as an animal or a machine. Teachers

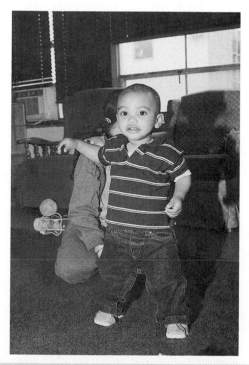

***Figure 5–3*** Young toddlers respond to music by "dancing."

**Figure 5–4**  Toddlers can participate in simple circle games.

can play music that represents various animals and the children can move as they think the animal would move. This opens an entirely new realm of possibilities for movement.

The use of props, such as scarves, while moving will be discussed in the next chapter. In general, the use of props with toddlers can be distracting (Pica, 2000). Additionally, if props are used, they should not be attached to the child, such as tying a scarf on his wrist (Pica, 2000). Toddlers need to be able to get rid of props if they wish, and do not like to be attached to them (Pica, 2000).

## ▌ Try this One!

### Moving with Ribbons

Collect the following:

- Shower curtain rings
- Brightly colored ribbons in 16-inch lengths

1. Tie several ribbons on each curtain ring.
2. Clear enough space for the children to be able to move freely.
3. Play a recorded composition and give the ribbons to the children to wave while they move around.

Select a short and lively composition. Some suggestions include:

- "Hens and CocKerels" from *The Carnival of the Animals* by Saint-Saëns.
- "Ballet of the Unhatched Chicks" from *Pictures at an Exhibition* by Mussorgsky.
- *The Flight of the Bumblebee* by Rimsky-Korsakov.
- "Champagne Aria" from *Don Giovanni* by Mozart.

Movement activities can be performed with or without music. When music is available, the children hear the music while they are doing the activity, but it does not necessarily follow that they are listening to the music. Moving to music and listening to music while moving are two distinct activities. Let me explain.

By listening to music, I mean that the child is attending to the music and that the music is not merely in the background or an accompaniment to an activity. Therefore, the teacher has to decide on her reason for using a piece of music. Is her objective for the children to listen to the music or to use the music as an accompaniment for movement? Movement can accompany music to which the children are listening, but when it does, the movement interprets the music. This is very different from singing a song and putting movement to it or using music as an accompaniment to walk, run, skip, or jump and then mindlessly stamping about the room while the music plays, amid giggles. If the teacher wants the children to listen to the music, she must facilitate their listening abilities. Gaining the attention of toddlers in order to present a piece of music or song can be time-consuming. However, if the teacher begins moving to a recording or begins singing and moving to a song, the children usually join her in much less time than if she tried gathering them all together first.

In addition to moving while listening to music, music should be played for listening, even when movement activities are not planned. Children should not be forced to listen, but on the other hand, the music should not be turned off just because the adult does not think the child is paying attention to it (Gordon, 1990). The child will not be hurt by hearing too much music. The harm occurs when he hears too little music (Gordon, 1990).

Choose times for playing music that will enhance the atmosphere of the classroom by choosing music that complements the time during which you are playing it. You can play music during snack time or lunchtime as background music. The music should be calm and conducive to supporting good table manners and healthy digestion. Nap time is another time when music listening can be incorporated into the daily routine. Using music with which the children are already familiar will help encourage focused listening. Toddlers are accepting of all styles of music. Teachers should take advantage of this characteristic by introducing children to music from many different cultures, styles, and tonalities. Music can be played throughout the day and while the child sleeps. In fact, a child will become musically acculturated much more quickly if he sleeps with music than if he sleeps in silence (Gordon, 1990). The preparation for movement and listening activities requires the teacher to use her imagination and a great deal of thought, and some time to review recordings.

As with chants and songs, I suggest that child care centers develop a basic list of orchestral pieces that are used in every classroom throughout the year. By presenting a variety of activities with the same musical pieces at each age level, the child will develop a familiarity with good music. Remember, children like repetition and we all feel comfortable with things that are familiar to us. If teachers help infants and toddlers engage in appropriate music activities, then the children will be able to respond naturally to music on their own when they are old enough (Feierabend, 1996). See the Resource Guide in Appendix D for suggested recordings.

## Summary

This chapter described the music development process through which toddlers travel when they are cared for in an ideal situation that includes a rich and varied musical environment coupled with informal music guidance. It is a time when music babble is as important to a child's future music ability as his language babble is to his language ability. How soon a child emerges from the music babble stage and begins to actively participate in music can determine how musical he will be for the rest of his life (Gordon, 1990). Gordon theorized that a child who was deprived of a rich and varied early musical environment would be able to learn about music, but it would be more difficult for him to learn to perform musically. This is not a reference to a child's ability to become a professional performer, but simply to being able to participate in the music of everyday life, such as singing happy birthday to a friend.

## Key Concepts

- Many musical activities begun in the infant child care room can be continued in the toddler room.
- Toddlers should be stimulated with a variety of good music.
- When music is a natural part of daily routines, it helps make transitions less stressful.
- A variety of sound toys can be made for toddlers to explore.
- Toddlers need time and space to explore sounds.
- Toddler rooms should have more than one of each musical instrument or sound exploration toy.
- Singing with toddlers helps them begin to find their singing voices.
- Toddlers use music babble as well as speech babble and it is important for teachers to recognize this babble and respond.
- Select songs that are age appropriate for toddlers such as songs with repetitive phrases.
- Toddlers enjoy participating in simple chants and finger plays.
- Toddlers naturally move to music.
- Children with special needs can be included in musical activities, with or without special accommodations.

## Suggested Activities

1. Observe a toddler classroom. Note the various ways in which music is used in the classroom. Do the children initiate music activities on their own? Do the teachers respond to the children's attempts to make music? Is it encouraging? What suggestions would you make to the teachers regarding the music nurturing or lack of music nurturing you observed? Write a short summary of your visit.
2. Make several sound toys that are suitable for use by toddlers.
3. Prepare an activity that is suitable to use with toddlers. Share the activity with your class peers.
4. In the toddler room, there are many transition times. Select a chant or song that you would use to transition toddlers from one activity to another. Write a paragraph telling when you would use the chant or song and what you hope to accomplish by using it during that specific transition.
5. Journal reflective question 5: Do you remember any rhymes or chants from your childhood? Where did you learn them? Do you remember being bounced on someone's knee to a rhyme?

## Music Lab #5

Welcome to Lab #5! In this lab, we will explore keyboard instruments and continue our journey through music history as we enter the twentieth century.

### Activity #1: Exploring Keyboard Instruments

Keyboard instruments include pianos, harpsichords, organs, accordions, and electric keyboards. Although they all have a keyboard, they are different from each other. A keyboard is unique, because several notes can be played at one time.

## Discovering Instruments

### Keyboard Instruments

- Harpsichord: From 1500 to 1775, the harpsichord was an important instrument in concert chambers and homes. The harpsichord has one or two keyboards that control small wedges called plectra. The plectra pluck the strings of the harpsichord to create a sound. Gradually, the harpsichord was replaced by the piano as the most popular instrument for concert and home.
- Pipe Organ: Around 1600, the pipe organ became prominent. That prominence lasted until approximately 1750. Although the pipe organ no longer holds the position of prominence it once held, it continues to be widely used in religious services around the world. Some of the largest organs in the world have six or seven keyboards, a footboard that is played with the feet, and more than 28,000 pipes. The organ can sound like various instruments, such as trumpets. Knobs called stops are pulled out or pushed in to change the sound or tone color of the organ. The keyboards control valves that blow air across openings in specific pipes to make the various sounds.

- Piano: The piano was invented around 1700. The original pianos were smaller than those we know today. By 1850, the piano had been perfected. Throughout the years 1700 to 1850, the evidence of the changes in and growth of the piano is noticeable, particularly in the piano music of Beethoven. He composed his music to fit his newest piano. By 1850, the piano keyboard spanned 88 keys, as it does today. Like the harpsichord, the body of the piano contains strings; however, instead of plucking the strings, the keys are connected to felt hammers that strike the strings and cause them to vibrate. Once the string is struck and the key released, a felt damper touches the string and causes it to stop vibrating. The piano also has three foot pedals. When the damper pedal is depressed, the dampers are lifted off the keys, allowing them to vibrate until the damper pedal is lowered again. The una corda pedal, also called the soft pedal, softens the sound when the string is struck. The third pedal, or sustenuto pedal, does not exist on all pianos. When it does exist, it allows the pianist to lift the dampers on some strings to allow them to continue to vibrate, while others are dampened as soon as the key is released. The piano was originally called the pianoforte. This is a combination of two Italian words used in music, piano and forte. The Italian words *piano* and *forte* are descriptive words used in music to describe the dynamics (loud or soft) of the music to be played.
- Accordion (see Figure 5–5): Accordions have existed in one form or another since the early 1800s. Although they have been used for religious ceremonies, they are used primarily to play the folk music of many cultures. Free-vibrating steel reeds are controlled by a small keyboard that is played by the right hand. The bass keyboard is played by the left hand. The reeds vibrate when air generated by the bellows opening and closing blows over them.
- Electric Keyboard: In addition to traditional keyboard instruments, there are many electric instruments with keyboards. Many battery-run models have keyboards that fit the small fingers of young children. Usually, these small keyboards are inexpensive enough to allow several to be

**Figure 5–5**    Accordion

purchased for a classroom. Additionally, some will accommodate headphones, allowing the child to explore the keyboard without disturbing others.

The sources for this activity are Accordions Worldwide (2005), Laird (2004), and Kamien (2003).

**For You**

1. Spend time exploring various keyboard instruments, such as pianos or electric keyboards.
2. Visit a large church to see a pipe organ. If you cannot find a pipe organ near you, the next best thing is to visit the Web site http://theatre organs.com/laird/top.pipe.organs.html. This site has categorized the largest organs in the world. In some instances, you can click on another site that gives information about the organ.

**In the Preschool and in Out-of-School Programs**

1. Take a field trip to see a pipe organ. Arrange for the organist to meet you and play the organ for the children.
2. Bring small keyboards that are battery-run into the classroom and allow the children to explore the sounds they can make on them.
3. Invite an accordionist to visit the classroom and play for the children.

## A Closer Look

### Dynamics

The word *dynamics* refers to how loud or soft the music is and the various degrees of loudness or softness. Traditionally, Italian words are used by composers to represent how loud or soft to sing or play their music. For example: The Italian word *piano* means soft and the word *forté* (for-tay) means loud. The dynamic soft or piano is represented by the symbol *p* and the dynamic loud or forte is represented by the symbol *f*. Variations of these dynamics are also used. For example: *mp* means moderately soft and *mf* means moderately loud, while *pp* means very soft and *ff* means very loud.

---

## Activity #2: Learning About Music

We have explored sound, played rhythm instruments, listened to music, and learned about the beginnings of the music of Western culture, as we know it today. However, in order to continue with keyboards and other pitched instruments, we have to learn more about music.

*The Musical Alphabet*  To begin with, we will talk about the **musical alphabet**. The musical alphabet has only seven letters in it and they happen to be the first seven letters of the English alphabet (A, B, C, D, E, F, G). These letters are important because they are the names of the notes and scales in our music. We have just learned that there are 88 keys on the piano keyboard. However, there are not 88 names for all of those keys. The keys are all named using these seven letters. As you know, there are white keys and black keys on the piano keyboard. Look at Figure 5–6. This is not an 88-key keyboard, but it will serve our purpose. Notice that the black and white keys are arranged in a pattern that repeats. There are two black keys and then a group of three black keys. The pattern helps us know the names of the keys. Many piano books teach the names of the keys beginning with the note **middle C**. However, I like to start with D. D is easy to find.

> Hey, diddle, diddle.
> D's in the middle.
> In the middle of what can it be?
> In the middle of the two black keys.

**For You**

1. Look at the keyboard in Figure 5–6 and find the group of two black keys. The white key in the middle of them is D.
2. Make a copy of the keyboard so you can write on it, and write *D* on every key that is in the middle of the two black keys.
3. Now that you know where D is, you can name all of the other keys. We are only naming the white keys today. The notes go up in pitch to your right and down in pitch to your left. It is the same with the alphabet. The white key to the right of D is E, then F, then G. G is the last letter in the musical alphabet, so we start over again. The next key is A, then B, then C, and we are back to another D.

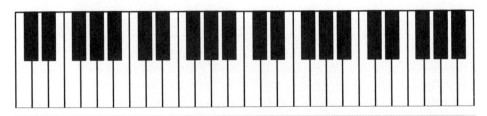

*Figure 5–6*  Keyboards have a pattern of two and three black note groups.

**4.** Fill in the names to all of the white keys on the keyboard. I have mentioned middle C. Middle C is the C in the middle of the piano keyboard. This is not true with all keyboards. Small keyboards may begin with middle C on the far left of the keyboard. We usually sing the notes from just below middle C and up. Therefore, by placing middle C on the far left of a small keyboard, it allows the keyboard to contain many of the notes we sing.

### For Out-of-School Programs

Some of these children may already know about the musical alphabet because they are taking lessons or they learned them in school. If some children are interested in the keyboard, you can teach them the names of the keys using the method described above.

## Activity #3: Musical Notation

With 88 keys on the piano keyboard and many other notes that other instruments can play, there has to be a way to know which ones to play. Well, there is! This is called music notation. There are many parts to music notation and we cannot learn them all at once, but we will begin.

Music is written on a **staff** (see Figure 5–7). A staff has five lines and four spaces. You should always count the lines and spaces from the bottom up. The bottom line is number one and the space between line one and line two is space number one.

### For You

Draw a staff or copy Figure 5–7. Number the lines and spaces on the staff.

*Figure 5–7*  A staff has five lines and four spaces.

## Activity #4: More Notation

Notes are placed on the lines and in the spaces to tell which key to play on an instrument or which pitch to sing. There are different notes, but we will learn about the four basic notes.

First, let's learn about a note's anatomy. Every note has a head. Some notes have white heads and others have black heads. Most notes also have a stem. Some notes have a flag or even two or three flags. Today, we will only be concerned with notes that have one flag. (See Figure 5–8.)

Finally, to learn the names of the notes think of a pie. In Figure 5–9, there is a whole pie and a **whole note**. When the pie is cut in half, the two halves still equal a whole pie. The two **half notes** also equal one whole note. (At this point, just remember the basic stuff. One whole note equals two half notes and vice versa. It will all become clear, eventually.)

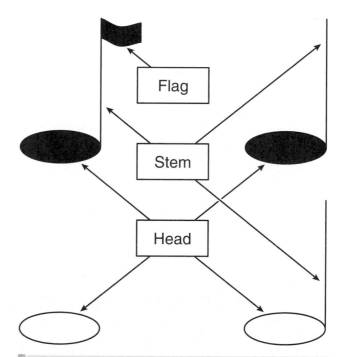

*Figure 5–8*  All notes have a head, some notes have a stem, and other notes have a stem and a flag.

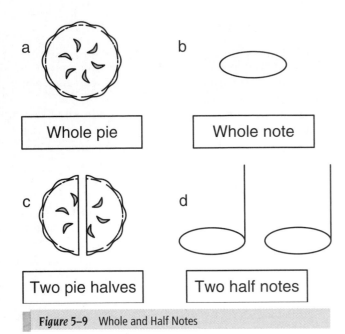

**Figure 5-9**    Whole and Half Notes

In Figure 5–10, the pie has been cut into quarters. The four parts still equal a whole pie. The four **quarter notes** equal a whole note. Finally, the pie is cut into eight parts, which still equal a whole pie. Similarly, the 8 **eighth notes** equal a whole note. Notice, the eighth notes are the only ones with a flag and the whole note has only a head.

**For You**

1. Draw some whole, half, quarter, and eighth notes.
2. Can you explain their relationship to each other?
3. How many quarter notes equal a half note?
4. How many eighth notes equal a half note? A quarter note? A whole note?

## Activity #5: Music Appreciation

Our journey through musical history has brought us to the twentieth century. The twentieth century brought about more fundamental change to the music world than any other era since the beginning

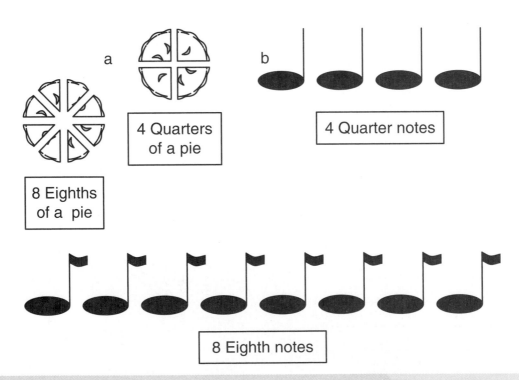

**Figure 5-10**    Quarter and Eighth Notes

of the Baroque Era. The sources for the history presented in this activity are Kamien (2003), Sadie (1986), and Sherrane (2004).

## Musical History

### Twentieth-Century Music (1900–2000)

The music from 1900 to 1950 was revolutionary. Some pieces broke so much from the traditional sounds that they were met with violence. The most famous of all stories is that of the premier of Stravinsky's ballet, *The Rite of Spring,* in Paris on May 29, 1913. The event caused a huge riot. The police had to be called to stop the booing, laughing, animal sounds, and fighting among audience members. Stravinsky's supporters wanted to hear the composition and others thought it was hideous. Take time to listen to the composition yourself. It has since been proclaimed a masterpiece. Our ears are so accustomed to the musical sounds of the early twentieth century that we accept them. The rhythms and chords included in this composition are used in the music we hear on the radio today.

Many musical styles existed side by side during the first half of the twentieth century. As the world became more accessible, composers were influenced by sounds and music from other cultures. Music of Asia and Africa was accepted and incorporated into Western compositions. Nationalism was still strong and composers included folk songs and popular music of their countries into their concert hall music. American jazz also influenced composers of this period. Jazz became the "American Sound," but the style was used by American and European composers (Kamien, 2003 p. 252). Debussy used elements of jazz in his *Golliwogg's Cakewalk* from his suite *Children's Corner* in 1908, while Gershwin included jazz elements in his concert hall compositions.

Another change during the twentieth century was the audience taste. In past centuries, music was the main source of entertainment. The audiences demanded the newest and latest compositions. However, as we have seen, many audience members did not understand or like the experiments of twentieth-century composers. Audience taste created a new circumstance in concert and operatic programming. For the first time in music history, it was not the latest and newest music that dominated the concert and operatic repertoire, but the music of the past. Many twentieth-century composers also work as conductors, teachers, and performers in order to make a living. Beginning in the 1950s and 1960s wealthy individuals and organizations commissioned new works in an effort to sponsor contemporary music, but the repertoire of most symphony orchestras and opera groups remains based on the music of the past.

Compared with the first half of the twentieth century, the second half brought about further-reaching changes in musical innovation. The end of World War II saw an explosion of technology. Radios, televisions, long-playing records, audio tapes, eight-track tapes, compact disks, video, DVDs, and computers have brought music to nearly every man and woman on earth. The ability to record music is so accessible that nearly every band has its own album to sell at performances.

In America, there are many styles of music performed and recorded daily. The most influential style is jazz. Jazz is an American form of music that came out of the dance halls, bars, brothels, and streets of southern towns such as New Orleans. It was created by predominantly African American musicians. Jazz probably existed before 1900, but since the style is improvisational it only existed in performance. In other words, the performers made it up while they played. There was nothing written down and the first recording of jazz was made of the Dixieland Jazz Band in 1917.

Jazz grew out of a combination of various musical elements borrowed from the music of the West African, American, and European cultures. The drumming and improvisation of African music was combined with European and American folk songs, hymns, popular songs, dances, piano pieces, the American band influence, ragtime, and the blues to create early jazz.

The substyles of jazz include Dixieland, swing, bebop, jazz rock, free jazz, and cool. Well-known performers include Louis Armstrong, John Coltrane, Duke Ellington, Charlie Parker, and Benny Goodman. Jazz has influenced popular music and concert hall music alike. This influence can be heard in the works of Maurice Ravel, Darius Milhaud, and Aaron Copland.

In addition to jazz and its substyle, rock, the other important American contribution to twentieth-century pop culture is the **musical comedy**. The forerunners of the American musical comedy were the operetta, a comic opera in which there was singing, dancing, and dialogue; vaudeville, a variety show of various acts with no plot; and the revue, a variety show with no plot, but having a theme.

From 1930 to 1960, the musical comedy was at its peak. Dance was more important to this musical style and was integrated into the plot. After World War II, plots were set in other lands, such as *South Pacific* and *My Fair Lady*. The plots changed from unrealistic boy-meets-girl plots to realistic and serious plots as in *West Side Story*. Well-known composers of musical comedy include Irving Berlin, Jerome Kern, George Gershwin, Richard Rogers, Frank Loesser, Oscar Hammerstein II, and Leonard Bernstein.

### For You

1. Many musical comedies are available on video. Select one and watch it.
2. Choose one of the children's books about a twentieth-century composer and read it.
3. Select a composition by that composer and listen to it.
4. Think about how and when you would present this composition to the children in your classroom.

### For the Preschool Program

1. Read one of the books about a twentieth-century composer to the children.
2. Play a selection of that composer's work for the children.
3. Ask the children to tell you how the music makes them feel.
4. Have the children move to the music.

### For the Out-of-School Program

1. Teach the children songs from a particular musical comedy.
2. Have them work on a short version of the musical and present it to their parents or another out-of-school program in the town.

## References

Accordions Worldwide. (2005). *History*. Retrieved February 23, 2005, from http://www.accordions.com/index/his/his_acc_his.shtml

Aronoff, F. W. (1969). *Music and young children*. New York: Holt, Rinehart & Winston.

Bailey, P., Cryer, D., Harms, T., Osborne, S., & Kniest, B. A. (1996). *Active learning for children with disabilities*. Parsippany, NJ: Dale Seymour Publications.

Berk, L. E. (2001). *Development through the lifespan*. Boston: Allyn & Bacon.

Bowe, F. G. (2000). *Birth to five: Early childhood special education*. Clifton Park, NY: Thomson Delmar Learning.

Cave, C. (1998, Summer). Early language development: Music and movement make a difference. *Early Childhood Connections: Journal of Music- and Movement-Based Learning, 4*(3), 24–29.

Choksy, L. (1981). *The Kodály context*. Englewood Cliffs, NJ: Prentice-Hall.

Feierabend, J. M. (1996, Fall). Music and movement for infants and toddlers: Naturally wonder-full. *Early Childhood Connections: Journal of Music- and Movement-Based Learning, 2*(4), 19–26.

Gordon, E. E. (1990). *A music learning theory for newborn and young children*. Chicago: G. I. A. Publications.

Heyge, L., & Sellick, A. (1998). Music: A natural way to play with babies. *Early Childhood Connections: Journal of Music- and Movement-Based Learning, 4*(4), 8–13.

Honig, A. S. (2001, January). Building relationships through music. *Scholastic Early Childhood Today, 15*(4), 24–25.

Kamien, R. (2003). *Music, an appreciation*. New York: McGraw-Hill.

Laird, M. (2004). *The world's largest pipe organs*. Retrieved December 12, 2004, from http://www.theatreorgans.com/laird/top.pipe.organs.html

Levinowitz, L. M. (1998). The importance of music in early childhood. *General Music Today, 12*(1), 4–7. Retrieved September 11, 2004, from http://www.westsidemusictogether.com/importance.html

McDonald, D. T. (1989). *Musical growth and development: Birth through six.* New York: Schirmer Books.

Music Educators National Conference, MENC. (1994). *National standards for art education.* Reston, VA: Author. Retrieved September 24, 2004, from http://www.menc.org/publication/books/ performance_standards/prek.html

National Association for the Education of Young Children (NAEYC). (1997). *Developmentally appropriate practice in early childhood programs* (Rev. ed.). S. Bredekamp & C. Copple (Eds.). Washington, DC: Author.

Pica, R. (2000). *Experiences in movement: With music, activities, and theory* (2nd ed.). Clifton Park, NY: Thomson Delmar Learning.

Sadie, S. (1986). *Music guide, an introduction.* Englewood Cliffs, NJ: Prentice-Hall.

Scott-Kassner, C. (1993). Musical characteristics. In M. Palmer & W. L. Sims (Eds.), *Music in prekindergarten: Planning and teaching* (pp. 7–13). Reston, VA: Music Educators National Conference.

Sherrane, R. (2004). *Music history 102: A guide to Western composers and their music.* Internet Public Library. Retrieved September 16, 2004, from http://www.ipl.org/div/mushist/middle/index.htm

# Musically Nurturing Preschool Children (Three to Six Years of Age)

## Key Terms

| | | |
|---|---|---|
| bar lines | interval | self-listening |
| chest voice | ledger line | timbre |
| common time | measure | time signature |
| ethnomusicologists | musicology | vocal exploration |
| head voices | octave | |

Sabrina is a new teacher in the four-year-old room. She has been having difficulty getting the children to stay on their mats and be quiet at nap time. After talking with some of her more experienced colleagues, she plans to try something new today. When lunch is over and the children have been to the bathroom, she asks them to sit in a circle so she can read a story to them. It has been snowing and the children are excited about the snow, so she has chosen *The Snowy Day* by Ezra Keats. After reading the story, she asks the children if they would like to be a snowflake. "Snowflakes are soft and quiet," she explains. Sabrina turns on her tape recorder and begins to play "Aquarium" from the *Carnival of the Animals* by Saint-Saëns. She talks the children through their movement. She tells them they are fluffy snowflakes falling gently through the sky. As the music continues, she asks the children to drift to their mats and as the music ends, she tells them they are gently falling onto the ground. The music has ended and the children are on their mats. Sabrina tells them that she is going to replay the music so they can close their eyes and imagine snowflakes falling in their heads. This time, Sabrina lowers the volume slightly and replays the music for the children to fall asleep to it.

Sabrina's problem is normal in early childhood classrooms. By leading the children into a calming musical experience, Sabrina not only solved her problem by preparing the children for a rest, but also provided them with valuable musical nurturing. Currently, teachers like Sabrina all over the United States are responsible on a daily basis for the musical nurturing of millions of preschool children. The music used in this story, "Aquarium" from *The Carnival of the Animals,* is the same music used in an activity in Chapter 3. The same composition can be used in various classrooms for various activities. When teachers use the same composition throughout a child care center, the children become more familiar with the music and it adds to the consistency of the child's experience.

## Musical Nurturing of Preschool-Age Children

Until the 1960s, most preschool children stayed home until they entered public kindergarten or first

---

## Standards and Other Professional Guidance

### What the Standards Say

The National Music Standards set for prekindergarten are meant to ensure that children entering kindergarten are prepared to participate in the normal music classes.

The standards in this section are intended for age four.

1. *Content Standard: Singing and playing instruments*

   Achievement Standard:
   Children
   a. use their voices expressively as they speak, chant, and sing.
   b. sing a variety of simple songs in various keys, meters, and genres alone and with a group, becoming increasingly accurate in rhythm and pitch.
   c. experiment with a variety of instruments and other sound sources.
   d. play simple melodies and accompaniments on instruments.

2. *Content Standard: Creating music*

   Achievement Standard:
   Children
   a. improvise songs to accompany their play activities.
   b. improvise instrumental accompaniments to songs, recorded selections, stories, and poems.
   c. create short pieces of music, using voices, instruments, and other sound sources.
   d. invent and use original graphic or symbolic systems to represent vocal and instrumental sounds and musical ideas.

3. *Content Standard: Responding to music*

   Achievement Standard:
   Children
   a. identify the sources of a wide variety of sounds.
   b. respond through movement to music of various tempos, meters, dynamics, modes, genres, and styles to express what they hear and feel in works of music.
   c. participate freely in music activities.

4. *Content Standard: Understanding music*

   Achievement Standard:
   Children
   a. use their own vocabulary and standard music vocabulary to describe voices, instruments, music notation, and music of various genres, styles, and periods from diverse cultures.
   b. sing, play instruments, move, or verbalize to demonstrate awareness of the elements of music and changes in their usage.
   c. demonstrate an awareness of music as a part of daily life.

From *National Standards for Arts Education.* Copyright © 1994 by Music Educators National Conference (MENC). Used by permission. The complete National Arts Standards and additional materials relating to the Standards are available from MENC—The National Association for Music Education, 1806 Robert Fulton Drive, Reston, VA 20191.

grade. Some children attended part-time preschools in order to socialize. They usually attended two or three days a week for about three hours a day. Prior to the 1960s, preschools, including kindergartens, were nearly nonexistent in many communities. By the 1970s, the number of preschools and child care centers began increasing rapidly, as women entered the workforce in growing numbers. By 1998, there were 7 million children of preschool age being cared for by someone other than their parents (Children's Defense Fund, 2004). Today, many of these children spend 10 to 12 hours a day, 5 days a week, in a child care setting.

Although the first three years of life have been identified as the most important in terms of laying a foundation for future learning, the preschool period is also extremely important. During this period, the child continues to build on the foundation that was established during the first three years of life, developing skills she will use the rest of her life. With so many preschool children spending so much time in child care settings, the responsibility for much of a preschool child's music nurturing falls on the shoulders of her early childhood teacher. If preschool-age children continue to receive music nurturing from their teachers, even when they are no longer small enough to be bounced on a lap or rocked to sleep with a song, then, according to Gordon (1999), their developmental music aptitude will increase and they will attain their fullest musical potential.

As we learned in Chapter 1, music has always been recognized as an important element in early childhood education. Nearly all preschool environments use music as a wonderful teaching tool. Often, through music a concept is taught and learned more easily than through any other teaching method. For example, in preschool settings, songs are used to teach children concepts, such as colors and shapes. Songs like "Mary Wore Her Red Dress" and "If You Have on Red" are popular songs for teaching a concept. More recently, researchers have suggested that music enhances cognitive development.

Throughout the 1990s, research demonstrated the importance of music in the overall development of preschool children. A sampling of this research includes:

- The presence of background music increased social interaction among preschool children (Godeli, Santana, Souza, & Marquetti, 1996).
- After four months of music instruction, children's visual-motor skills were enhanced (Orsmond & Miller, 1999).
- Music training specifically enhanced preschool children's spatial-temporal reasoning (Rauscher, et al., 1997).
- Preschool children retained sequential verbal information using melodies (Wolfe & Hom, 1993).
- Kindergartners who participated in a music program that supplemented the whole-language curriculum had greater reading accuracy. This study supports other research that music can facilitate recall and retention (Colwell, 1994).

## Snapshot of a Child

### Preschool Child (Three to Five Years Old)

The preschool child emerges from the toddler period with enthusiasm. She is independent, confident, and generally happy. She will state her first name, often without being asked. Preschool children have a zest for life that is contagious.

Physically, the preschool child continues to build her repertoire of skills. By the age of three, many children can kick a ball and climb stairs using alternating feet. Four-year-olds can pedal a tricycle, or they are learning this skill. When the child enters the three-year-old classroom, her toilet training has usually been completed, although accidents may still occur as she becomes interested in new challenges and does not get to the toilet in time. The young preschool child can and usually wants to dress herself, although she may require some help with snaps, buttons, and zippers. As she progresses to the age of five, the preschooler will gain better balance and coordination in her gross and fine motor skills. She will refine her eye–hand coordination and learn to catch a ball. She will learn to hop on one foot and eventually will learn to skip. Skipping is usually the last basic gross motor skill children learn. Additionally, the preschool child will refine the fine motor skills she learned as a toddler, such as turning the pages of a book, unscrewing lids, and holding a pencil correctly. She will also learn to write her name as well as other letters, draw figures using crayons and markers, copy shapes, cut with scissors, and use paste. During the preschool years, the child develops additional gross and fine motor skills and refines skills she learned as a toddler.

Cognitively, the preschool child increases her ability to understand her world. Throughout the preschool years, the child's attention span increases, making it easier for her to remain with a task until it is completed. As she moves through the preschool years, the child learns to count, match items that go together, recognize same and different, identify shapes, colors, letters, and numbers, match by category, understand more and less, identify emotions and gender, and pretend. Cognitively, the preschool child is in Piaget's preoperative stage. Classification, seriation, and conservation are concepts that develop over these years.

At the age of three, the typically developing child can understand approximately 1,200 words and speaks in 4- or 5- word sentences. By the time she is ready for kindergarten, she can understand at least 2,500–2,800 words and speaks in 5- to 8-word sentences. By the age of five, the child can tell long stories accurately. Additionally, the child progresses from being able to follow two-part instructions to being able to follow three-part instructions.

Socially and emotionally, the child has moved from parallel play through associative play to cooperative play. Friends are becoming more important to them and they enjoy playing with friends. They are able to follow instructions from their friends, answer questions posed by their friends, apologize, and settle conflict nonaggressively. In preparation for school, they learn to share, take turns, listen and follow group instructions, and participate in games, songs, and rhythmic activities.

The preschool years are busy years of growth and development in preparation for the school-age years. During this time, the child develops many of the skills she will need for the rest of her life and that she will spend her school-age years refining. (The material presented in this snapshot is from Berk, 2001.)

## Piaget's Preoperative Years

By the time a child is three years old, she is in Piaget's preoperational stage. During this stage, the child gathers knowledge through symbols. These symbols might be words she is adding to her vocabulary or they may be the many symbolic play situations in which she engages. Language is a means of encoding information, while symbolic play allows the child to come to an understanding of objects by incorporating them into familiar actions. Symbolic play and imitation are both important aids to being able to think. Singing games and rhythmic chants incorporate symbolic play and imitation. Often, children will combine the words of newly learned chants with tunes that are familiar to them. This is similar to what some early childhood teachers call "piggyback songs," although these songs are initiated by the children. D.Wolf and Gardner (1980) define the stage as a time when the child is a symbol user.

During the preoperative years, children also engage in classification. As the child's language skills develop, adults label objects for the child. Naming an object helps the child classify that object. It is equally as important to begin labeling musical concepts at this age. Labels help children code information about sounds and music. Some helpful music labels include: high–low, up–down, fast–slow, loud–soft, and even–uneven. Preschool children can also begin to classify rhythm instruments according to how they are played, the type of sound the instrument makes, or how long the sound lasts (Scott-Kassner, 1993). Additionally, the traditional instruments of the orchestra should be introduced to the children. As their abilities develop, children can learn to recognize the instruments by the sounds they make and classify them (Scott-Kassner, 1993). While children sing and practice pitches, tone, and volume, they are also sorting and classifying kinesthetic impressions (Cave, 1998). Additionally, by gaining these skills for singing, children will be able to transfer the skill to their verbal expressions (Cave, 1998).

Remember: During the early steps of classification, children are able to concentrate on only one attribute at a time. For example, they can classify types of shapes, such as circles and squares, but they cannot classify the colors and types of the shapes at the same time, for example, red and square buttons. Similarly, children can concentrate on only one musical attribute at a time, such as pitch, rhythm, or intensity. Once children understand these attributes, they can begin to categorize using more than one attribute, such as high and soft or low and loud sounds. Children are able to handle increased numbers of music concepts as their classification skills develop.

## Try This One!

### Classifying Rhythm Instruments

Place a variety of rhythm instruments (see Figure 6–1) on a table for children to classify. Remember, the age and stage of the child's development will dictate the number of attributes the child is able to classify at one time. For example, generally, young preschool children can classify only one attribute at a time, such as how the instrument is played (struck or shaken) or what the instrument is made from (metal or wood). Tables 6–1 and 6–2 are examples of classification charts.

**Figure 6–1**  Preschool children can begin to classify rhythm instruments.

Other research has examined the musical development of preschool children. A sampling of that research includes:

- Children generally develop musical concepts in the following order: volume (loud or soft), timbre (the distinct sound of voices or instruments), tempo (fast or slow), duration (long or short), pitch (high or low), and harmony (more than one voice sounding at the same time) (Zimmerman, 1984).
- When presented with a new song, children will first learn the rhythm and then the melody (Bentley, 1966; Davidson, McKernon, & Gardner, 1981). This is helpful to know when attempting to teach a song to preschool-age children.

**Table 6–1**  Classification chart for attributes shake and strike

| Shake | Strike |
|---|---|
| a | b |

**Table 6–2**  Classification chart for attributes metal and wood

| Wood | Metal |
|---|---|
| a | b |

- At the age of three, children reproduce a song in the same key it has been repeatedly presented to them, if the pitches of the song are within the correct singing range (Sergeant & Roche, 1973). Interestingly, five- and six-year-olds cannot do this. By this age, they store the song in their memory according to the shape of the melody and the relationships of the notes to each other (Sergeant & Roche, 1973). The shape of the melody refers to how the notes go up or down and the relationship of the notes to each other means how much higher or lower a note is from the one that precedes or follows it in a song. The distance between two notes is called an **interval**.

- Most children decrease their spontaneous singing (music babble) after age four, although at this point in their development, they have more control over their voices and sing melodies with greater accuracy and musical expression. At this age, children usually sing songs they have learned (Scott-Kassner, 1993).

- Preschool children develop their musical memory through musical activity (Sergeant & Roche, 1973). In other words, preschool children must be involved and active participants in music, rather than passive listeners.

- Three-year-olds seem to learn certain rhythmic tasks better when the rhythms are vocalized first (Rainbow & Owen, 1979). Rhythms should be performed using a nonsense syllable such as ta, da, ba, or la to speak the rhythm.

- Slower tempos are more difficult for three- to five-year-olds (Rainbow & Owen, 1979). This may be because young children move at a faster tempo than older children and adults. Perhaps it is easier for them to synchronize their movements with the music if the music's tempo is closer to their walking tempo (Scott-Kassner, 1993).

## A Closer Look

### Intervals

Figure 6–2 has three examples of intervals. In the first example, the interval between the first note and the second note is very small, because the second note is in the space right next to the first one. The first note is on a little line under the space, called a **ledger line**. This interval is called an interval of a second. When you count the lines and spaces from the first note to the second note, you count only one for the ledger line and two for the space where the second note sits. In example 2, the interval is a little greater, because the second note is a space, a line, and a space above the first note. This is an interval of a fourth, because if you start with the first note and count every line and space, the second note is on the fourth line or space above the first note. In the third example, the interval is much greater. This is an interval of an eighth, or as it is usually referred to, an **octave**, which means eight. If you begin with the first note and count every line and every space, the second note is the eighth line or space you count.

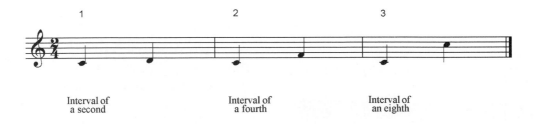

Interval of a second

Interval of a fourth

Interval of an eighth

**Figure 6–2**  Intervals are the spaces between notes.

• With age and experience, children can more accurately reproduce rhythms and maintain a beat (Scott-Kassner, 1993).

The more researchers find out about how children learn music, the better equipped teachers will be for the important job of music nurturing.

## Preschool Sound Exploration

Sound exploration does not end when the toddler developmental period ends. Preschool classrooms should offer children a place where they can continue this important exploration. The preschool classroom sound center should be a well-defined area, so the children know the boundaries and do not cross them unless they are using the center. It should be as private as possible, so the child using the center can become absorbed in the exploration process. Additionally, it should be placed away from quiet centers, so the children are free to make loud sounds if they wish. The walls of the center can be defined by using a large cardboard appliance box, a small indoor tent, or the backs of shelves that are being used in other centers. Large open-topped boxes can be constructed from plywood to make a more elaborate sound center (Andress, 1980). Regardless of how the center is formed, the teacher needs to have observational access to the area for safety as well as for observing the child.

Sound exploration is a hands-on activity for children. The materials should be safe and developmentally appropriate so the children can create and explore their own sounds. A large variety of sound-making materials and instruments should be available to rotate through the sound center. Rotating a variety of sound materials and instruments will keep the center interesting for the children. Some materials are of greater interest to the children than other materials. For instance, placing a drum in the sound center may excite more children than strings to pluck. A popular item may require special rules for use when the new sound materials are first introduced. This may have to include a time limit per child in order to give all children a chance to try the new materials. As the ardor for the instrument cools with time, children can be given more time to freely explore the instrument.

The walls of the center can be decorated with pictures from favorite stories or nursery rhymes, especially stories or nursery rhymes that lend themselves to sounds, such as the rhyme "Hickory, Dickory Dock." The children can retell the story or rhyme, enhancing it with their own sound effects. If the teacher tells a story during circle time and uses sound effects, the instruments used in telling the story can be placed in the sound center so the children can re-enact the story using their own sounds. By adding a tape recorder to the center, children can listen to a reading of the story while adding sound effects.

Materials should not be selected for the sound center in a haphazard manner. Teachers must carefully plan for the concepts they want children to learn. If they want children to know that there are differences between sounds, then they must provide materials that allow children to make these discoveries. For example, if the teacher wants the children to experience soft and loud sounds, then they must provide the materials and guidance to allow this to happen. Additionally, music is an art of sound. It is not noise. When children are working in the sound center, teachers should refer to what they are doing as making sounds, not noise, although they may be loud sounds. Along with the other sound-making materials, musical instruments should be available for exploration. These instruments should be of the highest quality possible. They should have clear and beautiful tones when played.

## Try This One!

### Seriating Resonator Bells

Place resonator bells on a table for the children to arrange in order of sound from lowest to highest or vice versa. Begin with only two bells and gradually add more bells as the children are able to seriate more items. When they first begin to seriate according to low to high sounds, it may be difficult for the children to hear the difference. To help the children distinguish the difference in tones make sure the bells are not close to each other in the scale and sound distinct from each other. Here are some suggestions for bell selection.

| Number of bells | Suggested Bells |
|---|---|
| 2 | Middle C and G |
| 3 | Middle C, E, and G |
| 4 | Middle C, E, G, and high C |

See Tables 6–3 and 6–4 for classification chart examples.

Often, teachers complain that they do not like to use rhythm instruments because the children just bang on them. This is true. What is wrong with this picture? We must remember that when preschool children are given a new object, they first explore it.

If rhythm instruments are made available to the children only when the teacher has a planned activity, then they will take that time to explore the instruments (see Figure 6–3) (Scott-Kassner, 1993). The music time usually ends up with a lot of banging. In general, children of this age have not arrived at a stage in their musical development that allows them to participate in structured musical activities. However, they will reach that stage sooner if they are given opportunities to explore sounds and are given musical instruments to play on their own (Scott-Kassner, 1993).

In addition to rhythm instruments that can be purchased through many reputable companies, materials can be made by the teacher or parents for the sound center. Preschool children can also make musical instruments in the art or woodworking center for use in the sound center. Preschool children continue to enjoy many of the sound materials used by infants and toddlers. However, they are beginning to organize and classify sounds by themselves. To accommodate this new skill acquisition, for example, when preschool teachers make the sound cans described in Music Lab #3, they should make them in sets of two. Put one color of contact paper on one set and a different color on the second set. This allows the sound cans to be used for comparison.

**Table 6–3**    Classification chart for attributes high and low

| High | Low |
|---|---|
| a | b |

**Table 6–4**    Classification chart for attributes high, medium, and low

| High | Medium | Low |
|---|---|---|
| a | b | c |

**Figure 6–3**  Children need to explore rhythm instruments to be ready to participate in teacher-planned activities.

## Try This One!

### Comparing Sound Cans

Three different activities can be presented to preschool children using sound cans.

1. Place one set of sound cans on a table in the sound center for children to explore sounds. Ask about the sounds the children are making. Use words to describe the sound such as *loud, soft, swishy, clinky,* and so on.

2. Place three sound cans from one set on a table in the sound center for children to arrange the cans in order from the loudest to the softest, or vice versa. To make this effective, there must be a clear difference in the sounds made by shaking the cans. For example, choose a can that contains nails, one that contains sand, and one that contains cotton. Do not place more than three cans on the table at first. Young children cannot seriate large numbers of items. They must learn this skill.

3. Using two sets, children can match the cans that sound the same. Place a matching color dot on the bottom of matching sound cans to make the activity self-correcting. (See Table 6–5 for chart examples.)

There is a growing collection of intriguing rhythm instruments from various countries available to preschool teachers. Teachers should select these instruments with care. The instruments should be purchased from a reputable music dealer who knows

whether the materials used to construct the instruments are safe for the children. Other countries do not always have the same strict standards as the United States does. As with all materials used with children, age-appropriateness of the musical instrument is of utmost importance. This is especially true if the instruments are placed in an area that is not under direct adult supervision at all times.

### The Teacher's Role

It is not enough to make instruments and sound toys available to children and allow them to explore the instruments at will. The teacher must be actively interested in what the children are doing in order to support their sound exploration. What does it mean to be actively interested in what the children are doing? It means that instead of merely looking on, the teacher is engaged in questioning about, commenting on, and demonstrating sounds. Here are some examples of supportive responses.

- Actively observe children as they explore sounds. Show an interest in what the child is doing. By showing an interest in what the child is doing, you are telling the child that what she is doing is important.
- Encourage the child to continue her exploration by making positive comments to her. These comments lay a foundation for musical understanding. For example, you can comment on how loud a sound the child made. You can also demonstrate or ask the child to make a soft or loud sound, or a high or low sound, or a fast or slow sound.
- Demonstrate other ways in which the child can make a sound with the object. For example, show the child who is pounding on a drum that she can make a different sound by rubbing the mallet on the head of the drum, using a different mallet, or using her hand.

Children are born into a world of sound. Learning to distinguish one sound from another, comparing and distinguishing between sounds, and labeling and classifying sounds are all part of the music development process. Opportunities must be presented for

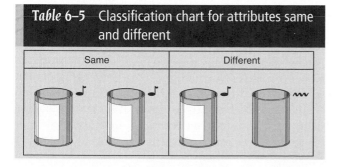

**Table 6–5** Classification chart for attributes same and different

| Same | Different |
|------|-----------|

children to explore a rich variety of sounds. Sound exploration is a hands-on process for young children. In addition to exploring various sound materials, children must be given the opportunity to explore high-quality musical instruments. Through this exploration process, they become familiar with instruments and musical terms. Through sound exploration, children begin to experience and understand that sounds can be organized to communicate ideas and feelings.

## Rhythmic Chants and Singing with Preschool Children

Rhythmic chants and singing are two of the most important activities for musical development in which teachers and children can participate together. When teachers sing and chant to, with, and for young children, they help them learn to feel the beat and rhythm of music and sing with their singing voices. In the preschool classroom, it is important that we sing and chant, and then, sing and chant some more.

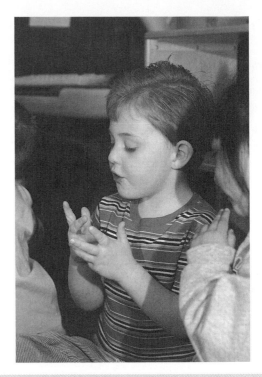

*Figure* 6–4    New chants or rhymes help expand the children's growing vocabularies.

### Rhythmic Chants

Rhythmic chants are songs without the melody. New chants or rhymes help expand the children's growing vocabularies. Once the children know a chant or rhyme, it can be used during transitions to move the children from one activity to another in a pleasant and fun manner. In addition to nursery rhymes and chants, many traditional playground chants are good to use with young children. Since transitions take up so much of the day, it is important to select worthwhile activities for transitions. The Resource Guide in Appendix D contains examples of chants and recommended sources for more rhymes.

Rhythmic chants, nursery rhymes, and finger plays that were introduced in the infant and toddler classrooms can also be used in the preschool classroom (see Figure 6–4). I recommend that each child care center have a selection of rhythmic chants and finger plays that are commonly used throughout the center. This

practice helps the children build a repertoire of rhymes to take with them throughout life. It also creates a sense of continuity as they move from one class to another.

Additionally, rhythmic chants, nursery rhymes, and finger plays should be shared with parents. When parents use these rhymes and chants at home, they serve as a transition and stress reducer between home and the child care setting. Teachers serve as an extended family by passing along the traditional rhymes and songs of various cultures.

Teachers must make these chants come alive for the children. The melodic sound of your voice gives life to the chant. Practice saying the chants until you not only have them memorized, but can perform them with a dramatic flair. By adding movement, children are more involved with the chant. Teachers who use a theme-based curriculum will find numerous chants, rhymes, and finger plays that fit nearly every preschool theme.

## The Young Child's Singing Voice

From birth, some children seem to be able to sing in tune and use their singing voice, while others must search for their singing voice through experimentation. This experimentation is called **vocal exploration** (Cave, 1998). A child's singing voice is different and very distinct from her speaking voice. The singing voice of preschool children is light and airy and not loud (Cave, 1998). Teachers must keep this in mind when encouraging young children to sing. Young children should be discouraged from shouting songs. Shouting strains children's voices and keeps them from finding their singing voice.

Young children have a small singing range. Their range begins around the pitches middle C or D at the lower end and goes to G or A above middle C (see Figure 6–5). A few children have a range as wide as D to D (Anderson & Lawrence, 2003) (see Figure 6–6). Teachers should choose songs that can be sung within the child's vocal range. Often, adults develop a habit of singing in a range that is too low for young children. Teachers should become aware of their own singing habits and, if necessary, use a pitch pipe to help them begin songs for young children at a higher pitch than the pitch with which the teacher might normally begin the song. Pitch pipes can be purchased in music stores and are not very expensive.

Even when the adult sets a good example, some children will consistently sing lower than middle C

C    A

**Figure 6–5**  Young children have a small singing range, usually from middle C or D at the lower end to G or A above middle C.

D    D

**Figure 6–6**  A few children have a range as wide as D to D.

(Ball, 1995). This is especially true of children who try singing popular music they hear on the radio. These children are singing in their **chest voice**. They should be discouraged from using their chest voice and encouraged to sing in a range that is normal for their age. When a child continually uses her chest voice, she can strain her voice and in extreme cases cause vocal damage. When a child sings in the normal range for young children, she is using her **head voice**. By having children imitate a siren and singing into higher pitches using "oo," you can help them experience their head voices (Ball, 1995).

The ability of infants to match pitches at the age of three to six months deteriorates by three and a half years of age if pitch-matching activities are not continued with children past infancy (Scott-Kassner, 1993). Playing imitation games with children not only helps them maintain this skill, but also helps those children who have a limited number of notes they can sing. By asking them to imitate sounds made by the teacher, such as sliding over several notes like a siren, children with limited singing ranges are able to experience other notes to sing.

By the age of three, most children can sing an entire song, but many will modulate or change from one key to another throughout the song (Scott-Kassner, 1993). Teachers can help young children learn to sing in tune by occasionally singing familiar songs using the neutral syllable "loo" (Scott-Kassner, 1993). The reason for using this particular syllable, "loo," is that the vowel sound "oo" is believed to be the easiest one with which to sing on pitch (Choksy, 1981). Ball (1995) used puppets named the "Loo Sisters" to lead children in songs sung on the syllable "loo." She suggests that teachers might also use a cow puppet and have the children sing "moo." When children are having difficulty singing in tune, using the puppet to sing for them is an emotionally "safe" technique (Ball, 1995). If the sound is not quite right, it does not really matter because the puppet did the singing.

Singing is a listening activity. When children listen to themselves as they sing, it is called **self-listening** (Cave, 1998). Self-listening helps children refine as well as find their singing voices (Cave, 1998). In order to sing in tune, children's ears must hear the song. This information is carried to their brains, where listening takes place. When the children are able to audiate, or think the musical sound, they can reproduce it. The information they are thinking is transmitted to their larynxes and the children attempt to reproduce the song. If they are to learn to sing in tune, the children must listen to themselves as they reproduce the song. This requires the opportunity for individual children to sing alone. It is difficult for children to hear their own voices when they are singing in a group. They must be able to hear in order to learn to listen. Teachers should provide time and space for children to sing alone and listen to themselves. A tape recorder in a quiet area may entice a child to sing to herself, for example. The addition of headphones will not only cut out other sounds in the room, but will also make it easier for the child to hear her voice, both as she sings and as she plays back her singing on the recorder.

The most important thing a teacher can do to help children learn to sing in tune is to provide an environment that values singing as a means of communication. In this environment, teachers guide chil-

dren in the proper use of their voices, model good singing techniques, and provide many experiences in which they sing to and with children.

## Echo Singing

Echo singing helps children learn to match pitches and is also an excellent way for young children to learn a song. Very young children learn songs in bits and pieces and need repetition. Usually, echo songs consist of short song snippets that are repeated. A well-known echo song is "Frere Jacques." While helping children learn to match pitches, you can also reinforce information about your curricular theme. For example, perhaps the weekly theme incorporates birds. Figure 6–7 is an example of an echo song that is based on the curricular theme about birds.

Echo songs can be based on the universal children's song. Two or three notes are all that is necessary when singing with young children. For example, sing: "Time to clean up" (see Figure 6–8).

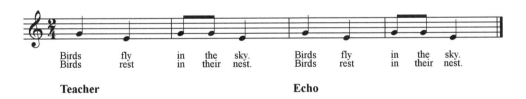

Figure 6–7    Example of an echo song made up by the teacher.

Figure 6–8    Example of an echo song about cleanup time.

Teacher             Child

*Figure* 6–9   Example of roll call echo singing.

Finally, echo songs are a good way to help children begin to improvise. You can put words to a familiar echo song such as "Frere Jacques," sing a question to individual children, and encourage them to answer by singing back to you (Andress, 1980). When echoing an answer, the music remains similar to the music of the question, but the words may change. This type of activity can take place throughout the day. For example, while taking roll, you sing, "Where is Maria?" and the child answers, "Here I am." See Figure 6–9 and 6–10.

### Improvised Singing

When children have been exposed to a musical environment, they will begin to improvise their own songs. They sing to themselves while they work and play. They may even sing to each other. Improvisation cannot be taught in a formal manner, but we should encourage and support children's attempts at improvisation. To be supportive, we need to be aware of what children are doing and learn to listen to and for their improvisations.

As an experiment, I asked two teachers to think about their classroom of three-year-olds and describe the musical activities in which children engaged. They were unaware of these activities. Inconspicuously, a tape recorder was set up in the room for half an hour. Within that period, the following occurred:

- Several children experimented with their voices.
- One child walked past the recorder as he sang nonsense syllables to himself.
- Two children sang bye-bye to each other. They were using the first two notes of the universal children's song. They made a game out of it. One child sang, then the other answered, though not always imitating the notes, as shown in Figure 6–11.
- Another child sang fragments of a Christmas song while he worked at the woodworking bench.
- While these children sang, a fourth child had set up pots, pans, and cymbals to "play." He could be heard experimenting with them. He first listened to the sound produced when he hit his various

*Figure* 6–10   Maria answers, "Here I am!"

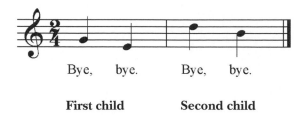

Bye,    bye.    Bye,    bye.

**First child**        **Second child**

*Figure* 6-11    Musical example of what two children sang when singing bye-bye.

"instruments." He was exploring the timbre of his instruments—in other words, how different they sounded from each other. Finally, he settled into a rhythm, which he maintained for several minutes.

The teachers were amazed at the rich musical activities that were going on under their noses! If teachers are going to support the musical efforts of young children, they must not only create an environment that is accepting, but also must be aware of those efforts when they occur, so they can encourage and support the children's efforts.

## Try This One!

### What's Going on in Your Room?

Set up a tape recorder in an inconspicuous, but active place in your classroom. Let it run during free-play time. Did you capture any children participating in musical activities? What were they? Were you aware of them at the time they were happening? What did you learn from this experiment?

Renowned music educator John Feierabend uses a play microphone for a prop to encourage improvisation (Ball, 1995). He sings the first phrase or question into the mike and then points it to the children when it is their turn to sing. In addition to the entire class singing, individual children can be chosen to sing back an answer. Children are motivated to sing because they want to use the microphone. Although children are encouraged to sing their answers, they

should not be forced. The children will usually join in because this becomes a game to them. Microphones can be made by rolling a small piece of poster paper into a cone shape, gluing a Styrofoam ball on top, and spray-painting it. Several can be made and placed in the dramatic-play corner. This will also encourage children to sing and engage in self-listening.

Another way to encourage improvisation is to create a singing chair by cutting the legs shorter on a fancy chair to make it child-size (Andress, 1980). Children are asked to sit in the chair and sing a song to the class. Sometimes the song will be a learned song. Sometimes the child will make up the song on the spot. The more practice they have improvising, the easier it will become. A play microphone can be used with the singing chair as well.

## Try This One!

### Sing-a-Story Books for the Library

To help with improvisation, develop sing-a-story books for your library area. Teacher supply stores carry nursery rhyme sequencing books for young children. The rhymes are usually in simplified form and consist of four pieces.

Collect the following:

- 8 × 11 piece of tag board or poster paper
- Sequenced nursery rhymes
- Glue
- Clear contact paper or laminating film

Do the following:

1. Select a nursery rhyme with which the children are familiar.
2. Fold the poster paper in half to make a four-page booklet.
3. Cut out the nursery rhyme sequences.
4. Glue each section of the rhyme on a page of the booklet.
5. Laminate or cover the booklet with clear contact paper for endurance.
6. Introduce the book during circle time.

7. After introducing the book, chant the rhyme with the children.
8. Tell the children you are going to sing the rhyme.
9. Improvise a song to the words of the rhyme.
10. Invite the children to improvise their own song.
11. Place the booklet in the library where the children can look at it and sing.

## How to Teach a Song to Young Children

There are several approaches to teaching a song, but they are not all appropriate for the abilities of young children. The ages of the children will always influence how you teach the song. The manner in which most songs are learned by young children is by rote. This means that they learn as the teacher sings the song over and over, teaching them a section at a time. The more repetition in the song, the easier it is for the children to learn and the faster they begin to respond. The trick is to make the process interesting. Find a different way of presenting the song each time so the children do not lose interest. Find a part of the song that can engage the children. After you have sung the song for them, ask them to sing that part every time you come to it. Involve the children by giving them a motion to perform as they sing.

## Try This One!

### Teaching a Song to Young Children

Another echo song is "Who has the penny?" You will find it in the Resource Guide in Appendix D. This is an old singing game. It is not quite the same as "Frere Jacques," because the children only echo the music, not all the words.

Pass out three items. To go along with the song, the items would be a penny, a key, and a thimble. You could just as easily use a crayon, a ball, and a dump truck, as I did in the second verse in the Resource Guide (see Appendix D). You can use any object; just change the rhythm to match the name of the object when you sing the song.

1. Tell the children to put their hand up when you ask who has it. Older toddlers may not do this

alone, at least not at first. Some preschool children will not do it either. In that case, you can point to them when it is their turn. Sing their name in answer to your question, such as "John has the penny."
2. Sing the song through once, pointing to the children with the items. Shake your finger when you say "Don't let us see it" and ask the other children to sing and shake their fingers with you.
3. Redistribute the items. This time, before you begin to sing, tell the children that you want to practice "Don't let us see it." Again, shake your finger for emphasis and have the children shake theirs. This gets all of the children involved. As you sing the song again, one or two times, giving different people a chance to hold the items, encourage all of the children to sing with you when you tell who has the item. Gradually they will begin to pick up the song.
4. Older toddlers will be happy to play the game in this manner. Once they know the song, preschool children can stand or jump up and reply on their own when their item is sung about. Make their reply a surprise by standing in a circle and passing the items around after each time you sing, so no one knows who has the item until they sing. Older children will be able to do this immediately.

## Folk Songs and Nursery Rhymes

Songs that help teach a concept make good teaching tools, but often they are not the best songs to help children learn to sing. The most beneficial songs for helping children learn to use their singing voices are generally short, simple, narrow in pitch range, repetitive, and sung in the range of the young child's voice.

As we learned in Chapter 5, simple songs such as folk songs and nursery rhymes are the best songs to sing with young children (Aronoff, 1969; Feierabend, 1996). Folk songs are easier to sing than many composed songs, because they usually have a small range of notes and so are within the singing ability of young children. Folk songs and nursery rhymes have stood the test of time and there is a good chance the child will be able to sing them at home with mom, dad, or

## Music of the World

### Folk Songs from Other Countries

Using folk songs from other countries is a good way to enrich your multicultural program. Here are some books and recordings to get you started.

- Delacre, L. (1992). *Arroz con Leche: Canciones y Ritmos Populares de América Latina.* New York: Scholastic Press
- Frazee, M. (1999). *Hush Little Baby: A Folk Song with Pictures.* Harcourt Children's Books
- Nikola-Lisa, W. (1995). *Bein' with You This Way.* New York: Lee & Low Books
- Nikola-Lisa, W. (1996). *La Alegría de Ser Tú y Yo* (Translated from *Bein' with You This Way*). New York: Lee & Low Books
- Orozco, J. L., and Kleven, E. (1997). *Diez Deditos = 10 Little Fingers & Other Play Rhymes and Action Songs from Latin America.* East Rutherford, NJ: Dutton Books
- Orozco, J. L., and Kleven, E. (1999). *De Colores and Other Latin-American Folk Songs for Children.* East Rutherford, NJ: Puffin Books
- Syverson, J., and Hall, N. A. (1999). *Los Pollitos Dicen / The Baby Chicks Sing.* New York: Little, Brown
- Jenkins, E. (1995).*Multicultural Songs for Children* Jenkins, E. (2003). *Sharing Cultures with Ella Jenkins*
- Wolff, A. (2003). *Oh, the Colors/ De Colores: Sing Along in English and Spanish!/ Vamos a Cantar Junto en Ingles y Espanol!*

### San Serani: Puerto Rican Singing Game

In this singing game from Puerto Rico, children take turns acting out different professions. Form a circle and either have one child in the middle perform an action and the rest imitate the child or have all of the children do the same action in a circle. Have the children decide ahead of time what action they think they should do. (See "San Serani" on page 128.)

Doctores (doc-tor-rays) = doctors

Zapateros (zah-pah-tay-ros) = cobblers or shoemakers

Pescaderos (pes-cah-day-ros) = fishermen

Carpenteros (car-pen-tay-ros) = carpenters

Pintores (pin-to-rays) = painters

Bailerinos (bay-le-ree-nos) = ballerinas

Aviadores (ah-vee-ah-dor-rays) = pilots or aviators

---

other members of her family. As with rhythmic chants, I recommend that child care programs should develop a basic list of well-known folk songs and nursery songs to be sung in every classroom, beginning with the infant room. As children are promoted from one room to the next, they will find comfort in these familiar songs. In turn, they will be ready to learn new songs from their new teacher.

## Singing for Young Children

Finally, it is important for teachers to sing for children. Let me explain the difference between singing to children and singing for children. I believe that singing *to* children is an intimate activity, usually done with an individual child or a small group of children. The songs chosen are simple and those that the teacher wants the children to eventually learn to sing. On the other hand, singing *for* children is an activity in which a song is performed for the children that is currently beyond their ability, but a song they will enjoy hearing. Many songs you know can add to the listening repertoire of young children as well as help develop their musical neural network. Perhaps it is a special song that your mother, father, grandmother, or grandfather sang to you; a song not heard in the normal repertoire of young children. Many of the songs from the 1930s to 1950s are fun songs and excellent to share with young children. Some songs from that era include "Button Up Your Overcoat," "Singin' in the Rain," "Winter Wonderland," and the "Alphabet Love Song" ("A, you're adorable, B, you're so beautiful...") (J. Wolf, 2000). Teachers should choose songs that they enjoy singing. The children will enjoy listening to you sing and will not judge your singing ability. Sing with expression, or as I have told my vocal students: "Sell the song." The children will beg you for more.

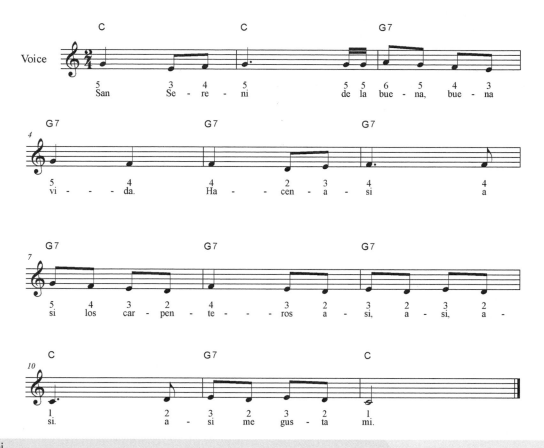

San Serani

## Moving and Listening to Music for Preschool Children

Movement to music takes two forms in early childhood, creative movement and synchronized movement. Creative movement allows children the freedom to respond to music, freely, in a creative manner (McDonald, 1989). Synchronized movement means to be synchronized with the beat of the music (McDonald, 1989). It is important to plan for both kinds of movement activities in the preschool classroom.

## A Closer Look

Here are four favorite songs redone as children's books.

- Kaye, B., Wise, F., Lippman, S., and Alexander, M. (1998). *A You're Adorable*. Cambridge, MA: Candlewick Press
- Rogers, R. (2001). *My Favorite Things*. New York: HarperCollins
- Rogers, R. (2002). *Getting to Know You*. New York: HarperCollins
- Weiss, G. D., and Thiele, B. (1995). *What a Wonderful World*. New York: Atheneum

## A Closer Look

### Suggestions for Creative Movement

The following are some suggestions for creative movement. Involve the children in the decision process when moving creatively. Ask the children to demonstrate the movement they think they should make.

1.  "Things" children can "become"

    a.  Animal
    b.  Balloon
    c.  Birds
    d.  Bubble
    e.  Crayon
    f.  Music box
    g.  Rain
    h.  Robot
    i.  Snowflake
    j.  Various machines (Washing machine, blender, car wash, vacuum cleaner)
    k.  Wind-up toy or doll

2.  Ways for children to move

    a.  Swing arms or legs
    b.  Sway upper body
    c.  Roll head, shoulder
    d.  Turn upper body
    e.  Turn entire body
    f.  Tiptoe
    g.  Run
    h.  Walk
    i.  Skip
    j.  Leap
    k.  Hop

Among other benefits, moving to music helps a child develop her listening skills (Cave, 1998). Moving to music helps children practice their listening skills because it focuses their listening. Focused listening involves doing a structured activity to musical excerpts. Focused listening is perceptive or active listening. When someone engages in focused listening, she is thinking about or perceiving the sounds. Hearing is different from listening because it does not require you to think. It is truly in one ear and out the other!

## Creative Movement to Music

Creative movement for children is concerned with interpreting the music, not with keeping the beat. However, children must develop a repertoire of movements before they can be told to "move the way the music makes you feel." McDonald (1989) calls this "preparing the instrument" (p. 100). Without a movement repertoire, children have no idea how to move to music, unless the teacher tells them what to do and then, it is no longer a creative activity. To build a movement repertoire, children need many chances to walk, run, march, gallop, dance, clap, hop, jump, and slide to music. They also need chances to explore their bodies and discover what the various parts can do.

Young children are already interested in themselves, so body exploration is a natural part of the preschool curriculum. Daily, teachers in preschools lead children in finger plays, rhymes, songs, chants, and games that explore their body parts or require children to move them, such as wiggling their fingers or shaking their feet. These activities include songs such as "Head, Shoulders, Knees, and Toes," rhymes such as "It's Me," and singing games such as "Make a Pretty Motion."

Imagery is another way to help children discover what their bodies can do and add to their movement repertoire. Using imagery, teachers guide children through various scenarios that require them to "become" an object, while the teacher describes what happens to the object. Some objects that children can become are, for example, an ice cube that melts on the floor or a doll that is wound up and moves about the room. In addition to adding to the children's movement repertoire, the use of imagery helps children learn to move freely (Gordon, 1990). Through imagery, teachers can calm and relax preschool children as a preparation for nap time or help children creatively imitate animals and objects in their world.

Another manner in which young children add to their movement repertoire is by watching older children and teachers move to music (Scott-Kassner, 1993). Teachers should plan to model movements to music for young children on a regular basis. The teacher can play a recording and begin to move to the music, inviting children to join when they wish. When selecting movements to model, teachers should keep in mind the stage of each child's physical development and coordination. An important outcome of successful music movement activities is the reinforced self-esteem of each child. The child's ability to be successful is dependent on the teacher selecting developmentally appropriate movements. In general, a child's stage of development is determined by the amount of movement experience she has (Scott-Kassner, 1993). Teachers will find that during these early years, girls tend to be more coordinated than boys are (Scott-Kassner, 1993).

With their teacher's guidance, children learn to move to music in a creative manner. During creative music movement time, teachers can guide children by leading them to move quickly during a fast piece of music and slowly during a slow piece. Children begin to understand musical dynamics when they are led to respond to loud and soft music with appropriate movements such as marching to loud music and tiptoeing to soft music. Activities such as these also engage children in focused listening. The ability to listen for and recognize the phrasing in music can be developed when the teacher leads children to change direction or change movements at the end of each phrase.

As children gain more experience and a repertoire of movements, it is easier for them to move using their own creative ideas. Now, they can become a part of the movement decision process. When the teacher involves them in purposeful movement to music, children can develop their creative movement ideas (Weikart, 1988). This means that before moving to a piece of music, the teacher and the children discuss and decide on what movement will be done to the music. Children are more successful in this planning process when they are working with a familiar piece of music. Beyond the fact that young children have short attention spans, this is another reason to keep music excerpts short. It allows the piece to be played several times so the children will become familiar with it. I recommend that child care programs select specific pieces of music for listening and moving for use in all classrooms. Thus, children are introduced to music as infants and they continue to experience the same music throughout their preschool years. The selection of these musical works should be made very carefully. There should be a wide variety in the selections and they should be of the highest quality. See the Resource Guide in Appendix D for suggestions.

## Synchronized Movement to Music

Through synchronized movement to music, children develop their "hearing-feeling connection" (Weikart, 1995, p. 7). This connection helps the child develop a steady beat later in her music education (Weikart, 1995). The ability to identify and perform the beat in music is "the most basic of all music skills" (Choksy, 1981, p. 24). The child goes through four levels when learning this skill (Choksy, 1981). By recognizing the various levels of achievement, which are listed as follows, the teacher can plan appropriately for the individual children in her classroom. Choksy (1981):

1. Unable: At this stage, the child is unable to demonstrate a feeling of the beat. It is rare to see this inability even at the age of three.
2. Gross response: This is not usually a response to the beat, but a response to the tempo of the music. The child will move bodily to the fastness or slowness of the music.
3. Smaller bodily response: The child taps her body in response to the music.
4. Highly specific response: The child is able to step or clap on the beat of the music.

Over the past 30 years, there has been a significant decline in the ability of people in our society to keep a steady beat to music or chants (Weikart, 1995). Our changing society may be blamed for much of this decline, as well as the decline in basic coordination, balance, purposeful movement, such as skipping (Weikart, 1995). Children spend much less time playing outdoors and, as in the past, are not involved in neighborhood games. Furthermore, many of these neighborhood games are not being passed on to new generations. Children not only enjoyed playing these games, but through their play, their bodies became better coordinated and they learned to move with ease. Preschool children are in the process of developing and refining their fundamental movements. It is a process and, if children are given opportunities for movement experiences, the product will be seen in the future.

## Try This One!

### American Singing Game—"My Aunt Came Back!"

You will find the song "My Aunt Came Back" in the Resource Guide in Appendix D. This singing game is also an echo song, so the children can perform it immediately. Often, older children enjoy making up other verses. Another fun thing to do is to build the motions one upon the other instead of doing them separately. Use a chart to help children remember what my aunt brought back (see Table 6–6).

Here are the various places my aunt visited and the items she brought back with her:

| | | |
|---|---|---|
| Old Japan: | a great big fan | (wave hand like a fan) |
| Holland, too: | a wooden shoe | (tap foot on the floor) |
| Old Algiers: | a pair of shears | (make a motion like cutting scissors) |
| Niagara Falls: | a basketball | (pretend to bounce a basketball) |
| County Fair: | a rocking chair | (pretend to rock in the chair) |
| Timbuktu: | a nut like you | (point to the children) |

In actuality, synchronized movement training should begin with very little movement. Rhythmic speech activities are the best way to begin synchronized move-

ment with young children because "language is a natural bridge to movement" (Weikart, 1995, p. 15). Chanting the rhythm of a rhyme is the easiest way for preschool children to feel the beat (McDonald, 1989). Researchers found this to be much easier for young children than marching to the beat or playing it on rhythm sticks (McDonald, 1989). The ability to clap while walking to a beat requires many movement experiences and good coordination (Choksy, 1981). Chanting can and should be integrated throughout the day, starting at circle time. Once the children know a chant, it can be used during transitions. Many of the jump rope chants of the past are being rediscovered and published in chant books. They provide a wide variety of entertaining chants to use with young children. As the children move from saying the rhythm to clapping and playing the rhythm or the beat, use a variety of activities to express the beat in order to keep this type of activity fun and interesting. For example, by sitting with their legs crossed, they can play the beat on their "lap drums." See the Resource Guide in Appendix D for sources of chants.

## Try This One!

### Chanting—"Sing a Song of Sixpence"

Many nursery rhymes can be chanted. Chant the rhyme while you clap or play a hand drum.

Sing a song of sixpence,
A pocket full of rye.
Four and Twenty black birds
Baked in a pie.

When the pie was open,
The birds began to sing!
Wasn't that a dainty dish
To set before the king!

The king was in his counting-house,
Counting all his money.
The queen was in the parlor,
Eating bread and honey.

The maid was in the garden,
Hanging up the clothes.

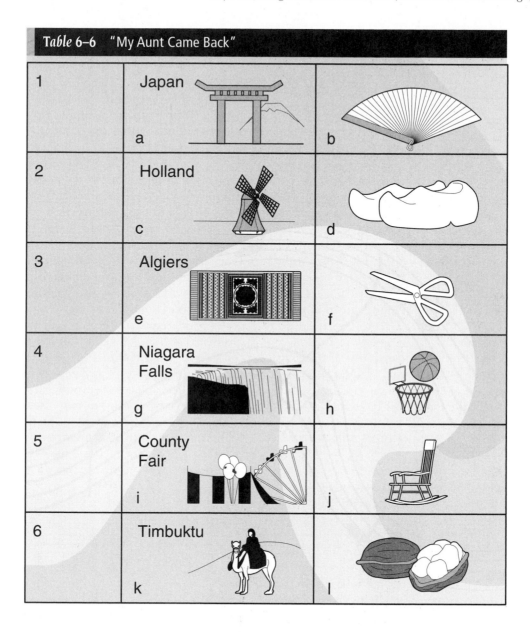

**Table 6–6** "My Aunt Came Back"

| | | | |
|---|---|---|---|
| 1 | Japan<br><br>a | | b |
| 2 | Holland<br><br>c | | d |
| 3 | Algiers<br><br>e | | f |
| 4 | Niagara Falls<br><br>g | | h |
| 5 | County Fair<br><br>i | | j |
| 6 | Timbuktu<br><br>k | | l |

Along came a black bird
And snipped off her nose!

The goal of synchronized movement is for children to be able to feel the beat and rhythm of music with accuracy and independence. Children will imitate the performance of the teacher, so it is important for teachers to be precise and dynamic in their performance of chants. Practice saying the chants and rhymes in an expressive manner, before performing them for the children. To help children feel the beat, it must be evident in the teacher's performance. For children to achieve accuracy and independence in performing rhythmic patterns, Choksy (1981) outlines three steps to achieving this independence.

1. Performing the skill in a group with a leader
2. Performing the skill in a group without a leader
3. Performing alone

The final and most important step is usually omitted (Choksy, 1981). This step can be accomplished by playing a game with the children. For example, form a circle and have the children take turns performing the rhythmic pattern or beat of a song in the middle of a circle. Although synchronized movement should include gross motor movement to music, the best strategy for introducing synchronized movement is to begin with chanting, clapping, and tapping activities.

Feeling the beat while moving is an important next step. To help children begin to feel the beat with their entire bodies, the teacher can make a game out of it, for example. She can have the children move to the beat of a drum in a circle. When the drum stops, the children should stop. The teacher should vary the tempo of the beat by making it faster or slower.

## Using Props for Movement to Music

As preschool children become more adept at moving to music, the use of props helps maintain their focus on the music (Gordon, 1990). Teachers can incorporate the use of props into their music movement program. Props that are normally found in the early childhood classroom include scarves, ribbons, and streamers. Preschool children have difficulty moving freely (Gordon, 1990). The use of scarves helps give children freedom in movement as well as continuous flow. The child needs help to "recapture the feelings that he had when he moved as an infant" (Gordon, 1990, p. 79). Infants move in graceful, continuous motions, but that ability disappears. This may be due to societal restrictions put on young children (Gordon, 1990). Those limits may include the amount of time children have for freedom of movement as well as the behavioral expectations that are enforced by parents and teachers in our progressively "indoor" society. Teachers need to help

children learn to move to music freely, continuously, and with flexibility (Gordon, 1990).

The use of parachutes has gained in popularity in child care settings. Just a few possible movements with a parachute include raising and lowering, walking in a circle, making waves and ripples, standing in one place and rotating the parachute, and moving a ball on the parachute, as in Figure 6–12. Children enjoy using a parachute in movement activities. There is a variety of activities possible with a parachute, making it an excellent prop for movement and focused listening to music.

With the use of some props such as scarves, slower tempos can be introduced to the children. Teachers should call on their imaginations to find new ways to help children feel music as they move to it. Feierabend suggested giving children a paper cup filled halfway with water to carry while they moved to slow music (personal communication, 1995) This works very well to slow down the pace and allow the children to feel the music.

As children mature and gain experience moving to music, their ability to reproduce the rhythms of the music they are listening to increases (Scott-Kassner, 1993). This might be evident in the manner that they begin to play rhythm instruments *with* the music. This is much better than the typical rhythm band

**Figure 6–12** Parachutes offer a variety of activities for movement and focused listening to music.

experience of banging away in spite of the music. Whether performing or listening, the children will become more actively involved in the music when they begin to feel the music as well as hear it.

## Try This One!

### Parachuting to Music

Gather all of the children around the parachute. Place a ball in the center of the parachute. Try playing these pieces from Saint-Saëns's *Carnival of the Animals* and moving the ball to the music. Be sure to listen to the music before playing it for the children.

- Kangaroos (52 seconds): stop and go bouncing
- Fossils (1:27): jerky bouncing
- The Elephant (1:35): more regular bouncing

### Listening

Listening activities that do not involve movement are also important to include in the preschool curriculum. When movement is absent, the children can concentrate totally on listening to the music. Brain research has taught us the importance of stimulating young children to develop neural pathways. If we want to develop a child's musical intelligence, then we must stimulate her musical mind through listening to music as well as through singing and moving to it (Feierabend, 1995). As in the infant and toddler rooms, music can be played during various activities. Nap time is not only a good listening time but is a good time to introduce a new piece of music to the children that may be used for movement later. The teacher should match the music to the activity and prepare the children to listen to the music. Imagery can be used to calm them and clear their minds for listening.

By singing to children, playing an instrument for them, or playing good musical recordings, teachers can help children develop their attentive-listening skill. Because preschool children accept all styles of music, music from other cultures should be included in the music-listening program for early childhood.

Children develop their preferences for a particular style of music through their listening experiences. Therefore, children should be exposed to high-quality performances in a variety of musical styles (Baney, 2002).

## Musically Nurturing Children with Special Needs

Children with special needs deserve a chance to participate in music activities and it is the law. In 1975, Public Law 94–142 mainstreamed children with medical, physical, and cognitive disabilities into music classrooms across United States. Many music teachers were unprepared in their schooling to adapt their teaching methods and materials to serve the needs of these children. In 1979, Pierre Rabischong, dean of faculty of medicine in Montpellier, France, proposed that a symposium for special music educators/music therapists and medicine be arranged (Pratt, 1991). As a result, in 1980, the International Association of Music Education for the Handicapped (IAMH) was founded by two physicians and two music educators. That same year, the association held its first symposium at the University of Montpellier, France. In 1991, this organization merged with The International Arts Medicine Association (IAMA), whose purpose was "to provide a forum for interdisciplinary, international communication between arts and health professional" (IAMA, 2002, p. 1). Some of the studies and information brought forth from this relationship of music and medicine included, for example, the effects of certain rhythms on muscular response, the effects of music on surgical patients, the relationship between cognitive and motor activities, and the responses of autistic children to music, just to mention a few (Pratt, 1991). While this research is important, the implications and information for teaching in an inclusive early childhood classroom have not reached the majority of teachers in early childhood classrooms. Currently, this organization is not a membership organization but does maintain a Web site and referral services. As the interest in arts in health care has grown, so have the number of organizations.

## A Closer Look

**Organizations for the Arts in Health Care**

- Society for the Arts in Healthcare: http://www.societyartshealthcare.org/
- International Expressive Arts Therapy Association: http://www.ieata.org/

- The American Association for Integrative Medicine: http://www.aaimedicine.com/
- American Holistic Medical Association: http://www.holisticmedicine.org/

---

Their memberships include clinicians, educators, researchers, and artists who have an interest in the relationship between the arts and medicine.

Not all special-needs children require accommodations to participate in music activities and not all special-needs children require accommodations all of the time. For those times when accommodations are required, there are some simple remedies. The very first step a teacher should take is to learn about the child. Each child is an individual with her own strengths and weaknesses. Talk with the child's parents and previous teachers and observe the child. Some children are born with a disability while others become disabled through an accident. Some disabilities are severe and some are mild. Some disabilities involve several domains of development, while others involve only one domain. Knowing the child's strengths will help determine alternative ways to facilitate the child's participation in music activities.

## Children with Physical Disabilities

The accommodations needed for children with physical disabilities depend on the severity of the disability and the part of the body affected. Some ideas for helping children with physical disabilities include:

- Make sure there is enough space for children in wheelchairs to participate in movement activities (see Figure 6–13).
- Have children in wheelchairs "dance" in their chairs, either by themselves or with a partner pushing them.
- Give them a special movement to do with their arms or heads.

**Figure 6–13** All children with special needs benefit from participation in music activities.

- Help children play instruments by, for example, attaching larger knobs on sandblocks and cymbals and using bells that attach around the wrist.
- Supply a doorstop or rubber teething ring for strumming an autoharp (Andress, 1998).
- Pair special-needs children with nondisabled partners who can help them manipulate the instruments. For example, one child can hold an instrument while the other strikes it.

- Give children an instrument to play if they cannot sing.
- Children with hearing loss can feel the vibrations even though they do not hear the sound. Let them place their hands on the vibrating surface of an instrument.
- Teach the children some songs using sign language.
- Have them move near the audio speaker so they can feel the vibrations of the music.
- If hearing loss is mild, special accommodations may not be necessary.
- Assign partners to children with visual impairments for movement activities.
- Use ropes when playing circle games to give the visually impaired child a sense of security, in the same way that ropes are used to keep children together when going for a walk.

## Children with Cognitive Disabilities

The child with cognitive disabilities may also have other affected developmental domains, since the brain is the center of all activity. They may feel frustrated as they attempt various activities during the day. Music, however, is special for them because there is not a right or wrong way to participate in music (Bailey, Cryer, Harms, Osborne, & Kniest, 1996). Some things to keep in mind when working with children with cognitive disabilities include:

- Break the instructions for an activity down into small steps.
- Teach songs with repetitive parts. Repetition is very important for children with cognitive disabilities.
- Use pictures to help the children remember the words of a song.
- All young children have difficulty following more than one instruction at a time, but children with cognitive disabilities have more difficulty with this, so request only one task at a time.

## Children with Learning Disabilities

Learning disabilities make up the largest number of exceptional children served in schools today (Bailey et al., 1996). Learning disabilities is a term that covers a wide range of behaviors. To meet each child's needs, the teacher must get to know the individual child. Children with learning disabilities may have difficulty receiving information and translating it from one or more of their senses. The more variety you use in your teaching strategies, the better chance you have to reach each individual child. Use techniques that allow them to see, hear, move, or touch sequentially or simultaneously.

Music should be a time when there is no stress on the child to perform. Music is joyful and all children deserve the opportunity to participate in music activities without judgment.

## Summary

Throughout the preschool years, children continue to develop in all domains. This may be the most important time for teachers to nurture the musical development of young children. A good music-nurturing curriculum includes many opportunities for preschool children to explore various sounds; sing and be sung to; play rhythm instruments; perform chants and nursery rhymes; experience creative and synchronized movement to music; and practice the skill of focused listening to music. Preschool teachers face a big challenge, but the integration of music in their classrooms will bring joy to their days and lasting benefits to the children they teach.

## Key Concepts

- Preschool children should continue to explore sounds and the instruments that make them.
- Preschool children should be sung with, to, and for by their teacher.
- Folk songs and nursery rhymes are good songs for young children's vocal range.
- Preschool children should be given the opportunity to move to music.
- Preschool children should begin to use focused listening with music.

## Suggested Activities

1. Make a sing-a-song storybook to share with the class.
2. Visit a child care center. List all of the songs you hear being sung in the center. How many of those songs appear on the suggested list from this textbook? How many are folk songs? How many were used to teach a concept and how many were sung for the joy of singing?
3. Learn three new chants or rhymes and perform them for your class.
4. Observe children of various preschool ages on the playground. What movement skills do they use?
5. Journal reflective question 6: If you designed a music program, what are the most important elements to include and how would you do it?

## Music Lab #6

Welcome to Lab #6! In the previous lab, we began to learn about music notation so we could understand pitches and play pitched instruments. In this lab, we

will continue that discovery process. We also begin to explore the instruments that make up the symphony orchestra.

### Activity #1: The Instruments of the Orchestra—Percussion Family

The orchestra is made up of instruments that are divided into four families: strings, woodwinds, brass, and percussion. The orchestra's seating chart is always the same in front of the conductor (see Figure 6–14). The first instrument family we will examine is the percussion family. As the conductor sees them, the percussionists are behind the left half of the string section.

Percussion instruments are the most basic of instruments. The percussion instruments used by early humans evolved into drums around 6000 BC (Iben, 1997). Drums have played an important role in many cultures. They have been used to protect African tribal royalty, communicate long distances, and lead soldiers into battle (Iben, 1997).

Anything that produces sound when it is struck or shaken can be used as a percussion instrument. Classroom rhythm instruments are percussion instruments. We know from our study of these instruments that they can be pitched or nonpitched. The pitched orchestral percussion instruments include the marimba, xylophone, bells, and tympani. With the

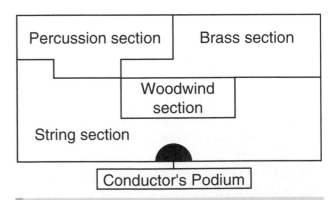

*Figure* 6–14    The orchestra is always seated in the same manner in front of the conductor.

exception of the tympani, all of these instruments have been discussed previously.

## Discovering Instruments

Tympani (see Figure 6–15): These large, tunable drums are fondly referred to as "kettledrums." The original kettledrums were the forerunner of the modern tympani. These single-headed drums were shaped like a bowl on the bottom. Arabic kettledrums that were used in Medieval Europe eventually developed into tympani drums. The first tympani were drums placed on wooden stands. Eventually, the stand and drum became a single unit. In the nineteenth century, the machine tympani was invented. This reduced the time needed to tune the instrument because it had handles placed around the head that could be turned to ensure that the head of the drum had equal tension on it all around the rim. Foot pedals for tuning were the final addition to the instrument that made it the instrument we know today. As late as the seventeenth century in Europe, tympani symbolized royalty (Iben, 1997; Kamien, 2003).

The nonpitched orchestral percussion instruments include the snare drum, bass drum, cymbals, gong, and auxiliary instruments. Previously, cymbals and auxiliary instruments were discussed as part of the classroom rhythm band. Auxiliary instruments can be any instrument from the rhythm band that the composer calls for in his composition. For example, we discovered in the music appreciation activity in Chapter 3 that Haydn used auxiliary instruments in his *Toy Symphony*.

Snare drum: This was the first instrument to be called a drum. Its ancestor was the medieval tabor. This was a double-headed drum with a snare inside. A snare is a string made of animal gut that is attached by wire under the head. When the head is struck, the snare begins to vibrate as well, giving the drum its unique sound. From the sixteenth century, the snare drum has been associated with the military and has accompanied soldiers into battle. It was not until the eighteenth century that the first snare drum was used in the orchestra.

Bass drum: The bass drum has two ancestors. The first was a Turkish drum that had a wide head, but the body or shell of the drum was not very tall if sat on the ground. This drum was known in Europe as the Turkish drum until the nineteenth century. The second ancestor had a shell that was twice as high as its head was wide. This drum was changed over the years until it resembled the Turkish drum. The bass drum was first used in the orchestra in the eighteenth century at a time when Turkish military music was popular.

Gong (see Figure 6–16): Believed to be of Middle Eastern or Southeast Asian origin, the gong first appeared in China, brought by the barbarians in the sixth century. From China, the gong spread through Asia and Africa and eventually reached Europe where it became a part of the orchestra in the nineteenth century. There are various types of gongs, but in general, the gong is a hammered metal disc of various sizes. The orchestral gong is at least 3 feet in diameter (Iben, 1997; Kamien, 2003).

**For You**

1. Select an orchestral piece for listening. Concentrate on the percussion instruments and listen to how they are used in the music.
2. Choose one of the children's books about the orchestra and read it.

*Figure 6–15* Tympani

**Figure 6–16**    Gong

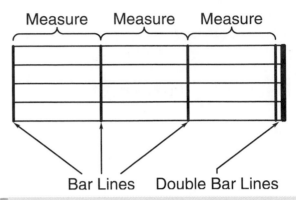

**Figure 6–17**    Example of a staff with bar lines dividing it into measures

**In the Preschool and in Out-of-School Programs**

1. Read one of the children's books about the orchestra to the children.
2. Listen to a short orchestral piece or part of one and have the children listen for the percussion instruments. You can make it a game. Have the children stand up or raise their hand when they hear a drum or gong or cymbals. Of course, you should listen to the music first because, obviously, not all orchestral pieces feature the percussion section.

## Activity #2: Learning About Measures

In the last lab, we learned that music is written on a staff that has five lines and four spaces, which are counted from the bottom up. Music is organized sound and one of the ways it is organized is by dividing the staff into sections so we can keep track of all those notes. Vertical lines called **bar lines** are drawn through the staff. A double bar line is found at the end of a piece of music to indicate that it is the end. The space between the bar lines is called a **measure** (see Figure 6–17).

**For You**
Look at the music in Appendix D. Can you count the measures in a piece of music? Professional musicians have to count the measures as the orchestra plays so they know when it is their turn to play. Sometimes there are little numbers written above the measures throughout the composition. This helps the musicians keep count, especially if they are not playing all of the time. It also helps the conductor at rehearsal. The conductor can ask the musicians to begin to play at a certain measure, so they can rehearse from a particular place in the music. The musicians do not have to count all of the measures to find the place the conductor wants to rehearse.

## Activity #3: Learning About Time Signatures

Each measure contains a certain number of beats. The number is determined by the **time signature**. Time signatures are very important, because without them, musicians cannot count the beats or play the rhythm of the music. In the last lab, we learned about the four basic notes and how they are related to each other (see Figure 6–18).

Before we can read the rhythm in music, we have to first understand time signatures. Time signatures are the set of two numbers at the beginning of each piece of music. The numbers vary, but the meaning is the same (see Figure 6–19). The top number always tells us how many beats should be in each measure.

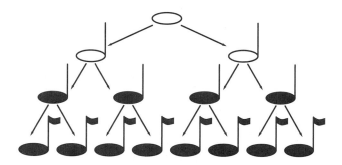

**Figure 6–18**   Relationship of notes to each other

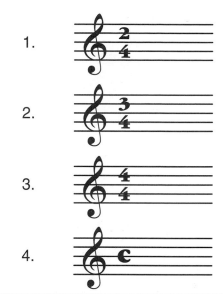

**Figure 6–20**   Examples of time signatures

Let's practice. Look at Figure 6–20. How many beats are in each measure for time signature 1? How about time signatures 2 and 3?

In time signature number 1, there should be two beats in each measure. Therefore, if you were playing music with that time signature, you would count 1, 2, and then you would be in the next measure where you would count 1, 2, again. That would be the beat of the song. We know the beat is steady and unchanging so, just because you come to a bar line, you do not stop, unless it is a double bar line. For time signature 2, the count of the beat would be 1, 2, 3, 1, 2, 3, etc. For time signature 3, the count of the beat would be counted 1, 2, 3, 4, 1, 2, 3, 4, etc.

---

# 2 = Number of beats in a measure

# 4 = Symbolizes the note that gets one beat

**Figure 6–19**   Time signature anatomy

Now, what about time signature 4? It has a *C* instead of numbers. The *C* has come to stand for **common time**. Originally, it was a musical symbol from the medieval times. It is shorthand for time signature number 3. Now, can you answer the following: How many beats are in a measure for time signature 4? If you said four, you are correct.

The bottom number does not stand for the number of anything. It is a symbol for a note. As you can see in Figure 6–21, the number 4 stands for a quarter note, the number 2 stands for a half note, the number 1 stands for a whole note, and the number 8 stands for an eighth note. Whatever the note is, quarter, half, whole, or eighth, depending on the number, that note is equal to one beat.

For now, we will just concentrate on a 4 as the bottom number. That means a quarter note gets one beat. If we were to read the time signature for Figure 6–22, we would say: Four beats to a measure and a quarter note gets one beat.

## Activity #4: Reading Rhythm

Believe it or not, you are ready to begin reading rhythms. You just have to combine what you have

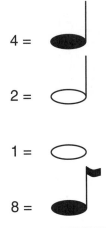

4 =

2 =

1 =

8 =

**Figure 6–21**     Bottom number of time signature and the note it symbolizes

learned about time signatures and the relationship of notes to each other. This is where we call upon our math skills. Do not worry! You do not need to know algebra!

When the bottom number of a time signature is a 4, we know that a quarter note gets one beat. If there are four beats in the measure, how many quarter notes can there be in one measure? Right, four! Each quarter note gets a beat.

**For You**

1. Look at Figure 6–22.
2. Count the beats for these four measures.
3. Next, instead of counting, we are going to chant the rhythm. Here's how: we will use a method that Kodály used. For each quarter note say "Tah." Now, chant Figure 6–22.
4. Now that you have counted and chanted these four measures, can you clap them?

Using only quarter notes could be very boring. If you were going to have only half notes in a measure, where the time signature has a bottom number of 4, how many could you have? Right, two, because each half note is equal to two quarter notes. This time look at 6-23. These measures have half notes.

**For You**

1. Count the beats for the half notes. We still have four beats in each measure, so the counting sounds the same as when we were counting quarter notes.

1.          2.          3.          4.
Tah,     tah,     tah,     tah.
Clap,   clap.   clap,   clap.

1.          2.          3.          4.
Tah,     tah,     tah,     tah.
Clap,   clap,   clap,   clap.

1.          2.          3.          4.
Tah,     tah,     tah,     tah.
Clap,   clap,   clap,   clap.

1.          2.          3.          4.
Tah,     tah,     tah,     tah.
Clap,   clap,   clap,   clap.

**Figure 6–22**     Quarter note rhythm pattern

1,2,          3,4.
Tahah,     tahah.
Clap,        shake.

1,2,          3,4.
Tahah,     tahah.
Clap,        shake.

1,2,          3,4.
Tahah,     tahah.
Clap,        shake.

1,2,          3,4.
Tahah,     tahah.
Clap,        shake.

**Figure 6–23**     Half note rhythm pattern

*Figure 6–24*    A mystery tune

**2.** This time chant the half notes. Again, we will use a syllable that Kodály taught. Because each half note is two beats, we have to make the sound longer, so say "Tah-ah" for each half note.

**3.** Now it is time to clap the measures. Only clap the first time you count the note, then shake your clutched hands once. The first measure would be clap, shake, clap, shake.

Finally, look at Figure 6–24. It combines both quarter and half notes. Can you chant the pattern? Can you clap the pattern? Do you recognize the song this rhythm comes from?

### Activity #5: Guessing the Song

The song you just guessed was "Twinkle, Twinkle, Little Star."

**For You**
Take turns with your classmates clapping the rhythms of songs and guessing what the name of the song is.

**In the Preschool and in Out-of-School Programs**
Clapping rhythmic patterns is a wonderful activity with young children. Once they have experience clapping names and songs, you can play the guessing game with them.

**1.** Clap a one-measure rhythm for the children and have them clap it back to you. You can begin circle time by leading the children in several clapping exercises to get their attention. This type of exercise helps children learn to listen carefully.

**2.** Clap names and have the children guess what name you are clapping.

**3.** When they can listen longer, you can try the first few measures of a song. School-age children will not need as much time performing rhythmic

clapping before they will be able to play the game.

## Try This One!

### Singing Instead of Talking

Here is an interesting experiment that you can try in your own classroom.

I asked a teacher in a preschool classroom to sing to the children about their painting activity. This was a new experience for the children and the teacher. The teacher was asked to use the notes of the "universal children's song" as the basis for her singing and to sing everything she wanted to say to the children. There was no prior explanation to the children. Without being asked to sing back, the children gradually responded with singing. At one point, the teacher was asking a little boy what colors he had used. She would sing, "What color is this?" When he could hear the word as sing-song in two syllables such as yellow or orange (this became or-ange), he had no problem singing back. Even the color green was not a problem, probably due to the long vowel sound. However, he had difficulty when the color was a single-syllable word with a short vowel sound, such as red or brown. He would simply say the word. The entire sung conversation did not last more than two minutes, but the child became so involved singing back and forth with the teacher that the second time she asked about the color red, he immediately came up with a musical solution. He sang the word three times in a descending chord (see Figure 6–25). By involving the child in this manner, the teacher stimulated his musical intelligence. Somewhere in his neural network, he had stored away the information

**Figure 6–25**    Chord child sang

needed to solve this musical puzzle. He was able to respond to the teacher with a pattern she had not sung for him. In addition, when he used this information, his musical network was reinforced. By reinforcing information that the brain has stored, there is a greater chance that the information will be retained. This is truly a use-it-or-lose-it situation.

## Music Appreciation

We have explored Western European music history from the Middle Ages through the twentieth century. In this lab, we will begin the music history of other cultures. We begin with a look at the music history of Native Americans. The sources for the history presented in this activity are Bierhorst (1979), Pearson Education (2005), and Spotted Eagle (1997).

## Musical History

### Native American Music

Music is an important part in the lives of Native Americans. Until the late 1960s, the music of Native Americans was unknown by many outside of the culture. What was known was usually generalized and inaccurate. Although there were museums, no books existed about Native American music. For most people, their only exposure to Native American music was the inaccurate interpretation used in films. Over the past 50 years, the music of indigenous people all over the world has been studied by **ethnomusicologists**. **Musicology** is the study of music and its effects on society; ethnomusicology is a branch of musicology that studies the music of world cultures of the past and present. After extensive listening to Native American songs, ethnomusicologists have discovered that Native American music can be grouped geographically. Although the musical characteristics of one group may occasionally blend with another group, each group has its own unique style.

The central part of all Native American music is the song. Traditionally, in the Native American community, everyone must have songs. It is believed that songs come from the Creator, often through dreams. Among the many groups, there are songs for dancing, healing, good hunting, war, and entertainment. There are also children's songs and lullabies. Songs are property that can be lent, sold, or inherited. Often, songs are given to children by a relative. That song belongs to the child for the rest of her life and no one else may use it, unless she sells her song.

Most traditional Native American songs fall into one of two categories, social and religious. Social songs are sung at different times, but particularly at powwows. Powwows provide a time for Native Americans to come together and rejoice in who they are. Among other reasons, powwows are held for celebration, for honoring elders, for birthdays, and just for fun. Religious songs are sacred and their sources are secret. All Native American songs are believed to have the power to make things happen.

Instruments are important as accompaniments to songs. The most important instrument is the drum. To some Native Americans, the drums are so important that they are given individual names and thought of as human. Other than the flute, Native American instruments cannot play melodies. They are strictly for accompaniment. Next to drums, rattles made from gourds, turtle shells, cow horns, deer hooves, and rawhide are the most prevalent. Other instruments include rasps with scrapers and snapsticks. A rasp is a piece of wood with grooves cut in it and a scraper to rub against it. A snapstick is a stick with a slit in it that makes a sound when snapped with the wrist.

Native Americans make flutes from reeds, cane, bones, bamboo, clay, and wood. Flutes are used to play love songs. Traditionally, only men play the flute. Flutes are played to steal the heart of a young girl.

Native American music has gained in popularity over the past 30 years. Books and recordings are readily available and provide much more detail than the scope of this book allows. The Resource Guide in Appendix D provides sources of recordings and books.

**For You**

1. Spend time listening to the music of Native Americans.
2. Visit with a Native American and ask if they have a song of their own they would sing to you.

**In the Early Childhood Classroom**

Share the music you listen to with all of the children in your care. Read books about Native Americans to the children. See the Resource Guide in Appendix D for suggestions.

## References

Anderson, W. M., & Lawrence, J. E. (2004). *Integrating music into the elementary classroom*, 6th ed. Belmont, CA: Thomson Schimer.

Andress, B. (1980). *Music experiences in early childhood.* Fort Worth, TX: Holt, Rinehart & Winston.

Andress, B. (1998). *Music for young children.* Clifton Park, NY: Thomson Delmar Learning.

Aronoff, F. W. (1969). *Music and young children.* New York: Holt, Rinehart & Winston.

Bailey, P., Cryer, D., Harms, T., Osborne, S., & Kniest, B. A. (1996). *Active learning for children with disabilities. A manual for use with the Active Learning Series.* Parsippany, NJ: Dale Seymour Publications.

Ball, W. (1995, Fall). Nurturing musical aptitude in children. *Dimensions, 23*(4), 19–24.

Baney, C. E. (2002). *Wired for sound: The essential connection between music and development.* Retrieved October 1, 2004, from http://www.gymboreeplayuk.com/wired.html

Bierhorst, J. (1979). *A cry from the earth: Music of the North American Indians.* Santa Fe, NM: Ancient City Press.

Bentley, A. (1966). *Musical ability in children.* New York: October House.

Berk, L. E. (2001). *Development through the lifespan.* Boston: Allyn & Bacon.

Cave, C. (1998, Summer). Early language development: Music and movement make a difference. *Early Childhood Connections: Journal of Music- and Movement-Based Learning, 4*(3), 24–29.

Children's Defense Fund. (2004). *Child care basics.* Retrieved September 11, 2004, from http://www.childrensdefense.org/earlychildhood/childcare/basics.asp

Children's Center for the Visually Impaired. (2000). *Opening new doors* [Brochure]. Kansas City, MO: Author.

Choksy, L. (1981) *The Kodály context.* Englewood Cliffs, NJ: Prentice-Hall, Inc.

Colwell, C. M. (1994). Therapeutic application of music in the whole language kindergarten. *Journal of Music Therapy, 31,* 238–247.

Davidson, L., McKernon, P., & Gardner, H. (1981). The acquisition of song: A developmental approach. In *Documentary report of the Ann Arbor Symposium: Applications of Psychology to the Teaching and Learning of Music.* Reston, VA: Music Educators National Conference.

Feierabend, J. M. (1995, Spring). Music and intelligence in the early years. *Early Childhood Connections: Journal of Music- and Movement-Based Learning, 1*(2). Retrieved September 11, 2004, from http://www.giamusic.com/music_education/feierabend/articles/intelligence.html

Feierabend, J. M. (1996, Fall). Music and movement for infants and toddlers: Naturally wonder-full. *Early Childhood Connections: Journal of Music- and Movement-Based Learning, 2*(4), 19–26.

Godeli, M. R., Santana, P. R., Souza, V. H., & Marquetti, G. P. (1996). Influence of background music on preschoolers' behavior: A naturalistic approach. *Perceptual and Motor Skills, 82,* 1123–1129.

Gordon, E. E. (1990). *A music learning theory for new-born and young children.* Chicago: G. I. A.Publications.

Gordon, E. E. (1999, September). All about audiation and music aptitudes. *Music Educators Journal, 86*(2), 41–44.

Iben, H. (1997). *The guide to symphony orchestra instruments.* Retrieved September 15, 2004, from http://www.mathcs.duq.edu/~iben/auxil.htm

The International Arts Medicine Association (IAMA). (2002). *What is IAMA?* Retrieved December 12, 2004, from http://members.aol.com/iamaorg/index.html#TOP

Kamien, R. (2003). *Music, an appreciation.* New York: McGraw-Hill.

McDonald, D. T. (1989). *Musical growth and development: Birth through six.* New York: Schirmer Books.

Music Educators National Conference, MENC. (1994). *National standards for art education.* Reston, VA. Retrieved September 24, 2004, from http://www.menc.org/publication/books/performance_standards/prek.html

Orsmond, G. I., & Miller, L. K. (1999). Cognitive, musical and environmental correlates of early music instruction. *Psychology of Music, 27,* 18–37.

Pearson Education. (2005). *Music of countries and cultures.* Retrieved February 22, 2005, from http://www.sbgmusic.com/html/teacher/reference/cultures.html

Pratt, R. R. (1991, January). Music education and medicine. *Music Educators Journal, 77(5),* 31–36.

Rainbow, N., & Owen, D. (1979). *A progress report on a three year investigation of the rhythmic ability of pre-school aged children.* Council for Research in Music Education (Bulletin No. 59), 84–86.

Rauscher, F. H., Shaw, G. L., Levine, L. J., Wright, E. L., Dennis, W. R., & Newcomb, R. L. (1997). Music training causes long-term enhancement of preschool children's spatial-temporal reasoning. *Neurological Research, 19,* 2–8.

Scott-Kassner, C. (1993). Musical characteristics. In M. Palmer & W. L. Sims (Eds.), *Music in prekindergarten: Planning and teaching* (pp. 7–13). Reston, VA: Music Educators National Conference.

Sergeant, D., & Roche, S. (1973). Perceptual shifts in the auditory information processing of young children. *Psychology of Music, 1(2),* 39–48.

Spotted Eagle, D. (1997). *Voices of Native America.* Liberty, UT: Eagle's View Publishing.

Weikart, P. S. (1988). *Key experiences in movement: A sequential approach.* Ypsilanti, MI: High/Scope Press.

Weikart, P. S. (1995, Fall). Purposeful movement: Have we overlooked the base? *Early Childhood Connections: Journal of Music- and Movement-Based Learning, 1(4),* 6–15.

Wolf, D., & Gardner, H. (1980). Beyond playing or polishing: A developmental view of artistry. In J. Hausman (Ed.), *Arts and the schools* (pp. 47–77). New York: McGraw-Hill.

Wolf, J. (2000). Sharing songs with children. *Young Children, 55(2),* 28–30.

Wolfe, D. E., & Hom, C. (1993, Summer). Use of melodies as structural prompts for learning and retention of sequential verbal information by preschool students. *Journal of Music Therapy, 30(2),* 100–118.

Zimmerman, M. P. (1984, June 28–30). *State of the art in early childhood music and research.* Paper presented at the Music in Early Childhood Conference Provo, UT. (ERIC Document Reproduction Service No. ED250068)

# Music Nurturing for Out-of-School Time (Five to Nine Years Old)

## Key Terms

| | | |
|---|---|---|
| belly dancing | rote | sitar |
| clefs | round | staves |
| koto | shakuhachi | |
| pentatonic scale | shamisen | |

Today is a teachers' work day at the local elementary school and the children who are normally at the center before and after school will be here all day long. Judy and Marcia have been planning for this day, because they want the day to be a worthwhile experience for the children. They do not want them to just be putting in time until they are picked up at the end of the day. At the same time, they do not want the children to feel as if they are in school. The day is full of activities that are enriching and interesting for this age range.

The children who attend this school-age program are in a program run by teachers who care. Programs for school-age children must employ the kind of planning that these two teachers have employed. Children of this age range are "out of school more than half of their waking hours when families are at work or otherwise unavailable. Many hours . . . half a lifetime" (Bender, Flatter, & Sorrentino, 2000, p. ix). Half of a lifetime is too much time to be wasted.

The demand for school-age care in the United States is growing at least as fast as the demand for infant and toddler care (NAEYC, 1999). With the exception of year-round school systems, most school-age children are in school 180 days and out of school 185 days a year. In addition, the child's school day is shorter than his parents' workday, which means that many children may spend up to six hours or more out-of-school on a school day while their parents are at work. Weekly, an estimated 2 million kindergarten through third-grade children spend their out-of-school time in a child care situation (National Institute on Out-of-School Time [NIOST], 2000). For most of these children, out-of-school time includes before- and after-school time, including half-day kindergarten care, summer vacation break, holiday breaks, and teacher workdays. These children are fortunate. The U.S. General Accounting Office (1997) estimated that in 2002, only 25 percent of the demand for out-of-school care would be met in urban areas. An estimated 8 million children, ages 5 to 14, are without supervised care weekly (NIOST, 2000). Communities are working to establish enough school-age care to meet the demand. For those in care, teachers need to be trained, so these children will not be wasting half a lifetime as well.

## The Role of Out-of-School Programs

Researchers have found that children who regularly attend after-school programs have higher grades and self-esteem when compared with children who have lower attendance rates (Center for Policy Alternatives, 2003). Quality out-of-school programs:

- keep school-age children safe during out-of-school hours.
- provide enrichment activities.
- provide opportunities to develop positive relationships with other children and with adults.
- offer opportunities for school-age children to explore their interests.
- offer opportunities for school-age children to develop skills.
- offer school-age children physical recreation and unstructured playtime.
- promote the development of positive character traits and life skills.
- help school-age children strengthen academic skills (NIOST, 2000).

The youngest age group in school-age care is the five-year-old group. This group usually attends kindergarten part of the day, sometimes in the morning and sometimes in the afternoon. Public school kindergarten schedules create unique planning situations for before- and after-school programs. In school districts that offer half-day kindergarten, the children may arrive before school, perhaps as early as 6:00 AM (see Figure 7–1). Some of the children will leave for morning kindergarten, while the others are left behind to wait for afternoon kindergarten. The morning kindergarten group returns around noon for lunch, at which time the afternoon kindergarten group leaves, usually returning around 3:30 PM. At that

*Figure 7–1*   Often, kindergarten children spend most of their days in out-of-school programs.

time, the group combines again, until parents arrive to take the children home. Further scheduling complications arise because some of the children only require before-school care, while others only require after-school care.

## Snapshot of a Child

### Five-Year-Olds (Kindergarten School Years)

The kindergarten child is still a preschool child, however they end up in out-of-school programs because they attend kindergarten in elementary schools and their schedules are disruptive when they are placed in preschool classrooms.

Physically, five-year-olds have a more streamlined body than 3- and 4-year-old children. It is proportioned more like an adult's body. They continue to combine skills learned earlier into increasingly more complex physical skills. Most children this age can ride a bicycle with training wheels, run with greater speed, gallop, are beginning to skip, and can throw and catch in a more mature manner. Their first permanent teeth have also arrived. The five-year-old's fine motor skills allow him to begin writing simple words and numbers, tie his shoes, draw a person with six parts, and use a knife to cut soft food.

Cognitively, the five-year-old is still in Piaget's preoperational stage. As he moves through the stage, he acquires more information with which to understand his world. Increasingly he is aware of the difference between reality and make-believe. Magical beliefs are beginning to decline. The five-year-old's abilities to classify, seriate, and conserve are increasing. The ability to recognize differences between objects and events, recall events, and describe an event are skills the five-year-old is developing. By the time he reaches his sixth birthday, the child will have accumulated a vocabulary of 10,000 words, having learned approximately 5 words a day since the age of two.

Socially and emotionally, the kindergartener is turning outward toward others. His ability to interpret, predict, and influence the emotions of others has improved. He can express empathy through his use of language. Moral rules have been learned and are adhered to in his behaviors. Gradually, five-year-old children divide themselves into gender-related groups. They take on the beliefs and behaviors of their gender. They are also gender constant, because they now grasp that gender is genital related. (The material presented in this Snapshot is from Berk, 2001.)

---

Ideally, kindergarten children should have their own room in a school-age program. Kindergarten children are closer to preschool children in their skills and thinking than they are to children in the primary grades. They need activities that offer them opportunities to function at their own level of development and to be successful. Activities for five-year-olds were included in Chapter 6, on preschool children and music. However, this chapter addresses five-year-olds as they fit into before- and after-school programs.

Teachers in before- and after-school programs should take into consideration the child's entire day when planning activities for kindergarten children in the before- and after-school program. Several things to keep in mind when planning before- and after-school activities for kindergarten children include:

- Morning activities should not tire the children. The children must be fresh for their afternoon kindergarten and not worn out from their before-school program.
- Afternoon activities should take into consideration that children who attend a morning kindergarten may arrive at the after-school program tired out from their school day.
- Before- and after-school care should not be a duplication of the kindergarten classroom.

## Primary-Grade Children in Before- and After-School Programs

The primary grades include children who are six, seven, and eight years old. Often these children are dropped off at a before-school program as early as

6:00 AM by their parents on the way to work. Others may arrive just in time for breakfast (Figure 7–2) and then transportation to school. Many programs arrange to have the children transported to school by school bus or the program transports the children. Generally, the children have left for school by 8:30 AM. By approximately 3:30 in the afternoon, the after-school group is back. The same children may not return in the afternoon, depending on the needs of the family, so the teacher may have a slightly different group in the morning and afternoon. During summer vacation and on teacher workdays, all of the children served by the program may attend. In some school districts, one day a week is a partial day, giving schoolteachers time for planning. This means that the children may return to the program on that day about 1:00 PM. It is important to understand the various scheduling combinations in order to plan for the use of music with primary children in out-of-school care settings.

## Snapshot of a Child

### Six-, Seven-, and Eight-Year-Olds (Primary School Years)

The last three years of early childhood do not exhibit the vast amount of development and growth as the first three years of early childhood, so they can be considered together.

Physically, children in this age group slowly gain weight and height. Gradually, their baby teeth are replaced by permanent teeth. As their fine motor skills improve, their writing becomes smaller and more legible and any tendency to reverse letters declines. Their drawings become more detailed and organized and as their perceptions develop, their drawings include depth cues. This age group enjoys games that have rules.

Cognitively, their thinking is more logical and is demonstrated in their ability to solve problems that require the use of classification, seriation, and conservation. They can give clear and organized directions, due to their improved understanding of spatial concepts. These children are able to plan and they use memory strategies to help them remember. Their memory strategies include rehearsal, which involves repeating the information over and over again, and organization, which involves grouping related items together. They not only use these techniques, but they also have an awareness of the connection between the level of their performance and how well they use memory strategies, pay attention, and are motivated. As they mature, their use of language improves and their vocabulary increases.

Socially and emotionally, they look at themselves in a more realistic manner. For example, they may self-evaluate regarding their academic achievements, their social relationships, and their physical abilities. Through this self-evaluation process, they develop a general feeling of their self-esteem. Friends become increasingly important and their interactions with peers

*Figure 7–2*  Playing music during breakfast and snack time helps children relax.

become more pro-social and less physically aggressive, although at this time, children begin to discriminate between who "belongs" to the group and who does not. (The material presented in this Snapshot is from Berk, 2001.)

## Activities to Enhance Musical Intelligence During Out-of-School Time

In programs that offer high-quality before- and after-school care and summer vacation care, children are given opportunities to enrich and expand their school experience. Additionally, these programs present opportunities for children to participate in activities that may be minimal at school, such as art, music, and sports (Center for Policy Alternatives, 2003).

### Exploring Sounds

The exploration of sounds is as important for school-age children as it is for infants, toddlers, preschool children, and their teachers. Through exploration of sounds, children experiment with a wide variety of sound-making materials. The information they gather through sound exploration allows them to begin experimentation with improvisation and composition.

*Sound Center*   The sound center should be located in an area that allows the children freedom to explore sound without restraint and without bothering others. School-age children can participate in any of the sound exploration activities described for teachers in the music workshops of this textbook. Primary-grade children work independently and follow simple directions without needing constant help from the teacher. However, the teacher must set up the materials and prepare the center for the children. The materials should include sound-making objects found around the home or school, pitched and nonpitched rhythm instruments, and materials with which children can create sound-making materials and instruments. In addition, teachers should provide various orchestral, folk, and keyboard instruments for the children to explore. Children of this age enjoy exploring various instruments. Occasionally, making instruments from each of the instrument families available for the children to explore not only gives the children additional sounds to explore but also allows them to become familiar with various instruments. Finally, a tape recorder with headphones should be available for children to record their playing and to accompany recorded music. The sound center should always be available for the children, but materials in the center should be changed frequently to maintain the children's interest.

Primary-age children also enjoy exploring sounds they can make with their bodies. The teacher can lead children to these discoveries by asking questions about what sound can be made with hands, feet, mouths, and fingers. Songs that lend themselves to clapping and other body sounds are good for exploring various sounds.

## Try This One!

### Singing Cups

Collect the following:

- Disposable plastic cups of various sizes
- Several strings in 2-foot lengths
- Pencil
- Water or violin rosin

1. Make a very small hole in the bottom of the cup with a pencil.
2. Thread a length of string through the hole.
3. Tie a knot in the string to keep it from coming out of the cup when you pull hard on it.
4. Wet the string with water or violin rosin.
5. Hold the cup with one hand while you grip the string between your forefinger and thumb, beginning at the top of the string near the cup.
6. Slide your fingers down the string and hear the sound made when the cup vibrates.
7. Try this with different sizes of cups and see if there is a difference in sounds made depending on the size of the cup.

# Standards and Other Professional Guidance

## What the Standards Say

The National Music Education Standards for grades K-4 include:

1. *Content Standard: Singing, alone and with others, a varied repertoire of music*

   Achievement Standard:
   Students

   a. sing independently, on pitch and in rhythm, with appropriate timbre, diction, and posture, and maintain a steady tempo.

   b. sing expressively, with appropriate dynamics, phrasing, and interpretation.

   c. sing from memory a varied repertoire of songs representing genres and styles from diverse cultures.

   d. sing ostinatos, partner songs, and **rounds.**

   e. sing in groups, blending vocal timbres, matching dynamic levels, and responding to the cues of a conductor.

2. *Content Standard: Performing on instruments, alone and with others, a varied repertoire of music*

   Achievement Standard:
   Students

   a. perform on pitch, in rhythm, with appropriate dynamics and timbre, and maintain a steady tempo.

   b. perform easy rhythmic, melodic, and chordal patterns accurately and independently on rhythmic, melodic, and harmonic classroom instruments.

   c. perform expressively a varied repertoire of music representing diverse genres and styles.

   d. echo short rhythms and melodic patterns.

   e. perform in groups, blending instrumental timbres, matching dynamic levels, and responding to the cues of a conductor.

   f. perform independent instrumental parts while other students sing or play contrasting parts.

3. *Content Standard: Improvising melodies, variations, and accompaniments*

   Achievement Standard:
   Students

   a. improvise "answers" in the same style to given rhythmic and melodic phrases.

   b. improvise simple rhythmic and melodic ostinato accompaniments.

   c. improvise simple rhythmic variations and simple melodic embellishments on familiar melodies.

   d. improvise short songs and instrumental pieces, using a variety of sound sources, including traditional sounds, nontraditional sounds available in the classroom, body sounds, and sounds produced by electronic means.

4. *Content Standard: Composing and arranging music within specified guidelines*

   Achievement Standard:
   Students

   a. create and arrange music to accompany readings or dramatizations.

   b. create and arrange short songs and instrumental pieces within specified guidelines.

   c. use a variety of sound sources when composing.

5. *Content Standard: Reading and notating music*

   Achievement Standard:
   Students

   a. read whole, half, dotted half, quarter, and eighth notes and rests in 2/4 , 3/4 , and 4/4 meter signatures.

   b. use a system (that is, syllables, numbers, or letters) to read simple pitch notation in the treble clef in major keys.

   c. identify symbols and traditional terms referring to dynamics, tempo, and articulation and interpret them correctly when performing.

   d. use standard symbols to notate meter, rhythm, pitch, and dynamics in simple patterns presented by the teacher.

6. *Content Standard: Listening to, analyzing, and describing music*

   Achievement Standard:
   Students

   a. identify simple music forms when presented aurally.

   b. demonstrate perceptual skills by moving, by answering questions about, and by describing aural examples of music of various styles representing diverse cultures.

## Standards and Other Professional Guidance   *(Continued...)*

**c.** use appropriate terminology in explaining music, music notation, music instruments and voices, and music performances.

**d.** identify the sounds of a variety of instruments, including many orchestra and band instruments, and instruments from various cultures, as well as children's voices and male and female adult voices.

**e.** respond through purposeful movement to selected prominent music characteristics or to specific music events while listening to music.

**7.** *Content Standard: Evaluating music and music performances*

Achievement Standard:
Students

**a.** devise criteria for evaluating performances and compositions.

**b.** explain, using appropriate music terminology, their personal preferences for specific musical works and styles.

**8.** *Content Standard: Understanding relationships between music, the other arts, and disciplines outside the arts*

Achievement Standard:
Students

**a.** identify similarities and differences in the meanings of common terms used in the various arts.

**b.** identify ways in which the principles and subject matter of other disciplines taught in the school are interrelated with those of music.

**9.** *Content Standard: Understanding music in relation to history and culture*

Achievement Standard:
Students

**a.** identify by genre or style aural examples of music from various historical periods and cultures.

**b.** describe in simple terms how elements of music are used in music examples from various cultures of the world.

**c.** identify various uses of music in their daily experiences and describe characteristics that make certain music suitable for each use.

**d.** identify and describe roles of musicians in various music settings and cultures.

**e.** demonstrate audience behavior appropriate for the context and style of music performed.

From *National Standards for Arts Education.* Copyright © 1994 by Music Educators National Conference (MENC). Used by permission. The complete National Arts Standards and additional materials relating to the Standards are available from MENC—The National Association for Music Education, 1806 Robert Fulton Drive, Reston, VA 20191.

## ▌Try This One!

### Teacher-Led Sound Improvisation

After the children have sufficient experience exploring sounds on their own, the teacher can facilitate an experience in improvisation.

**1.** Choose a small group of no more than four children who have shown interest in the rhythm instruments.

**2.** Play a beat on a drum for the children. For example, play a measure of four quarter note beats several times. (If you count—1, 2, 3, 4, 1, 2, 3, 4— the children will hear how long each measure is.)

**3.** Ask the children to figure out a short rhythm to play with the beat on their choice of rhythm instrument. You can demonstrate what you mean by playing one of these two rhythms.
  **a.** quarter (note), quarter (note), two eighths (notes), quarter (note)
  **b.** quarter (note), two eighths (notes), quarter (note), quarter (note)

Figure 7–3 illustrates one measure of each rhythm. These rhythms are one-measure rhythms that are repeated over and over. Practice them before you play them for the children the first time. You can also clap the rhythms for all of the children to participate with you. Clapping helps the children feel the rhythm.

Tah,    tah,    tee - tee - tah.    Tah    tee - tee - tah    tah.

*Figure 7–3*    Rhythm Examples

Getting the children started on a rhythm may be the most difficult part of this activity. On a previous day, you may want to spend time with them playing and improvising rhythms together.

4. Each child should play his rhythm while the teacher beats the drum, just for practice.

5. After each child has the chance to practice, ask the children to be quiet while the teacher begins with a steady drumbeat.

6. One by one, each player should begin to play his rhythm when the teacher nods until everyone is playing together.

7. This activity may require repetition until the children begin to experiment on their own.

8. Going through this exercise with the children, gives them a formula to begin their own improvisations.

9. This is also a good way to introduce them to jazz. (Suggested book: Weatherford, C. B. (2003). *The Sound That Makes Jazz*. New York: Walker & Company).

## Rhythmic Rhymes and Chants

Chanting rhymes continue to be an enjoyable activity for primary-grade children. Although they still enjoy some of the same rhymes they learned as preschool children, primary- grade children are able to remember longer and more complicated rhymes. A wonderful source of rhymes and chants for this age group are jump rope rhymes and hand clap games. These can be taught as an impromptu beginning to a group gathering. Once the children learn the rhyme, rhythm instruments and body sounds, such as clapping and stomping can be added for interest. Teach

children to use the chant on the playground for rope jumping as in Figure 7–4. Children will enjoy the chants and hand-clapping games and, in return, their ability to feel the beat and rhythm of music will be enhanced. The Resource Guide in Appendix D lists sources of these chants.

## Try This One!

### "Johnny Over the Ocean"

Children enjoy saying jump rope chants such as "Teddy Bear, Teddy Bear" and "The Lady with the Alligator Purse." Here is another chant they will enjoy. Begin the rhyme by beating a hand drum. Keep the beat going throughout the chant. Have the children select rhythm instruments to accompany the chant

*Figure 7–4*    Jump rope chants are good rhythmic exercises.

once they know it; you can also teach them the hand claps in parentheses.

> Johnny over the ocean, (Slap thighs, clap, slap thighs, clap)
> Johnny over the sea. (Slap thighs, clap right hand with partner's right, slap thighs, clap left hand with partner's left)
> Johnny broke a milk bottle (Slap thighs, clap, slap thighs, clap)
> Blamed it on me. (Slap thighs, clap right hand with partner's right, slap thighs, clap left hand with partner's left)
> I told Ma, (Slap thighs, clap, slap thighs, clap)
> Ma told Pa. (Slap thighs, clap right hand with partner's right, slap thighs, clap left hand with partner's left)
> Johnny got a lickin' (Slap thighs, clap, slap thighs, clap)
> Haw, Haw, Haw! (Clap both hands with partner's hands three times)

## Singing in Out-of-School Time

Singing is an activity through which children can learn while enjoying themselves. Through singing children can learn about musicianship. They also learn to use music to express their feelings. Songs teach them about their own culture and history as well other cultures. When teachers choose songs wisely, the children's vocabulary and language skills are expanded (Campbell & Scott-Kassner, 1995). Singing is also an activity in which all of the children can participate.

## Including Children with Special Needs

### Singing with Special-Needs Children

Some children with special needs may not be able to sing, but they still enjoy the experience of being in a group of children who are singing. They can be given a special role by having them play a rhythm instrument. They will probably not play with the beat, but they will feel a part of the group.

Children who are hearing impaired may also have difficulty singing, depending on the level of impairment. Those children who are studying a sign language can be asked to sign the words of the song for the other children to learn.

Singing can be used as a transition aid as children are moved from the bus in the afternoon into the after-school classroom. Children are arriving at the program after a school day, which has made demands on them. Singing can help the children begin to relax and yet maintain discipline as they move into the afternoon program. In addition, singing can be used at any time during the morning or afternoon of the before- and after-school program as a large-group, small-group, or individual activity. Teachers in school-age programs must be sensitive to the mood and energy level of the children as they arrive in the morning or afternoon and reflect that mood and energy in the music selected.

Due to the fluctuation in the class attendance as children arrive in the morning and leave in the afternoon at various times, singing is a good activity for arrival and dismissal times since it does not involve a tangible material to put away or get out. Children also enjoy this activity, whether they are active participants or not. During the summer vacation program and on teacher workdays, longer and more intricate singing activities that involve teaching new songs and using instruments for accompaniment can be planned.

When children sing a song, they tend to sing it the way the song was first sung for them (Campbell & Scott-Kassner, 1995). Therefore, teachers must keep some things in mind when presenting a new song to children.

- Sing in tune and use the correct rhythm of the song. Children will learn the song the way in which it is sung.
- Sing the song in the correct style and voice quality. If the song is a lullaby, then it should be sung in that style and in a voice that would coax a baby to sleep.
- Use good posture. Sit or stand straight, but not stiff. The body is the instrument and it should be in the correct position.

- Reflect the mood of the song and tell the story. If children are to learn expressive singing, they need a good model.
- Use facial expressions, gestures, and the right energy level to fit the song. This is important to gaining the children's interest in the song.

*The Primary Child's Singing Voice*    Children in the primary grades continue to develop their singing voices. Most of these children can sing in tune, at least better than they did as preschool children. Those who cannot sing in tune will develop the ability by the end of second grade if they are given the chance to sing every day (Campbell & Scott-Kassner, 1995).The same techniques described in Chapter 6 to help children find their singing voice can be used with primary-grade children as well. Children should never be labeled as a nonsinger. Generally, the problem is not with the voice, but with the ear. Often, the child who cannot sing in tune needs to train his ear by listening to his own voice.

With each passing year, the primary child's vocal range gradually widens, as shown in Figure 7–5. Usually, first graders (six- and seven-year olds) can sing in tune within the vocal range of d to b. Second graders (seven- and eight-year-olds) can sing an octave in tune, usually C–c' or d–d'. Third graders (eight- and nine-year-olds) have a range of B–e. Not all of the children will be able to sing the complete range of their age group. Teachers should choose songs that do not use the highest or lowest notes of the vocal ranges very often (Campbell & Scott-Kassner, 1995).

*Appropriate Songs for Out-of-School Time*    As with songs chosen for younger children, songs for the out-of-

school program should be chosen for their musical, textual, and developmental appropriateness (Campbell & Scott-Kassner, 1995). Some of the same songs sung with preschool children can be used in the out-of-school program, such as "If You're Happy." Other songs that can be used for young primary children include: "Johnny Works with One Hammer," "Ring Around the Rosies," "London Bridge Is Falling Down," "The Bear Went Over the Mountain," and "Paw, Paw Patch." Teachers should be careful to select songs that the children will not consider "baby" songs. A visit to the music program in the school where the children attend is a good way to become familiar with the songs the children are learning. As their friends become more important to them, singing is a way for primary children to socialize and they enjoy combining their voices with others in a communal songfest.

The primary years are a perfect time to introduce songs that children will eventually learn to sing as a round. A round is a song for which one group begins the song, such as "Row, Row, Row Your Boat," and after that group reaches a certain point in the song, another group begins the song. Normally, this type of singing is begun in the third grade. However, in order to perform a round, the children must know the song very well. By the end of the school year, simple rounds may be sung by having the first and second graders sing a familiar song together and the third graders sing the second part.

Children enjoy singing. When teachers enjoy singing and enthusiastically lead children in this activity, singing will enrich the out-of-school time of primary children. When teachers choose to teach songs that reflect the children's culture, they are bestowing a gift of many enjoyable moments

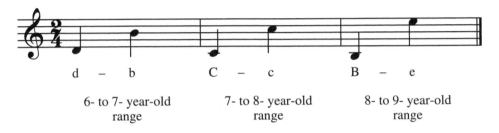

d  –  b          C  –  c          B  –  e

6- to 7- year-old          7- to 8-year-old          8- to 9- year-old
range                     range                    range

**Figure 7–5**  Vocal Ranges of Primary Children's Voices

## A Closer Look

### Men Singing for Children.

Due to the number of single mothers and long work hours of many fathers in this country, many children do not have a consistent male role model in their lives. Men who work in schools and in the care of young children play an important role in the lives of many children. Men are actively recruited for these teaching positions. It is therefore important to address this subject.

During early childhood, some children may have trouble matching the tones sung by men, because men sing an octave below children. Some children may try to sing in the lower octave. Other children are confused enough by the sound that they try to

sing pitches somewhere in between the pitches they should be singing and the pitches the male voice sings. When working with children in early childhood, men should listen to the children and verify that they are singing in their head voices and not in their chest as discussed in Chapter 6. Additionally, teachers should pay the same attention to the children's singing voices when they use recordings of men's voices. By the fourth grade, children have enough experience that they can reproduce the male voice sound in the correct register and this is not such a problem. (The material presented in this Closer Look is from Campbell & Scott-Kassner, 1995.)

that children can carry with them throughout their lives.

## Moving to Music in Out-of-School Time

By the time school-age children arrive at the out-of-school program, they have usually sat most of their day and are ready to move. It is the teacher's job to channel the children's desire to move into a worthwhile activity. Allowing the children time to move and have a snack before attempting to complete homework assignments will help settle them into their assignments much faster. This thinking may have to be explained to parents who demand that their child not do anything until their homework is completed.

## A Closer Look

### Appropriate Songs for Out-of-School Time

When choosing songs for out-of-school time, consider the interests of the children and their ages. Additionally, songs should be chosen that could be built on in the future, such as songs to be used as rhymes. Camp songs consist of good selections for this age group.

"Hokey Pokey"
"Go Tell Aunt Rhody"
"This Old Man"
"Row, Row, Row Your Boat"
"Hey, Ho, Nobody Home"
"Kookaburra"
"Down by the Station"
"The Bee and Pup"
"Scotland's Burning"

"Bingo"
"I Bought Me a Cat"
"Clap, Clap, Clap Your Hands"
"Home on the Range"
"Little Wheel A-Turning"
"Pick a Bale of Cotton"
"Peanut Song"
"Riding in a Buggy"
"Tinga Layo"
"This Land Is Your Land"
"Sweetly Sings the Donkey"
"White Coral Bells"
"Tell Me Why"
"We're All Together Again"
"Yankee Doodle"

Instead of allowing them to run out of control on the playground, the teacher can lead the children in movement and music exercises that will promote their physical well-being and allow them to get rid of their tensions before settling down to homework and yet maintain enough structure to lead them into doing their homework. All of the children should be encouraged to move after spending their day sitting most of the time. Additionally, this time allows children to discover the movements they can make with their bodies. These discoveries will build their repertoire of movement and prepare them for longer and more intricate music and movement experiences when they are at the program all day.

Games such as Simon Says can begin a session. Movement to fast music, such as running or jumping in place, can follow. Next, have the children imagine that they are something, such as an inanimate object, or have them pretend they are walking in fog or rain or mud. All of this can be accompanied by music. Finally, have a cooling-off exercise that will calm the children down and prepare them for homework time. Use relaxing music to have them imagine that they are melting, floating, or lying on their back watching clouds float overhead.

## ▌ Try This One!

### Do the Limbo

Have children hold a broom while the rest of the class does the limbo to music from the Caribbean. See the Resource Guide in Appendix D for suggested music.

---

When children spend the full day in the program, the teacher can plan movement activities that require a longer time. Interspersing sections of the activity throughout the day, will allow the teacher to complete the full activity without the children losing interest.

Children who are not used to moving in a group may feel self-conscious with this activity. Therefore, the teacher needs to be sensitive to those children and give them the support they require to feel enabled. However, most schools provide physical education classes in which the children participate, so this may not be a problem.

## Listening to Music in Out-of-School Time

Until the age of nine, when friends become an influence, children are accepting of various styles of music. That makes early childhood a good time to introduce children to many different styles of music and develop their active listening. Additionally, using music to set a mood in the classroom is helpful. For example, in the morning, some children may still be sleepy when they arrive. Playing quiet music sets a mood that allows those children a chance to rest before eating breakfast and going to school. This is particularly necessary when children arrive at the program as early as 6:00 AM and have at least two hours before they go to school, where they may be under pressure throughout the day.

Many programs have a period during the afternoon for homework completion. Playing music such as Mozart's *Sonata for Two Pianos in D*, K 448, may prove relaxing and more conducive to good study habits than a teacher trying to maintain quiet. This composition happens to be the one used by Drs. Rauscher and Shaw in their research with college students in 1993. That research project was one of several that initiated the term Mozart effect. I am not suggesting that playing this music will make the children smarter or that their homework will be better, I merely suggest that the music might be tried at homework time to create an atmosphere.

As mentioned above, during the primary years focused listening should be encouraged. A listening center should be available to children where they can listen to good music in a variety of styles. Tape recorders or CD players with headphones facilitate focused listening.

## ▌ Try This One!

### Music Detectives Club

Prepare cards with questions about several pieces of music in the listening center. Prepare checklists for the children to listen for specific portions of the music. For example, for Haydn's *Toy Symphony*, children can check off when they hear the toy trumpet or the bird whistle or the ratchet. After several children have listened, the teacher can gather those children to discuss what they heard. Together they can listen to the piece of music, pointing out certain features to those who did not hear it when they listened alone. Take Mozart's *Ah vous dirais-je Maman* for another example. Have children listen to this piece and count the number of variations of "Twinkle, Twinkle Little Star" they hear.

Numerous compositions can be used for this purpose. Many twentieth-century composers used folk songs within their compositions, which children can listen for after they have been taught the song.

## Music Projects in Out-of-School Time

Many ongoing music activities should be made available to children. Several activities in which children can participate as they wish include:

- The Rhythm Band Section: Provide an area where children can make their own instruments and play them. Supply a recorder so they can record their music. Additionally, supply music from cultures that use rhythm instruments, such as Africa and the Caribbean.
- Music and Art Area: Provide children with recorders and headphones so they can listen to a variety of music as they paint.
- Name That Composer Center: Provide children with books about a composer and make the composer's music available on recordings. Change the composer and music in the center as the use of the center dictates.
- Musical Computer: Set up musical programs on the computer for the children to use. Some programs, such as Finale's *Print Music*, allow children to hear their own music as they compose it and then print it out.
- Singing Club: Provide a karaoke machine and children's sing-along CDs for those who enjoy singing. Be sure to select songs that will not

strain the young child's voice, as many popular songs will do.

These are just a few of the activities that can provide musical nurturing during out-of-school time. Many schools have music programs that teach the children fundamental music education. The job of the out-of-school program is not to teach music, but to enhance what the school has already taught. Collaborating with the school music teacher will help out-of-school teachers meet this challenge.

Another way in which out-of-school programs can enrich and enhance children's music education is to provide instruction on musical instruments. Children of this age may be ready to begin lessons on the guitar or the piano. Making instruction available to those who want it also provides a service to the parents. By providing this service while the child is at the out-of-school program, the parent does not have to take the child to lessons after work. This could be a time savings of at least an hour and a half, giving the parent and child more quality time together.

## Summary

Nearly 8 million school-age children spend half of their waking hours unsupervised by adults. An additional 2 million spend much of the same time in out-of-school care settings. These children will also be wasting this precious time if early childhood teachers are not trained to stimulate these children through enhancing activities. Out-of-school time should not duplicate the school day. Children who have spent the day sitting at a desk require time to exercise and enjoy interesting activities. Music can play a large part in the out-of-school program. Music can be used to help children move and exercise. It can be used to calm children after a stressful day. And, music can be a part of the program for its own sake. Children in out-of-school programs should be presented activities that will extend their school learning. In regard to music, this means that children should be given the chance to learn to play an instrument, sing, listen to and write music. Out-of-school program settings are the ideal settings for nurturing children with music.

## Key Concepts

- Children in out-of-school programs need enriching activities that enhance and extend what they learned in school.
- Often, children arrive at the out-of-school program after a stressful day and need time to calm down.
- Children need time to exercise in out-of-school programs.
- Music can fulfill many needs in out-of-school programs.
- Out-of-school programs are good places for children to learn to play instruments.

## Suggested Activities

1. Visit an out-of-school program. List the activities in which you observe the children engaged. Are any of the activities connected to music? If you were the director of the program, would you change anything? If yes, how would you change it? If no, why?
2. Interview a six- to nine-year-old child. Ask the child what they do after school. Ask them what they would like to do. Ask them if they would like to learn to play an instrument and, if yes, which one and why.
3. Interview a parent of a school-age child. Ask them what they worry about in regard to their child's out-of-school time. Ask if their child is in an out-of-school program. Ask if their child is taking lessons on an instrument.
4. Journal reflective question 7: How would you encourage a shy child to join in on a movement activity?

## Music Lab #7

Welcome to Music Lab #7! In this lab, we will explore the instruments of the string family. We will also continue to learn about music notation in preparation for playing pitched instruments. Our exploration of music in world cultures takes us to the Middle East and Asia.

### Activity #1: The Instruments of the Orchestra—String Family

The first type of string instrument was simply a stick with a string that ran from one end to the other (Iben, 1997). This instrument is still played in parts of Africa and South America. About 5,000 years ago, the harp and lyre appeared in Egypt and Sumeria and a box with one or more strings attached were used in ancient Egypt, Greece, and India (Iben, 1997). During the tenth century, for the first time a bow was used on a lute. The lute is a pear-shaped instrument with strings like a guitar. It is normally played by plucking the strings. From this experiment, the modern string family was developed. During the Baroque Era, the orchestra evolved. This performing group was centered around the instruments of the string family (Kamien, 2003). In the Classical Era, the strings continued to be the most important group of instruments in the orchestra (Kamien, 2003). However, by the Romantic Era, the other orchestral families began taking on more prominent roles in the music (Kamien, 2003).

The string section of the orchestra is made up of four instruments: the violin, viola, cello (or violoncello), and the double bass viol (or the bass fiddle or bass). They all consist of a hollow body and a tailpiece. Gut or wire strings are stretched from a bridge at one end of the body to the end of the tailpiece. The bridge lifts the strings off the body so they can vibrate. (We have learned what happens when we touch a vibrating instrument—it stops vibrating and so does the sound.) The long tailpiece is a fingerboard for the musician to press on the string, moving her fingers up and down to lengthen or shorten the string, which changes the pitch of the tone. The string instrument can be played by plucking the strings or with a bow. The bow is a curved stick that is strung with horsehair. The bow is pulled across the strings, making them vibrate. The four string instruments differ in size, which affects their range and tone color or timbre.

## Discovering Musical Instruments

- Violin: The violin is the smallest instrument in the string family (see Figure 7–6). Because it is the smallest, the strings are shorter and thinner, making it the highest-sounding instrument in the family. For more than 300 years, the violin has

remained unchanged. More music has been written for this instrument than any other instrument in the orchestra.
- Viola: The viola is the second-smallest instrument in the string family. Around 1550, string instrument makers began to make instruments that corresponded with the human voice. The viola was the alto-tenor of the violin family. During the seventeenth century, composers used the viola to add a mellow tone to their compositions. Today, the viola is used for harmonizing with the melody.
- Violoncello: The violoncello or cello was developed in the 1500s by Andrew Amati. The name comes from *violone*, which means "big viola." The cello became a favorite solo instrument during the 1700s. In addition to the body and tailpiece, the cello has a peg on the bottom that allows the musician to sit a chair with the cello sitting on its peg between the musician's knees. The large body of the cello makes it a very resonante instrument.
- Double Bass Viol - Instrument makers first tried to create the double bass using the violin as the pattern, but this did not work. In the 1500s, the bass was patterned, with slight changes, from the violoncello, hence the name, double bass viol. The bass is six feet tall and the musician must stand to play (see Figure 7–7). The strings are very thick and do not allow for a wide range of expression. Occasionally, a composer has written a solo for the bass. This instrument is also used in jazz assembles. (The material for this section is from Iben, 1997.)

### Activity #2: Learning More About Reading Rhythms

In Lab #6, you learned how to read rhythms when using quarter and half notes. Now, we will practice using eighth and whole notes. For our purposes, we will continue to use the number 4 as the bottom number of the time signature. Remember, that means a quarter note is equal to one beat.

Using only quarter and half notes for rhythm is almost as boring as using quarter notes alone. These notes are rather slow in tempo. For example, if you

*Figure 7–6*    Violin

*Figure* 7–8    Example of Beamed Eighth Notes

*Figure* 7–7    Double Bass Viol

are playing a drum or triangle, you only strike it once for each note. That means for the half note, you have to count two beats (when the bottom number of the time signature is 4) before striking the instrument again. The quarter note is twice as fast. You would strike the instrument on every beat if you were playing quarter notes and the bottom number of the time signature is 4. The half note's head is white. White notes are slower than black notes. Notes with stems are faster than notes without stems. That brings us to the eighth note. Because notes with stems and flags are faster than notes with only stems. If you were to give a child a flag or streamer, they might run with it to see it fly. Well, that is what the eighth note does, it runs. When I teach young children, I tell them that the eighth note runs so fast that

sometimes it gets its flag tangled up with another eighth note (see Figure 7–8). We say these eighth notes are beamed together.

The eighth note is twice as fast as the quarter note. Therefore, if the quarter note receives one beat, the eighth note receives only a half beat, so when you count it, you count the beat and then add "and" in between. Example: 1, and, 2, and, 3, and, 4, and. Now, let's look at Figure 7–9. I have mixed in some quarter notes to keep the exercise interesting.

**For You**

1. Count the beats using eighth and quarter notes. There are still four beats in each measure.
2. Chant the rhythm. Again, we will use a syllable that Kodály taught. Because each eighth note is equal to half a beat, we have to make the sound shorter than a quarter note. For eighth notes that are joined together, say "Tee-tee" for the pair or for each beat.
3. Clap the measures. Clapping eighth notes is faster, because you will clap twice for each beat. It will help if you count the beats, like you did above, as you clap.

Finally, we come to the whole note. You have probably guessed that this is the longest note of the four basic notes. It is played four times as long as the quarter note. If there are four beats in a measure,

*Figure* 7–9    Practice reading rhythms with eighth and quarter notes.

how many whole notes can be in one measure? Right, 1! Look at Figure 7–10.

**For You**

1. Count the beats in Figure 7–10 using whole notes. There are still four beats in each measure.
2. Chant the rhythm. Again, we will use a syllable that Kodály taught. Because the whole note is four times longer than a quarter note, we have to make the sound four times longer when we chant the note. For each whole note say "Tah–ah–ah–ah."
3. Clap the rhythm. Clap the first time you count the note, then shake your clutched hands three times. The first measure would be clap, shake, shake, shake.

4. Look at Figure 7–11. These examples contain all four of the notes we have been counting. Count the beats in the examples in Figure 7–11.
5. Look at Figure 7–12. Clap and chant the rhythm in this example.

## Activity #3: Playing the Keyboard

Can you guess the name of the song in Figure 7–12? It was "Hot Cross Buns". Now, like magic, you are going to play hot cross buns by using only the rhythm pattern from Figure 7–12 and a keyboard.

**For You**

1. Look at your keyboard.
2. Find a group of three black keys.

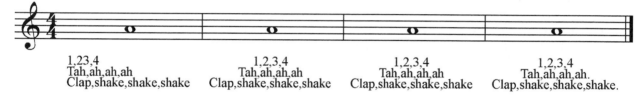

*Figure 7–10*   Practice reading rhythms with whole notes.

*Figure 7–11*   (a-c) Rhythm-Reading Practice

**Figure 7-12**   Mystery Rhythm

**3.** Look at Figure 7–13. Here you will find the same rhythm as in Figure 7–12. The only difference is that I have added words under each note; high, middle, low. High stands for the highest note of the three black keys, middle, of course, the middle, and low the lowest. The highest note is the black key to the right of the middle key. The lowest note is the black key to the left of the middle key.

**4.** Using those words as your guide, play the song, using the three-black-key group of a keyboard instrument. Once you have mastered that, you can sing the words of the song, while you play the song.

**In the Early Childhood and Before- and After-School Program**

Teach the children to play "Hot Cross Buns" by rote. Teaching by rote means to teach it through repetition. Use the method you used above to learn how to play the song.

## Try This One!

Share one of the following books with the children and then teach them "Hot Cross Buns" while you play it on the keyboard! If you are using a piano, be sure to select three black keys just to the right of the middle. On a small electric keyboard, you will probably need to select three black keys to the far left. By doing this, you should be within the singing range of the children. Try this before you have the children in front of you because you want to make sure you select notes that they can sing.

Morris, A. (1993). *Bread, Bread, Bread.* New York: HarperTrophy

Paulsen, G., and Paulsen, R. W. (1998). *The Tortilla Factory.* Dallas, TX: Voyager Books

Romendik, I. (2003). *The Musical Muffin Man.* Los Angeles: Straight Edge Press

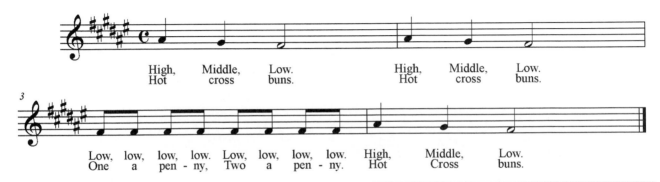

**Figure 7-13**   "Hot Cross Buns" on the Three Black Keys

Wing, N. (1996). *Jalapeño Bagels*. New York: Athenium
dePaola, T. (1996). *Tony's Bread: An Italian Folktale*.
   New York: Putnam Publishing

## Activity #4: Learning About Music Notation: Clefs

If you want to play music on a keyboard, or any other instrument, you have to learn to read the notes on the staff. Let's review: A staff has five lines and four spaces. We have been reading rhythms placed on the staff, but we have not paid any attention to the pitch of the notes. You may have heard about the lines and spaces having names. They are named after the letters in the musical alphabet. The question is: how do you know the name of a line or space? The answer is: by knowing the clef sign. There are different clef signs (see Figure 7–14). The clef sign appears on the staff right before the time signature and at the beginning of each staff.

*Note*: The time signature appears only at the beginning of a piece of music or, it might appear in the middle of a composition if the composer wants to change the time signature. Don't worry! For nearly all music you will use in early childhood education, there will only be one time signature and it will appear at the beginning of the piece of music.

Now, back to clef signs. When there is only one staff used in a piece of early childhood music the clef sign will be the treble clef. Treble stands for the highest pitches. Since children's voices are high, the

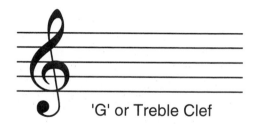

**Figure 7–15**    Example of a G Clef

songs we sing with them will use the treble clef to accommodate their singing range. The treble clef is also called the "G clef." This information is important because this is how the lines and spaces get their names. Look at Figure 7–15.

The G clef is a curvy thing, but notice where the last curve on the clef is. It curves around the second line of the staff. It always curves around that line, because the treble or G clef is an immovable clef. In other words, it is always drawn in exactly the same place. Can you guess what the name of that line is? Right, G! The treble or G clef tells us which line is G. This G is the one right above middle C on the piano keyboard. (Refer to Lab #5 for information about middle C.) Now that you know where G is, you can find out the names of all the other lines and spaces. You merely go forward or backward through the musical alphabet, just as we did when we named the keys on the piano keyboard after we knew where to find D. (See Figure 7–16.)

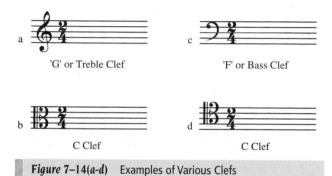

**Figure 7–14(a–d)**    Examples of Various Clefs

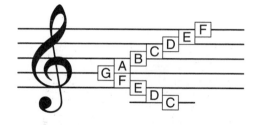

**Figure 7–16**    Names of Lines and Spaces on the G Clef Staff

## A Closer Look

Notice that middle C has it own little ledger line below the staff (see Figure 7–18). Not only is middle C in the middle of the piano keyboard, but in early music notation, it was actually written on a line in the middle of the two staves, hence, the name middle C.

The notes on the treble staff correspond to notes on the keyboard that are on the right-hand side of the piano keyboard. These are the higher notes. All of the songs in Appendix D only use one staff, the treble staff with a G or treble clef.

However, piano music is normally written using two **staves** (plural for *staff*) as in Figure 7–17. In general, the right hand plays the notes on the treble staff and the left hand plays the notes on the bass or bottom staff. Notice that there is a different clef for this staff, so the lines and spaces of the bass or F clef staff have different names. You will be happy to know that for our purposes, one staff is all you will use!

### Activity # 5: Playing Music Written on the Treble Clef

**For You**

1. Look at the piece of music in Figure 7–19. It is "Hot Cross Buns." This time, the notes are actually written on the treble staff the way you will play them. You will not use any black keys, only white keys. What note do you start on? Right, E! It is two white keys below the G marked by the treble clef. (See Figure 7–16 for help.)
2. Find E on your keyboard.
3. Put the third finger of your right hand on E.

**Figure 7–18**  Middle C

4. Now, play D with your second finger and middle C with your thumb. Try it.
5. Now you are ready to play the song by reading the notes.
6. Remember the rhythm and begin on E. This is the same as when you played on the black keys; it is just another key and one you can read at this point on the treble clef staff.

## Music Appreciation

This lab's musical journey takes us to the Middle East and Asia. This area of the world is rich in musical traditions that can only be touched on briefly. The Resource Guide in Appendix D lists sources and music that support further exploration into this fascinating music. The sources for the history presented in this activity are International Academy of Middle Eastern Dance (2005), Manas (2002), Pappas (2002), Pearson Education (2005), and Wikipedia (2005).

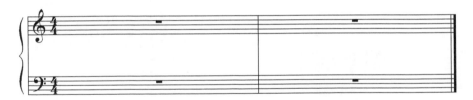

**Figure 7–17**  Example of Two Staves

## Making Musical Instruments

### Flower Pot Bells

*For You*

Collect the following:

- Clay flower pots of various sizes.
- Mallets of various types.

1. Line up the flower pots according to size.
2. Using the mallet, gently strike each one to hear the sound.
3. Try to find the pitches you would need to play "Hot Cross Buns" (you need only three.)
4. Try to find enough different sizes to be able to form an entire scale (do-re-mi, etc).

### *For the Preschool and Out-of-School Programs*

1. Once you have identified the best pots to use, have the children select their own pots.
2. Paint the pots.
3. Have the children play their pots.

### *Hanging Pot Instrument*

1. Thread a rope through the pots.
2. Tie knots at intervals so the pots stay in one spot on the rope.

3. Allow the pots to cover each other just a bit.
4. Hang up the pots and play by gently striking with a mallet.

### Flower Pot Wind Chime

1. Make three or four bell clappers out of clay.
2. Unbend a paper clip and bend it into a U-shape.
3. Insert the two ends of the U well into the clapper, leaving about a 1/4-inch loop on one end.
4. Allow the clappers to thoroughly dry.
5. Select three or four tiny clay flower pots.
6. Decorate the pots.
7. Tie one end of a piece of string to the hook on the clapper.
8. Thread the string from the inside out through the hole in the flower pot.
9. Tie a knot on the outside of the pot, leaving enough string to allow the clapper to swing.
10. Repeat the same procedure with each flower pot and clapper.
11. Attach the loose end of each string to a chain or other rope, spacing the flower pots on the chain so they do not touch.
12. Hang your wind chime.

## Music History

### Music of the Middle East and Asia

*Music of the Middle East*   The Middle East includes the countries that we know of as Turkey, Iran, Iraq, Saudi Arabia, Syria, Lebanon, and Egypt. The influences of the culture can be found in Morocco, Tunisia, and Algeria. The main religion of the area, Islam, affects the production of music and limits its use. Often Koran chanting is mistaken for singing by Westerners, but religious fundamentals do not consider it singing. Ancient chants with improvisation are used to inspire worshipers. Often, singing is not allowed as a secular activity. Formal poetry readings may be accompanied by instrumental music and enjoyed by many Muslims, as are traditional ensembles that play conservative classic Middle Eastern music. Muslim women do not participate in public music performances. However, within the home, there are traditional musical roles for the

*Figure 7–19* "Hot Cross Buns" Written on the Staff

children and women. Usually, the ritualistic songs and dances of the women are performed for other women and no men are allowed. This includes the dance called **belly dancing**. This dance as well as other folkloric dances are performed by women for women during rituals of preparation for marriage, fertility, and childbirth.

*Music of India*    Music is an integral part of life in India. The music reflects the feelings and moods of the people throughout the day and year. Indian music can be divided into two distinct types, classical and folk.

Classical Indian music has a tradition 5,000 years long and is primarily played and enjoyed by people from the upper class. The most famous Indian instrument used to play classical music is the **sitar**. This instrument is a string instrument with a long neck. It has two rows of strings. Seven strings on top are played by the musician. Below the main strings are 12 tuned strings that vibrate along with the main strings, producing a shimmering sound.

Indian folk music is the ceremonial music heard throughout a person's life. Due to the many religions, social classes, and languages found in India, there is a wide variety of styles. Additionally, the Indian culture has produced more than 500 folk instruments. The most commonly known Indian music is Indian film music. Indian films would be considered musicals in the Western world and are seldom without songs.

*Music of Thailand*    Thailand, once known as Siam, also has two styles of music, classical and folk. The classical style was heard only in the courts until the monarchy was ended in 1932. Thai classical music is the music used to represent Thailand to outsiders. Thai folk music is very diverse due to regional traditions. Thai folkmusic remains the music of the countryside and little is known about it.

*Music of Japan*    Although the current music of Japan reflects the Western European culture, Japan has traditional art music. The music is based on a **pentatonic scale**, meaning it has five notes in the scale. If you play the five black keys on a keyboard, starting with the lowest pitched of the two black keys, you will play a pentatonic scale. Harmony is not used in traditional Japanese music. Traditional Japanese music is important to all three types of Japanese theater, Noh, Kabuki, and Banraku. In all three forms, instruments play an important role. In addition to percussion instruments, three melodic instruments are used to play Japanese traditional music, along with the voice.

- **Koto**: a board zither with 13 or more strings
- **Shakuhachi**: a bamboo flute
- **Shamisen**: a long lute with three strings

**Taiko**: (see Figure 7-20) In Japanese, this word means "great drum". Although drums migrated to Japan from China, the Japanese improved the sound of this drum by making it from a single piece of wood from the trunk of a very large zelkova tree. Cow hide is used for the heads of these large drums. In addition to being used in Japanese theater along with other percussion instruments, these large drums were used to motivate warriors in battle during the time of feudal Japan. Recently, a new art-form has emerged in the form of Japanese drum ensembles called "kumi-daiko". Currently, there are around 10,000 of these drum ensembles in Japan.

*Figure 7-20*    Taiko

*Music of China and Taiwan*  The importance of music's role in making life better is respected in China. Like Japanese music, Chinese music is based on the pentatonic scale. The music is uncomplicated; however, it varies from one part of the country to another. The language of the people influences the differences in the music. Although most of the people speak Mandarin, the minority of people speak more than 60 different languages, each with its own musical style. Traditional music is based on legends, stories, nature, and true occurrences. Chinese instruments can be divided into three types.

- Strings: these include lutes, dulcimer, and zithers.
- Woodwinds: these include bamboo flutes and recorders.
- Percussion: these include drums, beaters, gongs, cymbals, and clappers.

Taiwan has a close history with China. Sometimes it has been considered a part of China and, other times, it is considered independent. This close history has brought to bear a great deal of Chinese influence on the music on Taiwan. However, in the mountains, the people maintain their folk music. Since they do not have their own written language, the history of the people is passed from generation to generation through their folk music.

*Music of Vietnam*  Vietnam partly borders on China, which has had a great influence on the music of Vietnam. In addition, as a French colony, it was influenced by Western European traditions. Traditional Vietnamese music is nearly always taught by rote with the teacher singing or playing the song and the student repeating. Vietnamese folk song traditions demonstrate the differences between the country's various regions. These songs also express the wish of people to live in the villages of their ancestors. Songs for children usually include a game or a lesson. Often, the Vietnamese language is taught in schools through singing.

**For You**

Listen to music from the Middle East and Asia. How does it make you feel? Is the sound different from what you are used to hearing? Here are some suggested recordings:

- *The Sounds of India* by Ravi Shankar (Sony)
- *Classical Chinese Folk Music* by Various Artists (Arc Music)
- *The Planet Sleeps* by Various Artists (Sony)

**In Early Childhood Classrooms**

- Select music to play for the children.
- Read stories from the culture while playing the music. Here are some story suggestions.

Vietnam

- Shea, P. D. (2003). *Ten Mice for Tet!* San Francisco, CA: Chronicle Books
- Hanh, N. (2003). *The Hermit and the Well.* Berkeley, CA: Parallax/Plum Blossom Books

Japan

- Say, S. (1993). *Grandfather's Journey.* New York: Houghton Mifflin
- Takabayashi, M. (2001). *I Live in Tokyo.* New York: Houghton Mifflin
- Friedman, I. R. (1987). *How My Parents Learned to Eat.* New York: Houghton Mifflin

China

- Demi. (1996). *The Empty Pot.* New York: Henry Holt.
- Hong, L. T. (1993). *Two of Everything: A Chinese Folktale.* Morton Grove, IL: Albert Whitman

Iraq

- Winter, J. (2005). *The Librarian of Basra : A True Story from Iraq.* Fort Worth, TX: Harcourt Children's Books

## References

Bender, J., Flatter, C. H., & Sorrentino, J. M. (2000). *Half a childhood: Quality programs for out-of-school hours.* Nashville, TN: School-Age NOTES.

Berk, L. E. (2001). *Development through the lifespan.* Needham Heights, MA: Allyn & Bacon.

Campbell, P. S., & Scott-Kassner, C. (1995). *Music in childhood*. New York: Schirmer Books.

Center for Policy Alternatives. (2003). *Family and work: An investment strategy for communities*. Washington DC: Author. Retrieved September 24, 2004, from http://www.cfpa.org/issues/workfamily/childcare/Chldcare.pdf

Iben, H. (1997). *The guide to symphony orchestra instruments*. Retrieved September 15, 2004, from http://www.mathcs.duq.edu/~iben/auxil.htm

International Academy of Middle Eastern Dance. (2005). *What is belly dancing?* Retrieved February 22, 2005, from http://www.bellydance.org/aboutus.php

Kamien, R. (2003). *Music, an appreciation*. New York: McGraw-Hill Book Company.

Manas. (2002). *Indian music*. Retrieved February 22, 2005, from http://www.sscnet.ucla.edu/southasia/Culture/Music/Music.html

Music Educators National Conference, MENC. (1994). *National standards for art education*. Reston, VA: Author. Retrieved September 24, 2004, from http://www.menc.org/publication/books/performance_standards/prek.html

National Association for the Education of Young Children (NAEYC). (1999). *Developing and implementing effective public policies to promote early childhood and school-age care program accreditation*. Washington, DC: Author. Retrieved September 24, 2004, from http://www.naeyc.org/resources/position_statements/psacrpol.htm

National Institute on Out-of-School Time (NIOST). (2000). *Making an impact on out-of-school time*. Washington, DC: Corporation for National Service. Retrieved September 24, 2004, from http://www.niost.org/publications/cns_1.pdf

Pappas, L. (2002). *The forbidden dance*. Retrieved February 22, 2005, from http://innerself.com/Fitness/The_Forbidden_Dance.htm

Pearson Education. (2005). *Music of countries and cultures*. Retrieved February 22, 2005, from http://www.sbgmusic.com/html/teacher/reference/cultures.html

U.S. General Accounting Office. (1997). *Welfare reform: Implications of increased work participation for child care*. Abstracts of GAO Reports and Testimony, FY97. Retrieved September 25, 2004, from http://www.gao.gov/archive/1997/he97075.pdf

Wikipedia. (2005). *Taiko*. Retrieved July 22, 2005, from http://en.wikipedia.org/wiki/Taiko

# The Role of Caregivers: Parents and Early Childhood Educators

## Key Terms

| | | |
|---|---|---|
| form | major scales | sharp |
| genre | minor scales | transposition |
| half step | rests | whole step |
| key signature | scales | |

Monique, the teacher in the three-year-old classroom, is on a home visit with Luis, who will be entering her classroom in a week. The purpose of her visit is to get to know Luis and his single-parent mother and allow them to become comfortable with her. She is also gathering information that will help her plan for Luis's development. In addition to the normal questions about his likes, dislikes, and the skills he has achieved, Monique asks Carlota questions about herself and her goals for Luis. Some of the questions Monique asks include what kind of music Carlota enjoys, how often she plays music, and if she ever plays different music. Monique also asks Carlota if she sings to Luis and, if so, what song is his favorite. Monique is beginning to build a partnership with Carlota that will benefit Luis as he progresses in her three-year-old classroom.

## Standards and Other Professional Guidance

### Music Educators National Conference Position Statement on Early Childhood Education

In July 1991, the Music Educators National Conference's (MENC) National Executive Board adopted a formal position statement regarding music and early childhood education. The statement consists of six sections, Introduction, Early Childhood Education, A Music Curriculum for Young Children, Beliefs About Young Children and Developmentally and Individually Appropriate Musical Experiences, The Music Teachers of Young Children, and Coda.

The position statement specifically discusses the role of parents, teachers, and early childhood music specialists in the young child's musical education. The following are excerpts from five of those six sections.

1. Introduction: "Musical experiences should be play-based and planned for various types of learning opportunities such as one-on-one, choice time, integration with other areas of the curriculum, and large-group music focus. The best possible musical models and activities should be provided. Adults responsible for guiding these experiences may range from parent, to caregiver, to early childhood educator, to music specialist."

2. Early Childhood Education: "Music educators should take the initiative to network with parents and early childhood professionals to disseminate developmentally appropriate materials and techniques for use in curriculum planning."

3. Beliefs About Young Children and Developmentally and Individually Appropriate Musical Experiences: "Children need effective adult models. Parents and teachers who provide music in their child's life are creating the most powerful route to the child's successful involvement in the art."

4. From the Music Teachers of Young Children:

    a. "It is desirable that individuals with training in early childhood music education for young children be involved in providing musical experiences for the children, either directly or as consultants."

    b. "Often it is the parent, certified teacher, higher education professional, Child Development Associate (CDA), or other care provider who is primarily responsible for guiding the musical experiences of the young child. These persons should:
        - love and respect young children,
        - value music and recognize that an early introduction to music is important in the lives of children,
        - model an interest in and use of music in daily life,
        - be confident in their own musicianship, realizing that within the many facets of musical interaction there are many effective ways to personally affect children's musical growth,
        - be willing to enrich and seek improvement of personal musical and communicative skills,
        - interact with children and music in a playful manner,
        - use developmentally appropriate musical materials and teaching techniques,
        - find, create, and/or seek assistance in acquiring and using appropriate music resources,
        - cause appropriate music learning environments to be created,
        - be sensitive and flexible when children's interests are diverted from an original plan."

5. Coda: "The Music Educators National Conference is committed to the implementation of this position statement. This goal can best be accomplished through the combined efforts of parents, music educators, and early childhood professionals. MENC supports policies and efforts that will make it possible for all children to participate in developmentally and individually appropriate practice in early childhood music education."

(MENC, 1991, reprinted by permission)

---

Monique is correct to build a partnership with Carlota. Parents are a child's first and most important teachers. They have been with the child since birth and can share information with the teacher that will help them reach their mutual goal of guiding the child to his full potential. Monique also included questions about music in the home to discover how much musical stimulation and nurturing Luis has received before entering her classroom. Monique understands that the arts, including music, are fundamental to a child's education. Additionally, she understands that through music she can help Luis feel comfortable in her classroom.

## Parents

In the past, parents have been the primary source of music education for their children (Levinowitz, 1998). Past generations musically nurtured their young children without the benefit of an education in early childhood music (Feierabend, 1996). Intuitively, parents, particularly mothers, played, sang, and danced with their young children and consequently promoted their musical growth (Feierabend, 1996). Extended family members lived near each other and when they gathered, music was often an important part of family life and entertainment. In this manner, families passed traditional songs, lullabies, rhymes, and chants from generation to generation (Feierabend, 1996). Today, we live in a highly mobile society that separates family units from extended family and friends. The culture of nearly 100 years ago supported the music nurturing of young children, but the culture that was prevalent 80 to 100 years ago in this country rarely exists today (Feierabend, 1996).

Not only have the past 100 years seen a loss of musical traditions through separation of extended family members, but additionally, an increased use of technology has helped to decrease, generation by generation, the musical ability and music appreciation of our society (Feierabend, 1996). This decrease makes it unlikely that parents will musically nurture their children during their time together (Feierabend, 1996). Furthermore, even if they had the inclination, most of them would not know what to do (Feierabend, 1996). Making music together used to be a major part of all family gatherings and celebrations. Members of the family would play various instruments and sing together. Today, for many families, music is a commodity that is enjoyed passively rather than actively, and parental musical nurturing is usually nonexistent or of low quality (Feierabend, 1996).

Another condition of modern society is that more parents are spending less time with their children. In both single-parent and two-parent families, the parents spend long hours at work and commuting to and from work, and more than 13 million children under six years of age daily spend as much time or more in child care (see Figure 8–1) (Children's Defense Fund, 2004). Additionally, millions of school-age children spend their out-of-school hours in a care setting (Children's Defense Fund, 2004). Once the family arrives at home in the evening, there is barely enough time to prepare and eat dinner and put the children to bed. Often, the longest period spent with the child is during the commute to and from home. Listening to music in the car may be the only time that parents engage their children in music.

### How Parents Can Musically Nurture Their Children

Chapter 4 discussed musically nurturing the prenatal infant. Many parents need guidance to engage in this

*Figure* **8–1**   Families used to pass traditional songs and chants from generation to generation.

activity. Programs such as Early Head Start that work with pregnant women should teach expectant parents how to musically nurture their unborn child. Library materials should be made available for expectant parents to borrow, such as literature about prenatal music stimulation, videos, and recordings of folk songs and a variety of good instrumental music. Classes should be conducted by a music specialist or music therapist that will help the mother through her pregnancy, including labor and delivery.

After the baby is born, parent meetings in child care centers should occasionally include labs by a music specialist or music therapist. Parent meetings present an opportunity to teach parents the importance of musically nurturing their children as well as a time to teach them how to fit musical nurturing into their busy schedules. Parents should be taught that through spontaneous singing and dancing with their child, music could be used as a transition and a help to calm a fussy or distressed child. Children's songs, lullabies, and rhymes should be taught to parents and they should be encouraged to share the childhood songs and rhymes from their culture. A variety of good instrumental music should be introduced to parents and a borrowing library should be established to maintain these recordings.

Parents should be encouraged to take their children to musical events (Scott-Kassner, 1999). Often, parents do not have extra money to spend on musical concerts; however, many musical events are free to the public. In addition, many of these events are held outdoors in parks, presenting a good setting for young children. However, parents do not always know about these events. This is information the child care centers should provide for parents. The center can also arrange for parents to attend a musical event as a group, thus providing them with a social outlet, making it more likely they will want to attend.

Actively involving parents in the musical nurturing of their children may lead them to seek future lessons for their child (Scott-Kassner, 1999). Those parents who cannot afford lessons should seek scholarships for their children when the time is appropriate for lessons.

An important outcome of parental involvement in the musical nurturing of their child is the message received by the child that her parents think music is valu-

able (Scott-Kassner, 1999). Children look up to their parents and model their actions. Children learn about their culture and the values of that culture from their parents. Parental involvement is essential to the musical nurturing of every child and for establishing a solid musical foundation (Scott-Kassner, 1999). When early childhood programs develop good partnerships with parents, they become family extensions and help parents musically nurture their young children.

## Try This One!

### The Marching Band Take-Home Box

One way in which teachers can help parents musically nurturing their children is to prepare plastic boxes filled with music materials for parents to borrow. Collect the following and place them in the box:

- A large plastic box that can be fastened shut
- Books
  a. *Our Marching Band* by Lloyd Moss, Putnam Publishing Group (2001)
  b. *Ty's One-Man Band* by Mildred Pitts Walter, Simon & Schuster Children's Publishing (1987)
  c. *John Philip Sousa (Getting to Know the World's Greatest Composers)* by Mike Venezia, from Children's Press (1999)
- CD: *Sousa's Greatest Hits* (ASIN: B0000296U6)
- Party hats
- Small washboard, two wooden spoons, a tin pail, and a comb to go with the book, *Ty's One-Man Band*
- Index cards with information on how to make simple instruments at home
- Any other materials you can think of that would facilitate the parents' musical time with their child
- Instructions for using the box

## Music Education Specialists

Where should music education specialists fit into the picture of preschool music nurturing? Music education

---

## A Closer Look

### Suzuki Association of the Americas

More information about Shinichi Suzuki and his music program is available online at http://www.suzukiassociation.org/. Materials, including a video about Shinichi Suzuki, titled *Nurtured by Love: The Life and Work of Shinichi Suzuki,* are available for purchase.

---

specialists are musicians who naturally want to encourage young children to become involved with music. Their purpose is to enhance children's understanding of music so that the children are better prepared to be future performers or music consumers (audiences). Ideally music education specialists would work with young children on a daily basis. However, in most cases, the situation is much less than ideal.

## Suzuki's Exciting Demonstration

For over 45 years, there has been a slow awakening in the field of music education to the importance of music in early childhood. The excitement began in 1958 when a group of Ohio music educators was shown a film of young children playing violins (Wood, 2003). The person responsible for this accomplishment was Shinichi Suzuki. In 1964, he brought a group of young violinists to the United States to play for a music education conference. Many of the children had begun violin lessons at age three or younger and were able to play very proficiently (Wood, 2003). Within a short time, the Yamaha and Baldwin piano companies began to develop courses for early childhood music. Community preschool music programs and university music lab–based early childhood courses were developed and sprung up across the United States. These classes, under the direction of early childhood music specialists, continue to be a good musical experience for the children who are able to attend them. However, these specialists cannot make up for a lack of daily music nurturing required for the children in their program with only an hour-long lesson each week.

## Specialists in Child Care Settings

Though most child care centers cannot afford to have a music education specialist on their staff full-time, some large child care centers do hire a music teacher to work with the children, usually on a weekly or monthly basis (Scott-Kassner, 1999). Unfortunately, many music teachers working in child care centers, community music schools, and private studios are highly trained musicians, but they have little or no training in early childhood and often approach young children with a watered-down version of an elementary school music curriculum (Scott-Kassner, 1999). In 1999, *Music Educators Journal,* the official magazine of MENC, released a special edition that addressed early childhood music education. The music education community was warned that many approaches being used with preschoolers went against best practices for early childhood music (Scott-Kassner, 1999). Due to a lack of training in early childhood music, music education specialists were emphasizing the product—that is whether the children could perform accurately— rather than the process of music development.

Music education specialists cannot effectively influence the musical nurturing of young children until they have been trained properly. They must know how to apply developmentally appropriate teaching methods when working with young children. As part of their preparation to work with young children in a developmentally appropriate manner, music education specialists should: (a) examine successful early childhood music education programs and (b) receive early childhood music courses as a required part of their training (Levinowitz, 1998; Scott-Kassner, 1999). Additionally, music education specialists have a particular duty to study the impact that early music development can have on a child's development in all domains

(Scott-Kassner, 1999). When they have a clear under-standing of the crucial impact of music on the lives of children, music education specialists must become advocates for the musical development of all children (Scott-Kassner, 1999) (see Figure 8–2).

Even if child care centers have enough discretionary funds to hire sufficient music education specialists to work with all of the children on a daily basis, training music education specialists to work in the early childhood arena is not the definitive answer to this problem. In early childhood classrooms, music experiences can and should occur at any time and not just when the music education specialist is present. Young children should be musically nurtured by the adult with whom they spend the most time daily (Stauffer, Achilles, Kujawski, & Watt, 1998). That is usually the classroom teacher (McDonald & Simons, 1989).

Many children spend more time with their teachers than they do with their parents, sometimes as much as 10–12 hours a day (Children's Defense Fund, 2004). Therefore, the responsibility to help children develop a love of music and culture falls on the shoulders of early childhood educators. If these teachers do not take up this responsibility, our culture could be cheated out of future performers and audiences and the children may be cheated out of a lifetime of musical experiences and life-enhancing enjoyment.

So, what is the answer to the question concerning the realistic fit of music education specialists into the picture of preschool music nurturing? Their role becomes supervisory in the child care setting. Once music specialists are armed with the knowledge necessary to teach early childhood music, they can help train and influence the teachers who must carry the responsibility to musically nurture young children, daily (Levinowitz, 1998). Through the intervention of the early childhood music specialist, early childhood classroom teachers can become more conscious of, and therefore more effective with, the use of music in the early childhood classroom (Coulter, 1995). When early childhood music specialists make planned visits to child care centers, they can observe musical interactions between teachers and children, give advice, and model responses and activities (Scott-Kassner, 1999). Training combined with observations and modeling can help teachers become more confident in their attempts at musical nurturing. This confidence should make it more likely that the teachers will try to enhance the children's musical growth (Scott-Kassner, 1999).

## Early Childhood Educators

Music and early childhood have always gone hand in hand. When you envision an early childhood classroom, it is easy to see children and teachers sitting in a circle singing or playing "Ring Around the Rosies." For years, early childhood educators have recognized that good musical experiences have a profound influence on the language development, cognitive development, and the social and emotional maturation of young children. Additionally, as more is discovered about the nature of rhythmic organization in movement, it is believed that research will show that musical experiences have important effects on children's motor skill development (see Figure 8–3) (Arkansas Department of Education, 1997). Music facilitates skill development in these areas because children are naturally attracted to music, making information

***Figure 8–2*** Large child care centers hire a music teacher to work with the children, weekly or monthly.

***Figure 8-3***  Musical experiences have important effects on children's motor skill.

and skills more easily learned through music. Music also enhances the early childhood program through its multicultural appeal and influences.

However, early childhood providers have merely stuck their big toes into the bucket where music in the early childhood classroom is concerned. Research has shown how necessary it is for teachers to jump into music nurturing with both feet. Two leading organizations in early childhood education, the Council for Professional Recognition (the Council, 1996) and NAEYC, (1991) support the importance of the use of musical activities in the early childhood classroom. Both encourage caregivers to use music to facilitate skill development in various developmental domains and as a creative activity that is important for its own sake. Unfortunately, many early childhood providers believe that by simply using music as a teaching tool in their classroom, they are encouraging creativity. Music is a wonderful teaching tool and

teachers should not stop using it in this way. Music helps make transition times more pleasant and children do learn other skills through music. However, as Section I of this textbook has established, skill development is not the sole reason for music to exist in the early childhood classroom.

For the majority of children in child care, their early childhood educators stand alone as they shoulder the responsibility to musically nurture these children daily. However, early childhood educators are not usually as familiar with a child's musical development as they are with her physical, cognitive, social, and emotional development (McDonald & Simons, 1989). Early childhood teachers, in general, receive insufficient training regarding music experiences for young children and little or no information about recent research in the field of early childhood music (McDonald & Simons, 1989).

In one study of infant and toddler teachers, they were found to have little or no musical repertoire with which to engage children (Greata, 1999). These caregivers suffered the same disconnection from past generations as Feierabend found in the rest of our society (Greata, 1999). The personal musical background and experiences of a teacher affect the kind of musical nurturing the young children in her care will receive (McDonald & Simons, 1989; Stauffer et al., 1998). This same study found that:

- Most teachers had limited, if any, musical background of their own. This affected their confidence to initiate a variety of musical activities and limited the scope of musical activities they thought they could or should attempt with the children (Greata, 1999).
- Most teachers did not have sufficient training in early childhood music to understand the relationship of a child's musical development to the development of the whole child (Greata, 1999). If teachers are expected to have an interest in developing the musical potential of children, they must have an understanding of the important contribution this potential can make to the child's entire life (Carlton, 1995).
- Most teachers did not understand the value of musical nurturing for its own sake and that it

should not be regarded merely as a teaching or transition tool (Greata, 1999).

- Most teachers did not understand what it meant to musically nurture young children and use appropriate musical activities (Greata, 1999).

If early childhood educators are expected to undertake this responsibility, they must be trained and given the tools to teach the enjoyment of music to children. They must be taught how to expose children to the kind of music that will nourish them for a lifetime. Researchers in the field of early childhood music education emphasized that:

- The teacher should be taught to observe children so they can discover the link between the musical nature of children and the theories and concepts learned in class (Stauffer et al., 1998).
- Teachers need to learn to deliberately teach what is in most cases only being indirectly taught, if it is taught at all (Gordon, 1996).
- Regardless of insufficient and low-quality past musical experiences, through training, teachers can develop their musical ability (Stauffer et al., 1998).
- Teachers should learn a larger repertoire of songs, chants, and rhymes to supplement their limited knowledge (Stauffer et al., 1998).
- Teachers should learn how to sing; learn to use the best key for young children to hear and imitate; and learn how to play rhythm instruments in an expressive way (Stauffer et al., 1998).
- Teachers should experience moving to music, rhymes, and songs in order to feel free in their movement (Stauffer et al., 1998).
- Additionally, to be able to musically nurture young children, teachers require more than information and teaching skills. They must develop a commitment to music nurturing of young children and an understanding of the importance of doing so. Only with that commitment and understanding will teachers seize the information presented to them and use the skills they have been taught (Greata, 1999).

### Partnering with Parents

As children spend more time in care out of their homes, early childhood educators have a greater influence on their futures. Additionally, parents must be actively involved in their child's education. Both teachers and parents must form partnerships to ensure that every child is able to reach her full potential, which is their mutual goal (see Figure 8–4). In this way, not only will each child receive her basic needs such as food, rest, and shelter, but the whole child will be nurtured and supported in her social, emotional, cognitive, and physical development. As parents and teachers work together to create rich environments to support every child in reaching her full potential, the arts must be a part of those environments. In particular, music should be included in the early childhood curriculum, not only because it helps the development of other skill areas, but also for the richness it brings to each child's life.

## Early Childhood Education and Music Education Collaborate

We have learned that parents and early childhood educators often do not have the experience or training to nurture children in music. Therefore, early

**Figure 8–4**    Parental involvement is essential for establishing a solid musical foundation.

childhood music education specialists must become an integral part of this nurturing process. Although there has always been a flirtation between the field of music education and the field of early childhood education, these two fields have remained separate for the most part. As early childhood educators and music educators have come to understand that the teacher who spends the most time with the child is the person who can contribute the most to her musical understanding, these two fields have begun to work together toward their mutual goals. In 1993, music specialists and early childhood educators were urged to work together to assure quality musical experiences for all young children, as a support of America's Goals 2000 National Education Goals (Andress & Feierabend, 1993). The strategy was directed toward enhancing the chances of children attaining future academic success and a higher quality of life (Andress & Feierabend, 1993).

In 2000, an early childhood music summit was held in Washington, DC. This summit was cosponsored by MENC, NAEYC, and the U.S. Department of Education. The summit was called to bring advocates for music education and early childhood education together to develop a "proactive approach to music education as both a worthy enterprise in its own right and as an essential educational component of early childhood development" (Boston, 2000, p. 1). The core idea of the summit was that "music education is basic education and is therefore integral to the education of children at any age" (Boston, 2000, p. 2). Research has shown that not only are the early years an important foundation to future learning, but additionally that music should be an integral part of that education (Boston, 2000). Although the summit consisted of experts from the early childhood and music education fields, the role of parents in early childhood music education was not excluded in the discussions. Attendees unanimously agreed that "unless the positive learning engendered by music in the earliest years is nurtured by those in the best position to provide it, i.e., parents, music teachers, and professional caregivers, the educational power of music and its potential for sound development can be diminished and diluted" (Boston, 2000, p. 3)

## Summary

Together, parents, early childhood educators, and early childhood music specialists have the opportunity to nurture this generation musically. In doing so, they also nurture future generations. Hope for future generations lies in children who are musically nurtured, and therefore have the experience and knowledge to personally ensure that their own children are musically nurtured (Gordon, 1996).

## Key Concepts

- Caregivers who spend the most time with children must be responsible for their music nurturing.
- Many children spend more time with their teachers than with their parents.
- Early childhood music specialists should train and influence early childhood educators to musically nurture young children.
- To carry out their responsibility, early childhood educators must be trained.
- Parents and early childhood educators must form partnerships to ensure that every child develops to her full potential, including her musical development.

## Suggested Activities

1. Visit the Web site http://www.menc.org/guides/startmusic/stmreport.htm, read about the 2000 Early Childhood Music Summit, and discuss the results of the report with your classmates.
2. Locate and visit an early childhood music program that is specifically for teaching music to young children. Write a report about your experience.
3. Journal reflective question 8: In what ways would you involve parents in the musical education of their young children?

## Music Lab #8

Welcome to Lab #8! In Lab #7, you began to read music and play a keyboard instrument. In this lab, you will learn about the woodwind family of the orchestra and continue learning about musical notation. And in this lab, our musical journey takes us to Africa.

### Activity #1: The Instruments of the Orchestra—Woodwind Family

Woodwind instruments are hollow pipes or tubes. The musician blows into a mouth piece or across a hole to start the column of air moving to cause vibration. All orchestra woodwind instruments have a reed or two in the mouthpiece, with the exception of the flute and piccolo. A reed is a thin piece of wood, which vibrates when the musician blows into the mouthpiece. The flute is played by blowing across the hole on one end. This is similar to the manner in which ancient woodwind instruments were played. How high or low the instrument can play is determined by the length and diameter of the pipe. This is similar to the strings of the string family. The thinner

and shorter the string is, the higher the pitch will be. In woodwind instruments, various pitches are played by covering holes along the body of the instrument with the fingers. In essence, this shortens the pipe.

Woodwind instruments called bone whistles first appeared around 6000 BC in the New Stone Age (Iben, 1997). Eventually, early man discovered that hollow reeds, which were closed at one end, would make a sound, when they blew across the hole at the open end (Iben). The earliest musical instrument was the Pandean pipes (Iben). The instrument consisted of a group of reeds of various lengths that were lashed together and played by blowing over the holes. The Romans and Greeks had many woodwind instruments (Iben). They were called flutes. The term woodwind came about, because the original instruments of the family were made of wood. The modern orchestra has eight woodwind instruments. These instruments are the flute, piccolo, oboe, clarinet, bass clarinet, English horn, bassoon, and contrabassoon.

## Discovering Instruments

### Woodwinds

- Flute and piccolo: When it was discovered that holes pierced into the hollow reed at various intervals would produce different pitches, the flute was born (Iben, 1997). Ancient Egyptian statues contain replicas of the oldest flutes known. These flutes are still played by Arabs (Iben, 1997). The instrument is held vertically and played by blowing across the open end (Iben, 1997). In Europe, during the Middle Ages, the flute was a military instrument, along with the drum (Iben, 1997). It was first played in the orchestra during the seventeenth century (Iben, 1997). The piccolo, the smallest instrument in the orchestra, is the flute's little brother. The modern flute is made of metal and is 27 inches long. The piccolo, which can play very high notes due to its size, is about 12 inches long.

- Oboe and English horn: The oboe (see Figure 8–5) and English horn are reed instruments.

**Figure 8–5**   Oboe

They have a mouthpiece out of which two reeds project. When the musician blows through these reeds, they vibrate and make a sound. The Egyptians made the ancestor to these instruments by flattening barley straws and sticking them into the end of a reed (Iben, 1997). The Crusaders brought the first double-reed instrument, the shawm, back to Europe in the twelfth century (Iben, 1997). The first oboe was made by a French family of musicians and instrument makers and used in the court of Louis XVI (Iben, 1997). The oboe and English horn are similar. These instruments are made from ebonite, a hard rubber. The oboe is about 2 feet long and the English horn is a little over $2\frac{1}{2}$ feet long. The English horn is larger than the oboe and has a lower, richer sound, although the oboe's reedy sound has made it a favorite of composers for 300 years (Iben, 1997).

- Clarinet and bass clarinet: Although the first instrument to resemble a clarinet can be traced back to ancient Greece, Persia, and India, the clarinet of the orchestra was not fully developed until 1840 (Iben, 1997). This version of the instrument is still used today. The first bass clarinet was constructed in Dresden in 1793 (Iben, 1997). It developed and evolved alongside its cousin, the clarinet. They are single-reed instruments.

Instead of blowing through two reeds, the musician blows through a single reed and its mouthpiece. The clarinet is a versatile instrument, due to its three very distinct ranges. Both instruments are made from granadilla wood or African blackwood. The clarinet is about 2 feet 3 inches and the bass clarinet is about $4\frac{1}{2}$ feet long.

- Bassoon and contrabassoon: The bassoon (see Figure 8–6) is the tenor of the oboe family. Its ancestor was the bass shawm (Iben, 1997). During the early sixteenth century, the tubing of the bass shawm was bent back upon itself and the first instrument similar to the bassoon of today was born (Iben, 1997). The instrument was called the curtail and had only two keys (Iben, 1997). During the eighteenth century, German instrument makers were experimenting with the bassoon. The model developed by Heckel was the most successful and that instrument is used today. The first contrabassoon was made in 1739, using the bassoon as its pattern (Iben, 1997). This is the bass of the oboe family. Eventually, it was made by doubling the tubing back on itself several times to make it easier to handle (Iben, 1997). Both instruments are made of ebonite or rosewood. They are double-reed instruments and played by blowing through two reeds attached to

**Figure 8–6**   Bassoon

## Music of the World

### Flutes of the World

Around the world, nearly every culture has developed its own version of a flute. Flutes can be found made from bamboo, reeds, wood, and clay. The ancient Greeks told the story of the god named Pan, who was part goat and part man. Pan fell in love with a beautiful nymph, Syrinx. When he asked her to marry him, she ran away. With Pan in pursuit, Syrinx came to a deep stream where she begged the water nymphs to help her escape from Pan. Just as Pan reached out to embrace Syrinx, the water nymphs turned her into a bundle of reeds. When Pan realized that all he had caught was a bundle of reeds, he sighed in despair. His breath caused the reeds to produce such a sweet sound that he tied them together as a remembrance of his lost love. And thus, so the legend says, the panpipe was born (see Figure 8–7).

- Flutes of Reed or Bamboo

  **a.** Panpipes called siku (see-ku) are also native to South America in the area surrounding Lake Titicaca between Peru and Bolivia. These pipes are divided into two separate halves and played by two musicians who weave the melody between themselves. The pipes can be played by one musician, but the two halves must be held together.

  **b.** In Japan, the shakuhachi is the most famous woodwind instrument. It is a flute made of bamboo. Bamboo is hollow except at the nodes. These are eliminated to make a completely hollow tube. The shakuhachi has four finger holes and a mouthpiece on top of the instrument. The name is derived from the words *shaku*, meaning the length of a foot, and *hachi*, meaning eight parts of a foot. Although there are other flutes longer than a foot, they are all referred to as shakuhachi.

  **c.** Bansuri flutes from northern India are also made of bamboo. These flutes have mouthpieces on the side of the flute.

- Flutes of Clay

  **a.** In Italy, the ocarina, invented during the 1850s by Donati, is played. Ocarina means "little goose." This clay vessel is shaped liked an elongated egg, hollow inside with finger holes and a mouthpiece. The size of the finger holes determines what pitches the instrument can make.

  **b.** Other cultures have made clay flutes, including China and native South and Central American peoples. In China, the flutes called xun were made from wood, gourds, bone, shell, and stone and were used in Confucian religious ceremonies. Over thousands of years, the natives of South and Central America developed their craft of clay flute whistle making to such a high degree that musical acousticians have a difficult time explaining their complex designs. In Europe, ceramic bird water whistles can be traced back to at least the seventeenth century. The body of the bird is filled with water and when the mouthpiece is blown, the sound is like a bird warbling. Duplicates of these whistles can be found today made from plastic. An interesting Web site by *Ceramics Today* features an article called "How to Make a Clay Whistle." The site can be found at http://www.ceramicstoday.com/articles/clay_whistle.htm

- Flutes of Wood: During the 1950s and 1960s, the wooden Irish flute was revived in popularity. These flutes are made to specifically suit Irish music, which does not require as many holes as the more traditional flute. By eliminating the extra holes, the tone of the flute is better. The Irish flute is similar to flutes of nineteenth century Europe.

- Native American flutes are discussed in chapter 6. These flutes have been found made from many materials. Today, there is an increasing demand for flutes tuned in the Native American tradition. These flutes are now being made from resin in an effort to accommodate the growing demand.

*Figure 8–7*    Pan pipes

## Music of the World (continued)

- Suggested listening:
    a. *Bamboo Flute Lullabies of Japan* by Ron Berger and Ricky Frystack (ASIN: B00003OTDN)
    b. *Contentment Is Wealth* by Matt Malloy (Irish Folk Melodies) (ID: HR-GLCD1058)
    c. *Changes: Native American Flute Music* by R. Carlos Nakai (#2933-720-615; available from Matoska Trading Company at http://www.matoska.com)

    d. *Medicine Woman, V.2* by Medwyn Goodall (folk melodies and instruments of South America, available from Sunstar at http://1800sunstar.com/)

The material for this box is from Burnt Earth (2005) Henley (1999), Pearson Education (2005), and Standing Stones (2002).

---

the mouthpiece. The bassoon's tubing is almost $7^{1}/_{2}$ feet long until it is put together, when it is about 4 feet 4 inches long. The contrabassoon's tubing is 16 feet long and 10 feet after it is put together.

## Activity #2: Learning More About Reading Rhythms

Music is organized sound, but among the sounds, occasionally there is silence. The manner in which these silences are conveyed to the musician is through symbols called rests.

You have learned to count the beat using the four basic notes. Now, we will add rests to our rhythms.

Each note has a corresponding rest. The rest is as long as its corresponding note. The only difference is that you do not make a sound during a rest. Figure 8–8 shows the four basic notes and their corresponding rests.

**For You**

Let's practice counting rests. Begin with Figure 8–9 example 1, and continue with examples 2, 3, and 4. With each example, do the following:

1. Count the beats, including the rests.
2. Chant the rhythm, but say "Sh" during the rest for as long as the note would be held.
3. Clap the rhythm. When you come to a rest, do not clap; instead, turn your hand outward and upside down, like you are throwing away the beat. If there is more than one rest or if the rest is longer than one beat, repeat the throwing-away motion for the duration of the rest.

## Activity #3: Learning About Music Notation: Key Signatures

The next important piece of information about musical notation has to do with the key signature. The key signature tells us the key in which we are playing a piece of music. This will be more relevant to you in the next lab, when you begin to play the autoharp. You already know about the staff. In fact, you played "Hot

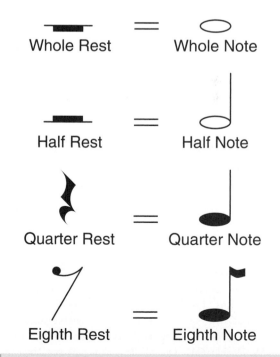

*Figure 8–8*  Four Basic Notes and Their Corresponding Rests

**Figure 8-9**    Four Exercises in Reading Rhythms

Cross Buns" by reading notes on the staff during the last lab. This is where we use the black keys on the keyboard. To learn about the key signature, we will first learn about **scales**. Do not moan! I will make this as painless as possible. First, there are two kinds of scales, major and minor. **Minor scales** are sometimes described as sounding sad. Since most children's songs are not sad, they are usually written using **major scales**. Therefore, we are going to talk only about major scales.

There is a formula for major scales. It is the same no matter what. The formula is **whole step** (W), whole step (W), **half step** (H), whole step (W), whole step (W), whole step (W), half step (H). When it is written like this—(W, W, H) (W) (W, W, H)–you can see that the first part is the same as the last part with a whole step (W) in the middle. Now, what does all of this mean?

**For You**

1. Look at the keyboard in Figure 8–10.
2. Start on the key below the two black keys. What is its name? Right, C! We are only going to play on the white keys. If your finger moves from C to the next white key, D, we skip over a black key in between. Because we skipped over a key, we say we moved a whole step. You play a whole step when you move from one key to the next and there is a key in between. It does not have to be a black key in between. If we were to go from the first black key to the second black key, we would also go a whole step, because we skipped over D. (Remember: D's in the middle of the two black keys!)

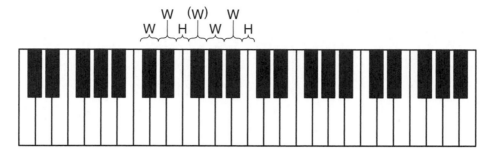

*Figure 8–10*   Keyboard showing the C-Major Scale

**3.** Start on C again. We move from C to D, which is a whole step. Then we move from D to E. What did we play? Right, a whole step!

**4.** Now, we will move from E to F. Whoops! There was no note in between. That is a half step. You just played whole step (W), whole step (W), half step (H)—the first part of our formula for a major scale.

**5.** Now, move from F to G. That is the whole step in between the two matching parts of the formula.

**6.** From G, we continue with the last part of the formula, whole step, which takes us to A (remember, we have to start the musical alphabet over again after G).

**7.** Then move another whole step, which takes us to B.

**8.** Finally, we finish at the next C by taking a half step from B. You have just played your first major scale using the formula: (W, W, H) (W) (W, W, H). Because you started on C and followed the formula, you played the C-major scale. No matter which major scale you play, you will always use the same formula.

The next question to consider is: when you played the scale, did you play any black keys? Right! The answer is no. You played only white keys. That is important, so remember it while we continue.

**1.** This time, find the G above middle C. (Hint: Look for the group of three black keys. It is the white key between the first two black keys in the group.) Now, you will play a scale based on G, a G-major scale. Play G, then a whole step to A,

**2.** then a whole step to B,

**3.** and half step to C.

**4.** Now, there is the whole step in between the matching patterns, which takes you to D. (You recognize D; he is between the two black keys!)

**5.** Now, begin the little pattern again. A whole step to E

**6.** and a whole step to—Whoops! You have to play a black key to make a whole step. Play the black key and then—

**7.** finish the pattern with a half step to G.

In Figure 8–11 the keys you played are marked. Normally, after playing E you would play F, but F was only a half step so you played the black key above F. That key is called F sharp. When you play a key (usually a black key) above or to the right of the key you would normally play, it is a sharp. To sharpen a key means to go up half a step from the original. In this case, instead of F, in order to play a whole step you had to play F sharp.

Figure 8–12 shows the notes you played as they are written on the staff. The symbol in front of the note on the F line is the sharp sign. To help children remember about sharps, they are asked, "If you sit on something sharp, which direction will you go?" Of course, the answer is "up." So, to make a note sharp, you go up half a step.

You now know that in order to match the major scale pattern, when starting on G you have to raise or sharp the F. The key of G major is based on the G-major scale. It would be very inconvenient to have to always place a sharp sign in front of every F in the music, so we have a key signature at the beginning of the music to tell us which notes are sharp. The key of G Major is the only major key signature that will have only one sharp. Other scales will have two, three,

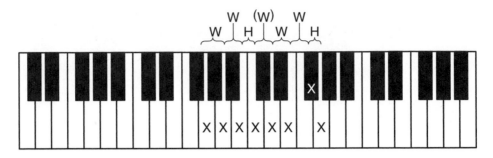

**Figure 8–11**    Keyboard Showing the G-Major Scale

**Figure 8–12**    G-Major Scale Written on the Staff

four, or five sharps. The key signature for G looks like Figure 8–13. The center of the sharp sign is placed over the top line, which is named F. Any time you see that key signature, you know to always play F sharp every time a note is written on a line or space of the staff that is named F.

*Review.* When you begin on some keys of the keyboard and want to play the major scale formula, you have to play one or more black keys in order for the formula to come out correctly. To indicate that the black key has to be played for certain major scales, there is a key signature. In the key of G, one black key had to be played in order to correctly play the formula and it was F sharp. Therefore, the key signature shows one sharp sign on the F line. This means that when you see a note written on the F space (Remember: the first space of the treble is also F.) or F line, you play F sharp instead. There is another symbol used in the key signature, but we will discuss that in the next lab.

Now, back to the scale and key of C. Remember, I told you that you had to remember that you did not play any black keys when you played the C-major scale using the formula. Because you did not play any black keys, that means there are no symbols in the key signature. C is the only major key that has no symbols in the key signature. The staff is empty of symbols in front of the time signature. Figure 8–14 shows the key signature for the key of C major.

## Activity #4: Playing the Keyboard

Now it is time to play a song in the key of G on your keyboard.

**For You**

1. Look at Figure 8–15. Does the rhythm look familiar to you? You are correct! It is "Hot Cross Buns", and this time it is written in the key of G.

**Figure 8–13**    Key Signature for G Major

**Figure 8–14**    Key Signature for C Major

**Figure 8–15**   "Hot Cross Buns" in the Key of G Major

2. Find the keys on your keyboard for playing Figure 8–15. (Hint: The first note, B, is the key above the three black keys.)
3. Play the song.
4. Now, you have not only read the rhythm and the notes, but you have played "Hot Cross Buns" in three different keys. You played it in one key when you played it on the three black keys, you played it in the key of C when you read it the first time, and now you played it in the key of G. It is the same song, just in a different key. Because they are in different keys, one song is sung on lower notes, while another is sung on higher notes. This is called transposition. When you transpose a piece of music, you play it in a different key than it is originally written. Which key did you like best for your voice range or the children's voice range?

## Try This One!

### Play Songs for the Children on the Keyboard

**For You**

Look at Figures 8–16, 8–17, and 8–18. The numbers under the notes on the staff correspond to their place in the scale of the key in which it is written.

- Choose a song to play.
- Look at the key signature and decide in what key you will be playing the song.
- The name of the key is the name of the first note in the scale for that key.
- Find that note on your keyboard.
- Using small removable stickers, write the numbers 1 through 8 on eight stickers.
- Place a sticker on eight notes beginning with the first note of the scale. For example, in the key of

C, the first note is C, so it will have a sticker with the number 1 on it. Go straight up the scale from there. D is 2, E is 3, F is 4, G is 5, A is 6, B is 7, and the next C is 8.

- Now, you can play the song by reading the numbers written under the notes.
- Practice your songs and then play them for the children in your room.
- *Note*: You can transpose the song you are playing into a different key by moving the numbers to the notes in that key.

### In the Infant and Toddler Rooms

- Allow the children to touch the keyboard and hear the sounds.
- Play a song for them.
- Sing the song and play it again.

### In the Preschool and in Out-of-School Programs

- Play your songs on the keyboard for the children.
- Tell them they can do the same.
- Copy the numbers of songs children know on 8 by 11 poster boards. You only have to copy the numbers, not the notes. Place a measure line in the proper place. As the children learn more about music, you can place the note values above the numbers. See Table 8–1. For easy reading, color-code the numbers. For example, 1 is red, 2 is blue, 3 is purple, 4 is green, 5 is yellow, 6 is orange, 7 is brown, and 8 is red. You can use whatever colors you wish, but keep numbers 1 and 8 the same since they are the same note, just played an octave apart.
- Place the cards sideways in a shoe box for storage.
- Place several small keyboards in the music center with numbers on the keys of various scales.
- Allow the children to choose songs to play on the keyboards.

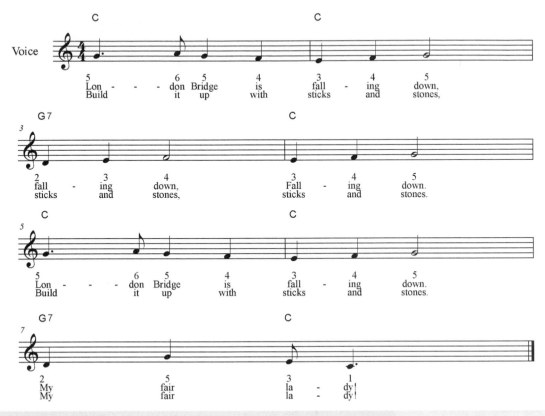

**Figure 8–16** "London Bridge"

## Try This One!

### Ding, Dong, Ding!

Select the two resonator bells that are marked middle C and the F above middle C. Play: F–C–F (Rest). Make it sound like "ding, dong, ding" at the end of "Frere Jacques." Now sing "Frere Jacques" as you play the two resonator bells throughout the song. Give two children one bell each. Practice with them by singing: ding, dong, ding. Have them play throughout the song while the rest of the class sings. Redistribute the bells and perform the song again. Do not worry if the children do not play exactly at the correct time.

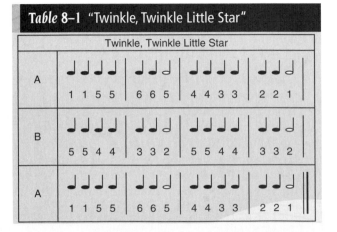

**Table 8–1** "Twinkle, Twinkle Little Star"

| | Twinkle, Twinkle Little Star | | | |
|---|---|---|---|---|
| A | 1 1 5 5 | 6 6 5 | 4 4 3 3 | 2 2 1 |
| B | 5 5 4 4 | 3 3 2 | 5 5 4 4 | 3 3 2 |
| A | 1 1 5 5 | 6 6 5 | 4 4 3 3 | 2 2 1 |

## A Closer Look

### Musical Form

Look at Table 8–1. Notice that the first and last lines of music are the same. The rhythm is the same and the notes you play are the same. The middle line is different. What I am pointing out to you is the **form** of the music. This is called ABA form, because you play one little melody section (A), then another little melody section (B), and then you repeat the first section, (A). *Note*: The double line at the end of the song denotes that it is the end.

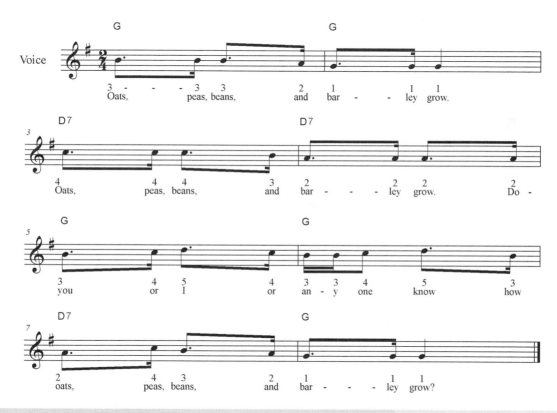

**Figure 8–17**  "Oats, Peas, Beans and Barley"

## Try This One!

### Sing a Song from Africa–"Kye Kye"

"Kye Kye" is an African call-and-response song (see Figure 8–19). Practice playing the song on the keyboard by reading the numbers. There are only five lines of words to learn and many of the words are re-peated. Here is a pronunciation guide for the words and a guide for the rhythms.

Words:          Kye, kye, kule
Pronounce:      Chay, chay, koo-lay
Rhythm:         Tah, tah, tah, tah

**Figure 8–18**   Little Red Caboose

| | | |
|---|---|---|
| Words: | Kye, kye, kofi sa | |
| Pronounce: | Chay, chay, koh-fee sah | |
| Rhythm: | Tee tah, tee, tah, tah | |

| | |
|---|---|
| Words: | Kofi sa langa |
| Pronounce: | Koh-fee sah lan-gah |
| Rhythm: | Tee tah, tee, tah, tah |

| | |
|---|---|
| Words: | Keke chi langa |
| Pronounce: | Kay kay shee lan-gah |
| Rhythm: | Tee tah, tee, tah, tah |

| | |
|---|---|
| Words: | Kum aden nde |
| Pronounce: | Koom ah-den day |
| Rhythm: | Tah- ah tee, tah, tah |

The pronunciation guide for this song was obtained from Jet (2005).

1. When you know the song, you are ready to teach it to the children.
2. Begin by chanting the rhythm using a syllable such as "Ba" or use the syllables I have used. Chant the call and have the children respond.
3. Play the rhythm on a hand drum as you chant.
4. Have the children play on their lap drums.
5. Depending on the age of the children, this may be sufficient for the first day.
6. The next time you introduce the song, chant the words in rhythm. Make sure your voice is animated to maintain the children's interest.
7. When you feel they are ready, sing the words and have the children respond to your call.

**Figure 8-19** "Kye Kye"

Once the children know the song, they can play the circle game played by children in many parts of Africa. In this game, the leader is in the middle of the circle. While standing, the leader performs a movement that the other children imitate, as they sing the song. Each time the song begins again, the leader performs a different movement for the other children to imitate. The leader makes his final movement while on the ground and then he jumps to his feet. The rest of the children jump up after making the final movement and the first one up is the new leader (Enrichment Through the Arts, 2005).

Follow up the song by reading a book about Africa to the children There are several listed in this box. The music on the *African Lullaby* (ASIN: B00000JCRJ) CD listed can be played at nap time or throughout the day. The CD features sounds of mbira, balaphone, kora, a capella vocals, guitar, bamboo flutes, dundun, and talking drum combined in songs of folklore, family, and village life in the traditional languages of the Ivory Coast, Mali, Senegal, Zimbabwe, Uganda, Guinea, Kenya, Nigeria, Zambia, and South Africa.

## Making Musical Instruments

### Pan Flute

#### For You

Collect the following:

- Bamboo about an inch in diameter
- Saw—coping saw is fine
- Glue—a low-temperature hot-glue gun is perfect for adults to use
- Twine or raffia in a variety of colors

1. Cut several (start with just 4 or 5) pieces of bamboo in various lengths. Make the first bamboo piece 3-4 inches long.  Make the next bamboo piece ½ inch longer and each successive piece ½ inch longer than the previous one. (i.e. 3 inches, 3½ inches, 4 inches, 4½ inches, etc.) Be sure to cut on either side of the nodes so you end up with hollow pieces.
2. Sand one end of the bamboo pieces to remove any roughness.
3. Plug the rough end with beeswax.
4. Place the pieces in order of size.
5. Line one end (the smoothed end) of the pieces in a straight line.
6. Glue the pieces together.
7. Secure the bamboo pieces by wrapping them with raffia or string and gluing the ends together.

Information that contributed to the instructions for making this instrument was obtained from Pighills (2004). More information about panpipes can be found online at http://www.pan-flutejedi.com/resources-page.html.

### How to Play the Instrument

Hold the flute near your chin, under your lips. Blow by bringing your upper lip over your lower lip to force the air down into the bamboo. As you blow, move the flute from side to side to make various pitches.

#### In the Preschool and in Out-of-School Programs

- Make the project part of the woodworking area.

- Have the children do the part of the project they are capable of doing. For example, young children can sand the bamboo piece ends, while older children can saw the bamboo into pieces.

### Plastic Straw Reed Instruments

#### For You

Collect the following:

- Box of plastic drinking straws with a wide diameter
- Box of plastic drinking straws with a slightly smaller diameter
- Scissors
- Hole punch

1. Make a reed for your instrument. The reed vibrates and causes the sound. Flatten about ½ to 1 inch of one end of a straw. Cut off a corner on each side to make a V-shaped end. Flatten your reed further by pulling it between your forefinger and thumb.
2. Put the straw far enough into your mouth so that your lips are resting on the round part of the straw. Don't bite down!
3. Blow hard. Did you make a sound?
4. Cut a hole in one side of your instrument using the scissors or the hole punch. Cut only one side! This time when you blow, cover and uncover the hole to change the sound. Did you feel the reed vibrating against your tongue?
5. Add more holes to increase the number of notes you can play.

### Variation: A Slide Instrument

Instead of punching holes in your instrument, add a slide to make different pitches.

1. Make a reed on a smaller straw as you did for the first reed instrument you made.
2. Slip the small straw into a larger one.
3. Blow in the same way you did before. This time change the pitches by moving the slide in and out.

Instructions for making a PVC flute can be found online at http://www.nativeaccess.com/ancestral/flute-adv.html.

Some stories to accompany the music are:

- *A Is for Africa* by Ifeoma Onyefulu, Puffin Books (1997)

- *Bringing the Rain to Kapiti Plain: A Nandi Tale* by Verna Aardema, Puffin Books (1983)
- *Why the Sun and the Moon Live in the Sky* by Elphinstone Dayrell, Houghton Mifflin (1990)

- *Zomo the Rabbit: A Trickster Tale from West Africa* by Gerald McDermott, Voyager Books (1996)
- *Mufaro's Beautiful Daughters* by John Steptoe, Amistad (1987)
- *Jambo Means Hello: Swahili Alphabet Book* by Muriel L. Feelings, Puffin Books (1981)

## Music Appreciation

Music is important in the daily lives of Africans. When Africans were abducted from their homes and taken all over the Western world as slaves, they took their music with them. Since that time, African music has influenced music all over the world. The sources for the history presented in this activity are Christo (2004), Microsoft Encarta Online Encyclopedia (2005), and Pearson Educational (2005).

# Musical History

## Music of Africa and Its Influence in America

The huge continent of Africa is divided by the Sahara Desert into what are now Black Africa in the south and the Arab north. The area south of the Sahara and particularly the west coast of Africa is the target of our musical journey. Migrations, wars, and colonization all had their effect on the musical culture of Africa. However, the slave trade that began when the Spanish first arrived after 1400 AD was responsible for the impact that African music would have on the Western world.

Although the instruments found in Africa are similar to instruments found all over the world, the reason for creating music is different. Music is usually combined with poetry or dancing. The African musician takes sounds from nature and puts them into the music, giving them a special meaning. Music is woven into every aspect of African life. Music is considered such a part of humanity that many languages do not have a word to describe it. It is simply not necessary. From birth, children are included in the musical life of the community. By the age of three, children begin making musical instruments and play-

ing musical games that prepare them to participate in the rituals of adult life.

Drums, bells, and rattles are the primary instruments found in West African communities. However, the drum is the most important. In fact, the drum is so important that in some communities it is equal to a man. Women must pay the drum the same respect they pay their men and they may not touch the drum. Drumming is done in ensembles that play for the many rituals of life. The ensemble usually consists of drums of various sizes and, of course, bells and rattles. A master drummer plays solos while the rest of the players play a pattern. Sometimes these patterns remain the same throughout the composition. It is also the master drummer's job to lead the other musicians and let them know when to switch tempos or patterns or stop. It is his job to coordinate with the dancers.

Solo and group singing are also an important part of African music. One style of singing consists of the soloist alternating with the group in a call and response. Harmony is also a prominent ingredient in African singing.

When slaves arrived in the United States, often they were not allowed to use their music. Slave owners were particularly afraid of letting them use drums, because they thought the drums would be used to send messages.

Frequently, slaves were taught Christianity. Although they did not accept all of the teachings, they accepted most of them and expressed their new-found religion in the same manner that they expressed their spirituality in Africa. Their religious meetings included dancing, clapping, singing, prayer, shouting, preaching, and stories. These were often held in secret.

Spirituals grew out of this tradition. The call-and-response style of many spirituals is a direct descendant of African singing. Although the words to spirituals were from European hymns or the scriptures, the spirituals were not used only for religious purposes. Spirituals were sung on work gangs to keep everyone working together and at the same pace. They also disguised hidden messages that told about a yearning for freedom, or an escape plan, or told an escapee where to find places of refuge.

After the Civil War, African-Americans moved into the northern states, and brought their spiritual tradition with them. The influence of this music led to the development of gospel music in three different forms: the gospel hymn, rural gospel, and Holiness-Pentecostal gospel. The gospel hymn was based on European hymns with choral responses. The rural gospel is sung in a blues style by a soloist who is accompanied by a harmonica or guitar. The Holiness-Pentecostal gospel style remained similar to the rural spiritual and includes dancing, singing, and instrumental music played on brass instruments, mandolins, and jugs.

The influence of African music can be found in many American music genres. In the next lab, we will see the impact it had on the music of the Caribbean.

## References

Andress, B., & Feierabend, J. (1993, December). Creating a link between elementary and preschool music. *Teaching Music*, pp. 27–28.

Arkansas Department of Education. (1997). *Did you know? A record number 47 states take serious steps toward improved music and arts education.* Retrieved October 15, 2004, from http://arkedu.state.ar.us/playagain/research .htm

Boston, B. O. (2000). *Start the music: A report from the early childhood music summit.* Washington, DC: Wordsmith, Inc. Retrieved December 12, 2004, from http://www.menc.org/guides/startmusic/stmreport.htm

Burnt Earth. (2005). *Flutes and whistles.* Retrieved February 26, 2005, from http://www.ninestones.com/flute.html

Carlton, E. B. (1995, Fall). Building the musical foundation: Music key experiences in active learning settings. *Early Childhood Connections: Journal of Music- and Movement-Based Learning, 1*(4), 16–20.

Children's Defense Fund. (2004). *Child care basics.* Retrieved September 11, 2004, from http://www.childrensdefense.org/earlychildhood/childcare/basics.asp

Christo. (2004). *African music: A historical perspective.* Retrieved February 22, 2005, from http://www.acslink.aone.net.au/christo/histmain.htm

Coulter, D. J. (1995, Winter). Music and the making of mind. *Early Childhood Connections: Journal of Music- and Movement-Based Learning, 1*(1), 22–26.

Council for Professional Recognition. (1996). *The child development associate: Assessment system and competency standards.* Washington, DC: Author.

Enrichment Through the Arts. (2005). Retrieved July 22, 2005 from http://www.enrichmentthroughthearts.com/ishangi11.html.

Feierabend, J. M. (1996, Fall). Music and movement for infants and toddlers: Naturally wonder-full. *Early Childhood Connections: Journal of Music and Movement-Based Learning, 2* (4), 19–26.

Gordon, E. E. (1996, Fall). Early childhood music education: Life or death? No, a matter of birth and life. *Early Childhood Connections: Journal of Music- and Movement-Based Learning, 2*(4), 7–11.

Greata, J. D. (1999). *Creating musically nurturing environments in infant and toddler childcare setting by providing training to caregivers.* Unpublished doctoral practicum report, Nova Southeastern University, Fort Landerdale-Savie, Florida.

Henley, C. (1999). How to make a clay whistle. *Ceramics Today.* Retrieved February 26, 2005, from http://www.ceramicstoday.com/articles/clay_whistle.htm

Iben, H. (1997). *The guide to symphony orchestra instruments.* Retrieved September 15, 2004, from http://www.mathcs.duq.edu/~iben/auxil.htm

Jet, D. (2005). *K-2 West Africa lesson plans: Music.* Retrived July 22, 2005 from http://home.earthlink.net/~debrajet/main.html.

Levinowitz, L. M. (1998). The importance of music in early childhood. *General Music Today, 12*(1), 4–7. Retrieved September 11, 2004, from http://www.westsidemusictogether.com/importance .html

McDonald, D. T., & Simons, G. (1989). *Musical growth and development: Birth through six.* New York: Schirmer Books.

Microsoft Encarta Online Encyclopedia. (2005). *Latin American music.* Retrieved: February 22, 2005, from http;//encarta.msn.com

Music Educators National Conference (MENC). (1991). *Position statement on early childhood education.* The National Association for Music Education, 1806 Robert Fulton Drive, Reston, VA 20191. Used by permission.

National Association for the Education of Young Children. (1991). Guide to accreditation. Washington, DC: National Association for the Education of Young Children.

Pearson Education, (2005). *Music of countries and cultures.* Retrieved February 22, 2005, from http://www.sbgmusic.com/html/teacher/reference/cultures.html

Pighills, D. (2004). *Making your own panpipes.* Retrieved September 10, 2004 from http://www.panflutejedi.com/david-pighills-tutorial.html

Scott-Kassner, C. (1999). Developing teachers for early childhood programs. *Music Educators Journal, 86*(1), 19–25.

Standing Stones. (2002). *What is an Irish flute?* Retrieved February 26, 2005, from http://www.standingstones.com/irflute1b.html#irflute

Stauffer, S., Achilles, E., Kujawski, S., & Watt, R. (1998, Spring). Preparing the caregivers: Music in early childhood education. *Early Childhood Connections: Journal of Music-and Movement-Based Learning, 4* (2)20–29.

Wood, E. (2003). *Background. Suzuki music: Learning with love.* Retrieved October 20, 2004, from http://suzukimusic.org.au/suzuki_method/frame_history.html

# Where?

The final section of this textbook answers the question where? Where do we musically nurture young children? Is it in the circle at the beginning or end of the day? Is it on the playground? Is it in the dramatic-play area? Is it in the block corner or the library, or on their resting mats, or at the lunch table? It is in all of these places. Music should be everywhere in the early childhood classroom.

Chapter 9 specifically examines the environment the teacher provides for music nurturing. It looks at the various components of the classroom environment and answers the question: where can music be incorporated into the classroom environment?

The fact that this section is the last section in the textbook does not make it the least important section. Where children are musically nurtured is just as important as why, what, or how.

# Planning the Music-Nurturing Environment

## Key Terms

| | | |
|---|---|---|
| arpeggio | leading tone | rumba |
| block chord | mambo | schofar |
| bomba | merengue | soca |
| calypso | plena | son |
| chords | reggae | tonic |
| flat | root | |

John and Wanda are working on their classroom. They are moving furniture and supplies, and examining the room. They team teach in an out-of-school program. Over the weekend, they both attended a lab that discussed classroom environment. After the lab, they sat together and talked about their classroom. Something was not working. Children seemed to walk around as if they had nothing to do, and yet there were plenty of materials and equipment. As they talked, they discovered that the problem might be the environment and the manner in which it was set up. They made a list of items to check and sketched out a floor plan for a new room arrangement. They also reviewed their materials and packed away some of the equipment and materials to rotate into the classroom later in the year. The children will arrive soon from school and they will be ready with a new and interesting environment.

Planning for a music-nurturing environment is just as important as planning the music-nurturing curriculum. The environment must be well-equipped, inviting, attractive, and child accessible or even the best curriculum plans might fail. What do we mean by the environment? Is it the furniture? Is it the equipment? Is it the materials? It is all of these and much more. All environments send out a message. Think about a place you visited and then said you never wanted to go back to again. What made you say that? Maybe the place was too loud. Maybe it smelled funny. Maybe the people were rude. All of this is a part of the environment. Now think of a place that you visited and could not wait to return to. What made you feel that way? The environment is everything that surrounds us. In addition to the furniture, equipment, and materials, the environment includes the amount of space available, the temperature of the room, the lighting, the people in the room, and the attitudes of those people.

## Attitude

Attitude is the first component of the environment to be addressed, because it may be the most important component. The most beautiful equipment and materials in the world cannot create a music-nurturing environment if the atmosphere in that environment does not convey acceptance of and respect for the activities of the children. I have visited classrooms that were filled with beautiful equipment and furniture, and yet most of it was unused due to the structured approach of the teacher. On the other hand, although an unstructured approach is desirable for fostering creativity, when the environment is not organized, it is difficult for the children to find the materials or the space they require to express their creativity.

To ensure the success of your music-nurturing program you should create your own philosophy about music nurturing in the classroom. "A philosophy of education is a set of beliefs about how children develop and learn and what and how they should be taught" (Morrison, 2001, p. 13). A philosophy is not based on your opinions, it is based on your "core values and beliefs" (Morrison, 2001, p.13). You form your core values through your life experiences, through the knowledge you gather reading books, attending class, and listening to those around you, especially those you admire, and through exchanging ideas with your colleagues. Your teaching is influenced by your beliefs. Putting your beliefs on paper and into a philosophy helps you clarify your ideas and gives you a guide and direction for making instructional decisions.

## Try This One!

### Writing a Philosophy Statement

Here is one way to get started with your statement of philosophy. It will probably not be your final statement, because as you study further and practice your art of teaching you will mold your beliefs and fine-tune them. Begin by concentrating only on the preschool years. Using single words and short phrases do the following:

1. Write down why you think music nurturing is important in early childhood education.
2. Write down all of the ways in which you believe (based on your studies) children learn.
3. Describe the environment you want to provide for music nurturing.
4. Write down all of the types of musical activities in which you believe (based on your studies) young children should be engaged.
5. Write down your expectations for the children in terms of future growth and development.

Look at what you have written. Take what you have written and plug the information into the following formula.

I believe music is important in the lives of young children because (put your words from item 1 here). Children learn best through (put your words from item 2 here). Therefore, I will provide an environment that supports their learning by (put your words from item 3 here). I will provide materials and space for music-nurturing activities such as (put your words from item 4 here). By providing opportunities for music exploration and experience, children in my care will (put your words from item 5 here).

You will need to arrange the words to make them sound correct, but this is a way to get you started on writing your philosophy of music nurturing in early childhood education.

---

Once you have your own philosophy, compare your philosophy with your school's education philosophy. Are they compatible? Are there any compromises to be made? In the end, the most important issue is that the needs of the children are fully met.

The next step in establishing your environmental attitude is to ask yourself questions about how you can carry out your philosophy in the classroom environment such as:

1. How can I set up an environment that will help children
   - Explore sounds?
   - Learn to sing in tune?
   - Learn to move expressively and rhythmically?
   - Learn about instruments?
   - Learn to listen?
   - Learn musical concepts in a developmentally appropriate manner?
   - Create music that enhances their self-esteem?
   - Develop a respect for music as a valuable part of everyday life?
2. How should I arrange my schedule to accommodate creativity and the exploration and experimentation of musical materials? Consider the following:
   - Is there time set aside in which children can explore and experiment with sounds and music?
   - Are there times within the schedule in which music would be a natural addition?
   - How many transitions are in my schedule and how can I use music during transitions?
   - Does my schedule provide time for me to work with small groups and individuals?
   - Does my schedule allow for a special group music time?

The attitude of the teacher is important regardless of the age of the children in the class. A personal philosophy reflects the teacher's attitude of respect for the importance of music nurturing in the early childhood classroom. Having a philosophy about music nurturing and being able to arrange the environment to support that philosophy is extremely important to the success of your music-nurturing program.

## Space

Space is an important consideration for effective music nurturing. The NAEYC accreditation criteria and procedures require a "minimum of 35 square feet of usable playroom floor space indoors per child" (NAEYC, 1998, p. 49). This is the minimum amount of space per child required for accreditation, but a minimum of 50 square feet of usable floor space is recommended (NAEYC, 1998).

The lack of storage is a common problem faced by teachers in early childhood centers. Often, as a result, teachers must keep all of their equipment in the classroom, either in freestanding cabinets to be rotated throughout the year or actually out on shelves in the classroom all year long. Teachers must be creative in the organization of their classrooms and judicious with the amount of "stuff" they make available at any one time.

When planning for music nurturing, teachers must consider how they will display and store the instruments and materials in the music center. Placing the rhythm instruments in a bin on a shelf does not invite children to use them. Rhythm instruments can be stored in bins, but the bins should be clearly marked with pictures and words so the children know what is in them. Similarly, pictures and words on the shelves illustrate where the instruments belong when the children are finished with them. Hooks on the backs of shelves can provide a place to hang large instruments and drums. Again, pictures can illustrate where certain instruments should be hung.

Think about how you want the children to use the materials. A table for tape or CD recorders, headphones, and tape and CD storage units provides a neat and organized listening center, but consider this instead. Remove the table and replace it with bean bag chairs for relaxing. A place on the shelves or a smaller table can accommodate the listening materials and the children will enjoy cuddling up in the chairs to listen to music.

How well you arrange the space also conveys your value of and attitude toward the importance of children being able to freely move to music. If the space is large and inviting, it says, "Come, let's move to music!" If the space is small, cramped, and uninviting it says, "You really are not allowed to do that here!" To be nurturing, we must be careful of the messages we convey through the environment.

Another consideration when setting up the classroom space is to remember that individuals react differently to the same environment. Teachers must know the children with whom they work. They must know the characteristics of the age and stage of development of those children. Nurturing environments invite all of the children to participate and help them feel comfortable doing so. The use of space and the equipment and materials that are placed in that space may differ from room to room, according to the age and stage of development of the children in the room.

## Infant, Toddler, and Preschool Environments

In the infant room, space is required for teachers to "dance" with the infants. Since this is usually on a one-to-one basis, the space does not have to be as large as in a classroom of toddlers or preschoolers where more children may be involved in an activity. In addition, there should be sufficient floor space away from cribs where infants can begin to explore sounds (see Figure 9–1).

Both toddler and preschool classrooms require space where children can spontaneously move to music. This is often a problem in early childhood classrooms, because there is no planning for open space. However, there is usually a space for group and circle times and this space can often double as the music center. Classrooms should be scrutinized for unnecessary clutter and organized in a manner that welcomes children and invites them to participate in activities or centers. Sometimes in our zeal to present many opportunities to children, our classrooms

*Figure* 9–1   Provide floor space away from cribs where infants can begin to explore sounds.

become so well stocked that they are confusing to the children.

## In the Out-of-School Time Environment

The out-of-school classroom requires a slightly different accommodation. Children in this age range (six to nine) are often self-conscious and do not move to music spontaneously, at least not in front of each other, unless they have been doing so since they were younger. This does not mean that a place for movement is not necessary. However, an area can be created that allows children to experiment with movement and music without feeling that they are on display. Higher shelving can create a place that encourages freedom of movement because it blocks the view from other children, but not the teacher.

Additionally, a place should be created where children can play music either from recordings or on instruments without disturbing children who must complete homework assignments. Separating these two sections with room dividers and using rugs and draperies to absorb the sound will make the experience better for everyone. Allowing students to listen to soft music through headphones while studying can also make it easier for them to concentrate. Another solution is to allow those who have no homework to take their music outdoors. Areas of the country in which mild weather exists all year long have the advantage of being able to use the outdoors as an extension of the classroom. Areas that experience winter weather should take advantage of the outdoors as much as possible.

By setting up several areas for outdoor listening, children can choose what they want to listen to without disturbing others. Another area, perhaps an outdoor gazebo, can be set up to allow children to play instruments and experiment with sounds.

## Try This One!

### Environment Message Investigation

- Select several locations to visit with a friend or classmate. You might want to visit two different stores together.
- Select locations that are very different from each other. Perhaps you will visit a hospital or an airport.
- Separately, write down the messages you each receive from the environment. The environment affects each person differently. Some people find an airport environment stressful. Other people feel excited at an airport, while others feel relaxed and calm.
- Compare your notes and see if you and your friend received the same message from the environments you visited.

## Equipment and Materials

For the sake of clarity, in this textbook the word *equipment* refers to large or expensive items that you do not want to replace often, such as furniture, instruments, tape recorders or CD players, and computers. The word *materials* refers to smaller and less expensive items that are rotated in the classroom throughout the year or are regularly replenished, such as paper, glue, and paint.

Here are some examples of equipment that might be found in a music-nurturing classroom:

- Piano
- Large keyboard
- Small keyboards
- Tape recorders
- Headphones
- Rhythm instruments
- Orff instruments
- Montessori bells and sound cylinders
- Music boxes
- Percussion instruments
- Guitar
- Autoharps
- String instruments
- Books
- Puppets
- Tapes and CDs and their players
- Computer software
- Pictures of paintings and sculptures of musicians, dancers, and musical instruments
- Karaoke machine
- Shelves and containers for storage
- Furniture, such as a table, tent, box, etc., for exploring sounds
- At least one rocking chair in the infant and toddler rooms, if not one for each teacher
- Unbreakable mirrors on the walls and perhaps on the ceiling to allow the children to view their own movements—something they really enjoy doing

Items that come under the heading of materials are almost endless. Materials may be used to construct teacher-made equipment, such as sound bottles and sing-along rhyme books, or for children to make their own instruments. Some examples of materials are:

- Paper
- Glue

- Paint
- Paper plates and plastic disposable plates
- Rubber bands
- Shoe boxes
- Milk cartons of various sizes
- Guitar strings
- Scarves and ribbons
- Cans with lids
- Various kinds of sandpaper
- Plastic bottles of various sizes
- Bells
- Brass pipes in various lengths
- Drum heads
- Various materials to make sounds, such as rice, beans, rocks, seeds, and sand
- Gift wrap tubes
- Toilet paper tubes
- Mailing tubes
- Any other materials the teacher can imagine using to help children explore sounds

Of course, the age of the children dictates what materials are available for the children to use. In the school-age room, many items can be available at all times for the children. It is important to keep the display and storage of equipment and materials in mind, so that they are inviting, accessible to the children, and yet do not clutter the classroom space. Many of the materials mentioned above are already found in most early childhood classrooms.

## Interspersing Music Throughout the Classroom

In addition to a large space for movement, smaller spaces should be established for children to explore instruments, listen to music, read musical stories, and make their own instruments. Look around the classroom and discover other places where musical activities can be inserted. These spaces should be inviting and comfortable with sufficient materials for exploration to keep the children coming back.

### Listening Centers

Places should be established in the classroom where children can quietly listen to music or musical stories. Within an older-toddler, preschool, or out-of-school classroom, the listening center should be equipped with at least two tape recorders and headphone sets. The listening center should be located near the classroom's open space, to allow children to listen and move at the same time if they wish. The teacher should monitor this area, so she can help children with the equipment. Often, preschool children can operate the tape recorders by themselves.

The listening center should be stocked with recordings of music used in movement lessons, or chants and songs that are introduced during circle time. School-age children will enjoy learning jump rope chants and using them with a jump rope on the

## A Closer Look

Here are some ideas for pictures to display in relationship to certain music.

- Haydn: *Toy Symphony*—pictures of bird whistles, rattles, a ratchet, toy drum, toy trumpet, triangle, small cymbals, a cuckoo horn, and harpsichord
- Saint-Saens: *Carnival of the Animals*—pictures of lions, hens and roosters, mules, turtles, elephants, kangaroos, fish, cuckoos, birds, pianists, fossils, swans

- Tchaikovsky: *Waltz of the Flowers*—pictures of flowers
- Mussorgsky: *Pictures from an Exhibition: Ballet of the Unhatched Chicks*—pictures of chicks
- Vaughn Williams: *The Wasps: March Past of the Kitchen Utensils*—pictures of kitchen utensils
- Kabalevsky: *The Comedians: Pantomime*—pictures of clowns or mimes
- Mozart: *Eine kleine Nachtmusik*—pictures of the moon and stars

playground. Limit the number of tapes available at any one time to preschoolers to make it easier for young children to choose, but do not limit the variety of music available. Code the tapes with a picture that represents the music, for easy identification by non-readers. Decorate the walls of the center with pictures that represent the music available at the time. When you change the music, change the pictures, so that the center retains its interest and continues to attract the children.

## Sound Exploration Centers

An area for sound exploration is important in all classrooms. This area may get loud at times, so it should be placed near other areas where the sound level is compatible. Placing this center near the block area or the dramatic-play area is a better choice than placing it near the library or listening centers. As with the other centers, change the materials often enough to keep it interesting. By monitoring the center, you will not take materials out of the center prematurely, before each child has sufficient time to thoroughly explore the sound materials that interest him. Section 3 discussed sound centers in detail.

## Dramatic-Play Areas

The early childhood dramatic-play area is a good place to include musical materials that are used in everyday life. Depending on the age of the children, musical items found in homes may be placed in this area, such as a music box, doorbell chimes, or a child-size piano. This area should have a rocking chair where "mommies and daddies" can rock and sing to their babies. A tape recorder should be nearby with recordings of lullabies and household appliance sound effects.

Funny hats and rhythm instruments, along with recordings of parade music, give children all the makings of a parade (see Figure 9–2). Every band needs a director and props can be included for imaginary play as a conductor. The addition of a music stand, a baton, a cassette recorder with tapes of recorded short orchestral excerpts, and an old pair of tuxedo tails could carry a child into the land of

**Figure 9–2** Children enjoy marching and playing instruments to parade music.

music. With a sound exploration center nearby, the conductor may have a live orchestra on occasions as children pick up rhythm instruments and play along.

The entire dramatic area can be changed into a recording studio. Television has exposed young children to the recording industry and they enjoy pretending to record their music. The recording console can be made from cardboard with dials drawn onto it. Pretend microphones or a karaoke machine, headphones, music stands, and instruments combine to create the scene. Ask the children what they think they need for their studio and have them help make the various pieces of equipment.

## Library Corner

In the library corner, place a tape recorder with headphone sets along with many picture books that are based on children's rhymes and songs, so children can listen to the stories while they read the book or look at the pictures. This quiet place is also good for listening to recordings of lullabies and nursery rhyme chants. Place teacher-made books, such as sing-along rhyme books, in the library center for children to use. As in the listening center, decorate the library center with pictures that reflect some of the rhymes and stories and change the pictures and the stories often enough to keep the area interesting. However, keep in mind that children like repetition and are willing to listen to their favorite stories and rhymes repeatedly. Be aware of the stories the children enjoy the most and which ones they do not listen to as much. The stories that are avoided may need to be introduced or reintroduced to the children at circle time. Do not rotate the favorite stories and music out of the listening and library centers as often as you might rotate less popular stories and music.

## Art Center

The art area is another place for musical nurturing. Taped music should be available for painting to music. In addition to painting on the easel, finger painting or playing with shaving cream, as in Figure 9–3, to music is fun as well. By including head-phones, children do not have to listen and paint to the same music. Many beautiful paintings and sculp-tures depict musicians, dancers, and musical instru-ments. Pictures of these pieces of art can decorate the art area. Keep the area interesting by changing the pictures as often as necessary. These pictures can also

**Figure 9–3**  Provide music for finger painting or working with shaving cream.

be used to decorate the dramatic-play area. In the preschool classroom, materials for making music in-struments should be included in the art area and woodworking area, along with rebus instructions on how to make them.

## A Closer Look

### Books Based on Songs for Infant and Toddler Libraries

- *Clap Your Hands* by L. B. Cauley
- *Down by the Bay* by Raffi
- *Head, Shoulders, Knees and Toes* by A. Kubler
- *I Know an Old Lady Who Swallowed a Fly* by N. B. Westcott
- *If You're Happy and You Know It* by D. Carter
- *Knick-Knack Paddywhack: A Moving Parts Book* by P. Zelinsky
- *Old MacDonald Had a Farm* by P. Adams
- *The Eensy Weensy Spider* by M. A. Hoberman
- *This Old Man* by P. Adams
- *Twinkle, Twinkle Little Star* by J. Taylor and A. Kubler
- *Wheels on the Bus* by Raffi

### Books Based on Songs for the Preschool Out-of-School Program Libraries

- *Anna Banana: 101 Jump Rope Rhymes* by J. Coles
- *Baby Beluga* by Raffi

- *Carnival of the Animals: By Saint-Saëns* by B. Turner and S. Williams
- *If You're Happy and You Know It* by A. Kubler
- *Miss Mary Mack* by J. Coles and S. Calmenson
- *Miss Mary Mack* by M. A. Hoberman
- *Over in the Meadow* by E. J. Keats
- *Over the River and Through the Wood (A Song for Thanksgiving)* by L. M. Child and N. B. Westcott
- *Peanut Butter and Jelly: A Play Rhyme* by N. B. Westcott
- *Peter and the Wolf* by V. Vagin
- *She'll Be Coming Around the Mountain* by P. Sturges
- *Skip to My Lou* by N. B. Westcott
- *The Lady with the Alligator Purse* by N. B. Westcott
- *The Wheels on the Bus* by P. Zelinsky
- *There Was an Old Lady Who Swallowed a Fly* by S. Taback
- *This Little Light of Mine* by Raffi
- *Tingalayo* by Raffi

## Try This One!

### Finger Painting or Shaving Cream Painting to Music

1. Prepare a table for children to finger paint with paint or shaving cream.
2. Set up a tape recorder with two different compositions. Select one with a moderately fast tempo and another with a slow, relaxing tempo. Select compositions that are only about three minutes long.
3. When the children are set up to paint, begin to play the first piece. Do not say anything to the children. Play the music loud enough for them to hear it well.
4. When the first composition ends, play the second one.
5. Observe the children and note their reaction to the music. Does it affect the way in which they paint? Do they paint faster to the faster music and slower to the slower music?

Some suggested recording selections are "Rondo" from *Eine Kleine Nachtmusik*, K. 525 by Mozart, for the faster piece; and "Andante" from *Cassation*, K. 63 by Mozart, for the slower piece.

## Try This One!

### Making Instruments by Using a Rebus

By placing the instructions for making various instruments in the art and woodworking areas, children are able to make the instruments when they wish. Rebus instructions can be written on 8 by 11 poster board sheets and laminated to protect them (see Figure 9–4). Place them lengthwise in a shoe box for storage so the children can easily look through them and select the instrument they wish to make.

## A Closer Look

### Fine Art That Features Music and Movement

Numerous works of art feature musicians and dancers. Prints can be purchased at reasonable prices to display in various areas of the classroom. This list contains a few of the better known pieces of art in many styles.

#### Musicians

- *The Old Guitarist* by Picasso
- *The Three Musicians* by Picasso
- *To the Rhythm* by Juarez Machado
- *Cuban Musician* by Sue Kennedy
- *Jammin, at the Savoy* by Romare Bearden
- *Thunder* by Steve Johnson
- *Jamming* by Steve Johnson
- *Bourbon Street Blues I* by Robert Brasher
- *Bourbon Street Blues IV* by Robert Brasher
- *Songs of Childhood* by Charles Curran
- *Lullaby* by Eng Tay
- *Lesson* by Eng Tay

- *Cuba, 1997* by Christina Rodero
- *Midnight Boogie* by Jeff Pykerman
- *Jazz It Up* by Norman Rockwell
- *Woman with Guitar* by Pierre-Auguste Renoir
- *Two Girls at the Piano* by Pierre-Auguste Renoir
- *Jazz Cat Alley I* by Will Rafuse
- *Street Musicians* by William Johnson
- *Man Playing Bongo Drum* by Wolfgang Otto
- *Creators of Jazz* by Jason DeLancey
- *The Fifer* by Edouard Manet
- *The Music Lesson* by Lord Leighton
- *Classical Sunlight* by Carson

#### Dancers

- *Rain Dancer* by Tom Philips
- *Rejoice* by Monica Stewart
- *The Star* by Edgar Degas
- *Four Tribal Dancers* by Marco

Prints of this art can be found online at http://www.art.com.

## A Closer Look

### Some Musical Software for the Computer Center

| | |
|---|---|
| Disney Interactive: | *Radio Disney Music Mix Studio* |
| Finale: | *Print Music!* |
| Harmonic Vision: | *Music Ace* |
| Microsoft: | *Magic School Bus in Concert* |

| | |
|---|---|
| Scholastic: | *Clifford Musical Memory Games* |
| Viva Media: | *Hearing Music—The Game That Teaches You How to Listen!* |
| | *Making Music: Create! Play! Experience!* |
| | *Making More Music* |

Here are instructions for making a toilet paper roll kazoo. Collect the following materials:

- 1 toilet paper roll
- 1 container of paint
- 1 sheet of wax paper
- 1 rubber band

1. Paint the toilet paper roll. Decorate when dry, if you wish.
2. Attach a piece of wax paper to one end with a rubber band.
3. To play the kazoo, lightly place the wax paper against your lips and hum with an open month.

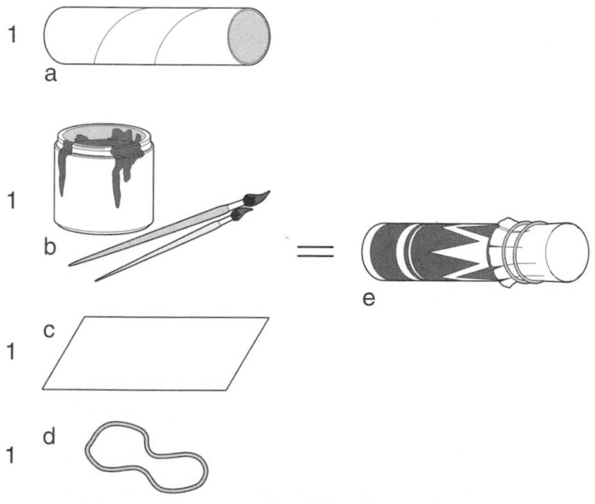

***Figure 9–4*** Rebus instructions for making a toilet paper kazoo.

## Computer Center

The computer area has become an area into which music can be inserted. Although there is a limited choice of music software for young children at this time, teachers should continually look for new materials as they become available. There was a time when having a computer in an early childhood classroom was questioned. Now it is an accepted practice and more software is continually being produced for young children. When looking for music software for young children, be sure the quality is excellent and that the activities are developmentally appropriate for the age and stage of the children in the classroom. Working at the computer is a social activity for young children (see Figure 9–5), so be sure there is more than one chair at the computer.

## Summary

Without a supportive environment, a music-nurturing curriculum may fail. Every component of the environment must be examined. This examination starts with the attitude of the administration and teachers and moves to the space, equipment, and materials available and the settings within the classroom where they are found. Planning a musically nurturing classroom requires that the teacher be creative and innovative. Time spent planning is time spent assuring that the musical goals for the children will be met. The environment speaks to children and adults and it tells them what is expected of them. If we want children to feel free

**Figure 9-5**    Music can be inserted into the computer area.

to move to music and to explore music, then the environment must be welcoming and supportive of these activities.

## Key Concepts

- The attitude of the teacher is maybe the most important part of the environment.
- Your attitude is reflected in your philosophy for music nurturing in the early childhood classroom.
- Music should be found throughout the classroom.

## Suggested Activities

1. Create a sound center for a toddler, preschool, or out-of-school-time classroom.
2. Visit a classroom. Sketch the classroom as it is arranged. Does this arrangement present an environment that nurtures young children musically? If not, using the same amount of space, redesign the classroom to be musically nurturing. Share your design with your class.
3. Select a book that is based on a song. Create a lesson plan and present the book to a group of children.
4. Make a sing-along book for your library. Share it with your classmates.

## Music Lab #9

Welcome to Lab #9! As we have moved through the labs, you have learned about basic music elements and notation. You have also learned how to play simple tunes on the keyboard. Our journey through musical history has taken us from the Middle Ages (450 AD) to beyond the twentieth century. We have also learned about Native American music and visited Asia, the Middle East, and Africa. In this lab, we will visit the Caribbean. Also in this lab, you will continue to experience playing simple songs on the keyboard and you will begin to play the autoharp. The introduction to the instruments of the orchestra concludes with the brass family.

### Activity #1: The Instruments of the Orchestra—Brass Family

The ancestors of the brass family existed thousands of years ago. The first horn was the horn of an animal. A hole cut in the small end of the horn was blown through. The earliest record of a horn is the Hebrew schofar, which was made from a ram's horn (Iben, 1997). This horn is still used in Jewish celebrations.

The brass family as it is known in the orchestra today was invented by William Weiprecht of Germany around 1828 (Iben, 1997). This instrument family got its name from the metal from which it was made. The four brass instruments normally found in the orchestra are the trumpet, trombone, French horn, and tuba.

## Discovering Instruments

### The Brass Family

- Trumpet: The trumpet (see Figure 9–6) is the smallest and highest pitched of the brass instruments. Trumpets date back to ancient Egypt and Rome. Several types were used for battle. Early trumpets had no holes or valves. By the seventeenth century, holes and valves had been added to the trumpet, making it easier to play. The trumpet of today's orchestra has about $4\frac{1}{2}$ feet of tubing in a very compact instrument.
- Trombone: The trombone is just a big trumpet. In fact, that is what the name means in Italian. Around the fourteenth century, the slide was added to the trumpet. A similar instrument was made in Germany called the sackbut. However, the name trombone prevailed and by the end of the eighteenth century in both Europe and England, the instrument was known as the trombone. At one time, valves were added to the trombone, but musicians did not like them. Today the trombone does not have valves. Since its invention, it has not changed. The trombone has 9 feet of tubing.
- French horn: The French horn (see Figure 9–7) evolved from animal horns, as the trumpet did. In England, it was used by the military, for hunting, and for signalling the arrival of someone. When the bell of the horn (the wide mouth) was widened by the French, it came to be known as the French horn. Other modifications included adding valves and slides in the tubing to alter the sound. The French horn has nearly $12\frac{1}{2}$ feet of tubing.
- Tuba: Through attempts dating from the Middle Ages to make a bass instrument, the tuba eventually evolved. The first instrument called a tuba was invented in 1845. The instrument underwent further improvements in the 1870s, resulting in the instrument we now know as the tuba. The tuba has 13 feet 9 inches of tubing, three valves, and a large bell. It is usually played standing up.

***Figure 9–6***   Trumpet

***Figure 9–7***   French Horn

## Try This One!

### "Tubby the Tuba"

"Tubby the Tuba" is a story written by Paul Tripp in 1948 and reissued in 1954. The original story is out of print and difficult to find; however, there are recorded versions available.

The Manhattan Transfer was nominated for best musical album for children in the 37th Annual Grammy Awards for its recording *Manhattan Transfer Meets Tubby the Tuba.*

1. Show the children a picture of a tuba and tell them that you have a story about a tuba named Tubby who was sad because he wanted to play a song in the orchestra.
2. Play the recording for the children.
3. Show the full-color story guide to the children as they listen.
4. Ask the children if they can play Tubby's tune on their pretend tuba.
5. As a transition, march the children to the next planned activity as they "play" Tubby's tune.

The children may not remember the tune, but will follow along as you pretend to play.

### Activity #2: Learning Key Signatures

In Lab #8, you learned about the key signatures G major and C major. In this lab, we learn the last key signature you will need to play any of the songs in a major key in this text. It is F major. The procedure is the same. The formula is the same. The only difference is the note on which we begin. You will begin on F and play a scale based on F, the F-major scale. You already know that you will have to play a black key, because you learned in the last lab that C major is the only major key that does not use any black keys.

For You

1. Look at Figure 9–8. The piano keyboard is marked showing the formula: (W, W, H) (W) (W, W, H). The keys that you will play are also marked.
2. Find F on your keyboard. (Hint: It is the note below the three black keys.) Play F, then a whole step to G,
3. then a whole step to A,
4. and a half step to—Whoops! To only play a half step, you have to play a black key. This black key is positioned above A. You cannot call it A sharp, because you already played A. You cannot have an A and an A sharp in the same scale. What is the next letter in the musical alphabet? Right, B! We will have to call it B—something. It is not a sharp, because we know a sharp takes a note up a half step. This time we call it a flat. Because B would be the next letter we use, we call it B flat. When a note is flat, that means we play a half step below the original note. To help children remember about flats, they are asked, "If your bicycle tire is flat, which direction does it go?" Of course, the answer is "down." Therefore, to make a note flat, you go down half a step. Let's continue by playing B flat.

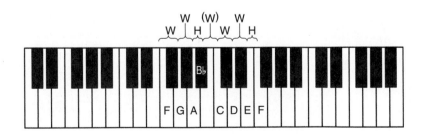

**Figure 9–8** Drawing of Piano Keyboard Indicating the Scale for F Major

5. There is that whole step in between the matching patterns, which takes you to C.
6. Now, begin the little pattern again. A whole step to D and
7. a whole step to E,
8. then a half step brings you back to F.
9. Look at Figure 9–9. It shows the notes you played as they are written on the staff.

The symbol of the note on the B line is the flat sign. Just as it would be inconvenient to place a sharp sign in front of every F in the music, when playing in the key of G Major, it is also convenient to place a flat in front of every B when playing the key of F Major. The key of F Major is the only major key signature that will have only one flat. Other scales will have 2, 3, 4, and 5 flats. You can see the key signature for F Major at the beginning of Figure 9.10. The center of the flat sign is placed over the line, which is named B. When you see the key signature for F Major, you know to always play B flat every time a note is written on a line or space of the staff that is named B.

## Activity #3: Playing the Keyboard

You have played "Hot Cross Buns" on the black keys without any notes to read, you have read the notes and played "Hot Cross Buns" in the keys of C major and G major, and now you are going to play "Hot Cross Buns" in the key of F major. If you cannot play anything else, you will be able to play "Hot Cross Buns"! I do not mean to bore you. I want you to experience the same song in various keys. Plus, you are already familiar with the melody and the rhythm,

which makes it easier for you to tell if you play the wrong note.

**For You**

1. Look at Figure 9–10. This is "Hot Cross Buns" in the key of F major.
2. Go ahead and play it, then look through Appendix D and find other songs that are written in the key of F major. Remember—look at the key signature to know the key in which the song is written.

## Activity #4: Exploring the Autoharp

The autoharp is a wonderful instrument for the early childhood teacher to use. It is easy to play and can be carried onto the playground or taken on a field trip. The autoharp is a harp of strings fastened to a wooden sound box. The strings are arranged from the longest and thickest to the shortest and thinnest. As on the violin and other string instruments, the longer and thicker strings produce the lowest-pitched sounds and the higher and thinner strings produce the highest-pitched sounds.

Bridging the strings are bars with a button on top and felt underneath. Autoharps come with either 12, 15, or 21 bars. A 12- or 15-bar autoharp is sufficient for the early childhood classroom. If you look at the bars from the side, you will notice that there are little tunnels cut into the felt. Each bar has tunnels over different strings. When the bar is pressed on, the felt stops some strings from vibrating, which you know means they will not make a sound. The tunnels allow particular strings to vibrate.

**Figure 9–9**   F Major Scale on the Staff

**Figure 9–10**   "Hot Cross Buns" in the Key of F Major

The autoharp is played by pressing the bars with fingers on the left hand, while the right arm crosses over the left and strums the strings. Press only one bar at a time. Practice strumming and pressing the bars on the instrument to get used to it.

The button on each bar has a letter and maybe a number beside it and the word *major* or *minor*. These are the names of chords. In order to know which buttons to press you have to know the key in which the song is written. You already know how to read three different major key signatures, so that is not a big problem. The next thing you need to know is what chords are used to play in any particular key. We will solve that problem in the next activity.

**For You**

1. Take time to examine the autoharp. Pluck a string and feel it vibrate. This is a good instrument to demonstrate the idea of vibration to young children. They can actually see and then feel the strings vibrate, especially the larger strings. Why? You know that answer—it is because lower sounds vibrate more slowly.

2. See Appendix C for more information on the care and tuning of the autoharp.

**In the Preschool and in Out-of-School Programs**

Young children can play the autoharp under the direction of the teacher. However, be sure to check the ends of the strings and make sure they are not sticking out. If they are exposed, the ends of the metal strings can be very sharp and can cut a child. Because children are not as coordinated as adults are, sometimes it is better to have one child press the buttons, while another child strums the strings. Some school-age children may be coordinated enough to play alone, but their arms are not long enough to allow them to cross the right arm over the left. Again, they can work in pairs, instead of learning to play the buttons with the wrong hand.

## Activity #5: Learning About Chords

Chords are two or more notes (usually three) that are played at the same time. You already know most of what you need to know in order to play chords.

- You know the formula for a major scale. Using the formula, you could figure out any major scale by starting on its tonic (the name of the scale or key) and playing the formula.
- You know how to read three major key signatures, C, F, and G. At least you know if you are to play in those keys!
- You know what the major scales of C, F, and G look like when they are written on the staff.

The last three questions you need answered are easy compared to what you have already learned. They are:

1. What makes up a chord?
2. What chords should be played for a particular key?
3. How are they played on the autoharp?

We will begin with the first question. What makes up a chord? Every chord has a root, just like a tree. It is the note for which the chord is named. Sometimes Roman numerals are used to name chords. If you come across a chord named with a Roman numeral, to know the letter name of the chord, you need to know the key in which the song is written. The Roman numeral refers to the position that the root of the chord holds in the scale of the key in which you are playing.

**For You**

Look at Figure 9–11. Here you see the C-major scale written on the staff. C is the first note, so it has the Roman numeral I for its name. This is the I chord. D is the second note in the scale and it has the Roman numeral ii for its name. The next note is E and—you guessed it! Its name is iii. The next note is F and its

*Figure 9–11*    C Major Scale on the Staff with Notes Numbered Using Roman Numerals

name is IV. The next is G and its name is V. The next is A and its name is vi. The next is B and its name is vii. That brings us back to C, which is still I.

Do you see something strange? The notes C, F, and G have capital Roman numerals for their names and the other notes have lowercase Roman numerals. That is because in any major key, the I, IV, and V chord are the major chords and the most important. In fact, that is the answer to the second question above. The I, IV, and V chords of whatever major key in which you are playing are the buttons you find on the autoharp and press. When you press them is another question, but that will be cleared up soon. However, first we need to build our chords.

## Activity #6: Building Chords

To build the I chord, we begin on C and then add every other note. You can play this on a keyboard: C, skip D and play E, skip F and play G. E is called the third of the chord, because it is three notes up from C (you count C). G is called the fifth of the chord, because it is five notes up from C (counting C).

**For You**

1. Look at example 1 in Figure 9–12. The notes of the chord are stacked, so you play them at the same time. The first chord is the C-major chord and it is the I chord in the key or scale of C major. Play the C-major chord. You can play each note alone, playing from the lowest note to the highest **(arpeggio)**, or you can play them all at once **(block chord)**.

2. Using the same procedure, you will now play the IV and V chords of the key of C major. To build the IV chord, we begin on F because it is the fourth note in the C scale. Now, add every other note. You can play this on the keyboard: F, skip G and play A, skip B and play C. A is called the

third of this chord, because it is three notes up from F (you count F). C is called the fifth of the chord, because it is five notes up from F (counting F). Look at example 2 in Figure 9–12. Play the F chord. This chord is the F-major chord and it is the IV chord in the key or scale of C major.

3. Next, we will build the V chord for the key of C major. To build the V chord, we begin on G because it is the fifth note in the C scale. Now, add every other note. You can play this on the keyboard: G, skip A and play B, skip C and play D. B is called the third of this chord, because it is three notes up from G (you count G). D is called the fifth of the chord, because it is five notes up from G (counting G). Look at example 3 in Figure 9–12. Play the G chord. This chord is the G-major chord and it is the V chord in the key or scale of C major.

4. Sometimes, you will see V7 instead of V. This means there are four notes in the chord. The seven stands for the seventh of the chord. In the G-major chord, the seventh note up from G is F. Look at example 4 in Figure 9–12. The seventh note of the V chord is called the **leading tone**. That is because it leads you back to the I chord.

5. Go back to example 1 of Figure 9–12 and play examples 1, 2, 3, and 4, then stop. If you stop playing after the fourth chord, your ear will not be satisfied. The leading tone is very strong and wants you to play the I chord again. This time play Figure 9–12 and end with the final chord (I chord). I would bet that your ear is much happier now!

## Activity #7: Playing Chords on the Autoharp

Now it is time for you to practice playing the chords for the key of C major on the autoharp. Before you

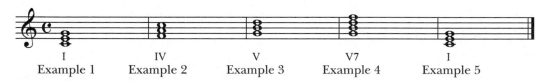

|   I   |   IV   |   V   |   V7   |   I   |
| Example 1 | Example 2 | Example 3 | Example 4 | Example 5 |

**Figure 9–12**   Chords of C Major on Staff

begin, here are three things to remember about where to place your fingers.

1. The index finger always plays the I chord of the key in which you are playing.
2. The ring finger always plays the IV chord of the key in which you are playing.
3. The middle finger always plays the V7 chord of the key in which you are playing.

**For You**

1. Place the index finger of your left hand on the button that says C major.
2. Place your ring finger on the button that says F major. Be sure it is F and not F7—that is the V7 chord for another key!
3. Place your middle finger on the button that says G7—you will want to use the V7 chord. Notice, your fingers fit just right!
4. Practice playing the chords of C major.

## Try This One!

When you play the autoharp, you only need to figure out the names of the I, IV, and V7 chords for the key in which you want to play the song. For a quick and easy way to figure out these chords, do this:

- Look at the key signature and figure out the name of the key.
- Using your fingers, start on the letter name of the key, such as G, and say the names of the notes in the scale. (Just follow the musical alphabet— G, A, B, C, D, E, F Sharp, G.)
- The first letter you said is the name of the I chord, the fourth letter you said is the name of the IV chord, and the fifth letter you said is the name of the V chord. You can play either the V or V7 chord by that name.
- In the key of G major, the name of the I chord is G, the name of the IV chord is C, and the name of the V chord is D, making the V7 chord D7.
- Find the correct buttons on the autoharp and practice playing the chords for the key of G. Practice playing the chords of G Major.

- Now, try doing the same thing for the key of F.
- Say the letter names of the scale, beginning with F (F, G, A, B flat, C, D, E, F). In the key of F major, the name of the I chord is F, the name of the IV chord is B flat, and the name of the V chord is C, making the V7 chord C7.
- Find the correct buttons on the autoharp.

Practice playing the chords for the key of F.

### Activity #8: Playing Songs Using the Autoharp

Knowing when to play each chord takes a little practice. When you place your fingers correctly on the buttons, the three chords you need are right under your fingers. You just need to listen to what your ear is telling you. However, if you need more help, you will find that the songs in Appendix D have the letters that represent the chord name written above the staff in various places. These are the names of the chords in the key the song is written. Until you get to know the songs better, you can use these letters.

*Hint:* Most children's songs begin and end by using the I chord, or in other words the chord that has the same name as the key in which you are playing the song. Often, the V7 chord is played right before the last chord.

There is one more thing you need to know before you begin to play the songs in Appendix D and that is how to strum the autoharp. How you strum the autoharp has to do with the time signature and the tempo at which you want to sing the song. We have talked about time signatures in which the bottom number is 4, meaning that a quarter note is equal to one beat. When you encounter one of these time signatures, do the following:

- 2/4 time: Depending on the song you are singing, either you can strum once for the entire measure and just let the strings vibrate for the second beat, or for a faster tune, you can strum on both the first and second beat.
- 3/4 time: Again, this depends on the song. For slow songs, you can strum once across all of the strings and let them vibrate for the second and third beats. For faster songs, strum three times.

The first stroke across the strings should be long and strong. The second and third strokes should be lighter and shorter. You can strum the second time on the lower strings and the third time on the higher strings, or strum both times in the same place.

- 4/4 time: A variety of ways of strumming can be done with this time signature. Again, for songs with a mood, or for slow songs, strum one long stroke across the strings and let them vibrate for beats 2, 3, and 4. You can also strum on every beat, making the first stroke longer and stronger and the other three shorter and lighter. You can move the shorter strokes along the strings from low to high. Or, you can strum on the first and third beat of the measure. If you strum this way, make the first stroke the strongest.

The other time signature with which you will be confronted on a regular basis has an 8 as the bottom number. This means that an eighth note is equal to one beat. The top number will usually be a 6, meaning there are six beats in a measure. See Figure 9–13.

In this time signature, the eighth notes are beamed together in groups of three instead of groups of two, as shown in Figure 9–13. Due to the way they are beamed, you would strum once for each beam of three eighth notes. In 6/8 time, that would be twice in each measure. The other option is to strum only once for an entire measure.

Your strumming techniques will develop as you practice and use the autoharp. Very soon, you will be making up your own strumming patterns or improvising. I know this all sounds very complicated, but you will quickly get the hang of it. Now, it is time for you to practice.

## Try This One!

### Play Your First Song on the Autoharp

You are now going to play your first song on the autoharp. Don't be nervous! You are ready. You are going to play "Mary Had a Little Lamb" in the key of F major.

1. Decide which chords you need to play on the autoharp: F (I), B flat (IV), and C7 (V7).
2. The notes are not going to be written on the staff. Instead, you will read the chart in Table 9–1. The chord you are to press appears in the corner of the square and the lines under the words tell you when to strum.
3. Play the chords without singing the song.
4. Now play the chords and sing the song as you play.
5. Go to the Resource Guide in Appendix D and find "Mary Had a Little Lamb" as it is written on the staff. Notice that the chords are written above the measures. If there is no chord written, continue to play the same chord until the chord name changes.

**For You**
1. After playing "Mary Had a Little Lamb" on the autoharp, go to Appendix D and find other songs you know and play them on the autoharp.
2. When you feel confident, play these songs for the children in your classroom.

**In the Preschool Program**
Have the children strum the strings while you change the chords of the song. Do this in small groups, because it will take the children a while to get used to strumming.

**Figure 9–13**   Example of 6/8 Time Signature and Beamed Eighth Notes

**Table 9-1** "Mary Had a Little Lamb" Written on a Chart with Strumming Indications

| | F | F | C7 | F |
|---|---|---|---|---|
| | Ma-ry had a | lit -tle lamb, | lit -tle lamb, | lit -tle lamb. |
| Strum: | \| | \| | \| | |
| | F | F | C7 | F |
| | Ma-ry had a | lit -tle lamb. Its | fleece was white as | snow. |
| Strum: | \| | \| | \| | |

**In the Out-of-School Program**

1. Teach the children how to play a song in the same manner you have learned.
2. Make a chart of the song as in Table 9–1 to help them find the right chords to play.
3. Use small, colored round dots to place on the fingertips of the children to help them remember which finger goes on which chord. Use a different color for each chord.

## Music Appreciation

In our final music history activity, we will visit the Caribbean. This area of the world has become famous for its music. There is a mixture of Native Islander, European, particularly Spanish, and African influence in the music. The sources for the history presented in this section are Elliott (1996), Mohn (2005), Pearson Education (2005), Welcome to the Caribbean (2005), and World History Archives (2005).

## Making Musical Instruments

### Maracas

#### For the Preschool Program

Collect the following items

- Two film canisters for each child
- Rice or small pebbles (you can get them at a craft store)
- Craft sticks
- Colored tape

1. Remove the tops of the canisters.
2. Fill about one-third of the canister with rice.
3. Cut a slit in the top of the canister.
4. Slip a craft stick into the top of each canister.
5. Place the top on the canister.
6. Use the colored tape to secure the top and stick.

#### For the Out-of-School Program

Collect the following

- Burnt out light bulbs
- Papier-mâché
- Paint in bright colors

1. Make papier-mâché and apply around the light bulbs.
2. Allow to dry and then paint.
3. Once the paint dries, hit the maracas to break the bulb inside for sound.

## Music History

### Music of the Caribbean

Long before Europeans set foot on the islands of the Caribbean, natives occupied the islands in large civilizations. The arrival of Europeans saw the demise of these civilizations. The islands of the Caribbean Sea were settled by various European nations such as Britain, Spain, France, and the Netherlands who were seeking gold and silver for their large kingdoms. Natives were forced into slave labor on the islands and some were taken as slaves to Europe. Island natives died by the thousands from overwork, disease, and mistreatment.

Beginning in the seventeenth century, the islands were affected by political changes in Europe. The Spanish gained the first foothold in the Caribbean and dominated trade, until England, France, and the Netherlands joined forces to disrupt this trade. Together, they hired privateers to attack Spanish ships and steal the gold and jewels for their governments. Eventually, these privateers developed their independence and became the famed pirates of the Caribbean.

Other Europeans arrived and began farming the fertile land. Large plantations developed and, because there were so few natives to work the plantations, slaves were imported from Africa. Unlike the slaves of North America, in general, the slaves of the Caribbean were allowed to maintain their culture. Additionally, whole tribes were imported, rather than splitting families and tribal units as was the custom in the north. Although a heritage of native music exists, African music had the greatest influence on the music of the Caribbean. In particular, the influence of African drumming and call-and-response singing can be heard in the music. This rhythmic music mixed with the Western European harmony and the guitar and dance forms from Spain has given the world various forms of Caribbean music.

Due to the different influences, the music varies from one island to the next. Some of the well-known styles come from these islands.

- Cuba: the musical style son includes the mambo. This style draws on the African call and response at the end of most compositions. The rumba is another dance with strong African beginnings.
- Dominican Republic, Puerto Rico, and Haiti: These islands have popularized merengue dance music. This music incorporates the use of drums, marimba, and accordions. The musical style, bomba, is based on the African call and response with drum accompaniment. This style comes from the island of Puerto Rico where we also find the plena, a style similar to ballads found in Mexico.
- Jamaica: Reggae, probably the most internationally famous music of the Caribbean, is exported from this island. A band named Bob Marley and the Wailers is responsible for bringing it to world attention.
- Trinidad and Tobago: The steel drum was born here. Steel drums are made from oil drums that are hammered into an instrument that produces many pitches. This is a popular instrument, especially in large bands. From these islands comes the calypso. Calypso lyrics told of political and social happenings and served to bring news to the people. A recent offshoot of calypso music is soca style, which emphasizes dance. The name soca comes from "soul of calypso" (Mohn, 2005, p. 49). A popular soca composition is "Hot, Hot, Hot" by Arrow.

Each year people from all over the world invade these islands for Carnival. The roots of Carnival have been traced to pagan rites to honor Dionysus, the god of wine. These pre-Christian rituals were adopted by Roman Catholics as a preparation for the Lenten season, which requires 40 days of strict diet and behavior. The ritual was brought to the Caribbean by

## A *Closer* Look

### The Steel Drums of Trinidad

The sources for the information presented in this section are Steel Drum Shoppe (2005) and Worldwide Destinations (2005).

The steel drum is an example of the ingenuity of humans and the need for humans to express themselves through music (see Figure 9–14). Trinidad had been a major slave trade center. The Africans who ended up in Trinidad brought with them their hand drum culture. During the late 1800s, Britain ruled the island of Trinidad. By that time, the hand drumming had become distinct among street gangs. Specific drumming was used to call members to street fights. In an effort to stop the gang warfare, the government outlawed the used of hand drums and other rhythmic instruments. Deprived of their drums, the people began to look for anything they could use for rhythm instruments such as pots and pans, biscuit tins, and hub caps. It is said that Spree Simon

discovered the various pitches he could make on his garbage can while trying to remove a dent with a hammer. Instead of removing the dent, he continued making more until he was able to play an entire scale. However, garbage cans were difficult to find and their metal was too thin. During World War II, U.S. forces abandoned oil drums in Trinidad. These proved to be perfect for making steel drums. These drums were not considered respectable and the violent rivalries that sprang up among the bands gave the instrument a bad name. If a young person was a member of steel band, he was labeled a possible criminal. Eventually, the instrument gained respect and is now recognized as a legitimate instrument. Major companies sponsor the bands with the encouragement of the Trinidad government. The Trinidadians claim that the steel drum is the only nonelectric instrument made in the twentieth century.

---

Catholic settlers. Traditionally, at this time of year, slaves were allowed to express themselves musically. These African-Americans used their music to express their hope and desire for social freedom.

Throughout hundreds of years of occupation, the islands have changed hands often due to politics in Europe. These changes have led to a unique mix of languages and cultures. In 1996, 400 Caribbean writers, artists, critics, and cultural experts gathered to discuss the influence of Caribbean arts on the world. One of the attendees read an English translation of a 150-year-old poem that was written by a mixed-race Spanish-speaking priest. This poem reflects the ethnic and sometimes confusing blend found in these islands.

Yesterday I was born a Spaniard
In the afternoon, I became French
At night, they said that I Ethiopian be
I am English, they say today
I do not know what will become of me
(Elliot, 1996, p. 1)

**Figure 9–14**   Steel Drum with Mallets

## Music of the World

### Sing a Song of Puerto Rico

1. Read one of these books to the children.
   a. Hooper, N. (2003). *Everywhere Coquis! / En dondequiera coquies.* New York: Omni Arts Publishers
   b. Mohr, N. (1995). *The Song of El Coqui and Other Tales of Puerto Rico.* New York: Viking Books

2. Teach the children the chorus to the song "El Coqui" ("coqui, coqui, coqui, qui, qui, qui").

3. Play the song "El Coqui" for the children. It can be found in the book by José-Luis Orozco titled *"De Colores" and Other Latin-American Folk Songs for Children* (New York: Puffin Books). The CD has the same name and is sung by José-Luis Orozco.

4. Have the children sing the chorus "coqui, coqui, coqui, qui, qui, qui" with the recording.

5. On other days, begin to teach the children other parts of the song in either English or Spanish.

---

Just as the islands once imported slaves from Africa, they now export the music that developed from the various cultures of these interesting people.

**For You**

1. Listen to music from the Caribbean. The Resource Guide in Appendix D lists suggested recordings.
2. Read books, such as James A. Michener's *Caribbean,* to become familiar with the island cultures.

**In the Preschool and in Out-of-School Programs**

1. Play music from the Caribbean for the children at appropriate times.
2. Read children's books about the Caribbean as you play the music.

## References

Elliott, J. (1996). *Experts examine global impact of Caribbean culture.* Reuters, August 8, 1996. Retrieved February 22, 2005, from http://www.hartford-hwp.com/archives/43/027.html

Iben, H. (1997). *The guide to symphony orchestra instruments.* Retrieved September 15, 2004, from http://www.mathcs.duq.edu/~iben/auxil.htm

Mohn, T. (2005). *Carnival!* Sky. February 2005. pp. 46–50. Omaha, NB: Pace Communications.

Morrison, G. (2001). *Early childhood education today* (8th ed.). Upper Saddle River, NJ: Prentice Hall.

National Association for the Education of Young Children (NAEYC). (1998). *Accreditation criteria & procedures.* Washington, DC: Author.

Pearson Education. (2005). *Music of countries and cultures.* Retrieved February 22, 2005, from http://www.sbgmusic.com/html/teacher/reference/cultures.html

Steel Drum Shoppe. (2005). *How did the steel drum instrument evolve?* Retrieved February 24, 2005, from http://www.steeldrumshop.com/pan_faq.asp

Welcome to the Caribbean. (2005). *Caribbean music.* Retrieved February 24, 2005, from http://www.welcometothecaribbean.com/music.htm

World History Archives. (2005). *The history of the Caribbean.* Retrieved February 24, 2005, from http://www.hartford-hwp.com/archives/43/

Worldwide Destinations (2005). *History of the steel drum.* Retrieved February 24, 2005, from http://www.yourtravelsource.com/About_YTS/Pandemonium/History/history.html

# Child Development

| Table A-1 | Piaget's Six Substages of the Sensorimotor Stage |
|---|---|
| Substage One: (Birth to one month old) | • From birth, the newborn possesses survival reflexes, such as sucking, hearing, seeing, crying, and grasping, to help him adjust to the world outside his mother. |
| Substage Two: (One to four months old) | • Gradually, the survival reflexes are replaced with intentional movements. The infant is more alert and begins to communicate with people around him. He also becomes more aware of his own body. He notices behaviors he performs by chance and then repeats them. For example, the infant may accidentally place his fist in his mouth and suck on it, that feels good, and so he does it again. Piaget called this primary circular reaction. Every time the infant notices one of his own behaviors that he finds interesting, such as blowing a bubble or opening his hand, he repeats the action. (Source: Boeree, 1999) |
| Substage Three: (Four to eight months old) | • The infant can now sit, reach, grasp, and manipulate objects. He begins to understand that he can affect his environment and he engages in secondary circular reactions, which involve people and objects in his environment. He repeats those actions and events that he finds interesting. For example, the infant discovers that if he throws his toy on the floor, someone will pick it up and give it back to him. Therefore, he throws it down, again. He learns that if he pushes a button on a toy the lid will pop open, so he does that over and over again. (Sources: Berk, 2001 and Boeree, 1999) |
| Substage Four: (Eight to twelve months old) | • During this stage, the infant continues to engage in secondary circular reactions, but his actions become organized and the child combines actions. Two important changes occur during this substage.<br><br>1) The infant engages in behavior that is intentional and with a goal in mind. For example, when shown a toy, which is then hidden, the infant will find it by first pushing the obstacle aside and second, grasping the toy. Piaget called this physical causality or the action of one object or person on another through contact. In the example above, the infant might push aside a covering over the toy. This is the beginning of problem solving.<br><br>2) The infant develops the ability to realize that something still exists, even when it cannot be seen. This is called object permanence. Prior to this point in the infant's development, if an object is out of sight, it is out of the infant's mind. One problem goes along with object permanence. Now that the infant can remember Mom when she leaves, he may suffer from separation anxiety. This means he becomes upset when she leaves, because he can now remember her. (Source: Berk, 2001) |

**Table A-1**   *(Continued)*

| | |
|---|---|
| Substage Five: (12 to 18 months old) | • Piaget described infants in this substage as "little scientists" because they begin to experiment with creative ways in which to repeat their actions (Essa, 2003, p. 301). The infant uses tertiary circular reactions. Now, when the infant drops an object, he will try various ways in which he can do that. His actions are deliberate and he is a better problem solver. As he continues his creative activities, the infant develops a "more advanced understanding of object permanence" (Berk, 2001 p. 151). (Sources: Berk, 2001 and Essa, 2003) |
| Substage Six: (18 months to 24 months old) | • This substage is more of a transitional period to the next stage. By the time the infant is in Substage Six, he has the ability to create mental representations of reality. This means that he can remember past events or missing objects. He solves problems less by trial and error and more through thinking. For example, if his push toy runs into something, he will think about it and then turn in a different direction, instead of continuing to push against the object randomly, until it moves, someone moves it, or he accidentally changes direction. The infant can also remember behaviors he has seen and copy those behaviors at a later time. At this point, the infant is capable of make-believe play. He imitates the actions of those around him. For example, he may rock a baby doll and put it in bed, or feed it. (Source: Berk, 2001) |

**Table A-2**   Characteristics of Piaget's Preoperational Stage (Ages 2–7 Years)

• **Symbolic representation** is an important ability of the child at this stage. A symbol might be a picture or a word, written or spoken, that represents an object, person, or animal. Daily, a child's language grows as he gathers language symbols for many objects. Dramatic play is another example of symbolic representation. In the dramatic corner, children play various roles. This helps them understand their world. (Source: Boeree, 1999)

• **Classification** is the process of grouping items according to a shared characteristic or attribute. Children begin to sort and classify objects at this time. The younger children in this stage can only classify objects by using one attribute at a time. For example, if they are sorting buttons, they may sort by using the attribute of color, putting all the red buttons in one pile and all of the blue ones in another pile, and so on. Or, they may sort by size, putting all the large buttons in one pile and all the small buttons in another pile. However, they are not able to sort using two attributes at once. For example, they cannot sort by placing all of the large, red buttons in one pile, large, blue buttons in another pile, small, red buttons in another pile, and small, blue buttons in the final pile. It is too much for them to keep in mind.

• **Egocentrism** is the term Piaget used to explain how children in the preoperational stage mentally view the world. Children in the preoperational stage have a limited perception of reality. It is limited to their viewpoint. The young child thinks that everyone sees the world as he does. Piaget believed this led to the child's thinking that inanimate objects also have feelings, desires, and goals. Egocentrism also leads to the inability of children in this stage to understand **conservation**. For example, if the child is shown the same amount of water in a tall thin beaker and in a squat, wide beaker, he will still say the tall beaker contains more. This is because from his viewpoint it looks like more. Conservation means that the child understands that although the appearance of an object changes, such as the shape of clay, other physical characteristics, such as volume, remain the same. (Source: Berk, 2001)

## *Table* A-3   Characteristics of Piaget's Concrete Operations Stage (Ages 7–11 Years)

- **Classification:** They continue to sort and classify, but now they can sort by several attributes at a time. Objects can be sorted and classified according to color, size, shape, and use. Through classification, children understand relationships and connections between objects, animals, and people.

- **Seriation:** This skill began during the previous stage. This is the ability to sort objects in a sequential order, according to a particular characteristic. For example, during the preoperational stage, a child might be able to sort three teddy bears according to size, small, medium, and large. However, if the child was given eight sticks of various sizes and was asked to place them in a sequential order, it would be too difficult for him. Children in the concrete operations stage are able to seriate various items, such as a list of months that contained rainy days, placing the month with the most rainy days first and the month with the least rainy days last. (Source: Berk, 2001)

- **Conservation:** This skill is achieved during this stage. For example, during the preoperational stage, if the young child is presented with two balls of play dough that are exactly the same size and then, one is flattened or rolled like a snake, the child would choose the round ball as the one with more play dough. If the same two balls of play dough were presented to the child in the concrete operations stage, he would understand that the balls remained the same in volume and that only the shape changed. (Source: Berk, 2001)

- **Reversibility:** This is the ability to understand that what is done can be undone, or to think through a process, backwards to the starting point. For example, in math, reversibility allows the child to understand that the equation, $2 + 3 = 5$, is the same as the equation, $3 + 2 = 5$. Additionally, reversibility allows the child to subtract $5 - 2 = 3$. If a child, who had developed the logic of reversibility, were using blocks to represent these equations, he would understand that he only needed five blocks to represent all of the equations above. Reversibility also helps the child in the concrete operations stage understand that the flattened or rolled ball of play dough in the example under conservation can be rolled back into a ball. (Sources: Berk, 2001 and Driscoll and Nagel, 2002)

## *Table* A-4   First Four Stages of Erikson's Psychosocial Theory

| | |
|---|---|
| Stage One: Trust versus Mistrust (Birth to 18 months) | During this stage, the infant's task is to develop trust in his world. Infants are helpless and must rely on the adults around them. If the adults are responsive, then the infant will be fed when hungry, changed when wet, kept warm, allowed to sleep when tired, and nurtured. When the infant is consistently and predictably cared for, he comes to trust the world. When the adults in his life do not provide consistent and predictable care, the infant learns to mistrust and he sees the world as a hostile place. A good balance between trust and mistrust results in a person who has hope that even when things are going wrong, sooner or later they will be fine. Too much trust and not enough mistrust results in a gullible person. Too much mistrust and not enough trust results in a withdrawn paranoid person. (Sources: Boeree, 1999, Essa, 2003, and Berk, 2002) |
| Stage Two: Autonomy versus Shame and Doubt (18 months to 3 years old) | During this stage, it is the task of the toddler to establish some autonomy or independence and to diminish shame and doubt. As children develop their language, cognitive, and motor abilities, they assert their independence from the adults around them. Of course, they cannot be totally independent at this point, but they try. At this age, children still enjoy being held and cuddled, but this may be on their terms. If adults do not understand the child's need for |

**Table A-4**   *(Continued)*

| | |
|---|---|
| | independence and instead, correct them or laugh at their efforts to be independent, the child can develop feelings of shame and self-doubt. A good balance between autonomy and shame and self-doubt results in a person who has determination. Too much autonomy and not enough shame and doubt leads to impulsiveness, or a child who jumps into things without considering his abilities. Too much shame and doubt and not enough autonomy leads the child to think he is not good for anything. (Sources: Boeree, 1999, Essa, 2003, and Berk, 2002) |
| Stage Three: Initiative versus Guilt (3 to 5 years old) | The child's task for this stage is to begin to take on responsibility, learn new skills, enjoy imitating adults, and learn to get along with others. That is initiative. Adults should encourage the child's curiosity and imagination and encourage him to try new activities and ideas. Children should be allowed to learn through their play and not taught in a formal manner. However, it is important to establish guidelines. If adults do not allow children to explore, experiment, and try out their ideas, or if they do not give children guidelines, the children will develop a sense of too much failure and guilt. A good balance between initiative and guilt results in a person who has a sense of purpose. Too much initiative and not enough guilt leads to ruthlessness, or a person who will step on anyone to get what he wants. **Sociopathy** is an extreme form of this unbalance. A sociopath, someone who exhibits the behavioral patterns of sociopathy, has an antisocial personality disorder. Too much guilt and not enough initiative leads to inhibition, or a child who will not attempt tasks. (Sources: Boeree, 1999, Essa, 2003, and Berk, 2002) |
| Stage Four: Industry versus Inferiority (6 to 12 years old) | The task for this stage is to develop competence in their work, rather than feeling inferior. At this time, children can plan projects and carry them through to the end. They develop habits of workmanship and persistence and learn to feel good about their accomplishments. They also develop citizenship and adhere to the rules of their society. Children of this age are engaged in activities outside of the home that can affect their development. If a child is rejected by his peers or a teacher does not allow him to be successful, he will develop a sense of inferiority. A good balance between industry and inferiority results in a person who has a sense of competence. Too much industry and not enough inferiority leads to **narrow virtuosity**, or a child who is not allowed to be a child and is pushed into a field of competence, but does not develop a broader spectrum of interests and abilities. This might be seen in the case of a child musical prodigy. The other side of this coin is too much inferiority and not enough industry, which leads to inertia. This child, like the child with inhibition, will not attempt anything. (Sources: Boeree, 1999, Essa, 2003, and Berk, 2002) |

## Table A-5   Infant Music Development

|  | Singing | Moving | Playing | Listening | Other Reactions |
|---|---|---|---|---|---|
| Birth to 3 Months |  | Responds to generalized body movement. |  | Differentiates between two tones about two octaves apart at 3–3.5 months. | Soothed by music. |
| 3 to 6 Months |  | Responds to generalized body movement. |  | Tones of an interval of a 5th distinguished at 4–6 months. | Looks for source of sound. |
| 6 to 9 Months | Between five and eight months they try to join in singing. | Initiates rhythmic movement to music about 5–8 months. |  | Differentiates between two notes 1.5 steps apart at 6–7 months. | Associates sound with its source. Enjoys listening to music—initiates cooing. |
| 9 to 12 Months | Imitates adult's vocalizations. | Responds rhythmically. |  |  |  |
| 12 to 24 Months | Babbles in irregular rhythmic patterns Imitates melodic phrases. Sings one- or two-word songs. | Rocks, nods, sways to music. | Shakes rattles and jingle bells. |  |  |

SOURCES: McDonald, D. T. & Simons, G. M. (1989). *Musical Growth and Development.* New York: Schirmer
Campbell, P. S. & Scott-Kassner, C. (1995). *Music in Childhood.* New York: Schirmer
Andress, B. (1998). *Music for Young Children.* Fort Worth, TX: Harcourt and Brace.

## Table A-6   Preschool Music Development

|  | Singing | Moving | Playing | Listening | Other Reactions |
|---|---|---|---|---|---|
| 2 Years of age | Sings in improvised style while playing. Sings repetitive words of a song and maybe the last word of a phrase. Explores his voice and its expressive abilities. Recognizes the difference between speaking and singing. | Moves spontaneously to many types of music. Improvises movement that shows an awareness of beat, tempo, pitch. Responds to music by rocking, bouncing, or waving arms. | Plays simple rhythm instruments (hand drum or sticks). Explores sounds of instruments. Creates sound from instruments and other sources. Plays random keys on a keyboard instrument. | Listens attentively to short musical excerpts and responds with movement. |  |

**Table A-6**  *(Continued)*

|  | Singing | Moving | Playing | Listening | Other Reactions |
|---|---|---|---|---|---|
|  | Uses phrases from learned songs. Babbles in extended phrases. Sings one- or two-word songs. | Tries to imitate clapping. Develops running and walking skills. |  |  |  |
| 3 Years of age | Sings in improvised style, using phrases from learned songs. Sings folk and composed songs. Explores her voice and its expressive abilities. Recognizes the difference between speaking and singing. Reproduces nursery rhymes and chants. Sings with others with increasing accuracy in pitch. Enjoys repeating familiar songs. | Moves spontaneously to many types of music. Practices movement by repeating. Invents new movements. Can perform simple action songs and singing games. Develops large muscle coordination for jumping, hopping, and galloping. | Plays simple rhythm instruments (hand drum or sticks). Explores sounds of instruments. Creates sound from instruments and other sources. Begins to play: Claves, Woodblocks, Tambourine, Gong, Cowbell, Sticks, Sandblocks, Guiro, Maracas. Plays mallet instruments. | Enjoys listening to music. Hears the orchestra as a whole entity. Cannot distinguish specific instruments when the entire ensemble is playing. | Has an increased ability to briefly maintain a steady beat. |
| 4 Years of age | Uses singing voice distinctly from speaking voice. Matches pitches and sings in tune most of the time. Enjoys singing nonsense songs, folk songs, and singing games. Returns answer in echo singing. Continues to improvise songs, but becomes more | Shows an awareness of beat, tempo, dynamics, pitch, and similar phrases through movement. Responds to music elements (pitch, duration, loudness) through movement. Describes through movement similarities and differences in music. Practices movement by repeating. | Shows an awareness of beat, tempo, dynamics, pitch, and similar phrases through playing instruments. Explores patterns on rhythm instruments. Expresses ideas or moods with instruments or other sound-making materials. | Gives attention to short selections. Listens attentively to own expanded repertoire. | Recognizes printed music and calls it music. Can classify rhythm instruments according to size, shape, pitch, and tone. Uses simple musical vocabulary to describe sounds. Describes in language |

**Table A-6** *(Continued)*

| | Singing | Moving | Playing | Listening | Other Reactions |
|---|---|---|---|---|---|
| | critical of self and begins to add traditional musical structure to his improvisations. | Invents new movements. Can perform simple action songs and singing games. Enjoys moving expressively to music. | Responds to music elements (pitch, duration, loudness) through instrument. | | similarities and differences in music. Can recognize some orchestral instruments. Demonstrates an awareness of beat, pitch, tempo, volume, and form. |
| 5 Years of age | Uses singing voice distinctly from speaking voice. Matches pitches and sings in tune most of the time. Enjoys singing nonsense songs, folk songs, and singing games. Improvises spontaneously during activities. Returns answer in echo singing. Acquires a large repertoire of songs. | Shows an awareness of beat, tempo, dynamics, pitch, and similar phrases through movement. Responds to music elements (pitch, duration, loudness) through movement. Describes through movement similarities and differences in music. Enjoys making up simple dances to music of other cultures. Can follow movement directions of simple traditional dances. | Shows an awareness of beat, tempo, dynamics, pitch, and similar phrases through playing instruments. Explores patterns on rhythm instruments. Expresses ideas or moods with instruments or other sound-making materials. Responds to music elements (pitch, duration, loudness) through instrument. Has better coordination and can play: Finger cymbals, Bongo drums, Timpani, Cymbals, Triangle, Keyboard. Plays simple tunes on bells. Uses rhythmic body sounds to accompany songs and chants. | Gives attention to short selections. Listens attentively to own expanded repertoire. | Can classify rhythm instruments according to size, shape, pitch, and tone. Uses simple musical vocabulary to describe sounds. Describes in language similarities and differences in music. Begins to read and write musical ideas. Can identify bands, orchestras, and choruses. |

### Table A-7  School-age Music Development

|  | Singing | Moving | Playing | Listening | Other Reactions |
|---|---|---|---|---|---|
| 6–7 Years of age | Sings in tune in the range of d–b. Begins to have expressive control of voice. With guidance, can develop head voice. | Begins to develop skipping skill. Responds to music with hand clapping. Can clap the beat. Can change movement to gradual pulse changes. | Performs the beat on drums and rhythm sticks. | Gives attention to short musical selections. | Can be involved in cooperative musical play. |
| 8–9 Years of age | Can perform simple harmony songs and rounds. Can accurately reproduce rhythms by chanting. | Can maintain a steady beat while tapping, clapping, stomping. Responds quickly to and accurately to musical changes during movement. Performs more complex folk dances. Can accurately reproduce rhythms by tapping, patting, clapping, or stepping. | Can play recorder and keyboard. Can play most instruments. | Gives attention to longer selections. Listens attentively to own expanded repertoire. | Can conduct with rhythmic accuracy. |

SOURCES: McDonald, D. T. & Simons, G. M. (1989). *Musical Growth and Development.* New York: Schirmer.
Campbell, P. S. & Scott-Kassner, C. (1995). *Music in Childhood.* New York: Schirmer.
Andress, B. (1998). *Music for Young Children.* Fort Worth, TX: Harcourt and Brace.

## References

Berk, L. E. (2001) *Development through the lifespan.* Boston: Allyn and Bacon.

Boeree, C. G. (1999). *Erik Erikson. Personality Theories.* Shippensburg University. Retrieved September 17, 2004, from http://www.shp.edu

Boeree, C. G. (1999). *Jean Piaget. Personality Theories.* Shippensburg University. Retrieved September 17, 2004, from http://www.shp.edu

Driscoll, A. and Nagel, N. G. (2002). *Early childhood education:* Birth - 8. Boston: Allyn and Bacon.

Essa, E. L. (2003). *Introduction to early childhood education.* Clifton Park, NY: Thomson Delmar Learning

# *Prenatal Music Nurturing*

## Singing to Prenatal Infants

Singing, moving, and listening to music are the key musical activities parents can carry out with their prenatal infants (Zemke, 1998). Of these three musical activities, singing is the primary activity. The fetus can hear by the second trimester (or fifth month). The closest sound to him and the one to which he becomes most accustomed is his mother's voice. A newborn will turn his head toward the sound of his mother's voice in the birthing room, selecting her voice over any other female voice (Thurman & Langness, 1986). His mother's voice is a comfort to the unborn baby. Through song, an expectant mother can let her baby know that he is wanted and loved and begin the bonding that will last a lifetime. Expectant mothers may sing to their prenatal infants as a natural routine, but for fathers this practice may not be as natural. However, fathers can and should join in on this important activity and form a bond with their unborn infants (Zemke, 1998).

### What Should Mothers and Fathers Sing to Their Unborn Baby?

Folk songs are excellent songs to sing to a prenatal baby. Most adults know folk songs and children's songs from their own childhood. Folk songs represent a wide variety of emotions, are about daily activities, and usually have simple tunes and repetitive words. Not only are folk songs simple and easy to sing, but they also include features common to the child's native language and culture. As the unborn child listens to his mother's or father's voice, he begins to learn the nuances of his language, or in other words, the rhythm and melody of his language (Zemke, 1998).

A lullaby is a form of folk song that encourages children to go to sleep. This form of children's song is discussed further in Chapter 4. Babies show a distinct preference for the music they hear in the womb, including the lullabies their mothers sang to them before they were born (Verny and Kelly, 1981 and Manrique, 2001). In one study, as much as 12 months after birth infants showed a preference for music heard in the womb (Lamont, 2001). It behooves expectant mothers to carefully choose the songs they sing to their unborn babies. After the babies arrive, those songs can be used to calm their babies, making life easier for the new mothers. Folk songs are widely available on children's recordings. If expectant parents want to learn more lullabies, usually a lullaby or two are included in recorded collections of folk songs. By purchasing and listen to these recordings, expectant parents can begin a music library for their child and learn more songs to share with their child in the process.

Finally, in addition to folk songs and lullabies, parents can improvise or make up their own songs. The song can be very short, perhaps only a few words, but it still communicates to the prenatal infant that he is loved and that he is special. If parents are not sure how to make up songs, they can start by using the tones of the 'universal child's song' discussed in Chapter 4. For example, a mother might sing the words, "Hello, Baby, Mommy wants to see you" to the tones of this children's song. The same song can be sung by the expectant father. This is a good way to start improvising songs.

## How Should Expectant Parents Sing to Their Unborn Baby?

Expectant mothers should sing anytime they wish. They should sing about what they are doing as they move through their day. They should sing about what they see, such as the moon and stars on a beautiful night or the bright sun through the window. Or, they can sing about how excited they are about the baby's arrival. Expectant fathers, of course, need to be near the mother in order to sing to the baby, but they can sing about the same subjects. Here are some tips on how to sing to an unborn baby.

- Begin as soon as the mother knows she is pregnant. This will allow her time to become familiar with some songs and be comfortable and spontaneous with the experience.
- Both expectant parents should build a small repertoire of songs that vary in mood and tempo. This will allow them the flexibility to change songs according to their mood and to fit their own words to various melodies.
- Once they become familiar with the melodies, parents can begin to make up their own words to the songs. This is made easier if their repertoire contains at least 10 songs. With practice, they will be able to fit the rhythm of their words to the rhythm of the melody. When singing a song, the words should sound natural, as if they were speaking them.
- Sing throughout the day and for enjoyment.
- The mother should sing a lullaby when she takes a rest or goes to bed at night. She can rock in a chair, gently rock back and forth on the bed, or massage her abdomen. This ritual may help establish a bedtime ritual for the baby after he is born.
- Nearly everything the mother says or sings is heard by her baby by the fourth or fifth month after conception. Not only can the baby hear sounds above a firm whisper (about 40 decibels—a firm whisper is about 35 decibels), but also, the higher pitch of the mother's voice makes it easier to hear. For the baby to clearly hear the expectant father, he must be very close to the mother, if not singing directly to the mother's abdomen (Thurman & Langness, 1986).

By singing to their unborn baby, expectant parents not only stimulate his musical intelligence, but also stimulate his language development and begin the parent-child bonding that is necessary for his total development.

## Moving with Prenatal Infants

Six months after conception, the prenatal infant already moves to the rhythms of his mother's speech (Heyge & Sellick, 1998). By moving (dancing or rocking, for example) while she sings, the mother gives her unborn child sensory stimulation for his rapidly developing brain (Heyge & Sellick, 1998). While in the womb, the fetus is already beginning to develop his senses of balance, spatial orientation, and muscular involvement (Thurman & Langness, 1986).

### How Can Expectant Parents Use Movement with Their Unborn Baby?

Movement by the mother is healthy for the fetus, because he is stimulated to adjust to the movement and use his developing physical senses (Zemke, 1998). Additionally, it is healthy for the mother to be engaged in exercise (Zemke, 1998). Here are different types of musical movement for expectant parents suggested by Zemke (1998).

- While listening to relaxing music, the mother breathes with the musical phrases and sways, stretches, and moves arms in an arc above her head or in front of her body.
- While singing or listening to music, the mother massages, taps, pats, rubs, or strokes her abdomen.
- While moving to music, the mother uses scarves as a prop to add interest. The mother should float and circle the scarves to express the music.
- While listening to slow tempo music, the expectant couple slow dances as a couple.
- While listening to slow-or moderate-tempo music, the couple performs metric dancing. In this type

of movement, the expectant parents move to a classical piece of music, either by stepping to the beat or rhythm of the music or by doing a dance step, such as step and bend.

## Listening to Music with Prenatal Infants

The expectant mother provides an enriching experience for her unborn baby when she listens to music, even before the fetus can hear (Zemke, 1998). Expectant mothers share hormones with their babies. Therefore, the emotional well-being of the mother is linked to the emotional well-being of her infant. The mother can help her unborn infant feel calmer and happier by setting aside time each day to listen and relax to music (Amphion Communications, 2003). From the time of conception, infants can feel loved and welcome through the relaxing musical experiences of their mothers (Manrique, 2001).

### How Can Expectant Parents Listen to Music with Their Unborn Baby?

Expectant mothers should set aside time to relax and listen to music on a daily basis. Although a variety of music can be played for their enjoyment, expectant parents should take time to carefully select the music they use for prenatal listening and movement. There has been speculation that in part, the level of a child's music aptitude may be a result of "his prenatal responsiveness to music as well as to the quality of the music environment that his mother experienced during her pregnancy" (Gordon, 1990, p. 10). Most expectant mothers reported that their fetuses seemed to prefer soothing music from the Baroque (Vivaldi, for example) and Classical (Mozart, for example) Eras (Zemke, 1998). Some music from the Romantic Era, such as music of Beethoven or Brahms, seemed to agitate the babies (Verny & Kelly, 1981). When expectant mothers attended rock concerts, they reported to researchers that their unborn babies reacted strongly to the music (Whitwell, 2003).

If the expectant parents want to be able to use music to relax and soothe their baby after it is born, relaxation time with music must be set aside. However, having the music playing is not enough if the mother is not relaxed and listening to the music. The mother must be in a relaxed state when she listens to the music. In fact, a different signal might be sent to the fetus about the music to which it is listening if the mother is upset while the music is playing. Remember, the baby shares her hormones.

Some researchers have experimented using small speakers placed on the mother's abdomen (Whitwell, 2001). This is not necessary for prenatal listening in the home, as long as the music is loud enough for the fetus to hear (40 decibels).

## Prenatal Classes and Labor/Delivery Room Music

The field of music therapy has brought music into prenatal classes and from there, into the labor/delivery rooms. The use of music in labor and delivery rooms is increasing, due to several perceived benefits (Schwartz, 1997). The use of music seems to accelerate the process of labor with a decrease in pain, and music relieves stress for both the mothers and the babies (Moltzahn, 2004; Schwartz, 1997; Zemke, 1998). When music is played during childbirth, the mother's anxiety is relieved, endorphins are released, and the need for anesthesia is reduced, making the experience better for both the mother and the infant (Amphion Communications, 2003). During Cesarean sections, usually mothers do not receive intravenous sedatives until the baby is born. Playing music helps the mother relax and endure discomfort as the uterus is manipulated (Schwartz, 1997). Finally, the expectant couple has a feeling of greater control over their environment when they are involved in choosing the music for their child's birth. This helps relieve anxiety when faced with a sterile and unfamiliar environment (Schwartz, 1997).

The music chosen should be based on what the parents like and want for their baby. Although

Dr. Schwartz, an anesthesiologist, suggests classical or new-age music for use in the delivery room, he cited one mother who said her baby liked rock and roll and she requested "Born in the USA" (1997).

Music educators offer classes such as Suzuki Prenatal Music Stimulation (Moltzahn, 2004), *Heartsongs* (Thurman & Langness, 1986), and "Lovenotes: Music for the Unborn" (Zemke, 1998) for prenatal music development. One of the projects offered in some prenatal music classes is the creation of a welcome baby ritual, which may include personal audio tapes for labor, delivery, and birth (Whitwell, 2003; de Gast, 2004). However, as shown above, any expectant couple can use music to soothe their unborn child, to relax his mother during labor and delivery, and to usher him into the world. If the infant experiences this prenatal stimulation, not only does he experience the many benefits mentioned in this appendix, but also he comes into the world ready to experience more music.

## Summary

Although the world of the prenatal infant continues to hold many mysteries, technology has allowed us to invade that world and make discoveries about the development of the fetus. Researchers continue to study the possibilities for enhancing the infant's life after birth through intrauterine stimulation before birth. Prenatal music stimulation is one approach that may hold benefits for both the mother and child. Both the fetus and the mother can benefit from the stress reduction and relaxation that music offers. Additionally, fathers should be encouraged to participate in this bonding process. There is some evidence that prenatal music stimulation may also enhance cognitive development in the fetus. In general, a growing amount of literature supports a revival of ancient prenatal bonding traditions and a growing number of expectant parents are seeking ways to bond with their baby before birth.

## References

Amphion Communications. (2003). *Make way for baby.* Retrieved October 11, 2004, from http://www.makewayforbaby.com/prenatalmusic.htm

de Gast, I. (2004). *Mother and baby sound connection.* Retrieved October 11, 2004, from http://www.ilkadegast.com/HTML/motherandbaby.html

Gordon, E. E. (1990). *A music learning theory for newborn and young children.* Chicago: G. I. A. Publications.

Heyge, L., & Sellick, A. (1998). Music: A natural way to play with babies. *Early Childhood Connections: Journal of Music- and Movement-Based Learning, 4*(4), 8–13.

Lamont, A. (2001). *How music heard in the womb is remembered by the child.* Retrieved September 11, 2004, from http://www.le.ac.uk/press/press/babiesmusic.html

Manrique, B. (2001). *Prenatal and postnatal stimulation research.* Make Way for Baby. Retrieved October 11, 2004, from http://makewayforbaby.com/research.htm

Moltzahn, J. (2004). *Suzuki early childhood development education* [Online]. Retrieved October 11, 2004, http://www.suzukimusiccentre.com/prenatal.htm

Schwartz, F. J. (1997). *Music and perinatal stress reduction.* Retrieved September 16, 2004 from http://www.birthpsychology.com/lifebefore/sound3.html

Thurman, L. & Langness, A. P. (1986). *Heartsongs: A guide to active pre-birth and infant parenting through. . .language and singing.* Englewood, CO: Music Study Services.

Verny, T., & Kelly, J. (1981). *The secret life of the unborn child.* New York: Delta.

Whitwell, G. E. (2001). *Prelude.* Center for Prenatal and Perinatal Music. Retrieved October 11, 2004, from http://www.prenatalmusic.com/prelude.htm

Whitwell, G. E. (2003). *The importance of prenatal sound and music.* Life Before Birth. Retrieved October 11, 2004, from http://www.birthpsychology.com/lifebefore/soundindex.html

Zemke, L. (Summer, 1998). Music and prenatal development. *Early Childhood Connections, Journal of Music and Movement-Based Learning, 4* (3), 19–23.

# Maintaining and Tuning Your Autoharp

The autoharp is probably one of the easiest instruments to maintain, tune, and play. That makes it a perfect instrument for the early childhood classroom and for the early childhood teacher who has little or no training in music.

The autoharp requires very little maintenance. Occasionally, a string will break and require replacing or a felt pad will need to be replaced, but this does not occur often when the instrument is used in a normal manner. Dusting the instrument and tuning it are the normal upkeep procedures. To dust the soundboard, you will need a flat stick such as a paint stir stick to reach under the strings. Wrap a thin piece of cloth or paper towel around the stick to catch the dust. Soft carrying cases can be purchased to keep the instrument from becoming too dirty between times of use.

Tuning the instrument requires some time and lots of quiet. A good time to tune your autoharp is when all of the children are sleeping in the afternoon. For those with little or no music training, the easiest way to tune the instrument is by using an electric tuner. The tuner indicates when the pitch of the string is correct. However, these tuners can be expensive. You can also use a pitch pipe to obtain the correct pitch or you can tune it to the piano or electric keyboard. If you are tuning to the piano keyboard, the pitch may not be accurate if the piano is out of tune, but the autoharp will be in tune with the piano.

The typical autoharp has 36 strings. Each string must be tuned individually. The strings are attached to the soundboard with metal pins. At the top of the harp (the side that slants on an angle), the pins have the name of the strings printed beside them. The tuner is a wrench with a handle that fits over the pins and turns them. We will tune the autoharp by

beginning with the F scale. As you learned in Chapter 9, the F scale consists of: F, G, A, B-flat, C, D, and E.

## Tuning the F-Major Scale

### Tuning the F Strings

- Begin with the lowest string, F. Place the tuner on the pin.
- Play the lowest F on the pitch pipe or small keyboard. On the piano, play two Fs below middle C. Now pluck the string. Does it sound the same? If not, do you think it is higher or lower? You might not know at first, especially if you are just beginning to listen to pitches. If you are sure it is different, pluck the string again. While the string vibrates, gently move the pin by turning to the left or right. Do not turn the pin far; just a slight movement is all that it takes to change the pitch. You can hear the pitch change as you move the pin. Turn right to make the pitch higher (you are shortening the string) and left to make the pitch lower (you are lengthening the string).
- Again, play F on the pitch pipe or keyboard and then pluck the string. Continue this process until you think they are the same pitch. Be aware that if you are playing an F that is higher or lower in pitch than the string, it will sound higher, but they will still be in tune with each other.
- Now, using the lowest F string on the autoharp as the base, tune all of the other strings that are named F to that string. Place your tuner on the next F string. Play the lower F string, play the next F string on the instrument, and adjust until they are in tune with each other. Continue until you have tuned all of the F strings.

### Tuning the G Strings

If you know how to sing the scale using solfa syllables—do (doe), re (ray), mi (mee), fa (fah), sol (sew), la (lah), ti (tee), do (doe)—it will help you with the tuning process. Just remember the song "Do, a deer, etc." In fact, once you have the F strings tuned, if you can sing the scale, you can tune the instrument to itself without any more use of the pitch pipe or keyboard.

- Play the F string, sing "do-re". Play the G string—does it match your "re"?
- If not, play the F, again, sing "do-re" and tune the G string.
- When you are satisfied that you can play do-re on F and G, tune all of the G strings to the first G string. You can check on yourself by playing the other F strings and then G strings right beside them. Do they sound like do-re?

### Tuning the A Strings

- Play the lowest F, then the G string and sing "do-re-mi."
- Play the A string. Does it sound like your "mi"? If not, go through the same procedure described above to tune the lowest A string.
- When you are satisfied that the string is in tune, use it to tune all of the A strings on the instrument. Again, check yourself by playing the F, G, and A strings and singing "do-re-mi."

### Tuning the B-Flat Strings

There is a possibility that your autoharp does not say B-flat beside any strings. If not, you should play the string marked A-Sharp. This is the same note as B-flat. Look on a keyboard and specifically at the three black keys. The highest of the three black keys can be either A-sharp, meaning you raised the A to sharpen it, or it can be B-flat, meaning you lowered the B to flatten it.

- This time play the lowest F, G, and A strings and sing "do-re-mi-fa."
- Play the B-flat string. Is it in tune?
- If not, use the procedure you have learned to tune it and then tune all of the B-flat strings.

### Tuning the Remaining Strings in the F-Major Scale

- Proceed through the scale, tuning the C, D, and E strings by using the procedure you have been following.
- When you have finished, you should be able to pluck the F scale (F, G, A, B-flat, C, D, E, and F) on the entire autoharp.

## Tuning the G-Major Scale

However, you are not finished! Some strings on the autoharp were not used in the F-major scale. You will now tune the G-major scale (G, A, B, C, D, E, F-sharp, and G). Notice there are only two strings you have not tuned in this scale, B and F-sharp.

- Begin on the lowest G. Play G, sing "do," play A, sing "re-mi," and then play B. Does it sound the same as your "mi"?
- If not, tune the B string and when you are satisfied, tune all of the B strings.
- Begin on G again. Play G, sing "do," play A, sing "re," play B, sing "mi," play C, sing "fa," play D, sing "sol," play E, sing "la-ti"; now, play F-sharp. Does it sound like your "ti"?
- If not, tune it as you did with the other notes and when you are satisfied, tune all of the F-sharp strings.
- Now you can pluck the G-major scale (G, A, B, C, D, E, F-sharp, and G) on the entire keyboard. You should also be able to pluck the C-major scale (C, D, E, F, G, A, B, and C).

If you are happy with these scales, we can finish the tuning by using the same procedure for the D-, A-, and E- major scales.

## Tuning the D-Major Scale

- The D-major scale is D, E, F-sharp, G, A, B, C-sharp, and D.
- As you can see, C-sharp is the only string that has not been tuned in this scale.
- Pluck the scale, sing the notes, and tune the C-sharp strings.

## Tuning the A-Major Scale

- The A-major scale is A, B, C-sharp, D, E, F-sharp, G-sharp, and A.
- In this scale, all of the notes have been tuned except G-sharp.
- Pluck the scale, sing the notes, and tune the G-sharp strings.

## Tuning the E-Major Scale

- The E-major scale is E, F-sharp, G-sharp, A, B, C-sharp, D-sharp, and E.
- In this scale, all of the notes have been tuned except D-sharp.
- Pluck the scale, sing the notes, and tune the D-sharp strings.

You are now finished tuning the autoharp. Unless the instrument is new, you should not have to tune it very often. New instruments take a while to hold their pitch and need more frequent tuning. At first the process may take you a while and seem tedious; however, the more you tune the autoharp,

the easier it will become and the faster you will be able to complete the tuning.

## Selecting Chords

Table C-1 in this appendix is meant as an aid in selecting the correct chords for various keys. Remember, when playing the autoharp, you normally play only three chords, the I, IV, and V7 of the key in which you are playing. The chords are listed for the corresponding keys.

| Table C-1 | | | |
|---|---|---|---|
| Key | I Chord | IV Chord | V7 Chord |
| C Major | C | F | G7 |
| G Major | G | C | D7 |
| F Major | F | B Flat | C7 |
| D Major | D | G | A7 |
| B Flat Major | B Flat | E Flat | F7 |
| a minor | a minor | D | E7 |
| e minor | e minor | A | B7 |

# D

# Resource Guide

## Suggested Recordings

*Music of Western European Historical Eras*

### Middle Ages and Renaissance

*Medieval Chants & Improvisations* (Centaur)
*Gregorian Chants: Medieval Voices* (Excel)
*Best of the Renaissance*, Tallis Scholars (Philips)
*From Chant to Renaissance*, Voices of Ascension (Delos Records)

### Baroque Era

**Bach (1685–1750)**
*Prelude and Fugue in G Major*
*Minuet in G*
*Suite No. 3 in D—Air & Gigue*
*Brandenburg Concertos*
*Bach for Babies: Fun and Games for Budding Brains*

**Handel (1685–1759)**
*The Royal Fireworks Suite—Overture & Menuetto*
*The Water Music Suite: Menuetto*
*Gavotte*

**Monteverdi (1567–1643)**
*Laetaniae della Beata Vergine* (Nuova Era)
*Gloria: Music from the 1600s* (Rivo Alto)
*Monteverdi: Madrigals* (Decca)

**Purcell (1659–1695)**
*Essential Purcell*, New College Choir Oxford (Hyperion)
*Fairy Queen* (Mundi)

**Pachelbel (1653–1706)**
*Pachelbel's Greatest Hits: Ultimate Canon* (RCA)

**Vivaldi (1678–1733)**
*The Four Seasons: Summer, Spring, Autumn, and Winter*

**Various Baroque Composers**
*25 Baroque Favorites* (Vox)

### Classical Era

**Franz Joseph Haydn (1732–1809)**
*Clock Symphony: Andante*
*Farewell Symphony*
*Toy Symphony*
*Trumpet Concerto in E Flat Major: Third Movement: Allegro*
*Symphony No. 94 in G Major (Surprise)*, Menuet

**Wolfgang Amadeus Mozart (1756–1791)**
*Minuet in G* (K. 1), written by Mozart at age five
*Minuet in F* (K. 2), written by Mozart at age six
*Allegro in B Flat* (K. 3), written by Mozart at age six
*Theme* from Sonata in A (K. 331)
*Rondo* from Sonata in C (K. 545)
*Eine kleine Nachtmusik* (K. 525), Menuetto
*Piano Concerto Number 21*, Andante
*Jupiter Symphony*, "Menuetto"
*German Dance No. 3* (K. 605, No. 3)
*Variations for piano (12) in C major on "Ah, vous dirai-je maman"* K. 265 (Tune of "Twinkle, Twinkle Little Star").
*Mozart for Mothers-to-be*, Neville Mariner & Alexander Gibson, conductors
*The Mozart Effect— Music for Babies—Playtime to Sleepy-time*, Children's Group

**Ludwig Van Beethoven (1770–1827)**
*Minuet in G*
*Für Elise*
*Eroica Symphony No. 3*, "Scherzo"
*Ninth Symphony*, "Ode to Joy"
*Beethoven for Babies: Brain Training for Little Ones*, Neville Mariner, conductor

### Romantic Era

**Bizet (1838–1875)**
"Leap Frog" from *Children's Games*

"The Ball" from *Children's Games*
"Impromptu—The Top" from *Children's Games*

**Brahms (1833–1897)**
*Hungarian Dances*
*Lullaby*

**Chopin (1810–1849)**
"Berceuse"

**Mendelssohn (1809–1847)**
"Nocturne" from *A Midsummer Night's Dream*

**Mussorgsky (1839–1881)**
"The Great Gate at Kiev" from *Pictures at an Exhibition*
"Limoges: The Market Place" from *Pictures at an Exhibition*
*Night on Bald Mountain*

**Offenbach (1819–1880)**
"Barcarolle" from *Tales of Hoffman*

**Rimsky-Korsakov (1844–1908)**
*The Flight of the Bumblebee*

**Saint-Saëns (1835–1921)**
"The Swan" from *Carnival of the Animals*
"Aquarium" from *Carnival of the Animals*
*Danse Macabre*

**Schubert (1797–1828)**
*March Militaire*

**Schumann (1810–1856)**
"Catch Me" from *Scenes from Childhood*
"The Wild Horseman" from *Album for the Young*
"Knight of the Hobby Horse" from *Scenes from Childhood*

**Tchaikovsky (1840–1893)**
"Dance of the Sugar Plum Fairy" from *Nutcracker Suite*
"March" from *Nutcracker Suite*
"Dance of the Little Swans" from *Swan Lake*
"The Bird's Funeral" from *Album for the Young*
"Marching of the Tin Soldiers" from *Album for the Young*

## Twentieth Century

### Copland (1900–1990)

*Appalachian Spring*
*The Cat and the Mouse*
*Billy the Kid Suite*
*Red Pony Suite*
*Rodeo*

**Debussy (1862–1918)**
*Prelude* from *Afternoon of a Faun*
"Golliwog's Cakewalk" from *Children's Corner Suite*

**Ellington (1899–1974)**
*Concerto for Cootie*

**Gershwin (1898–1937)**
*Rhapsody in Blue*

**Joplin (1868–1917)**
*Maple Leaf Rag*

**Kabalevsky (1904–1987)**
"Gallop" from *The Comedians*
"Clown" from *Twenty-Four Little Pieces, Op. 39, No. 20*
"Merry Dance" from *Twenty-Four Little Pieces, Op. 39, No. 20*

**Prokofiev (1891–1953)**
"March" from *Love for Three Oranges*
*Peter and the Wolf*
"Waltz on Ice" from *Winter Holiday*

**Ravel (1875–1937)**
*Bolero*
"Empress of the Pagodas" from *Mother Goose Suite*
"Hop o' My Thumb" from *Mother Goose Suite*

**Shostakovich (1906–1975)**
"Waltz" from *Six Piano Pieces for Children*
"Music Box Waltz" from *Ballet Suite No. 1*

**Stravinsky (1882–1954)**
Part I: "Omens of Spring" from *Le Sacre du Printemps (The Rite of Spring)*
Part II: "Sacrificial Dance" from *Le Sacre du Printemps (The Rite of Spring)*
"First Movement" from *Symphony of Psalms*
"Dance of the Ballerina" from *Petrushka*
*The Firebird Suite*

## Nature and Other Sound Recordings

### Laserlight Series: Echoes of Nature

*The Natural Sounds of the Wilderness*
*Ocean Wave*
*Thunderstorm*
*Morning Songbirds*
*Rainforest, Jungle Talk*
*American Wilds*
*The Sounds of Aquatic Mammals in the Wild*

*Wilderness River*
*Frog Chorus*
*Killer Whales*
*Bayou*
*Humpback Whales*
*Sampler*
*Beluga Whales*
*The North Coast*
*Tropical Lagoon*

## Other Sound Recordings

*Three Hundred Sound Effects*
*Hollywood Sound Effects*
*Authentic Sound Effects*
*Cartoon Sound Effects*
*Classic Sound Effects*

### Recordings of Native American Music

*Tribal Waters,* Various artists
*Red Sky Beat,* Blue Chip Orchestra
*Prophecy,* Blue Chip Orchestra
*Sacred Spirit Drums,* David and Steve Gordon
*Sacred Earth Drums,* David and Steve Gordon
*Drum Prayer,* Steve Gordon
*Drum Medicine,* David and Steve Gordon

### Recordings of Crystal Singing Bowls

*Crystal Spirit,* Yatri (music made with crystal singing bowls)

### Recordings Highlighting Various Instruments

*Ai Confini,* a compilation by the Municipality of Venice, including Steve Reich's *Music for Pieces of Wood,* which is a composition for five pairs of claves
*World of Drums and Percussion,* various artists
*Mondo Beat: Masters of Percussion,* various artists
*Il Trovatore* (Verdi) "Anvil Chorus," highlights the tambourine and the triangle
*Planet Drum,* Mickey Hart
*Nutcracker Suite* (Tchaikovsky), "Dance of the Sugar Plum Fairy," highlights the Celesta
*New World Symphony* (Dvorak), "Second Movement," highlights the English horn
*A Midsummer Night's Dream* (Mendelssohn) "Nocturne," highlights the French horn, cello, and bassoon

*Peter and the Wolf* (Prokofiev), highlights the oboe and bassoon
*Prelude and Fugue in G Major* (Bach), highlights the organ
*Carnival of the Animals* (Saint-Saëns), highlights the piano, double bass, strings, flute, clarinet, and xylophone at various times throughout the composition

### Recordings of Caribbean Music

*Caribbean Steeldrums: 20 Most Popular Melodies*
*Caribbean Steeldrums: 20 Famous Tropical Melodies*
*Caribbean Island Steel Drums Favorites*
*Drew's Famous Island Party Jams*

### Recordings of Middle Eastern Music

*Songs from the Middle East*
*Café Beirut*
*Faryad*

### Recordings of Asian Music

*Koto Music of Japan*
*Lullaby for the Moon: Japanese Music for Koto*
*Tegoto: Japanese Koto Music*
*The Art of Japanese Bamboo Flute and Koto*
*Masterpieces of Chinese Traditional Music*
*Eleven Centuries of Traditional Music of China*
*Classical Chinese Folk Music*
*The Silk Road: A Musical Caravan*
*Sitar Music from India*
*Indian Music for Sitar and Surbahar*
*Sound of the Sitar*
*Flute and Sitar Music of India*
*From Saigon to Hanoi, Traditional Songs and Music of Vietnam*
*Vietnamese Traditional Music*
*Air Mail Music: Thailand*
*Rough Guide to the Music of Thailand*
*Music from Thailand*
*Sufi Music of Turkey*
*Rough Guide to the Music of Turkey*

### Recordings of African Music

*Exotic Voices from Africa: 30 of the Best African Vocal Groups*
*African Tribal Music and Dances*
*African Groove*

*African Odyssey*
*Air Mail Music: African Drums*
*Africa: The Music of a Continent*

### Recordings of Lullabies

*African Lullaby,* Ellipsis Arts
*Brazilian Lullaby,* Ellipsis Arts
*Celtic Lullaby,* Ellipsis Arts
*Chinese Lullabies,* Wind Records
*Cuban Lullaby,* Ellipsis Arts
*Disney Baby Lullaby: Favorite Sleepytime Songs for Baby and You,* Disney
*Latin Lullaby,* Ellipsis Arts
*Lullaby Favorites,* Music for Little People
*Lullaby: A Collection,* Music for Little People
*Mediterranean Lullaby,* Ellipsis Arts
*The Planet Sleeps,* Sony Music Entertainment Inc.

### Story Recordings

#### Baroque Era

*Vivaldi's Ring of Mystery*
*Mr. Bach Comes to Call*
*Classical Kids: Hallelujah Handel!*

#### Classical Era

*Classical Kids: Beethoven Lives Upstairs* (1989)
*Classical Kids: Mozart's Magic Fantasy* (1994)
*Classical Kids: Mozart's Magnificent Voyage Fantasy* (1998)

#### Romantic Era

*Classical Kids: Tchaikovsky Discovers America* (1994)

### Recordings for Children

#### Classical Recordings

*Pavarotti's Opera Made Easy—My Favourite Opera for Children* (1994) (Decca)
*Classical Music for Children* (1997) (Entertainment Media Partners)
*25 Children's Favorites* (2000) (Vox)
*David Bowie Narrates Prokofiev's "Peter and the Wolf"* (1992) (RCA)
*Beethoven's Wig: Sing-Along Symphonies* (Rounder)
*Beethoven's Wig 2: More Sing-Along Symphonies* (Rounder)

#### Ella Jenkins—Smithsonian Folkways

*You Sing a Song and I'll Sing a Song*
*Multicultural Songs for Children*
*Songs Children Love to Sing*
*Sharing Cultures with Ella Jenkins*
*Early Childhood Songs*
*Jambo and Other Call and Response Songs and Chants*

#### Raffi (Rounder)

*The Singable Songs Collection*
*Baby Beluga*
*Singable Songs for the Very Young*
*One Light, One Sun*
*Rise and Shine*
*More Singable Songs*

### Music Classified for Movement to Music

#### Slow Movements

"Overture," *The Royal Fireworks Suite* (Handel)
*The Engulfed Cathedral* (Debussy)
"Samuel Goldenberg and Schmuyle" from *Pictures at an Exhibition* (Mussorgsky)
"The Great Gate at Kiev" from *Pictures at an Exhibition* (Mussorgsky)
"Third Movement" from *Symphony No. 1* (Mahler)
"Chorale" from *Album for the Young* (Schumann)
"The Bird's Funeral" from *Album for the Young* (Tchaikovsky)
*Lullaby* (Brahms)
"Nocturne" from *A Midsummer Night's Dream* (Mendelssohn)
*Allemande* (Beethoven)
*Prelude in A* (Chopin)
*Melody in the Mist* (Bartok)
"Menuetto" from *The Royal Fireworks Suite* (Handel)

#### Walking

*German Dance No. 3* (Mozart)
"Music Box Waltz" from *Ballet Suite No. 1* (Shostakovich)
"Merry Dance" from *Twenty-Four Little Pieces, Op. 39* (Kabalevsky)
"Gigue" from *Suite No. 3* (Corelli)
"Golliwog's Cakewalk" from *Children's Corner Suite* (Debussy)

"Clown" from *Twenty-Four Little Pieces, Op. 39, No. 20* (Kabalevsky)

"The Little Train of the Caipira" from *Bachianas Brasileiras No. 2* (Villa-Lobos)

"Empress of the Pagodas" from *Mother Goose Suite* (Ravel)

"Hop o' My Thumb" from *Mother Goose Suite* (Ravel)

"Menuetto" from *'Jupiter' Symphony No. 41* (Mozart)

## Marching

"Marching" from *Memories of Childhood* (Octavio Pinto)
*American Patrol* (F. W. Meacham)
*Semper Fidelis* (Sousa)
*March of the Toys* (Herbert)
"March" from *Love for Three Oranges* (Prokofiev)
*American Salute* (Gould)
*Children's March* (Goldman)
"Entrance of the Little Fauns" (Pierné)
"March" from *Nutcracker Suite* (Tchaikovsky)
"March Militaire" (Schubert)
"March of the Little Lead Soldiers" (Pierné)
*Soldier's March* (Schumann)
"Marching of the Tin Soldiers" *Album for the Young* (Tchaikovsky)

## Fast Movement

"Run, Run" from *Memories of Childhood* (Octavio Pinto)
"Gypsy Dance" from *Carmen* (Bizet)
"Scherzo" from *"Eroica" Symphony No. 3* (Beethoven)
"Limoges: The Market Place" from *Pictures at an Exhibition* (Mussorgsky)
"The Ball" from *Children's Games* (Bizet)
"Catch Me" from *Scenes from Childhood* (Schumann)
"Tag" (Prokofiev)
*Rondo in F* (Beethoven)
*Rondo* from *Eine Kleine Nachtmusik* (Mozart)
*Country Dance* (Beethoven)
"Flight of the Bumblebee" from *Tsar Saltan* (Rimsky-Korsakov)
*Contrasts for Violin, Clarinet, and Piano* (Bartok; fast dance)
"Clowns" (Kabalevsky)
"Impromptu—The Top" from *Children's Games* (Bizet)
"Tarantella" from *The Fantastic Toy Shop* (Rossini-Respighi)

## Skipping, Jumping, Galloping, and Hopping

*Hunting Song* (Schumann)
"Wild Horseman" from *Album for the Young* (Schumann)
"Gallop" from *The Comedians* (Kabalevsky)
"Knight of the Hobby Horse" from *Scenes from Childhood* (Schumann)
"Ballet of Unhatched Chicks" (Mussorgsky)
"Aragonaise" from *Le Cid* (Massenet)
"Leap Frog" from *Children's Games* (Bizet)
"Devil's Dance" from *A Soldier's Tale* (Stravinsky)

## Sliding/Gliding/Swaying and Rocking

"The Skater's Waltz" (Waldteufel)
"The Swan" from *Carnival of the Animals* (Saint-Saëns)
"Waltz on Ice" from *Winter Holiday* (Prokofiev)
"Barcarolle" from *Tales of Hoffman* (Offenbach)
"To a Water Lily" (MacDowell)
"Waltz" from *Six Piano Pieces for Children* (Shostakovich)
"Waltz of the Dolls" (Delibes)

## Dancing

*Minuet in F* ( Mozart)
*Minuet in G* (Bach)
"Danse Macabre" (Saint-Saëns)
*Nutcracker Suite* (Tchaikovsky)

# Videos

Babies Make Music (Video). 1996. Includes comments by Dr. Donna Fox, a leading early childhood music authority from Eastman School of Music. Available online from <http://www.vosa.org/>

Kids Make Music Too! (video). (1996). Available online from <http://www.vosa.org/>

New Screen Concepts (Producer) in association with The Reiner Foundation (1997). *The First Years Last Forever.* (Available from Parents Action for Children, formerly the "I Am Your Child Foundation"; at <http:// www.parentsactionstore.org>)

*Tubby the Tuba* (Video). (1977). Features the voices of Dick Van Dyke and Pearl Bailey. Available from Music for Little People

*Musical Baby.* Available from Music for Little People

*Music Play: Bah Bah Be-Bop.* (1999). Available from National Association for the Education of Young Children (NAEYC)

## Books for the Libraries of Children and Adults

### Books for Children

### Books About Sounds

Beeke, T. (2001). Roar Like a Lion!: A First Book About Sounds. New York: Sterling Publishing

Carle, E. (1990). *The Very Quiet Cricket: A Multi-Sensory Book.* New York: Philomel Books

Martin, B. (1988). *Listen to the Rain.* New York: Henry Holt

Spier, P. (1990). *Crash, Bang, Boom.* New York: Doubleday Books for Young Readers

Stolz, M. (1990). *Storm in the Night.* New York: Harper-Trophy

### Books About Instruments, Music, and People Who Make Music

Ackerman, K., & Gammell, S. (2003). *Song and Dance Man.* New York: Knopf Books for Young Readers

Aliki, (2003). *Ah, Music!* New York: HarperCollins

Aliki, (1986). *A Medieval Feast.* New York: HarperTrophy

Barrett, J. E., & Nelson, M. B. (2001). *Elmo's World: Music!* New York: Random House Books for Young Readers

Brown, R. (1993). *Old MacDonald Had a Farm.* New York: Viking

Carle, E. (1996). *I See a Song.* New York: Scholastic

Cauley, L. B. (1997). *Clap Your Hands.* New York: Putnam Publishing

Curtic, G. (2001). *The Bat Boy and His Violin.* Hong Kong: Aladdin Paperbacks, Simon & Schuster

Cutler, J., & Couch, G. (2004). *The Cello of Mr. O.* New York: Puffin Books

Garriel, B. S., & O'Brien, J. (2004). *I Know a Shy Fellow Who Swallowed a Cello.* Honesdale, PA: Boyds Mills Press

Gollub, M., & Hanke, K. (2000). *Jazz Fly.* New York: Tortuga Press

Gustafson, S. (1995). *Animal Orchestra.* Saskatoon, Saskatchewan, Canada: Greenwich Workshop Press

Hayes, A., & Thompson, K. (1995). *Meet the Orchestra.* Dallas, TX : Voyager Books

Hoffman, M. (1991). *Amazing Grace.* East Rutherford, NJ: Dial Books

Isadora, R. (1979). *Ben's Trumpet.* New York: Greenwillow

Johnson, T. (1991). *Grandpa's Song.* New York: Dial Books

Kalman, B. (1997). *Musical Instruments from A to Z.* New York: Crabtree Publishing

Koscielniak, B. (2000). *The Story of the Incredible Orchestra: An Introduction to Musical Instruments and the Symphony Orchestra.* New York: Houghton Mifflin

Kraus, R. (1990). *Musical Max.* New York: Simon & Schuster

Krementz, J. (1992). *A Very Young Musician.* New York: Aladdin

Kroll, L. (2004). *The Bremen Town Musicians.* Herndon, VA: Bell Pond Books

Kuskin, K. (1986). *Philharmonic Gets Dressed.* New York: HarperTrophy

Laskar, D. (1979). *The Boy Who Loved Music.* New York: Viking Press

McCloskey, R. (1978). *Lentil.* New York: Puffin Books

McDermott, G. (2000). *Musicians of the Sun.* Hong Kong: Aladdin Paperbacks, Simon & Schuster

Melmed, L. (1993). *The First Song Ever Sung.* New York: Puffin Books

Miller, J. P. (2000). *We All Sing with the Same Voice.* New York: HarperCollins

Moss, L., & Priceman, M. (1995). *Zin! Zin! Zin! A Violin* (Caldecott Honor Book). Riverside, NJ: Simon & Schuster Children's Publishing

Moss, L. (2003). *Music Is.* New York: Grosset & Dunlap

Pinkney, A. D., & Pinkney, B. (1997). *Shake Shake Shake: Family Celebration Board Books.* San Diego: Red Wagon Books

Plume, I. (1998). *The Bremen Town Musicians.* New York: Dragonfly Books

Raffi. (1988). *Shake My Sillies Out.* New York: Crown Books for Young Readers

Raschka, C. (1992). *Charlie Parker Played Be Bop.* New York: Scholastic

Rosenberg, J. (1993). *Dance Me a Story*. New York: Thames & Hudson

Rosenberg, J. (1996). *Sing Me a Story*. New York: Thames & Hudson

Sage, J. (1991). *The Little Band*. New York: Margaret K. McElderry Books

Sendak, M. (1975). *Really Rosie*. New York: HarperTrophy

Turner, B. C., & Williams, S. (1999). *Carnival of the Animals* (Book and CD). New York: Henry Holt & Company

Weatherford, C. B. (2003). *The Sound That Makes Jazz*. New York: Walker & Company

Williams, V. B. (1983). *Something Special for Me*. New York: HarperTrophy

Williams, V. B. (1988). *Music, Music for Everyone*. New York: HarperTrophy

Winch, J. (1994). *The Old Man Who Loved to Sing*. New York: Scholastic

Zemach, K. (2003). *The Question Song*. New York: Megan Tingley

### Books About Music and Rhymes

Adams, P. (2000). *This Old Man*. Wiltshire, England: Child's Play International

Aylesworth, J. (1994). *The Completed Hickory Dickory Dock*. Hong Kong: Aladdin Paperbacks, Simon & Schuster.

Celenza, A. H., & Kitchel, J. E. (2000). *The Farewell Symphony*. Watertown, MA: Charlesbridge Publishing

Celenza, A. H., & Kitchel, J. E. (2004). *The Heroic - Symphony*. Watertown, MA: Charlesbridge Publishing

Child, L. M. (1999). *Over the River and Through the Wood*. New York: Henry Holt & Company

Christelow, E. (1993). *Five Little Monkeys Jumping on the Bed*. New York: Clarion Company

Cole, J., & Tiegreen, A. (1989). *Anna Banana: 101 Jump Rope Rhymes*. New York: HarperTrophy

Cole, J., & Tiegreen, A. (1990). *Miss Mary Mack*. New York: HarperTrophy

Conover, C. (1976). *Six Little Ducks*. New York: Thomas Y. Crowell Company

Galdone, P. (1988). *Cat Goes Fiddle-i-Fee*. New York: Clarion

Hazen, B. S. (1972). *Frère Jacques*. New York: Lippincott

Hoberman, M. A., & Westcott, N. B. (1998). *Miss Mary Mack*. New York: Megan Tingley

Johnson, A. A. (1997). *Chinese Jump Rope*. Palo Alto, CA: Klutz Press

The Lady with the Alligator Purse (Compiler). (1998). *Jump Rope Rhymes*. Palo Alto, CA: Klutz Press

Kaye, B., Wise, F. Lippman, S., & Alexander, M. (1998). *A You're Adorable*. Cambridge, MA: Candlewick Press

Keats, E. J. (1989). *Over in the Meadow*. Dallas, TX: Voyager Books

Langstaff, J. (1955). *Frog Went A-Courtin*. New York: Gulliver Books

Lithgow, J. (2004). *Carnival of the Animals*. New York: Simon & Schuster

Raffi. (1992). *Five Little Ducks*. New York: Crown Books for Young Readers

Raffi. (1988). *Tingalayo*. New York: Knopf Books for Young Readers

Raffi. (1998). *Wheels on the Bus*. San Jose, CA: Crown Books for Young Readers

Rogers, R. (2001). *My Favorite Things*. New York: HarperCollins

Rogers, R. (2002). *Getting to Know You*. New York: HarperCollins

Rosen, M. (1998). *Vamos a Cazar Un Oso/We're Going on a Bear Hunt*. Caracas, Venezuela: Ediciones Ekare

Slavin, B. (1992). *The Cat Came Back: A Traditional Song*. Chicago: Albert Whitman & Company

Spier, P. (1994). *The Fox Went Out on a Chilly Night*. New York: Dragonfly Books

Sturges, P. (2004). *She'll Be Comin' Round the Mountain*. New York: Megan Tingley

Taback, S. (1997). *There Was an Old Lady Who Swallowed a Fly*. New York: Viking Books

Trapani, I. (1993). *The Itsy Bitsy Spider*. Watertown, MA: Charlesbridge Publishing

Trapani, I. (2002). *Froggie Went A-Courtin'*. Watertown, MA: Charlesbridge Publishing

Weiss, G. D., & Thiele, B. (1995). *What a Wonderful World*. New York: Atheneum

Westcott, N. B. (1998). *The Lady with the Alligator Purse*. Canada: Little, Brown & Company

Zelinsky, P. (1990). *Wheels on the Bus*. New York: Dutton Children's Books

**Books About Composers**

Cencetti, G. (2001). *Beethoven*. Columbus, OH: Peter Bedrick Books

Cencetti, G. (2001). *Mozart*. Columbus, OH: Peter Bedrick Books

Downing, J. (1991). *Mozart tonight*. Riverside, NJ: Simon & Schuster Children's Publishing

Hammond, S. (2004). *Mozart's Magnificent Voyage*. Pickering, Ontario, Canada: Children's Group

Isadora, R. (1997). *Young Mozart*. New York: Viking Books

Lynch, W. (2000). *Beethoven (Lives and Times)*. Chicago: Heinemann Library

Lynch, W. (2001). *Mozart (Lives and Times)*. Chicago: Heinemann Library

Nichol, B., & Cameron, S. (1999). *Beethoven Lives Upstairs*. New York: Orchard Paperbacks

Rachlin, A. (1992). *Haydn (Famous Children Series)*. Hauppauge, NY: Barron's

Rachlin, A. (1992). *Bach (Famous Children Series)*. Hauppauge, NY: Barron's

Rachlin, A. (1992). *Handel (Famous Children Series)*. Hauppauge, NY: Barron's

Rachlin, A., & Hellard, S. (1992). *Mozart (Famous Children Series)*. Hauppauge, NY: Barron's

Rachlin, A., & Hellard, S. (1993). *Tchaikovsky (Famous Children Series)*. Upper Saddle River, NJ: Silver Burdett

Rachlin, A., & Hellard, S. (1994). *Beethoven (Famous Children Series)*. Hauppauge, NY: Barron's

Rachlin, A., & Hellard, S. (1994). *Schubert (Famous Children Series)*. Hauppauge, NY: Barron's

Rachlin, A., & Hellard, S. (1996). *Chopin (Famous Children Series)*. Upper Saddle River, NJ: Silver Burdett

Venezia, M. (1995). *George Handel (Getting to Know the World's Greatest Composers)*. Danbury, CT: Children's Press

Venezia, M. (1995). *Peter Tchaikovsky (Getting to Know the World's Greatest Composers)*. Danbury, CT: Children's Press

Venezia, M. (1995). *Wolfgang Amadeus Mozart (Getting to Know the World's Greatest Composers)*. Danbury, CT: Children's Press

Venezia, M. (1996). *Duke Ellington (Getting to Know the World's Greatest Composers)*. Danbury, CT: Children's Press

Venezia, M. (1996). *Ludwig Van Beethoven (Getting to Know the World's Greatest Composers)*. Danbury, CT: Children's Press

Venezia, M. (1997). *Igor Stravinsky (Getting to Know the World's Greatest Composers)*. Danbury, CT: Children's Press

Venezia, M. (1998). *Johann Sebastian Bach (Getting to Know the World's Greatest Composers)*. Danbury, CT: Children's Press

Venezia, M. (1999). *Johannes Brahms (Getting to Know the World's Greatest Composers)*. Danbury, CT: Children's Press

Venezia, M. (1999). *John Philip Sousa (Getting to Know the World's Greatest Composers)*. Danbury, CT: Children's Press

Venezia, M. (2000). *Frederic Chopin (Getting to Know the World's Greatest Composers)*. Danbury, CT: Children's Press

Vernon, R. (2000). *Introducing Bach*. Langhorne, PA: Chelsea House Publications

Vernon, R. (2000). *Introducing Vivaldi*. Langhorne, PA: Chelsea House Publications

**Books About Native Americans**

Cohlene, T. (1998). *Dancing Drum: A Cherokee Legend*. New York: Troll Communications

Holling, H. C. (1980). *Paddle-to-the-Sea*. New York: Houghton Mifflin

Joosse, B. B., & Lavallee, B. (1998). *Mama, Do You Love Me?* New York: Chronicle Books

Scott, A. H., & Coalson, G. (2000). *On Mother's Lap*. New York: Clarion Books

**Books About Lullabies**

Aliki. (1968). *Hush, Little Baby: A Folk Lullaby*. Upper Saddle River, NJ: Prentice Hall

Beall, P. C. (2001). *Wee Sing Nursery Rhymes and Lullabies*. Upper Saddle River, NJ: Prentice Hall

Delacre, L. (2004). *Arrorro Mi Nino: Latino Lullabies and Gentle Games.* New York: Lee & Low Books

Feierabend, J. M. (2000). *The Book of Lullabies.* Chicago, IL: Independent Publishers Group

Frazee, M. (1999). *Hush Little Baby: A Folk Song with Pictures.* Fort Worth, TX: Harcourt Children's Books

Ho, M., & Meade, H. (2000). *Hush!: A Thai Lullaby.* New York: Orchard Books

Jaramillo, N. P. (1994). *Grandmother's Nursery Rhymes/ Las Nanas de Abuelita: Lullabies, Tongue Twisters, and Riddles from South America/Canciones de cuna, trabalenguas y adivinanzas de Suramerica.* New York: Henry Holt and Company

Joel, B., & Gilbert, Y. (2004). *Goodnight, My Angel: A Lullaby.* New York: Scholastic Press

Jordon, S. (2001). *Lullabies Around the World: Multicultural Songs and Activities.* Niagara Falls, NY: Sara Jordan Publishing

Kapp, R. (1997). *Lullabies: An Illustrated Songbook.* Fairbanks, AK: Gulliver Books

Larson, D. S. (2002*). Lullabies and Poems for Children* (Everyman's Library Pocket Poets). New York: Everyman's Library

McGill, A. (2000). *In the Hollow of your Hand: Slave Lullabies.* Boston, MA: Houghton Mifflin

Reiser, L. (1998). *Cherry Pies and Lullabies.* New York: Greenwillow Books.

Reiser, L. (1998). *Tortillas and Lullabies, Tortillas y cancioncitas.* New York: Greenwillow Books

Saport, L. (1999). *All the Pretty Little Horses.* New York: Clarion Books

Taylor, J., & Long, S. (2001). *Twinkle, Twinkle, Little Star: A Traditional Lullaby.* New York: Chronicle Books

## Books for Adults

Andress, B. (1998). *Music for young children.* Fort Worth, TX: Harcourt Brace College

Andress, B., & Walker, L. (Eds.). (1992). *Readings in Early Childhood Music Education.* Reston,VA: Music Educators National Conference

Andress, B. (Ed.). (1989). *Promising Practices: Prekindergarten Music Education.* Reston,VA: Music Educators National Conference

Bernstein, S. (1994). *Hand Clap!* Avon, MA: Adams Media Corporation

Bierhorst, J. (1979). *A Cry from the Earth: Music of the North American Indians.* Santa Fe, NM: Ancient City Press

Braun, S., & Edwards, F. (1972). *History and Theory of Early Childhood Education.* Belmont, CA: Wadsworth

Burton, B. (1993). *Moving Within the Circle: Contemporary Native American Music and Dance.* Danbury, CT: World Music Press

Carlson, L. (1994). *More Than Moccasins: A Kid's Activity Guide to Traditional North American Indian Life.* Chicago: Review Press

Choksy, L. (1981). *The Kodály Context.* Englewood Cliffs, NJ: Prentice-Hall

Edwards, L. C., Bayless, K. M., & Ramsey, M. E. (2005). *Music: A Way of Life for the Young Child.* Upper Saddle River, NJ: Pearson, Merrill Prentice Hall

Erdei, P. (Ed.). (1974). *150 American Folk Songs to Sing, Read and Play.* London: Boosey & Hawkes

Feierabend, J. (1990). *TIPS: Music Activities in Early Childhood.* Reston, VA: Music Educators National Conference

Feierabend, J. M., & Kahan, J. (2004). *The Book of Movement Exploration: Can You Move Like This?* (First Steps in Music series). Chicago: GIA Publications

Feierabend, J. M. (1986). *Music for Very Little People.* London: Boosey & Hawkes

Feierabend, J. M. (1989). *Music for Little People.* London: Boosey & Hawkes

Feierabend, J. M. (2000). *The Book of Bounces.* Chicago: GIA Publications

Feierabend, J. M. (2000). *The Book of Simple Songs & Circles.* Chicago: GIA Publications

Feierabend, J. M. (2000). *The Book of Tapping and Clapping: Wonderful Songs and Rhymes Passed Down from Generation to Generation* (First Steps in Music series). Chicago: GIA Publications

Feierabend, J. M. (2000). *The Book of Wiggles & Tickles.* Chicago: GIA Publications

Feierabend, J. M. (2003). *The Book of Call & Response* (First Steps in Music series). Chicago: GIA Publications

Feierabend, J. M. (2003). *The Book of Echo Songs* (First Steps in Music series). Chicago: GIA Publications

Feierabend, J. M. (2003). *The Book of Finger Plays & Action Songs* (First Steps in Music series). Chicago: GIA Publications

Gardner, H. (1983). *Frames of Mind. The Theory of Multiple Intelligences.* New York: Basic Books.

Gordon, E. E. (1990). *A Music Learning Theory for Newborn and Young Children.* Chicago: GIA Publications

Kamien, R. (2001). *Music: An Appreciation, Brief.* Columbus, OH: McGraw-Hill Humanities

Kamien, R. (2003). *Music: An Appreciation* (8th ed.). Columbus, OH: McGraw-Hill Humanities

Locke, E. G. (Ed.). (1989). *SAIL AWAY, 155 American Folk Songs to Sing, Read and Play.* London: Boosey & Hawkes

MacDonald, F. (2001). *Music and dance.* New York: Crabtree Publishing Company

Mayeski, M. (1998). *Creative Activities for Young Children.* Clifton Park, NY: Thomson Delmar Learning

Overby, L. (Ed.). (1991). *Early Childhood Creative Arts.* Reston,VA: Music Educators National Conference

Palmer, M., & Sims, W. (1993). *Music in Prekindergarten: Planning and Teaching.* Reston, VA: Music Educators National Conference

Pica, R. (2000). *Experiences in Movement with Music, Activities and Theory.* Clifton Park, NY: Thomson Delmar Learning

Purton, M. (2000). *Show–Me-How: I Can Make Music.* New York: Lorenzo Books

Schaberg, G. (1988). *TIPS: Teaching Music to Special Learners.* Reston, VA: MENC

Sobol, E. (2001). *An Attitude and Approach for Teaching Music to Special Learners.* Available: Reston, VA: MENC

Storms, J. (1995). *101 Music Games for Children: Fun and Learning with Music and Song.* Alameda, CA: Hunter House

Storms, J. (2001). *101 More Music Games for Children: Fun and Learning with Music and Song.* Alameda, CA: Hunter House

Warren, J. (1983). *Piggyback Songs.* Torrance, CA: Totline Publications

Warren, J. (1984). *More Piggyback Songs.* Torrance, CA: Totline Publications

Warren, J. (1985). *Piggyback Songs for Infants & Toddlers.* Torrance, CA: Totline Publications

Washington, V., & Andrews, J. D. (1999). *Children of 2010.* Washington, DC: National Association for the Education of Young Children

Weber, E. (1984). *Ideas Influencing Early Childhood Education.* New York: Teacher's College Press

Wortham, S. (1992). *Childhood 1892–1992.* Wheaton, MD: Association for Childhood Education International

**Resources for Making Instruments**

Hawkinson, J. (1969). *Music and Instruments for Children to Make.* Chicago: Albert Whitman & Company

Hawkinson, J. (1970). *Rhythms, Music, and Instruments to Make.* Chicago: Albert Whitman & Company

Mandell, M., & Wood, R. E. (1982). *Make Your Own Musical Instruments.* New York: Sterling Publishing

Purton, M. (2000). *I Can Make Music: Simple-to-Make and Fun-to-Play Musical Instruments for Young Children.* New York: Lorenz Books

## Informative Websites

### Websites about Art Works from Various Times and Cultures

http://www.metmuseum.org (the Metropolitan Museum of Art Web site)

http://witcombe.sbc.edu (Dr. Christopher L.C.E. Witcombe, Professor of Art History at Sweet Briar College, has compiled an extensive guide to art on this site.)

http://www.arthistory.net/ (The Art History Network is a guide to art history.)

http://www.baroquemusic.org

http://www.essentialsofmusic.com

http://www.ibiblio.org

http://artcyclopedia.com/ (Artcyclopeida is a guide to art on the Internet.)

### Websites about Brain Research

http://www.ez2bsaved.com

http://www.pbs.org

http://brainresearchinstitute.org/

http://brainresearchfdn.org/

*Websites for Purchasing, Making, or Learning About Musical Instruments*

**Catalogs of Recordings, Instruments, and Books**

GIA Publications, Inc.: http://www.giamusic.com
Kimbo Educational: http://www.kimboed.com
Music for Little People: http://www.mflp.com
Musician's Buddy: http://www.musiciansbuddy.com
Peripole-Bergerault, Inc.:
     http://www.peripolebergerault.com
Rhythm Band Instruments (RBI):
     http://www.rhythmband.com
Suzuki Musical Instruments:
     http://www.suzukimusic.com

**How to Make Instruments**

*Make Your Own Wind Chime* http://www.phy.mtu.edu

**Music Boxes and Singing Bowls**

For Small Hands http://www.forsmallhands.com

**Symphony Orchestral Instruments**

http://www.mathcs.duq.edu

*Website about Medieval Life*

http://www.yale.edu

*Websites about Music Research*

http://www.music-research.org/
http://www.educationthroughmusic.com

*Websites about People in Education*

**Jerome Bruner**

http://tip.psychology.org (search for Jerome Bruner)
http://www.infed.org

**Erik Erikson**

http://www.ship.edu

**Froebel**

http://members.tripod.com

**Howard Gardner**

http://www.indiana.edu
http://www.ed.psu.edu

**Edwin Gordon**

http://www.sc.edu
http://www.giml.org

**Maria Montessori**

http://www.montessori.org/
http://www.montessori-ami.org

**Pestalozzi**

http://www.newadvent.org

**Jean Piaget**

http://www.ship.edu

**Rudolf Steiner and Waldorf Schools**

http://www.waldorfanswers.com
http://www.consciouschoice.com
http://preschoolerstoday.com
http://www.steinercollege.com

**Lev Vygotsky**

http://www.kolar.org/vygotsky/

*Websites about Prenatal Music*

http://www.healthythoughts.com
http://expectantmothersguide.com

## Professional Organizations

American Orff-Schulwerk Association (AOSA)
PO Box 391089
Cleveland, OH 44139-8089
Journal: *The Orff Echo*
Web site: http://www.aosa.org/

Association for Childhood Education International
     (ACEI)
17904 Georgia Ave., Suite 215
Olney, MD 20832
Journal: *Childhood Education*
Web site: http://www.acei.org/

Dalcroze Society
Journal: *American Dalcroze Journal*
Web site: http://www.dalcrozeusa.org/

Music Educators National Conference (MENC)
1806 Robert Fulton Drive
Reston, VA 20191
Journal: *Music Educators Journal*
Web site: http://www.menc.org/

National Association for the Education of Young
    Children (NAEYC)
1509 16th St. N.W.
Washington, DC 20036
Journal: *Young Children*
Web site: http://www.naeyc.org/

Organization of American Kodály Educators (OAKE)
1612 - 29th Avenue South
Moorhead, MN 56560
Journal: *The Kodaly Envoy*
Web site: http://www.oake.org/

Suzuki Association of the Americas (SAA)
P.O. Box 17310
Boulder, CO 80308
Journal: *American Suzuki Journal*
Web site: http://www.suzukiassociation.org/

Early Childhood Music and Movement Association
    (ECMMA)
805 Mill Avenue
Snohomish, WA 98290
Journal: *Early Childhood Connections: Journal of Music
    and Movement-Based Learning*
Web site: http://www.ecmma.org/

## Songs for Young Children

### Traditional American Folk Songs

"A Frog Went a-Courtin"
"All the Pretty Little Horses"
"A Tisket, a Tasket"
"The Bear Went Over the Mountain"
"The Bee and the Pup"
"Bought Me a Cat"
"Bow Belinda Cindy"
"Clap, Clap, Clap Your Hands"
"Did You Ever See a Lassie?"
"Down by the Station"
"Down the River"

"Eency, Weency Spider"
"Erie Canal"
"Five Fat Turkeys"
"Go Round and Round the Village"
"Ha, Ha, This-A-Way"
"Head, Shoulders, Knee, and Toes"
"Hey, Betty Martin"
"Hickory, Dickory Dock"
"Hop Old Squirrel"
"Hot Cross Buns"
"Hush Little Baby"
"I Had a Little Rooster"
"If You're Happy and You Know It"
"It Rained a Mist"
"It's Raining"
"Jingle at the Window (Tideo)"
"Johnny Works with One Hammer"
"Lazy Mary"
"Little Redbird in the Tree"
"Love Somebody"
"Make a Pretty Motion"
"Mary Had a Little Lamb" (see Figure D-1)
"Mary Wore a Red Dress"
"Michael Finnegan"
"Miss Polly Had a Dolly"
"Oats, Peas, Beans and Barley"
"Old Brass Wagon"
"Old Gray Cat"
"Old MacDonald"
"Old MacDonald Had a Farm"
"Old Mister Rabbit"
"The Old Woman and the Pig"
"Over in the Meadow"
"Pawpaw Patch"
"Peanut Song"
"Pussy Cat, Pussy Cat"
"Rain, Rain, Go Away"
"Raining Again Today!"
"Ring Around the Rosies"
"Rock-a-Bye Baby"
"Row, Row, Row Your Boat"
"See-Saw, Margery Daw"
"Shoo Fly"
"Six Little Ducks"
"Sweetly Sings the Donkey"
"There Was a Frog"

# Mary Had a Little Lamb

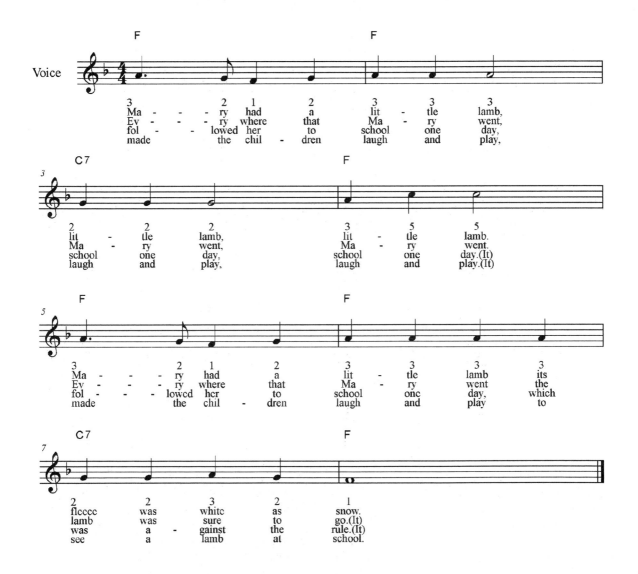

"There's a Little Wheel a-Turning"
"Three Blue Pigeons"
"Twinkle, Twinkle, Little Star"
"What Are Babies Made Of?"
"What Shall We Do?"
"Who's That Tapping at the Window?"
"Willowbee"
"Yankee Doodle"

### Traditional American Singing Games

"Frog in the Middle"
"Hokey Pokey"
"Jim Along Josie"
"Little Red Caboose"
"My Aunt Came Back" (see Figure D-2)
"Ring Around the Rosies"
"Rise, Sugar, Rise"
"Sing with Me"
"Skip to My Lou"

### Other Cultures and Languages

**Africa**

"A Ram-Sam-Sam"
"Zulu Lullaby"

**Chile**

"One Elephant"

**England**

"The Farmer in the Dell"
"Here We Go 'Round the Mulberry Bush"
"London Bridge"
"Looby Loo"
"The Muffin Man"
"Rig-a-Jig-Jig"
"Rock-a-Bye Baby"
"Round and Round the Village"
"Sally, Go 'Round the Sun"
"Sandy Maloney"
"This Old Man"
"Three Cheers for the Red, White, and Blue"
"We're All Together Again"

**France**

"Frère Jacques"
"Le Train"
"Les Feuilles D'Automne"
"Les Petites Marionnettes"
"Savez-vous"
"Ton Moulin"

**Germany**

"Mein Hut"
"Ringel, Ringel, Riehe"
"Schlaf, Schlaf, mein Kind"
"Tira Lira Lira"

**Ireland**

"Prettiest Boy in the County-O"

**Italy**

"Mira Ia don don della"

**Japan**

"Chi Chi Papa"

**Latin America**

"Friar Martin"
"Tinga Layo"

**Mexico**

"Los Patos"
"Rurru"
"Ti-ri-lin"

**Puerto Rico**

"El Coqui"
"Cat and Mouse"

**Scotland**

"Aiken Drum"
"Bingo"
"Bye O, My Baby"
"Noddin'"

**Spain**

"El Florón"
"San Sereni"

# My Aunt Came Back

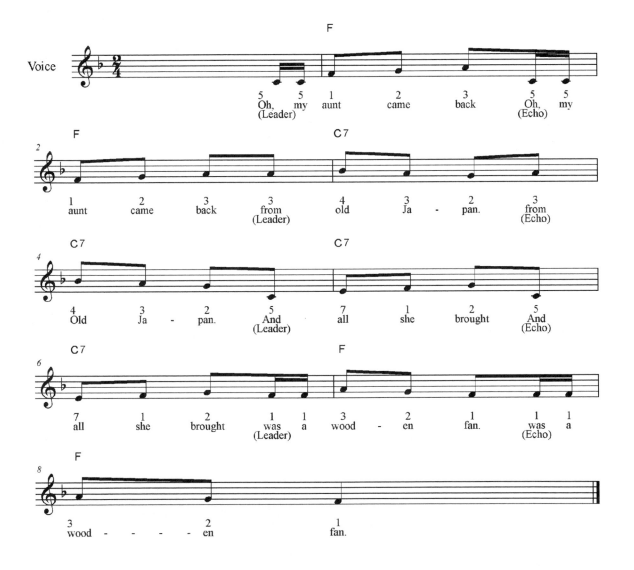

**Sweden**

"Dring, Dring, Dring"
"How D'You Do, My Partner?"
"Ritsch, Ratsch"

**Yiddish**

"I Had a Little Overcoat"

## Chants and Rhymes for Young Children

### "Ride a Cock Horse"

Ride a cock horse to Banbury Cross,
To see a fine lady upon a white horse.
Rings on her fingers and bells on her toes,
She shall have music wherever she goes.

### "Jack-in-the-Box"

Jack-in-the-box,
Sit so still,
Won't you come out?
Yes, I will!

### "The Family"

This is the father short and stout,
This is the mother with children about.
This is the brother, tall you see,
This is the sister with doll on her knee.
This is the baby sure to grow,
This is the family all in a row.

### "To Market"

To market, to market
To buy a fat pig.
Home again, home again,
Jiggitty jig.

To market, to market
To buy a fat hog.
Home again, home again,
Jiggitty jog.

To market, to market
To buy a plum bun.
Home again, home again,
Market's all done.

### "This Is the Way the Lady Rides"

This is the way the lady rides;
Prim, prim, prim, prim.
This is the way the gentleman rides;
Trim, trim, trim, trim.
This is the way the huntsman rides;
A gallop, a gallop, a gallop, a gallop.
This is the way the farmer rides;
Hobble-dee-gee, hobble-dee-gee.

### "This Little Piggy Went to Market"

This little piggy went to market,
This little piggy stayed home,
This little piggy had roast beef,
This little piggy had none,
This little piggy cried wee, wee, wee, all the
    way home.

### "Round a Ball"

Round a Ball,
Round a Ball,
Catch a little mousey.
Up the stairs,
Down the stairs,
And in his little housey.

### "Rub a Dub Dub"

Rub a dub dub
Three men in the tub;
And who do you think they be?
The butcher, the baker,
    the candlestick maker,
Knaves all three!

### "Grandma's Glasses"

These are Grandma's glasses,
This is Grandma's hat,
This is the way she folds her hands
And lays them in her lap.

These are Grandpa's glasses,
This is Grandpa's hat,
This is the way he folds his arms,
Just like that.

*"Shoe a Little Horse"*

Shoe a little horse,
Shoe a little mare,
But let a little colt
Go bare, bare, bare.

*"Peas Porridge Hot"*

Peas porridge hot,

Peas porridge cold,
Peas porridge in the pot,
Nine days old.

Some like it hot,
Some like it cold,
Some like it in the pot,
Nine days old.

# All the Pretty Little Horses

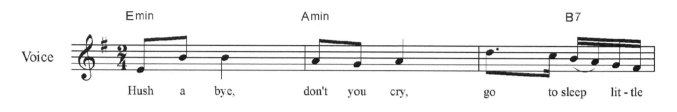

Hush  a  bye,  don't  you  cry,  go  to sleep  lit - tle

ba - - by.  When  you  wake,  you  shall  have

all  the pret - ty  lit - tle  hor - ses.  Black  and  bay,

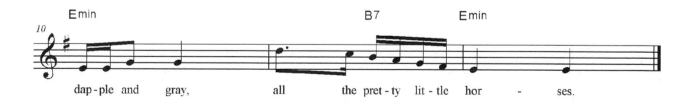

dap - ple and  gray,  all  the pret - ty  lit - tle  hor - ses.

# Tinga Layo

# Twinkle, Twinkle Little Star

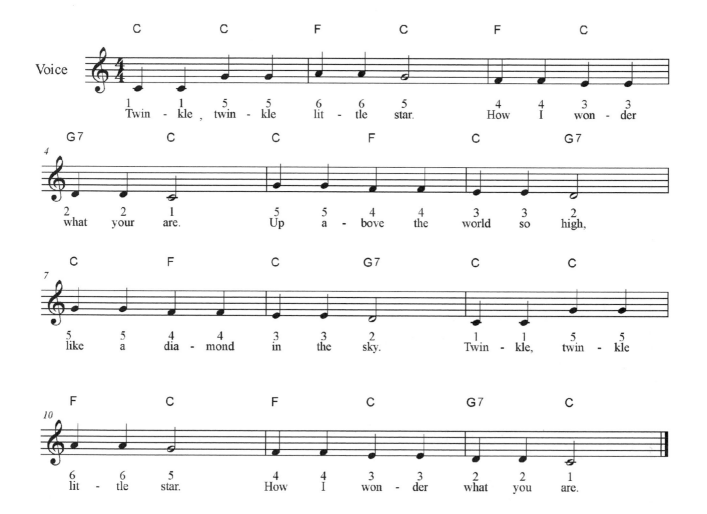

# Who has the Penny?

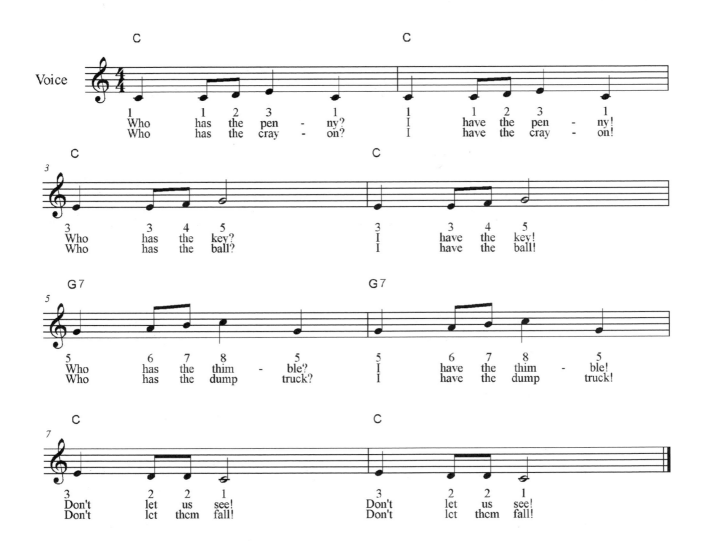

# Clap, Clap, Clap Your Hands

# Glossary

## A

**Absorbent mind:** a term used by Dr. Maria Montessori to describe how children learn

**Absorption:** the first stage of acculturation, during which time the child merely listens to music

**Accelerando:** to gradually play the music faster

**Acculturation:** the first type of preparatory audiation. It contains three stages: absorption, random response, and purposeful response

**Advocate:** someone who fights for the rights of others

**Anthroposophy (an-thro-pah-so-fee):** the belief that human beings are spiritual beings and can attain experience in the spiritual world through discipline and training

**Arpeggio (are-pay-jee-o):** playing the notes of a chord in succession instead of at the same time

**Assimilation:** the third type of preparatory audiation. It contains two stages, introspection and coordination

**Attentive listening:** means to pay attention to the music being played

**Audiate (ah-dee-ate):** the cognitive process by which we hear and comprehend music in our heads, even when there is no music playing

**Aural perception:** takes place when we hear music at the same time that the music is playing

## B

**Bar lines:** vertical lines drawn through the staff to divide it into measures

**Baroque (bah-rok):** a European historical period that is divided into three phases: early (1600–1640), middle (1640–1680), and late (1680–1750)

**Beat:** steady, unchanging pulse of the music

**Bell-shaped curve:** a theoretical distribution of natural occurrences represented by a curve

**Belly dancing:** a form of dancing from the Middle East, which women performed for other women

**Biomusicology (bi-o-mu-si-cal-o-gee):** a scientific field that studies why humans are musical and how music is used in the cultural and social rituals of various societies

**Block chord:** all notes of a chord played at the same time

**Bomba (bomb-ba):** a Puerto Rican musical style based on the African call and response with drum accompaniment

## C

**Calypso (cuh-lip-so):** a musical style from Trinidad and Tobago that served to bring news of political and social happenings to the people through its lyrics

**Chest voice:** singing by projecting the tone from the chest instead of into the head

**Child Development Associate credential:** a credential that requires 460 hours of experience and 120 hours of education, and is the first step to professionalism

**Child study movement:** an international movement from which sprang the theories on which the early childhood education field bases many of its beliefs

**Chord:** two or more notes played together in harmony

**Classification:** the process of grouping items according to a shared characteristic or attribute

**Clef:** a figure at the beginning of the staff that identifies the position of a note, thus identifying the rest of the notes on the staff

**Common time:** shown as a time signature: C and stands for 4/4 time

**Conservation:** understanding that although the appearance of an object changes, other physical characteristics remain the same

## D

**Diminishing intelligence:** the term used to express the loss of intelligence due to lack of stimulation of that area of the brain

**Dynamics:** how low or soft a piece of music is played

## E

**Eighth note:** a black note with a flag

**Enactive:** the first mode of learning from Bruner's theory of instruction during which children learn through concrete manipulation of materials

**Ethnomusicologists (eth-no-mu-sih-cal-o-gists):** a branch of musicology that studies the music of world cultures of the past and present

**Études (ay-toods):** a composition that is meant as a training piece for the pianist

**Eurhythmics (you-rhyth-mics):** a method of teaching music through body movement

**Eurythmy (you-ryth-mee):** a dancelike bodily movement used to express music and speech in which specific movements are made to particular notes or sounds

**Extrinsic reward:** a reward that comes from others, such as a smile, hug, pat on the back, or thumbs-up

## F

**Flat:** a symbol that lowers the pitch of a note a half step

**Form:** the way a composition is put together, its structure

**Forte (for-tay):** Italian word that means loud

**Frequency:** the number of vibrations a sound makes per second

## G

**Genre (zhan-ra):** another word for style

## H

**Half note:** a note with a white head and a stem

**Half step:** the interval from one note to the next one, chromatically

**Harmony:** describes what happens when two or more notes are played at the same time

**Head voices:** singing by projecting the sound into the head

## I

**Iconic:** the second mode of learning from Bruner's theory of instruction during which children learn through mental images

**Imitation:** the second type of preparatory audiation; contains two stages, shedding egocentricity and breaking the code

**Improvisation:** occurs when a piece of music is composed on the spot

**Interval:** the distance between two notes

**Intrinsic reward:** a reward that comes from inside a person, such as the feeling of accomplishment after solving a problem

## J

**Jazz:** a style of music developed in New Orleans that combines elements of European, American, and African music

## K

**Key signatures:** sharps or flats at the beginning of the staff that indicate the key of the composition

**Koto (kō-to):** a board zither with 13 or more strings

## L

**Largo (lar-go):** very slow tempo

**Leading tone:** the seventh note of a scale, major or minor

**Ledger line:** small lines added to the top or bottom of the staff to accommodate more notes

## M

**Major scale:** a scale built on the formula whole step whole step half step, whole step, whole step, whole step half step

**Mambo:** a Cuban musical style in which the African call and response is imitated at the end of most compositions

**Measure:** space created on a staff that is between two bar lines

**Melody:** the tune of a song that is made up of notes of varying pitches

**Merengue (mare-en-gay):** a musical style from the Caribbean islands of the Dominican Republic, Puerto Rico, and Haiti that incorporates the use of drums, marimba, and accordions

**Middle Ages:** a period of European history from AD 476 to 1450

**Minor scales:** each natural minor scale corresponds to a major scale. They use the same notes as their corresponding major scale, beginning on the sixth step of the major scale. For example A-minor corresponds with C major. A is the sixth step of the C-major scale. The A-minor scale uses the same notes (no sharps or flats) as the C-major scale, but begins on A, giving the notes a minor sound. The E-minor scale uses the same notes as the G-major scale, and the D-minor scale uses the same notes as the F-major scale

**Moderato (mo-der-a-to):** moderate tempo

**Monophonic (mo-no-fon-ik):** only one melody sung or played at a time

**Mozart effect:** refers to the power music may have on a person's health, education, and general well-being

**Multiple intelligences theory:** a theory that recognizes different ways in which humans are intelligent

**Music aptitude:** a child's innate, but not necessarily inherited, musical ability

**Music-learning theory for newborn and young children:** a theory of how children learn about music developed by Edwin Gordon

**Music therapy:** the occupation of allied health professionals who work in hospitals, both general and psychiatric, nursing homes, rehabilitation centers, mental health agencies, schools, and private practice to provide therapy in the form of music to help children and adults find relief from stress

**Musical alphabet:** seven letters of the alphabet that make up the names of the notes used in musical scales

**Musical comedy:** a style of entertainment that developed from the comic opera

**Musical intelligence:** one of eight intelligences described by Gardner, who theorized that it is the first intelligence to develop

**Musical notation:** various signs and words used to convey to the musician how the piece is to be played

**Musicology (mu-si-cal-o-gee):** the study of music and its effects on society

# N

**Nationalism:** a movement in the mid-nineteenth century in which composers felt compelled to insert folk tunes of their country into their compositions

**Neurons:** brain cells

# O

**Object permanence:** the ability to realize that something still exists, even when it cannot be seen

**Octave (ok-tive):** the interval between any note and the next note that has the same name

**Opera (op-er-a):** a story put to music and performed on stage with an orchestra, music director, costumes, scenery, lighting, and many singers

**Oratorio (or-a-tor-ee-o):** similar in musical style to an opera, but usually has a biblical text and does not require a stage setting with costumes and scenery

# P

**Pentatonic scale:** a five-tone scale

**Perceptive listening:** to understand the music as you listen to it

**Piano (pee-an-o):** an Italian word that means soft

**Pitch:** refers to the quality of a sound and the position of that sound in relationship to other sounds (i.e., higher, lower, same)

**Pitch pipe:** small circular instrument used to obtain the starting pitch or key of musical compositions

**Plena:** a musical style from Puerto Rico that is similar to ballads from Mexico

**Polyphony (po-lee-fo-nee):** more than one melody performed at a time

**Portfolios:** an alternate way of assessing a student's progress by gathering a student's work and comparing earlier work to current

**Preoperational stage:** second stage of Piaget's cognitive development theory (two to seven years of age)

**Preparatory audiation:** a period of development that young children progress through in preparation to participate in musical activities as described by Edwin Gordon

**Presto (pres-to):** very fast tempo

**Purposeful response:** the third stage of acculturation during which the child tries to match his movements and babble to the music in his environment

## Q

**Quarter note:** a note with a black head and a stem

## R

**Random response:** the second stage of acculturation during which the child begins to participate in music in addition to being a listener

**Recorder:** a simple instrument related to a flute that is played by blowing through a slit in one end and covering holes in the body of the instrument with fingers

**Reggae (reg-gay):** Jamaican musical style that was made internationally famous by a band named Bob Marley and the Wailers

**Renaissance:** a period of European history from approximately 1450 to 1600

**Requiem:** a mass for the dead

**Rests:** a silence between two tones signified by symbols

**Reversibility:** the ability to understand that what is done can be undone or to be able to think through a process backward to the starting point

**Rhythm:** refers to the pattern created when long and short sounds are combined

**Rhythm instruments:** basic instruments, which come from various cultures and are classified in one of two categories, nonpitched and pitched

**Rhythmic audiation skills:** skills that allow us to hear the rhythm of a melody in our heads

**Ritardando (rih-tar-dan-do):** to gradually play the music slower

**Root:** the lowest note in a chord

**Rote:** teaching through imitation

**Round:** a vocal canon

**Rumba (rum-ba):** a Cuban dance of African origin

## S

**Scaffolding:** the support given by adults to children as they try to learn to do something they cannot do alone at that point.

**Scales:** a series of tones that form a major or minor key

**Schofar (sho-far):** the earliest known horn. It was made from a ram's horn

**Self-concept:** knowing who you are and where you fit into your world

**Self-efficacy:** the feeling that you are capable

**Self-esteem:** the feeling that you are worthy

**Self-listening:** when children listen to themselves as they sing

**Sensorimotor stage:** first stage of Piaget's cognitive development theory (birth to two years of age)

**Separation anxiety:** the infant becomes upset when his mother leaves, because now he can remember her when she is no longer there

**Seriation:** to sort objects in a sequential order, according to a particular characteristic

**Shakuhachi (sha-koo-ha-chee):** a bamboo flute

**Shamisen (sha-mee-sen):** a long lute with three strings

**Sharp:** a symbol that raises the pitch of a note up a half step

**Sitar (sih-tar):** a three-stringed instrument from the Middle East

**Soca (so-ka):** recent offshoot of Calypso music

**Son:** a style of Caribbean music, which includes mambo and incorporates the African style of call and response at the end of compositions

**Sound wave:** the wave of movement that is caused by a vibrating object. Sound waves can move through any medium, including water and air

**Staff:** five lines and four spaces on which music is written

**Staves:** more than one staff joined by a bracket

**Style:** manner in which the musical elements are combined in a composition

**Symbolic:** the third mode of learning from Bruner's theory of instruction during which children learn through abstract thinking

**Synaptic gap:** the gap between the neurons over which sensory messages must jump from one cell to another using electrical impulses or chemical reactions

## T

**Taikyo:** the practice in Japan of pregnant women that avoids disharmony and helps them bond with their child before birth

**Tempo:** refers to how fast or how slow a piece of music is played

**Theme and variations:** a musical form in which a melody is played as the theme of the piece and then the composer writes several variations of the theme

**Timbre (tam-ber):** the distinct sound made by each voice or instrument

**Time signature:** the set of two numbers at the beginning of each piece of music. The top number always tells us how many beats should be in each measure and the bottom number signifies the note that receives one beat

**Tonal audiation skills:** skills that allow us to hear a melody in our heads

**Tonic:** the keynote or home tone of a key

**Transposition:** the act of playing or writing out a composition in a different key

## V

**Verismo:** works of art, but particularly operas that deal with the realities of life

**Vibration:** the repeated rapid rippling movement of an object

**Vocal exploration:** the child's search for his singing voice through experimentation

## W

**Whole note:** a white note with no stem

**Whole step:** an interval from one note to another with one note in between

**Windows of opportunity:** periods during children's development when it is easier for them to learn particular skills

## Z

**Zone of proximal development:** the zone within which Vygotsky believed that a child's learning takes place

# Index